STUDIES IN MODERN BRITISH RELIGIOUS HISTORY

Volume 40

CIVIL RELIGION AND THE ENLIGHTENMENT IN ENGLAND, 1707–1800

STUDIES IN MODERN BRITISH RELIGIOUS HISTORY

ISSN: 1464–6625

General editors
Stephen Taylor
Arthur Burns
Kenneth Fincham

This series aims to differentiate 'religious history' from the narrow confines of church history, investigating not only the social and cultural history of religion, but also theological, political and institutional themes, while remaining sensitive to the wider historical context; it thus advances an understanding of the importance of religion for the history of modern Britain, covering all periods of British history since the Reformation.

Previously published volumes in this series are listed at the back of this volume.

CIVIL RELIGION AND THE ENLIGHTENMENT IN ENGLAND, 1707–1800

ASHLEY WALSH

THE BOYDELL PRESS

© Ashley Walsh 2020

All Rights Reserved. Except as permitted under current legislation no part of this work may be photocopied, stored in a retrieval system, published, performed in public, adapted, broadcast, transmitted, recorded or reproduced in any form or by any means, without the prior permission of the copyright owner

The right of Ashley Walsh to be identified as the author of this work has been asserted in accordance with sections 77 and 78 of the Copyright, Designs and Patents Act 1988

First published 2020
The Boydell Press, Woodbridge
Paperback edition 2024

ISBN 978-1-78327-490-1 (Hardback)
ISBN 978-1-83765-149-8 (Paperback)

The Boydell Press is an imprint of Boydell & Brewer Ltd
PO Box 9, Woodbridge, Suffolk IP12 3DF, UK
and of Boydell & Brewer Inc.
668 Mt Hope Avenue, Rochester, NY 14620–2731, USA
website: www.boydellandbrewer.com

A CIP catalogue record for this book is available
from the British Library

The publisher has no responsibility for the continued existence or accuracy of URLs for external or third-party internet websites referred to in this book, and does not guarantee that any content on such websites is, or will remain, accurate or appropriate

This publication is printed on acid-free paper

For Richard, without whom this book would not exist

Contents

Acknowledgements ix
List of Abbreviations xi
Note on Dates xiii

Introduction: Hanoverian Civil Religion and its Intellectual Resources   1

1. Building Athens from Jerusalem: Anthony Ashley Cooper, Third Earl of Shaftesbury   40

2. The Politics of Priestcraft: John Trenchard and Thomas Gordon   59

3. The Church-State Alliance: Henry St John, Viscount Bolingbroke, and William Warburton   80

4. The Civil Faith of Common Sense: David Hume   108

5. The Legacy of Ancient Rome: Edward Gibbon and Conyers Middleton   137

6. Subscription, Reform, and Dissent: Civil Religion and Enlightened Divinity during the Late Eighteenth Century   166

Conclusion: Hanoverian Civil Religion and its Aftermath   193

Bibliography   208
Index   239

Acknowledgements

It is a pleasure to acknowledge the many debts that I have accrued in writing this book. My greatest debt is to Mark Goldie for his inexhaustible generosity, absolute support, and exacting standards. He encouraged me to study civil religion. I hope my performance has vindicated him. I am grateful to Stephen Taylor for his warm welcome at Durham University, support for this project, and providing extensive unpublished material. I thank Megan Milan, Michael Middeke, Emily Champion, Sean Andersson and my series editors at Boydell & Brewer. John Robertson and Brian Young have been generous and perceptive in their advice. Justin Champion read and commented on the manuscript. Sylvana Tomaselli provided valuable support with great humour. Katherine East established the Civil Religion Reading Group at Newcastle University and has commented on much of my work carefully. I thank Rachel Hammersley, Richard Tuck, Tim Stuart-Buttle, John Morrill, John Marshall, Andrew McKenzie-McHarg, Ariel Hessayon, Rachel Eckersley, Ross Carroll, Adam Morton, Gabriel Glickman, Emma Mackinnon, Callum Murrell, Gavin Hyman, and Ruth Smith. Giovanni Mantilla, who appeared unexpectedly, helped more than he can imagine, and my gratitude runs deep. I am very fortunate. I thank the Master and Fellows of Downing College, Cambridge, who provided a happy home for eight years, especially David Pratt, Paul Millett, Natalia Mora-Sitja, Ian James, and Michael Bravo. I must single out Kay Martin and Susan Lintott for their saint-like forbearance. I thank the staff of the College for making it such a special place. I have been very fortunate to work in the School of History, Archaeology and Religion at Cardiff University and, for their warm welcome and generous support, I would especially like to thank Jan Machielsen, Marion Loeffler, Keir Waddington, Lloyd Bowen, Mark Williams, Emily Cock, David Doddington, James Ryan, Bronach Kane, and James Hegarty. I am grateful to the staff of the West Room, Manuscripts Reading Room, and Rare Books Room at Cambridge University Library, the Bill Bryson Library at Durham University, the British Library, and Dr Williams's Library.

My parents have always understood the uses of literacy even if their son has still to learn to wear it lightly. They supported me even when they confronted the hardest of times themselves. I hope this book evidences their working-class aspiration. I seldom made things simple for Richard Johnson, to whom this book is dedicated. Since our relationship blossomed as undergraduates, he supported my research in every possible sense. He also helped me as I prepared the manuscript for publication. It is offered with deep thanks and great love.

ACKNOWLEDGEMENTS

In Cambridge, I was surrounded by dear friends made for life. The dearest, George Owers, is an accomplished intellectual historian of the eighteenth century and continues to act as sounding board and drinking companion. I thank Peter Sarris, who checked my French translations, and Mary Nathan and Bill Thompson, who volunteered to proofread the text. I am grateful to Turlough Stone, Nicola Bartlett, Andrew Howarth, Dan Ratcliffe, Holly Higgins, George Howes, Fred Jerrome, Jack Tunmore, Matthew Bird, Clare Walker-Gore, Marie Ferguson-Smith, Bridget Gorham, Sue Dennis, Paul Sales, Anne Campbell, and Ben Bradnack. Peter Roberts and Carina O'Reilly made space for me in their shared flat for several months. Ann Vinden and Frank Gawthrop twice welcomed me into their home as I completed the manuscript. David Doherty and Angela Huxtable – not forgetting my godson, Noel – put me up several times. Members of Petersfield Branch Labour Party almost certainly don't realise the ways in which I am grateful to them; members of Cambridge Constituency Labour Party even less so.

I am grateful for a series of research grants awarded for this research by the Sir John Plumb Charitable Trust. I reproduce Canaletto's painting *The River Thames with St Paul's on Lord Mayor's Day* (*c.* 1746) by permission of the Lobcowitz Collections and William Hogarth's engraving *The Sleeping Congregation* (1736) by permission of the Trustees of the British Museum.

Abbreviations

BJECS	*British Journal for Eighteenth-Century Studies*
CCS	Samuel Taylor Coleridge, *On the Constitution of the Church and State, according to the Idea of Each*, ed. John Colmer (Princeton, 1979)
Characteristics	Anthony Ashley Cooper, third earl of Shaftesbury, *Characteristics of Men, Manners, Opinions, Times*, ed. Lawrence E. Klein (Cambridge, 1999)
CL	John Trenchard and Thomas Gordon, *Cato's Letters or Essays on Liberty, Civil and Religious, and other Important Subjects*, ed. Ronald Hamowy (2 vols, Indianapolis, 1995)
Confessional	Francis Blackburne, *The Confessional* (3rd edn, London, 1770)
DF	Edward Gibbon, *The History of the Decline and Fall of the Roman Empire*, ed. David Womersley (3 vols, London, 1994)
DNHR	David Hume, *Dialogues* and *Natural History of Religion*, ed. J. C. A. Gaskin (Oxford, 1993)
HE	David Hume, *The History of England from the Invasion of Julius Caesar to the Revolution in 1688* (6 vols, Indianapolis, 1983)
HJ	*Historical Journal*
HPT	*History of Political Thought*
HS	*Hume Studies*
IJPR	*International Journal for the Philosophy of Religion*
IW	John Trenchard and Thomas Gordon, *The Independent Whig* (7th edn, 2 vols, London, 1743)
JBS	*Journal of British Studies*
JEH	*Journal of Ecclesiastical History*
JHI	*Journal of the History of Ideas*
JMH	*Journal of Modern History*

ABBREVIATIONS

JRH	*Journal of Religious History*
JSP	*Journal of Scottish Philosophy*
PH	*Parliamentary History*
SVEC	*Studies on Voltaire and the Eighteenth Century*

Note on Dates

England moved from the Julian to the Gregorian calendar in 1752, changing the start of the year from 1 March to 1 January. All dates have been presented in the New Style, taking 1 January as the start of the new year.

Introduction:
Hanoverian Civil Religion and its Intellectual Resources

> The twentieth century which has its own hairs to split may have little patience with Arius and Athanasius who burdened the world with a quarrel about a diphthong, but the historian has not achieved historical understanding, has not reached that kind of understanding in which the mind can find rest, until he has seen that that diphthong was bound to be the most urgent matter in the universe for those people.[1]

The problem of Jean-Jacques Rousseau

Jean-Jacques Rousseau most famously put the problem. In *The Social Contract* (1762), he argued that it was impossible for Christianity to become a civil religion. Christians could never profess faith in the *patrie*. Among the ancient pagans, 'every Religion was tied exclusively to the laws of the State which prescribed it' and no citizen distinguished between 'its Gods and its laws'. The church was an institution of the state and virtuous citizenship was compatible with religious piety. However, Christianity introduced a 'Spiritual Kingdom' that separated 'the theological from the political system'. The 'Kingdom of the other world' occasioned civil disorder as Christians fought over its nature.[2] Rousseau endorsed the claim of Niccolò Machiavelli in his *Discourses on Livy* (c. 1517) that Christianity was an otherworldly religion with no interest in civil life. Machiavelli had upbraided Christianity as a religion that made 'us place a lower value on worldly honour', glorified 'humble and contemplative men rather than active ones', and rendered 'the world weak'. It left sincere believers the pawns of priestly 'wicked men' who pursued temporal ambitions under sacerdotal guises. Christian revelation made slaves of men whereas Roman paganism had harnessed popular piety for patriotic *grandezza*.[3]

In the mood of the intense anticlericalism of the Enlightenment in France, Rousseau argued that Christian priests always sought to dominate the state.

---

[1] Herbert Butterfield, *The Whig Interpretation of History* (New York, 1965, orig. 1931), p. 17.
[2] Jean-Jacques Rousseau, *The Social Contract and Other Later Political Writings*, ed. Victor Gourevitch (Cambridge, 1997), pp. 143–4.
[3] Niccolò Machiavelli, *Discourses on Livy*, trans. Julia Conway Bondanella and Peter Bondanella (Oxford and New York, 1997), pp. 158–9.

Christian ecclesiology created a 'dual power' and 'a perpetual conflict of jurisdiction which has made any good polity impossible in Christian States'. Although some modern statesmen had attempted to restrain the church, nobody had 'succeeded in settling the question of which of the two, the master or the priest, one is obliged to obey'. In England, monarchs had 'established themselves as heads of the Church' since the Protestant Reformation. But they failed to create a civil religion because the priests believed the Church of England was superior to the state. Monarchs 'have made themselves not so much its masters as its Ministers; they have acquired not so much the right to change it as the power to preserve it; they are not its lawgivers, they are merely its Princes'.[4]

The only other thinker, believed Rousseau, to have attempted to create a civil religion was Thomas Hobbes in *Leviathan* (1651), the subtitle of which was *The Matter, Forme, & Power of a Common-Wealth Ecclesiasticall and Civill*. Hobbes 'dared to propose reuniting the two heads of the eagle, and to return everything to political unity'. But Hobbes came to understand that 'the domineering spirit of Christianity was inconsistent with his system, and that the interest of the Priest would always be stronger than that of the State'.[5] Hobbes realised that a Christian civil religion was an oxymoron.

For Rousseau, the civil religion must persuade all citizens to sacrifice their private interests for the public good. Within the social contract, 'it certainly matters to the State that each Citizen have a religion which makes him love his duties'. There must be 'a purely civil profession of faith' on pain of banishment or death. The dogmas of the civil religion should be neither complicated nor numerous, proclaiming 'the powerful, intelligent, beneficent, prescient, and provident Deity, the life to come, the happiness of the just, the punishment of the wicked, [and] the sanctity of the social Contract and the Laws'. They should condemn intolerance, 'a feature of the cult we have just rejected' in which 'Priests are the true masters' and 'Kings are but their officers'.[6]

However, Rousseau's argument would not have proven persuasive in Hanoverian England, where lay and clerical intellectuals hoped to construct a civil religion within a Christian commonwealth. By transforming the Church of England into a modern civil religion, they engaged in debates that connected ancient paganism with Italian Renaissance humanism and the Enlightenment. They believed that the state could secure its ascendancy over the church and prevent the domination of the priestly order. They claimed that the public faith of the Church of England could be one to which all English people should subscribe. They argued that Christians could prioritise wellbeing in this world over the prospect of rewards and punishments in the next one. The Christian sovereign, in the words of Rousseau, could secure a purely civil profession of faith.

---

[4] Rousseau, *Social Contract*, p. 145.
[5] Ibid., p. 146.
[6] Ibid., pp. 149, 150–1.

INTRODUCTION

The opportunity to create a Christian civil religion in eighteenth-century England lay in the unique status and role of the established church, which institutionalised a public faith predicated at once on catholic apostolicity and a recognition that its doctrines were contingent and imperfect. Theorists of civil religion believed that the Church of England rightly retained authority over the interpretation of revealed truth. But they also argued that the limits of human understanding rendered the truth of the creator unknowable in this world. The articles of faith of the Church of England were to be the civil religion of eighteenth-century England because they were products of fallible humans who interpreted imperfectly the nature of the divine being. The success of the civil faith turned on the prioritisation of shared rituals of public worship to express belonging within the Christian commonwealth over insoluble debates about the truth of the established articles of faith. Since their *jure divino* authority could not be proven, the clergymen of the Church of England owed their status as the public interpreters of the revealed faith to their *jure humano* legitimacy.

To pursue this argument is to develop the findings, by applying them to the eighteenth century, of two intellectual historians of Interregnum and Restoration England. A facet of Richard Tuck's longstanding interest in Rousseau's engagement with Hobbes has been the concept of civil religion. Tuck observed that Hobbes sought to transform Christianity into the civil religion of modern England by rendering the role of its doctrines as performative in the public worship of the commonwealth. Hobbes's civil religion was a solution to the problem of religious pluralism, charting a middle way between Independency and Laudianism.[7] Mark Goldie has revealed the republican dimensions of seventeenth-century English civil religion in the writings of James Harrington and his Restoration followers. Harringtonian civil religion combined a national church with liberty of conscience, prioritising civic service to the republic over theological wrangling about the nature of God.[8] Hobbes, Harrington, and their followers sought to imitate the ancient pagan civil religions in the modern Christian world. Although, as Rousseau argued, the source of the pagan faiths had come from within the state, seventeenth-century Englishmen insisted that primitive Christianity was reconcilable with civil order despite its otherworldliness.

Eighteenth-century English civil religion was neither the civil faith of Hobbes's covenanted subjects nor Harrington's republican citizens. It resulted

---

[7] Richard Tuck, 'The "Christian Atheism" of Thomas Hobbes', in Michael Hunter and David Wootton (eds), *Atheism from the Reformation to the Enlightenment* (Oxford, 1992), pp. 111–30; 'The Civil Religion of Thomas Hobbes', in Nicholas Phillipson and Quentin Skinner (eds), *Political Discourse in Early Modern Britain* (Cambridge, 1993), pp. 120–38.
[8] Mark Goldie, 'The Civil Religion of James Harrington', in Anthony Pagden (ed.), *The Languages of Political Theory in Early-Modern Europe* (Cambridge, 1987), pp. 197–222; 'Ideology', in Terence Ball, James Farr, and Russell Hanson (eds), *Political Innovation and Conceptual Change* (Cambridge, 1989), pp. 266–91; 'Priestcraft and the Birth of Whiggism', in Phillipson and Skinner (eds), *Political Discourse in Early Modern Britain*, pp. 209–31.

from the synthesis of civility and piety to develop a church whose structures and beliefs accorded with the state. Eighteenth-century civil religionists concerned themselves with how to make religion safe by civilising it.[9] Their religion was polite and free of its historical corruptions of superstition, enthusiasm, priestcraft, imposture, and intolerance. It was a repudiation of speculative dogma and ritualistic formalism. It was a religion of virtue, sociability, and happiness. It represented the Arminian rejection of the Calvinist insistence on the depravity of human nature and God's arbitrary use of grace. Sometimes, it located ethical power within human nature, independently of grace.[10] Irrespective of their inward views about the normative truths of the articles of faith of the Church of England, civil religionists sought to reconcile them with civil ends. Outward observance of the reformed religion was essential for belonging to the Christian commonwealth of Hanoverian England.

The construction of a Christian civil religion rested on intellectual resources bequeathed by the Protestant Reformation. Civil religionists believed that unreformed Christianity, above all, Roman Catholicism, preached spiritual subservience and tyranny. They abjured priestcraft, which signified the priestly fabrication of superstitious beliefs to advance their temporal power. It was not simply that popish priests peddled false doctrines, but also that, by their lies, they subverted the political order. In modern England, however, the idea of the priesthood of all believers gave Christian sanctification to membership of the commonwealth. The object of the civil state was the realisation of the primitive religion promised by Jesus Christ in the gospels in which every man was his own minister.

The terms 'popery' and '*imperium in imperio*', once deployed by Protestant reformers against the bishop of Rome, became general categories for the corrupt doctrines of impure Christianity and the priestly subjugation of the secular power. In England, the godly prince, who bestrode the church-state relationship by means of the royal supremacy, led the vanguard against corrupt religion. The civil church owed its structures to the magisterial Reformation. It was to be defended by the monarch, *fidei defensor*, who wielded the sword. Article XXXVII of the Church of England declared that 'The King's Majesty hath the chief power in this Realm of England and his other Dominions, unto whom the chief Government of all Estates of this Realm, whether they be Ecclesiastical or Civil, in all causes doth appertain'. God had instructed 'all godly Princes' to 'rule all estates and degrees committed to their charge by God, whether they be Ecclesiastical or Temporal and restrain with the civil sword the stubborn and evil-doers'.[11] It was because the loyalty of Roman Catholics lay not with the civil sovereign, but with the bishop of Rome, that civil religionists, concurring

---

[9] T. M. Bejan, *Mere Civility: Disagreement and the Limits of Toleration* (Cambridge, MA, 2017).
[10] Isabel Rivers, *Reason, Grace, and Sentiment: A Study of the Languages of Religion and Ethics in England, 1660–1780* (2 vols, Cambridge, 1991–2000).
[11] Diarmaid MacCulloch (ed.), *The Book of Common Prayer* (London, 1999), p. 564.

with John Locke, largely could not tolerate them.[12] It is a common refrain that anti-Catholicism was an integral aspect of the development of a multi-national British identity.[13] The suggestion that Roman Catholics could not be true citizens of the commonwealth was equally a feature of civil religion.

Civil religionists especially syncretised Roman republicanism with the gospel promise of Christ, fashioning a modern Christian version of Ciceronian *religio* stripped of *superstitio*. Hanoverian civil religion was that of the secular commonwealth at prayer. The institutional agents of its church, the parochial clergymen, were as much public officeholders as the Justices of the Peace or the overseers of the poor. Their church was an institution of the civil state. It would cleanse society of sanctimonious prelacy and ritualistic dogma, reorienting public life towards toleration, reason, and moral virtue. The two heads of Rousseau's eagle were thus to be reunited within a Christian commonwealth. The modern Elijah would slay the priests of Baal and the Christian would become the patriot.

The intellectual resources of Hanoverian civil religion

Hanoverian civil religionists took themselves to be concluding the long struggle of Christian reform to return the faith to primitive perfection. Article XIX of the Church of England proclaimed it a 'congregation of faithful men, in which the pure Word of God is preached and the Sacraments be duly administered according to Christ's ordinance in all those things that of necessity are requisite to the same'.[14] In the beginning, argued civil religionists, there was the apostolic purity of the primitive church. Error and corruption emerged as Christianity established itself in the world. The institutionalisation of Christianity as the official religion of imperial Rome under Constantine and the early church councils gave civil sanction to the theological wrongs of corrupt Christianity. These included the superstitions of Roman pagans, ancient Israelites, and the Pauline fusion of Christian theology with Greek philosophy.[15] In the language of Edward Gibbon in *The History of the Decline and Fall of the Roman Empire* (1776–88), Arius and Athanasius burdened the world with their quarrel about a diphthong.

The history of Christian reform was one of multiple attempts to beat back the corruptions of popery and the temporal usurpations of the bishop of Rome. English civil religionists were fond of drawing historical precedents for their

---

[12] John Locke, *A Letter Concerning Toleration and Other Writings*, ed. Mark Goldie (Indianapolis, 2010), pp. 117–18.
[13] Linda Colley, *Britons: Forging the Nation, 1707–1832* (New Haven and London, 1992); Colin Haydon, *Anti-Catholicism in Eighteenth-Century England: A Political and Social Study* (London, 1993); Ethan Shagan, *Catholics and the 'Protestant Nation': Religious Politics and Identity in Early Modern England* (Manchester, 2005).
[14] MacCulloch (ed.), *Book of Common Prayer*, p. 558.
[15] Dale B. Martin, *The Invention of Superstition: From the Hippocratics to the Christians* (Cambridge, MA, 2004); Euan Cameron, *Enchanted Europe: Superstition, Reason, and Religion, 1250–1750* (Oxford, 2010).

ecclesiology. They referred to the investiture controversy during the eleventh and twelfth centuries and the rivalries between the Guelphs and Ghibellines, which lasted for three subsequent centuries.[16] The influence of Marsilius of Padua on early modern English Protestant ecclesiology is well documented; he remained popular during the eighteenth century for resisting the papacy with Philip the Fair.[17]

Erastianism was a key legacy of Christian reform, broadly signifying the subjection of priestly power to the secular magistrate. Thomas Erastus was a sixteenth-century Zwinglian theologian who argued in Heidelberg against excessive powers of excommunication. His opposition was to the use of excommunication against an entire polity. He never argued for subjecting the church entirely to the secular power.[18] But in seventeenth-century England, especially at the Westminster Assembly during the 1640s and 1650s, the term 'Erastian' took a broader meaning.[19] In writing histories of England, civil religionists baulked at the power of superstitious priests over secular rulers. The images of Henry IV, king of the Germans, on the road to Canossa to bow in the snow before the pope and the whipping of Henry II of England for the death of Archbishop Thomas Becket loomed large.[20]

Civil religionists drew from other anti-papalist precedents, especially Paolo Sarpi of the Venetian republic. Sarpi's *History of the Council of Trent*, published posthumously in England in 1619, defended temporal sovereignty by attacking the Constantinean inheritance on primitivist grounds.[21] English church reformers drew on Sarpi's attack on the papal interdict of Venice (1606–7), his *History of the Interdict*. Three English translations of his *History*

---

[16] Uta-Renate Blumenthal, *The Investiture Controversy: Church and Monarchy from the Ninth to the Twelfth Century* (Philadelphia, 1988).
[17] Shelley Lockwood, 'Marsilius of Padua and the Case for the Royal Ecclesiastical Supremacy', *Transactions of the Royal Historical Society*, 5th ser., 1 (1991), pp. 89–119; Bettina Koch, 'Priestly Despotism: The Problem of Unruly Clerics in Marsilius of Padua's *Defensor Pacis*', *JRH*, 36:2 (2012), pp. 165–83.
[18] Charles D. Gunnoe, *Thomas Erastus and the Palatinate: A Renaissance Physician in the Second Reformation* (Leiden, 2010).
[19] J. N. Figgis, 'Erastus and Erastianism', *Journal of Theological Studies*, 2 (1901), pp. 66–101; Jeffrey R. Collins, 'The Restoration Bishops and the Royal Supremacy', *Church History*, 68:3 (1999), pp. 549–80; William M. Abbott, 'Anticlericalism and Episcopacy in Parliamentary Debates, 1640–1641: Secular versus Spiritual Functions', in Buchanan Sharp and Mark Fissel (eds), *Law and Authority in Early Modern England* (Newark, DE, 2007), pp. 147–85; Marco Barducci, 'Clement Barksdale, Translator of Grotius: Erastianism and Episcopacy in the English Church, 1651–1658', *The Seventeenth Century*, 25:2 (2010), pp. 265–80.
[20] Otto von Bismarck conjured the image of the road to Canossa during his *Kulturkampf* with Pope Pius IX. See Nicholas Hope, 'Prussian Protestantism', in Philip G. Dwyer (ed.), *Modern Prussian History, 1830–1947* (London and New York, 2001), pp. 188–208.
[21] J. L. Livesay, *Venetian Phoenix: Paolo Sarpi and Some of His English Friends* (Lawrence, KS, 1973); W. J. Bouwsma, 'Venice and the Political Education of Europe', in John R. Hale (ed.), *Renaissance Venice* (London, 1973), pp. 445–66; David Wootton, *Paolo Sarpi: Between Renaissance and Enlightenment* (Cambridge, 1983).

of the Inquisition, published posthumously in 1638, appeared over the following forty years. In *A History of Benefices*, published posthumously, and in English in 1736, he used medieval conciliarist texts in defence of secular regulation of clerical land ownership.

A further key resource was English ecclesiological scholarship. A common point of reference was Richard Hooker's defence of the royal supremacy in *Of the Lawes of Ecclesiasticall Politie* (1593–1662), especially his claim in the eighth book that 'within this *Realm* of *England* ... one society is both the *Church* and *Commonwealth*'.[22] The use of Hooker was problematic, since Hooker's conception of the unity of church and state assumed that all English subjects belonged to the Church of England. Although this assumption had been challenged, during the sixteenth century, by recusancy and puritanism, it ran alongside the aspiration for a comprehensive church settlement. Following the disorder of the mid-seventeenth century, the Restoration state reinforced this assumption by the penal laws against Protestant Dissent to force English subjects back into the state church. It was only with the passage of the Toleration Act (1689) that some Protestant Dissenters gained legal recognition. After 1689, English civil religion was Hookerian insofar as it required state offices to be filled by those who took Anglican communion and it prioritised external forms, including ecclesiology and liturgy, over doctrine.[23]

John Selden, the lawyer, parliamentarian, and Hebraist, was another common reference.[24] Selden's scholarship on the ancient Hebrews had influenced Hobbes and Harrington, especially his analysis of the Israelite priesthood in *De Successione in Pontificatum Ebraeorum* (1631) and his study of the civil and religious supremacy of the Sanhedrin in *De Synedriis et Prefecturis Juridicis Veterum Ebraeorum* (1650–5). But, during the eighteenth century, when the influence of the Hebrew republic declined by its association with Pauline superstition, English civil religionists were more apt to cite Selden's *History of Tithes* (1618) for the argument that tithing was a *jure humano* practice.

As much as Judaism was a uniquely difficult issue for the Enlightenment, English civil religionists, when discussing ancient Hebrews and modern Jews, were often uncivil.[25] On one hand, as the oratorios of George Frederick Handel demonstrate, the English might draw on Hebraic precedent in celebrating the

---

22 Richard Hooker, *Of the Laws of Ecclesiastical Polity*, ed. Arthur Stephen McGrade (3 vols, Oxford, 2013), vol. 3, p. 196.
23 John Gascoigne, 'The Unity of Church and State Challenged: Responses to Hooker from the Restoration to the Nineteenth-Century Age of Reform', *JRH*, 21:1 (1997), pp. 60–79.
24 Richard Tuck, *Natural Rights Theories: Their Origin and Development* (Cambridge, 1979), pp. 82–100; *Philosophy and Government, 1572–1651* (Cambridge, 1993), pp. 205–21; Reid Barbour, *John Selden: Measures of the Holy Commonwealth in Seventeenth-Century England* (Toronto, 2004); Jason P. Rosenblatt, *Renaissance England's Chief Rabbi: John Selden* (Oxford, 2006); G. J. Toomer, *John Selden: A Life in Scholarship* (2 vols, Oxford, 2009).
25 Adam Sutcliffe, *Judaism and the Enlightenment* (Cambridge, 2003), pp. 223–78.

Hanoverian order.[26] During the sixteenth and seventeenth centuries, interest had grown in the Hebrew language and republic, leading to the interpretation of the Hebrew Bible as a political constitution granted by God to the children of Israel in the Mosaic dispensation. The growth of Hebraism reinforced the idea that an Erastian unity between church and state could coexist with toleration.[27] Harrington's celebration of the Hebrew republic survived in the writings of John Toland, who supported Jewish naturalisation. Toland's position was ambiguous, since he sought, like Baruch Spinoza, to provide a secular and historicist interpretation of the Old Testament, undermining Jewish claims to divine election, but he celebrated the laws of the Hebrew republic.[28]

By the eighteenth century, Hebraism was associated with seventeenth-century enthusiasm. English puritanism had thrived on the Exodus narrative and Oliver Cromwell had readmitted the Jews during the 1650s.[29] The association with millenarian expectation made the case for Jewish naturalisation harder. Antisemitism reared its head during the controversy caused by the 'Jew Bill' in 1753 when the government introduced a Jewish Naturalisation Act, a measure by which the Whigs sought to allow a small number of foreign-born Jews to become citizens without taking the sacrament.[30] By his attempt to bridge the divide between Judaism and Christianity, the Unitarian Joseph Priestley did not help English Jewry and was rebuked by the likes of David Levi.[31]

The decline of Hebrew scholarship came with the rejection of the claim that the Jews, though they later lost his grace, had been initially chosen by God. It was routine to dismiss the Mosaic dispensation not as evidence of providential election but as the product of Egyptian statecraft. Moses, schooled in the art of Egyptian government, had been a wise legislator, instituting religion to keep a superstitious and cloudy people governable. English civil religionists tended to see the Jews as fanatical, intolerant, and haughty. Gibbon had dismissed their ancient forebears as a 'race of fanatics' whose 'stern temper' disposed them to embrace 'every

---

[26] Ruth Smith, *Handel's Oratorios and Eighteenth-Century Thought* (Cambridge, 1995).
[27] J. P. Sommerville, 'Hobbes, Selden, Erastianism, and the History of the Jews', in G. A. J. Rogers and Tom Sorell (eds), *Hobbes and History* (London and New York, 2000), pp. 160–88; Jason P. Rosenblatt, 'John Selden's *De Jure Naturalis ... Juxta Disciplinam Ebraeorum* and Religious Toleration', in Allison P. Coudert and Jeffrey S. Shoulson (eds), *Hebraica Veritas? Christian Hebraists and the Study of Judaism in Early Modern Europe* (Philadelphia, 2004), pp. 102–24; Eric Nelson, *The Hebrew Republic: Jewish Sources and the Transformation of European Political Thought* (Cambridge, MA, 2010), pp. 88–137.
[28] Sutcliffe, *Judaism*, pp. 197–205.
[29] Michael Walzer, *Exodus and Revelation* (New York, 1985), p. 5.
[30] Thomas W. Perry, *Propaganda and Politics in Eighteenth-Century England: A Study of the Jew Bill of 1753* (Cambridge, MA, 1962); David S. Katz, *The Jews in the History of England, 1485–1850* (Oxford, 1994), pp. 240–53; Frank Felsenstein, *Anti-Semitic Stereotypes: A Paradigm of Otherness in English Popular Culture, 1660–1832* (Baltimore, 1999), pp. 187–214.
[31] J. van den Berg, 'Priestley, the Jews and the Millennium', in David S. Katz and Jonathan I. Israel (eds), *Sceptics, Millenarians and Jews* (Leiden, 1990), pp. 256–74; Todd M. Endelman, *The Jews of Georgian England, 1714–1830* (Ann Arbor, 1999), p. 263.

opportunity of over-reaching the idolaters in trade'.³² The Nazarenes, who, while acknowledging Jesus as the messiah, followed ancestral Jewish ceremonies and rites, often wagged the pens of civil religionists like Gibbon.³³

With or without its Hebraic variations, the Erastian resources of civil religion stretched back into the 1530s. During the early Reformation, church reformers had defended the royal supremacy by the claim that the *imperator* was sovereign over the Christian commonwealth. The English monarchy defined itself by the image of Constantine as the Roman emperor who established Christianity. The closed imperial crown symbolised the Constantinean model as the king held both the sword and book.³⁴ The godly prince deployed temporal power to reverse the usurpations of the corrupt papacy and, by magisterial authority, returned the keys of heaven to the priesthood of all believers. In the eschatological iconography of John Foxe's *Actes and Monuments* (1563), Henry VIII defended the true faith by governing the visible church.³⁵ Repeated images of the pope or the papal tiara on the floor beneath the monarch symbolised the supreme governorship of Elizabeth I.³⁶ During the Restoration, Constantine remained the exemplification of the royal supremacy as the Church of England sought to move on from the chaos of the Interregnum.³⁷

But Constantine could be read as a quisling of priestly power. Uncivil priests were modern imitators of Athanasius and his ilk whose priestcraft at the council of Nicaea (AD 325) had so captivated Constantine. Histories of godly and ungodly kingship, in which Constantine struck an ambivalent pose, abounded during the eighteenth century. The history of the seventeenth-century wars of religion was the latest drama of the threat of popery. Whether James I at the Hampton Court Conference (1604), the power of Archbishop William Laud over Charles I, or Charles II at the Savoy Conference (1661), civil religionists feared the weakness of even Protestant kings in the face of priestcraft. Marsilian and Hookerian histories of the Christian church set the yardstick against which to measure the godliness of England's princes.³⁸

---

32 *DF*, vol. 1, pp. 515–17.
33 Ibid., pp. 449–56.
34 Patrick Collinson, *The Birthpangs of Protestant England: Religious and Cultural Change in the Sixteenth and Seventeenth Centuries* (Basingstoke, 1988), pp. 130–2; John N. King, 'The Royal Image, 1535–1603', in Dale Hoak (ed.), *Tudor Political Culture* (Cambridge, 1995), pp. 104–32, at pp. 104–7, 114, 129.
35 William Haller, *Foxe's Book of Martyrs and the Elect Nation* (London, 1963). But see Paul Christianson, *Reformers and Babylon: English Apocalyptic Visions from the Reformation to the Eve of the Civil War* (Toronto, 1978); Katherine Firth, *The Apocalyptic Tradition in Reformation Britain, 1530–1645* (Oxford, 1979).
36 Patrick Collinson, 'If Constantine, Then Also Theodosius: St Ambrose and the Integrity of the Elizabethan *Ecclesia Anglicana*', *JEH*, 30:2 (1979), pp. 205–29.
37 Jacqueline Rose, *Godly Kingship in Restoration England: The Politics of the Royal Supremacy, 1660–1688* (Cambridge, 2011).
38 Mark Goldie, 'Toleration and the Godly Prince in Restoration England', in John Morrow and Jonathan Scott (eds), *Liberty, Authority, Formality: Political Ideas and Culture, 1600–1900* (Exeter, 2008), pp. 45–66.

Having delivered England from popery, Whigs hailed William III as her latest godly prince. Whigs would use godly kingship to justify the Hanoverian succession in 1714 as a project of domestic reformation of manners and a larger brotherhood of European Protestantism against Bourbon France.[39] Despite the alliance between William III and Austria, the fear of a powerful convergence among the European Roman Catholic powers helped form the image of the magisterial state as a bastion of true religion. Gilbert Burnet, Williamite bishop of Salisbury, offered patronage to clergymen who believed in 'mid-Tudor ideals' of 'godly magistracy and moral reform'.[40] A similar concern with moral reformation emerged during the 1740s and 1750s in the aftermath of the second Jacobite rebellion in 1745 and as the Seven Years War pitted Britain, in an international coalition including Prussia, Portugal, and Hanover, against France, the Holy Roman Empire, Russia, and Spain.

Civil religion was tied to the international character of English Protestantism.[41] Churchmen, including Burnet, communicated with Swiss divines like Jean-Alphonse Turretini, Samuel Werenfels, and Jean Frederick Osterwald, who had campaigned for a repudiation of the strictly Calvinist *Formula Consensus Ecclesiarum Helveticarum* (1675). Francis Blackburne, archdeacon of Cleveland, defended Burnet and these Swiss divines in *The Confessional, or a Full and Free Enquiry into the Right, Utility, and Success of Establishing Confessions of Faith and Doctrine in Protestant Churches* (1767).[42] Upon his youthful conversion to Roman Catholicism, Gibbon's father sent him to Lausanne. Gibbon wrote in a letter that, while attending Protestant services there, he had had initial reservations about communing 'with Presbyterians as all the people of this country are'. But he 'at last got over it in considering that whatever difference there may be between their churches & ours, in the government & discipline they still regard us as brethren & profess the same faith as us'.[43]

In its domestic and international orientations, eighteenth-century civil religion was therefore a product of the process now known as the 'long Reformation', a process whose central themes included reformation of manners and godly

---

[39] Hannah Smith, *Georgian Monarchy: Politics and Culture, 1714–1760* (Cambridge, 2006), pp. 19–58.
[40] Tony Claydon, *William III and the Godly Revolution* (Cambridge, 1996), pp. 159, 231–2; Warren Johnston, 'Revelation and the Revolution of 1688–1689', *HJ*, 48:2 (2005), pp. 351–89; Andrew Thompson, *Britain, Hanover and the Protestant Interest, 1688–1756* (Woodbridge, 2006), pp. 25–60.
[41] B. W. Young, 'A History of Variations: The Identity of the Eighteenth-Century Church of England', in Tony Claydon and Ian McBride (eds), *Protestantism and National Identity: Britain and Ireland, c. 1650 – c. 1850* (Cambridge, 1998), pp. 105–28; W. R. Ward, 'The Eighteenth-Century Church: A European View', in John Walsh, Colin Haydon, and Stephen Taylor (eds), *The Church of England, c. 1689 – c. 1833: From Toleration to Tractarianism* (Cambridge, 1993), pp. 285–98.
[42] *Confessional*, pp. 83–5, 153–7, 214.
[43] Edward Gibbon to Catherine Porten, Feb. 1755, in J. E. Norton (ed.), *The Letters of Edward Gibbon* (3 vols, London, 1956), vol. 1, p. 3.

rule.⁴⁴ Further, as Robert Ingram has recently shown, it is salutary to conceive of eighteenth-century England as a post-revolutionary society whose members agonised over the causes, nature, and resolution of the wars of religion of the 1640s and 1650s as well as the bloody revolution of 1688–9.⁴⁵ The legacy of the seventeenth century mattered because the Reformation had not been settled; its unresolved religious and political consequences, especially the question of managing religious difference, had destabilised seventeenth-century England. Englishmen feared it could shatter the peace during the eighteenth century.

The development of the eighteenth-century English state continued the struggles of previous centuries; it cannot be understood without appreciation of ecclesiastical history between 1530 and 1689. It was the history of the battle of *imperium*, pitting *regnum* against *sacerdotium*. The concern with *praemunire*, or clerical subversion of secular power, was constant. To secularise eighteenth-century intellectual history by supposing that the Reformation broke the walls of the church is to misrepresent it. It would be wise to recall Duncan Forbes's warning against 'the fallacy of premature secularisation'.⁴⁶ The legitimacy of rulership turned at least in part on its godliness. The priestly state with its uncivil religion was to fall to the civil state of the evangelical prince and pious patriot. Sanctity lay in the political relationships of the civil community. In the words of Robert Molesworth in *An Account of Denmark* (1694), 'the Character of *Priest* [would] give place to that of true *Patriot*'.⁴⁷

Civil religionists were secularising the state insofar as they buttressed the sanctity of the civil magistrate. Despite the claim of Rousseau that Hobbes had failed to generate a civil religion, this was the process to which Hobbes contributed in *Leviathan*. Hobbes insisted that the civil sovereign was the highest priest and the ministers of the established church were his servants. Hobbes condemned the three 'knots' that had strangled the liberty of the true Christian: popery, prelacy, and presbytery. The Reformation had begun to untie these knots to restore Christians to 'the Independency of the Primitive Christians', which was 'perhaps the best'.⁴⁸ Hobbes's *Leviathan* thereby adapted Protestant eschatology for civil ends.⁴⁹

---

44 Jeremy Gregory, 'The Eighteenth-Century Reformation: The Pastoral Task of the Anglican Clergy after 1689', in Walsh, Haydon, and Taylor (eds), *Church of England*, pp. 67–85; *Restoration, Reformation and Reform: Archbishops of Canterbury and Their Diocese* (Oxford, 2000); Nicholas Tyacke (ed.), *England's Long Reformation, 1500–1800* (London, 1998); Robert G. Ingram, *Religion, Reform and Modernity in the Eighteenth Century: Thomas Secker and the Church of England* (Woodbridge, 2007).
45 Robert G. Ingram, *Reformation without End: Religion, Politics and the Past in Post-Revolutionary England* (Manchester, 2018).
46 Duncan Forbes, *Hume's Philosophical Politics* (Cambridge, 1975), p. 41.
47 Robert Molesworth, *An Account of Denmark, with Francogallia and Some Considerations for the Promoting of Agriculture and Employing the Poor*, ed. Justin Champion (Indianapolis, 2011), p. 14.
48 Thomas Hobbes, *Leviathan*, ed. Richard Tuck (revised edn, Cambridge, 1996), pp. 479–80.
49 J. G. A. Pocock, 'Time, History, and Eschatology in the Thought of Thomas Hobbes', in

The history of Christian reform converged with the classicising disposition of the eighteenth century. Historians are familiar with aristocratic fascination with ancient Rome, which expressed itself in the use of ideas of republican liberty and virtue to justify the Revolution settlement.[50] The idea of a sovereign Christian *imperator* was itself rooted in Roman law and it was a standard move of English Protestantism against the pope posing as *dominus mundi*. Precedents for the right relationship between church and state were found in ancient Rome, whose civil religion, it was claimed, at least before it had degenerated into popular superstition, had been a religion of the pious patriot. A popular choice was the legendary second king of Rome, Numa Pompilius, who had instituted the Roman religion following the death of Romulus.[51]

By far the most important figure was Marcus Tullius Cicero. But the legacy of Cicero was ambiguous.[52] Cicero's philosophy might be read by the orthodox in line with Stoic theism and, therefore, in support of a providential God or, by the heterodox, as a form of Academic Scepticism that rejected revelation for natural religion. The dialogue form of Cicero's work deepened the ambiguity. In *De Natura Deorum* (45 BC), Cicero wrote of three characters, Vellius, Balbus, and Cotta, representing the Epicureans, Stoics, and Academic Sceptics, and their discussion about the gods and the operation of the universe. In *De Divinatione* (44 BC), Cicero described a debate between Quintus Cicero, representing the Stoics, and Marcus Cicero, representing the Academic Sceptics, as they discussed the validity of divination and belief in divine providence in Roman religion.

English civil religionists tended to seize upon the distinction in these two works between *religio* and *superstitio*. In the first book of *De Natura Deorum*, Cotta distinguished between 'superstition, which implies a groundless fear of the gods', and 'religion, which consists in piously worshipping them'.[53] Later, in the second book, Balbus observed that 'religion has been distinguished from superstition not only by philosophers but by our ancestors'. The word 'superstition' came 'from *superstes*, a survivor', referring to parents 'who spent whole days in prayer and sacrifice to ensure that their children should outlive them'. But those 'who carefully reviewed and so to speak retraced all the lore of ritual were called "religious" from *relegere* (to retrace or re-read)'. Thus, superstition and religion

---

Politics, Language, and Time: Essays on Political Thought and History (Chicago and London, 1981), pp. 148–201.
[50] Reed Browning, *Political and Constitutional Ideas of the Court Whigs* (Baton Rouge, 1982); Philip Ayres, *Classical Culture and the Idea of Rome in Eighteenth-Century England* (Cambridge, 1997).
[51] Mark Silk, 'Numa Pompilius and the Idea of Civil Religion in the West', *Journal of the American Academy of Religion*, 72:4 (2004), pp. 863–96.
[52] K. A. East, *The Radicalization of Cicero: John Toland and Strategic Editing in the Early Enlightenment* (London, 2017), pp. 161–216; Tim Stuart-Buttle, *From Moral Theology to Moral Philosophy: Cicero and Visions of Humanity from Locke to Hume* (Oxford, 2019).
[53] Marcus Tullius Cicero, *De Natura Deorum, Academica*, trans. H. Rackham (London and Cambridge, MA, 1933), I.117–18.

'came to be terms of censure and approval respectively'.[54] The superstitious had failed to understand the true operation of the universe, leading to false doctrines and formalities with vicious ends.

Similarly, English civil religionists inferred from Cicero's work that it was the duty of he who loved his country to root out superstition. In *De Divinatione*, Marcus said:

> Speaking frankly, superstition, which is widespread among the nations, has taken advantage of human weakness to cast its spell over the mind of almost every man. This same view was stated in my treatise *On the Nature of the Gods*; and to prove the correctness of that view has been the chief aim of the present discussion. For I thought that I should be rendering a great service both to myself and to my countrymen if I could tear this superstition up by the roots. But I want it distinctly understood that the destruction of superstition does not mean the destruction of religion. For I consider it the part of wisdom to preserve the institutions of our forefathers by retaining their sacred rites and ceremonies. Furthermore, the celestial order and the beauty of the universe compel me to confess that there is some excellent and eternal Being, who deserves the respect and homage of men.[55]

It was the responsibility of the philosopher to purge superstition from society, leaving true religion intact. But, however superstitious the rites and ceremonies of the state, it was prudent to observe them. Marcus, who criticised augury and divination, respected these superstitions. 'I admit that Romulus,' he explained, 'who founded the city by the direction of auspices, believed that augury was an art in seeing things to come – for the ancients had erroneous views on many subjects.' However, 'the art has undergone a change, due to experience, education, or the long lapse of time'. It was 'out of respect for the opinion of the masses and because of the great service to the State that we maintain the augural practices, discipline, religious rites and laws, as well as the authority of the augural college'.[56] The prudent philosopher, however sceptical, must respect the superstitions of the poor.

Civil religion and the magisterial state

Away from classical scholarship, the construction of the right church-state relationship was yet more complex. England's magisterial Reformation had been deeply ambiguous from the outset. As J. G. A. Pocock has written, 'it is in the consequences of Henry VIII's Reformation that we find the enduring problematic of English political thought for the next three centuries'.[57] On one

---

[54] Ibid., II.72.
[55] Marcus Tullius Cicero, *De Senectute, de Amicitia, de Divinatione*, trans. William Armistead Falconer (London, 1923), II.148.
[56] Ibid., II.70.
[57] J. G. A. Pocock, 'A Discourse of Sovereignty: Observations on the Work in Progress', in

level, the upheavals of the 1530s might have placed the church entirely under the control of the crown. The Act of Submission of the Clergy (1534) mandated Convocation, the governing body of the Church of England, to meet only by royal assent, with further permission needed to pass new canon law. The crown controlled episcopal appointments and it seized the fiscal and juridical powers of the papacy. English courts received ecclesiastical appeals while the crown collected clerical 'first fruits and tenths'. Royal injunctions regulated worship and royal commissions discouraged dissent and recusancy. Most notoriously, the dissolution of the monasteries was by royal command.

Yet the crown was not the only agent in the Reformation. In 1533 the Act in Restraint of Appeals provided a legal formulation of English sovereignty by declaring England an empire with absolute jurisdiction over itself in temporal and spiritual affairs. But the meaning of the term 'empire' was vague: either the imperial crown symbolised royal authority over the church and the origins of that authority derived from within the church or it was the crown-in-parliament that governed the church according to the laws and customs of the realm.[58] The legacy of the magisterial Reformation was ambiguous and still contested as late as the eighteenth century because Anglican ecclesiology continued to render unclear the relationship between the monarchy, parliament, episcopacy, clergy, and laity.[59]

During the Restoration, a series of debates turned upon these unclear relationships. By now the established church was governed by the collection of laws known as the 'Clarendon code', which aimed to secure the ascendancy of the Church of England and discourage Protestant Nonconformity. The Corporation Act (1661) restricted civil office to Anglicans. The Act of Uniformity (1662) restored and required clerical subscription to the *Book of Common Prayer* (1549). It legislated for the rites, gestures, and ceremonies, including kneeling to take communion, signing the cross during baptism, and clergymen wearing the surplice, approved under Elizabeth I. It concluded the 'great ejection', between 1660 and 1662, of 2,000 puritan ministers and university dons. All clergymen were required to receive ordination from their bishops and repudiate the Solemn League and Covenant (1643). The Conventicle Act (1664) imposed penalties for those attending or allowing Nonconformist congregations on their premises. The Five Mile Act (1665) attempted to force Dissenters from towns where they had ministered congregations. It forbade them to teach and to host lodgers. The Test Act (1673) restricted military and civil office only to those who took the oaths of allegiance and supremacy and received communion by the rites of the Church of England. Although MPs were not required to receive communion, from 1678 the Test Act also applied to parliament.

Phillipson and Skinner (eds), *Political Discourse in Early Modern Britain*, pp. 377–428, at p. 381.
[58] John Guy, *Tudor England* (Oxford, 1988), pp. 132–4, 369–78.
[59] Rose, *Godly Kingship*, pp. 2–25.

These laws were passed by the crown-in-parliament. But when Charles II and James II issued declarations of indulgence in 1672 and 1687 to suspend the penal laws on Protestant Nonconformists and Roman Catholics by royal prerogative, a persecuting Anglican parliament found itself in a quandary. Either it could defend the Clarendon code in defiance of the crown or it could undermine the relationship between the king-in-parliament and the established church. Whigs and Protestant Dissenters might also choose to hail the godly prince acting independently of an unchristian parliament.[60] The fall of James II owed partly to the perception that he was undermining his own sovereignty over the church.[61] The Toleration Act finally provided relief for Trinitarian Dissenters. Crucially, it was called 'An Act Exempting his Majesties Protestant Subjects, Dissenting from the Church of England, from the Penalties of Certain Laws'. It was more a statute of indulgence carried out by the crown-in-parliament than a toleration act, since it merely suspended penal laws rather than reforming or repealing them.

There were further ambiguities in the magisterial state. The promise of godly kingship had been that the monarch would defend the exclusive relationship between the lay believer and God. This was rooted in Protestant soteriology, which, at least, demoted the role of the Christian minister in saving souls. The status of the public officeholders of the national church was deeply unclear. The debate turned upon two key positions. First, the idea that the church was a holy catholic order that comprised an apostolic clergy whose authority was *jure divino* and had been inherited directly from Christ himself. The church-state relationship, by this reading, was an alliance between two distinct societies. Second, the idea that the church was merely an earthly society, dependent upon human authority, established and governed by the magistrate. Either the supreme governor in or out of parliament or the bishops and clergymen were sovereign over the national church. This tension had origins in the Henrician Reformation itself. Whereas the Act of Appeals implied an alliance between separate temporal and spiritual societies, the Act of Submission of the Clergy placed the government and the legislation of the church establishment under the monarch-in-parliament. In the aftermath of the Revolution of 1688–9, these were the legal precedents to which competing divines appealed while debating the nature of the magisterial church-state relationship.[62]

Tory high churchmen defended the idea of an apostolic church as a distinct society.[63] Dr Henry Sacheverell, a fiery Oxford don whose sermonising and

---

[60] Andrew Marvell, *The Rehearsal Transpos'd* (London, 1672), p. 162; anon., *A Letter from a Person of Quality, to his Friend in the Country* (London, 1675), pp. 4–5.

[61] Mark Goldie, 'The Political Thought of the Anglican Revolution', in Robert Beddard (ed.), *The Revolutions of 1688* (Oxford, 1991), pp. 102–36.

[62] Mark Goldie, 'The Nonjurors, Episcopacy, and the Origins of the Convocation Controversy', in Eveline Cruickshanks (ed.), *Ideology and Conspiracy: Aspects of Jacobitism, 1689–1759* (Edinburgh, 1982), pp. 15–35.

[63] Geoffrey Holmes, *The Trial of Dr Sacheverell* (London, 1973); G. V. Bennett, *The Tory*

subsequent trial provoked riots in 1710, wrote: 'The *Civil* and *Ecclesiastical* State are the Two Parts and Divisions, that Both United make up One entire compounded Constitution, and Body Politick, sharing the same Fate and Circumstances, Twisted and Interwoven into the very Being and Principles of each Other.'[64] Francis Atterbury, bishop of Rochester, opposed 'the boundless authority of sovereigns in Church-matters'.[65] Convocation was 'as much a part of the constitution as a parliament itself'.[66] For the nonjuror, George Hickes, in his posthumous *The Constitution of the Catholic Church* (1716), the church was 'by its Constitution a Holy Royal or Regal Priesthood' and Christ had been 'a Sacerdotal Sovereign or Regal Priest' who 'committed the Government and administration of his Kingdom to Ministerial Priests'.[67]

Though not representative of all low-church Whig ecclesiology, Matthew Tindal argued in his *Rights of the Christian Church* (1706) that the legal framework of the magisterial Reformation showed that Queen Anne had 'no power in Ecclesiasticals except by the Laws of the Land, and can't divest her self of any part of it without Consent of our Parliament'.[68] The laws and usages of the realm governed the Church of England. Tindal's Whiggish defence of the church as an earthly society established by the crown-in-parliament appeared, like the arguments of Anthony Ashley Cooper, third earl of Shaftesbury, John Trenchard, and Thomas Gordon, during the post-Revolutionary wars of party. For Whig divines like Benjamin Hoadly, bishop of Bangor, who responded to Hickes in *A Preservative against the Principles and Practices of the Nonjurors both in Church and State* (1717), Christ's kingdom was not of this world. The church was a human institution and the authority of its clergymen was derived purely from the sovereign secular state. Christ had handed the keys of heaven not to a superior clerical caste but to the priesthood of all believers.[69]

These tensions within the magisterial state shaped variant forms of Hanoverian civil religion. Lay thinkers tended to demote Christian priests to ministers appointed by the human hands of the secular state. Such thinkers included Shaftesbury, Trenchard, Gordon, Gibbon, David Hume, and Henry St John, Viscount Bolingbroke. It included Whiggish clergymen like Conyers Middleton, Edmund Law, bishop of Carlisle, and Blackburne. Other eighteenth-century churchmen who engaged with civil religion defended the sacerdotal status of

---

Crisis in Church and State: The Career of Francis Atterbury, Bishop of Rochester (Oxford, 1975), pp. 103–12; Linda Colley, *In Defiance of Oligarchy: The Tory Party, 1714–60* (Cambridge, 1982).
[64] Henry Sacheverell, *The Political Union* (London, 1702), p. 9.
[65] Francis Atterbury, *The Rights, Powers, and Privileges of an English Convocation* (London, 1700), sig. A6r, p. 148.
[66] Francis Atterbury, *A Letter to a Convocation-Man, concerning the Rights, Powers and Privileges of that Body* (London, 1697), p. 50.
[67] George Hickes, *The Constitution of the Catholic Church* (London, 1716), p. 66.
[68] Matthew Tindal, *Rights of the Christian Church* (London, 1706), pp. ix, lxxxi.
[69] Andrew Starkie, *The Church of England and the Bangorian Controversy* (Woodbridge, 2007).

Christian ministers within the Church of England while conceding the supremacy of the secular civil magistrate. These included Edmund Gibson, bishop of Lincoln and then London, and William Warburton, bishop of Gloucester.

Learned ministers and pastoral clergymen

The long Reformation was also the context in which theorists of civil religion developed a positive vision for Christian ministry. Molesworth believed the central insight of republics was that they 'keep their *Ecclesiasticks* within their due bounds, and ... curb those, who if they had Power would curb all the World'.[70] But the ecclesiastics were still there. Although Whig and Enlightened religion in England could have strongly anticlerical moods, it would be more accurate to categorise such ecclesiology as anti-sacerdotal. Anticlericalism, when applied to the eighteenth century, is a term of art whose origins lay in the nineteenth century.[71] Overwhelmingly, eighteenth-century civil religionists believed that, while clergymen enjoyed no mediating position between God and the laity, they played a vital role in the civil state and civilised society.

The idea of the learned Christian minister was a crucial aspect of civil religion. The simple morality of the true faith could only be discovered by means of *sola scriptura* study of the gospels. History and theology were weapons in a war about the ecclesiological character and political status of the church. It was the responsibility of clergymen to study the history of scripture to identify and purge the corrupt accretions that had attached themselves to it since the days of the early church. Superstitious priests generated false doctrines by such corrupt means as scholasticism to subvert morality for their worldly gain. Learned ministers were to resist the superstition that was a product of priestly imposture and a cause of religious persecution. Theirs was the simple and reasonable religion of the gospel.

The attitude of English civil religion to scripture was Erasmian and, more broadly, humanist. Its English hero was the mid-seventeenth-century Oxonian scholar William Chillingworth. It took to heart Chillingworth's claim in *The Religion of the Protestants* (1637) that 'the Bible, I say the Bible only, is the religion of Protestants'. It was a 'vain conceit, that we can speak of the things of God better than in the words of God'. This 'deifying our own interpretations, and tyrannous enforcing them upon others' betrayed 'that latitude and generality, and the understandings of men from that liberality, wherein Christ and the Apostles left them'.[72] Civil religionists followed the philological

---

[70] Molesworth, *Account of Denmark*, p. 18.
[71] G. M. Ditchfield, 'The Changing Nature of English Anticlericalism, c.1750–c.1800', in Nigel Aston and Matthew Cragoe (eds), *Anticlericalism in Britain, c.1500–1914* (Stroud, 2000), pp. 93–114, at p. 93.
[72] William Chillingworth, *The Works of William Chillingworth* (10th edn, London, 1742), pp. 354, 203. See also Robert Orr, *Reason and Authority: The Thought of William Chillingworth* (Oxford, 1967).

instruction of John 5:39 to search the scriptures. Reason and critical enquiry were brought to bear on the claims and authorship of scripture, which was studied on similar terms to classical texts. The study of classical and scriptural languages was considered crucial for the contexts in which scripture was composed and the history of its subsequent corruption. Pious divines were to learn the arts of rhetoric and erudition in their sermonising and devotional literature. Religious knowledge was not simply valuable in and of itself, but it was to be made useful for the lay believer.

The battles between Anglicanism, Presbyterianism, and Nonconformity throughout the long Reformation lent urgency to the idea of learned Anglican ministry. For instance, John Goodwin of St Stephen's, Coleman Street, was a congregationalist divine whose humanism, Arminianism, and commitment to toleration and free inquiry showed that puritanism could threaten the learned hegemony of the Church of England.[73] No seventeenth-century Presbyterian would have welcomed being labelled a Nonconformist because Presbyterians defended the idea of a national church. Richard Baxter conceived of a national establishment in which 'Learned, judicious, Godly, able faithful men' were 'provided with their daily bread for food or raiment'. Learned ministers would 'manage God's word' and 'inform the people'.[74] Sometimes Whig civil religionists like Shaftesbury stood accused of weakness in the face of rebellious Presbyterians and puritans. But, in defending learned ministry, Whig civil religionists were trying to wrest back ground colonised especially by Presbyterians.

Concern about the universities, which remained Anglican seminaries, was a corollary of learned ministry. The caricature of Oxford and Cambridge was that they were cells for backward scholastics concerned with Platonic metaphysics and Aristotelian logic. Civil religionists castigated the study of patristics.[75] Cynicism about the priestly pettifogging of the universities had led to the grand tour as an alternative to a university education.[76] But Cambridge, which produced such civil religionists as Blackburne and Law, was more reliably Whig.[77] Oxford, where the young Shaftesbury suffered and the indolent Gibbon languished, was suspected of high-churchmanship and Jacobite disloyalty.[78] Reform remained an important goal of Whig anticlericalism throughout the

---

[73] John Coffey, *John Goodwin and the Puritan Revolution: Religion and Intellectual Change in Seventeenth-Century England* (Woodbridge, 2006).
[74] Richard Baxter, *A Holy Commonwealth, or Political Aphorisms, opening the True Principles of Government* (London, 1659), pp. 241–2.
[75] Jean-Louis Quantin, *The Church of England and Christian Antiquity* (Oxford, 2009).
[76] Jeremy Black, *The British and the Grand Tour* (London, 1985), p. 189.
[77] John Gascoigne, *Cambridge in the Age of the Enlightenment: Science, Religion and Politics from the Restoration to the French Revolution* (Cambridge, 1989).
[78] J. W. Yolton, 'Schoolmen, Logic and Philosophy', in T. H. Aston (ed.), *The History of the University of Oxford*, vol. 5, L. G. Mitchell and L. S. Sutherland (eds), *The Eighteenth Century* (Oxford, 1986), pp. 565–91.

eighteenth century.⁷⁹ The threat of the Dissenting academies lent urgency to the cause of reform.

A crucial part of the governance of the parish commonwealth, clergymen were also to be pastors for their parochial flocks. Much like ecclesiology, ideas of clerical pastoralism stretched into the contested legacy of the long Reformation. Anglicans, Presbyterians, and Nonconformists produced works on godly rule, devotion, moral reformation, and parochial care. The need impressed itself upon Anglicans to retake the ground seized by such Presbyterians as William Prynne and Baxter for godly ministry within the national church.⁸⁰ Burnet, in his *Discourse of the Pastoral Care* (1692), and Edward Stillingfleet, bishop of Worcester, in his *Charge to the Clergy of his Diocese* (1691), seized the initiative. Burnet aimed at 'the completing of our Reformation, especially as to the lives and manners of men'. Under the protection of princes, earlier reformers 'insensibly slackened' and, relying on legal succour, 'did not study to reform the lives and manners of their people'. Ministers must engage in 'the instructing, the exhorting, the admonishing and reproving, the direction and conducting, the visiting and comforting of the people of the parish'. These functions fell beyond 'the cognizance of the law'.⁸¹

The importance of pastoral ministry lay above all in the battle against enthusiasm. If superstition was one enemy of civil religion, enthusiasm was the other. Shaftesbury and Hume exemplified the tendency of civil religionists to defeat both enemies by their efforts to cast superstition with its priestliness and enthusiasm with its frenzy as inversions of true religion. Enthusiasts destabilised civil society by their claim to be inhabited directly by God's spirit.⁸² They were the causes of mysticism, sectarianism, and radicalism.⁸³ Commitment to the principles of freedom of conscience and the vernacular availability of the Bible undermined the integrity of the interpretations of the established church. Sectarians developed theologies with millennial and antinomian tendencies.⁸⁴ Civil religionists often referred to a group of French Huguenot refugees,

---

79 John Gascoigne, 'Church and State Allied: The Failure of Parliamentary Reform of the Universities, 1688–1800', in A. L. Beier, David Cannadine, and J. M. Rosenheim (eds), *The First Modern Society: Essays in English History in Honour of Lawrence Stone* (Cambridge, 1989), pp. 401–29.
80 William Lamont, *Marginal Prynne, 1600–69* (London, 1963); *Godly Rule: Politics and Religion, 1603–60* (London, 1963); *Richard Baxter and the Millennium* (London, 1980).
81 Gilbert Burnet, *A Discourse of the Pastoral Care* (3rd edn, London, 1692), sig. A4, pp. xiv–xvi, 184–91, 193–4, 205.
82 Michael Heyd, *'Be Sober and Reasonable': The Critique of Enthusiasm in the Seventeenth and Early Eighteenth Centuries* (Leiden and New York, 1995); J. G. A. Pocock, 'Enthusiasm: The Antiself of Enlightenment', in Lawrence E. Klein and Anthony La Vopa (eds), *Enthusiasm and Enlightenment in Europe, 1650–1850* (San Marino, 1998), pp. 7–28.
83 Liam P. Temple, *Mysticism in Early Modern England* (Woodbridge, 2019).
84 Ronald A. Knox, *Enthusiasm: A Chapter in the History of Religion* (Notre Dame, IN, 1950); Keith Thomas, *Religion and the Decline of Magic* (London, 1971), p. 141; Warren Johnston, *Revelation Restored: The Apocalypse in Later Seventeenth-Century England* (Woodbridge, 2011).

known as the Camisards, who appeared in London during the 1700s. Aside from their apocalyptic ecstasy, the group engaged in the developing free press to denounce the supremacy of rationalism in favour of personal revelation and primitive Christian enthusiasm. Since many of these 'prophets' continued to appeal to Anglicans to create a universal church, Lionel Laborie has rightly concluded that they can be classified neither as sectarians nor dissenters. They showed the potential for enthusiasm within the religious establishment in an age before Methodism.[85] Civil religionists defended the Church of England as a *via media* between the superstitious priestcraft of the Church of Rome and the frenzied enthusiasm of the Protestant sects. The outward worship of the Christian commonwealth celebrated this *via media*.[86] Sermons on 30 January commemorated the execution of Charles I to remind the laity of the dangers of enthusiasm. On 5 November, clergymen celebrated the demise of Roman Catholicism by the failure of the gunpowder plot. Instead of the puritan emphasis on grace or the priestly insistence on doctrine, soteriological weight was now to be placed on practical devotion. By marrying gospel precepts with pastoral care, the Church of England might generate polite and tolerant religion without leaving the laity recourse to 'mechanic preachers'. In the towns, especially London, where Dissenting interests flourished in the context of mercantile trade, there had developed a marketplace in 'conventicling' and sermonising. Here the Church of England was one among many, and the need to counteract 'sermon-gadding' laymen became a challenge for the establishment.[87] In these contexts, the challenge of pastoralism was one to which theorists of civil religion developed a response.

A religion of politeness, sociability, and latitude

By their emphasis on practical devotion, civil religionists were attempting to create a religion of politeness, sociability, and latitude. In the public sphere, polite religion was a feature of debate in the periodicals and coffeehouses.[88] Equally, Whigs and Tories competed for the banner of politeness.[89] The urban world of the commercial centre complemented the rational religion preached at the pulpit as a means of inculcating virtue and devotion. Superstition and enthusiasm were to be subjected not to the fiery damnations of the sanctimonious prelate but the good-humoured ridicule of the witty gentleman.[90] The censorial

---

[85] Lionel Laborie, *Enlightening Enthusiasm: Prophecy and Religious Experience in Early Eighteenth-Century England* (Manchester, 2015).
[86] Matthew Neufeld, *The Civil Wars after 1660: Public Remembering in Late Stuart England* (Woodbridge, 2013), pp. 203–42.
[87] Jennifer Farooq, *Preaching in Eighteenth-Century London* (Woodbridge, 2013).
[88] Nicholas Phillipson, 'Politics and Politeness in the Reigns of Anne and the Early Hanoverians', in J. G. A. Pocock with Gordon Schochet and Lois Schwoerer (eds), *The Varieties of British Political Thought, 1500–1800* (Cambridge, 1996), pp. 229–35.
[89] Markku Peltonen, 'Politeness and Whiggism, 1688–1732', *HJ*, 48:2 (2005), pp. 391–414.
[90] Joseph M. Levine, *The Battle of the Books: History and Literature in the Augustan Age*

public were agents in the generation of civil religion in the literary universe of *The Spectator* (1711–12) of Joseph Addison and Richard Steele.[91] Religious belief and political practice would be subjected to the culture of sociability. In the spirit of *doux commerce*, trade and commercial exchange were solvents of religious conflict as religion was put to the service of worldly civilisation.[92]

The Church of England was an institution of civil society. Civil religionists encouraged the voluntary aspects of pious devotion in the context of charitable service.[93] Good works were to replace controversial tracts and the traditional disciplinary structures of the Church of England. These developments in Anglican culture expressed themselves in such new organisations as the Society for Promoting Christian Knowledge (SPCK). The SPCK, encouraged especially by Gibson, harnessed a message of Christian primitivism in the face of Tory high-churchmanship, which itself sought to model its sacerdotalism on gospel principles. The goal of civil religion was a godly nation at prayer and one defended by its church establishment against enthusiasm.[94]

However, the involvement of Dissenters in the movement for the reformation of manners left it open to the high-church and Tory charge that low-church Whigs risked endangering the Church of England by their latitude.[95] In *The Character of a Low Churchman* (1702), Sacheverell argued that the Church needed to return to its 'ancient, primitive discipline' to secure its flocks 'from vice and immorality, schism and heresy'. It should not rely on 'a society for the reformation of manners, wherein every tradesman and mechanic is to take upon himself the gift of the Spirit, and to expound the difficult passages of Scripture, and every justice of the peace is allowed to settle its canons and infallibly decide what is orthodox and heretical'. The movement for the reformation of manners was a 'mongrel institution' that aimed to 'insinuate an insufficiency in the Church's discipline' and 'betray its power into the hands of a lay-eldership

---

(Ithaca, NY, 1991).
[91] Jürgen Habermas, *The Structural Transformation of the Public Sphere* (Cambridge, MA, 1989, orig. 1962); Edward Alan Bloom and Lilly D. Bloom, *Joseph Addison's Sociable Animal: In the Marketplace, on the Hustings, in the Pulpit* (Providence, RI, 1971), pp. 151–202.
[92] A. O. Hirschmann, *The Passions and the Interests: Political Arguments for Capitalism before Its Triumph* (Princeton, 1977).
[93] Brent Sirota, *The Christian Monitors: The Church of England in the Age of Benevolence, 1680–1730* (New Haven and London, 2014).
[94] Eamonn Duffy, 'Primitive Christianity Reviv'd: Religious Renewal in Augustan England', in Derek Baker (ed.), *Renaissance and Renewal in Christian History* (Oxford, 1977), pp. 287–300; 'Correspondence Fraternelle: the SPCK, the SPG and the Churches of Switzerland in the War of the Spanish Succession', in Derek Baker (ed.), *Reform and Reformation in England and the Continent*, c.*1500*–c.*1750* (Oxford, 1979), pp. 251–80; 'The SPCK and Europe', *Pietismus und Neuzeit*, 7 (1981), pp. 28–42; David Hayton, 'Moral Reform and Country Politics in the Late-Seventeenth-Century House of Commons', *Past & Present*, 128:1 (1990), pp. 48–89; Craig Rose, 'The Origins of the SPCK, 1699–1716', in Walsh, Haydon, and Taylor (eds), *Church of England*, pp. 172–90.
[95] A. G. Craig, 'The Movement for the Reformation of Manners, 1688–1715' (PhD thesis, University of Edinburgh, 1980).

and fanaticism'.[96] Sacheverell's charge rehearsed high-church anxiety that Anglican voluntarism threatened church institutions like the ecclesiastical courts, which declined rapidly after the Revolution, and old anti-puritan fears of religious activity outside the formal structures of the church. Whereas Tory high churchmen tended to suspect enthusiastic conventicling wherever Christians worshipped and performed works without the guidance of Anglican priests, Whig churchmen like Gibson placed their faith in the voluntary capacity of Christians in civil society.[97]

Civil religionists emphasised latitude as a means of rendering the Church of England a national church. However, the term 'latitude' must be understood carefully. Historians are tempted to trace a tradition of 'liberal' and 'rationalist' divinity from seventeenth-century England into the Enlightenment. This tradition supposedly encompassed 'Cambridge Platonists', including Ralph Cudworth and Henry More, and 'latitudinarians' during the seventeenth century through to deists and freethinkers during the eighteenth century. This argument first took hold during the nineteenth century.[98] The idea that there was a distinct group of 'latitudinarian' Anglican clergymen in Restoration England remained powerful throughout the twentieth century. But, as John Spurr has shown, the term 'latitudinarianism' is largely redundant in describing a self-conscious ecclesiastical grouping or mode of divinity.[99] Those associated with 'latitudinarianism' tended to be integrated within the main currents of Restoration Anglican divinity. Further, as Dmitri Levitin has argued, Cambridge Platonists were more accurately a loose collection of scholars connected by standard academic relationships and a commonplace seventeenth-century opposition to Calvinism, whose interests extended far beyond neo-Platonism.[100]

To use the term 'latitudinarianism' in discussing the eighteenth-century Church of England is less controversial. To speak of latitude was to invoke the vogue for moderation, following Philippians 4:5, which expressed itself in eirenic tolerance.[101] The children of God could err and, since there was no divine institution on earth, nobody could reasonably persecute sincere

---

[96] Henry Sacheverell, *The Character of a Low Churchman* (London, 1702), pp. 10–12.
[97] Tina Isaacs, 'The Anglican Hierarchy and the Reformation of Manners, 1688–1738', *JEH*, 33:3 (1982), pp. 391–411; John Spurr, 'The Church, the Societies, and the Moral Revolution of 1688', in Walsh, Haydon, and Taylor (eds), *Church of England*, pp. 127–42.
[98] See Scott Mandelbrote, 'Biblical Hermeneutics and the Sciences, 1700–1900: An Overview', in Scott Mandelbrote and Jitse van der Meer (eds), *Nature and Scripture in the Abrahamic Religions* (4 vols, Leiden, 2008), vol. 2, pp. 3–40.
[99] John Spurr, 'Latitudinarianism and the Restoration Church', *HJ*, 31:1 (1988), pp. 61–82; '"Rational Religion" in Restoration England', *JHI*, 49:4 (1988), pp. 564–58; *The Restoration Church of England* (New Haven, 1991), pp. 296–311. See also John Marshall, 'The Ecclesiology of the Latitude-Men, 1660–89: Stillingfleet, Tillotson and "Hobbism"', *JEH*, 36:3 (1985), pp. 407–27.
[100] Dmitri Levitin, *Ancient Wisdom in the Age of the New Science: Histories of Philosophy in England, c. 1640–1700* (Cambridge, 2015), pp. 13–17.
[101] Mark Knights, 'Occasional Conformity and the Representation of Dissent: Hypocrisy, Sincerity, Moderation and Zeal', *PH*, 24:1 (2005), pp. 41–57. See also Ethan Shagan, *The*

Christians who earnestly searched the scriptures. Hanoverian latitudinarians insisted that a certain set of doctrinal differences were permissible within the Church of England. They conjured a mood comparable with that of Addison's Mr Spectator, who, while dreaming, imagined himself in the Great Hall of the Bank of England. At the upper end of the hall was the Magna Carta 'with the Act of Uniformity on the right Hand, and the Act of Toleration on the left'. Later in the dream, Mr Spectator witnessed spectres of discord and images of accord. In front of the latter were 'Liberty with Monarchy at the right Hand' and 'Moderation leading in Religion'.[102]

Among civil religionists as much as latitudinarians, there were limits to toleration. The Toleration Act was a compromise that pleased few. It had initially formed a pair with a bill for comprehension within the Church of England, providing toleration for the small number of Protestants who could not reconcile their tender consciences with the established church. Comprehension having failed in 1689, the Toleration Act excluded those who 'shall deny in his preaching or writing the doctrine of the blessed Trinity, as it is declared in the aforesaid articles of religion'.[103] Dissenters tended to argue that the legislation had not gone far enough while Tories and high churchmen believed it had gone too far.[104] In defending an unstable compromise that upheld the national church, civil religionists, unless they were willing to argue for doctrinal reform to enable a comprehensive church, imposed limits to toleration.

While not necessarily indicating a programme or a party, there were shared eighteenth-century latitudinarian commitments that overlapped with civil religion. In its more reformist iterations, as in the cases of Blackburne or Law, latitudinarianism could have comprehensive tendencies.[105] It was adiaphorist in orientation, since its exponents claimed that the essentials of Christianity were simple and readily apprehensible; all else was of human creation. It emphasised latitude for tender consciences both within the fold of the establishment and beyond. Its keynotes were charity, practical Christianity, moderation, tolerance, free inquiry, and rationality. It insisted on the Erasmian and Chillingworthian emphases on *sola scriptura* study of the Bible. It often equated primitive Christianity with natural religion, though this was almost always attended by revelation. It remained suspicious of sacerdotalism. These were all the principles, argued Burnet, of low churchmen, who 'think no humane

---

Rule of Moderation: Violence, Religion and the Politics of Restraint in Early Modern England (Cambridge, 2011).
[102] Joseph Addison and Richard Steele, *The Spectator*, ed. Gregory Smith (4 vols, London, 1907), vol. 1, pp. 11, 13.
[103] E. Neville Williams (ed.), *The Eighteenth-Century Constitution* (Cambridge, 1960), p. 46.
[104] John Spurr, 'The Church of England, Comprehension and the Toleration Act of 1689', *English Historical Review*, 104:413 (1989), pp. 927–46; Ralph Stevens, *Protestant Pluralism: The Reception of the Toleration Act, 1689–1720* (Woodbridge, 2018).
[105] Mark Goldie, 'John Locke, Jonas Proast, and Religious Toleration, 1688–1689', in Walsh, Haydon, and Taylor (eds), *Church of England*, pp. 143–71.

constitution is so perfect but that it may be made better'.[106] Latitudinarian churchmen believed the doctrines of the Church could be purified by clearing them of scholastic, sacerdotal, and superstitious trash. But the impulse to defend a broad-based establishment left them unwilling, between the Bangorian controversy (1717–21) and the subscription controversy of the 1760s and 1770s, to propose reform.[107]

Yet more care is necessary in defining the terms 'high' and 'low church'. As William Bulman has intimated, the debate that took place among Anglican churchmen in the aftermath of the seventeenth-century wars of religion was an effort to design civil religion. In this battle, various Anglican divines hoped to reconcile religion with civil peace by harnessing erudite scholarship, church history, and pastoral ministry.[108] It might seem counter-intuitive that a commitment to toleration did not depend upon secularisation and, specifically, the separation of church and state. But, in England, whether by royal indulgence or the Toleration Act, the magisterial church-state heralded toleration. Until the age of Enlightened Dissent during the late eighteenth century, Englishmen saw nothing contradictory in marrying Erastianism with toleration. But it was possible to conceive of intolerant Erastianism. There were sophisticated theological justifications, taken largely from Augustine, for coercion and persecution as legitimate means of Christian ministry, but which balanced them with pastoralism.[109] Henry Dodwell developed these themes in opposition to 'open hostilities against the truth'.[110] Similar arguments can be found in Stillingfleet's *The Unreasonableness of Separation* (1680). Since many aspects of Christian worship had not been laid down as necessary by Christ, they argued that the secular magistrate could forcibly impose creeds, worship, and ceremonies on hateful schismatics in the interest of godly unity.

The label of Anglican high-churchmanship belongs to the intense ecclesiological disputes that attended the Revolution settlement. The Revolution produced a unique arrangement by which the established church acquiesced to a degree of statutory toleration. The Church of England at once recognised legitimate religious pluralism and claimed single jurisdictional authority. Whigs and Tories were debating the most prudent way to handle Protestant Nonconformity by means of learned culture and pastoral care in a project of Christian moral renewal to settle the church-state relationship.[111] The mainstay of intolerant Anglican clergymen who cautiously accepted the Revolution were

---

[106] Burnet, *Pastoral Care*, New Preface, p. 9.
[107] Martin Fitzpatrick, 'Latitudinarianism at the Parting of the Ways: A Suggestion', in Walsh, Haydon, and Taylor (eds), *Church of England*, pp. 209–27.
[108] William J. Bulman, *Anglican Enlightenment: Orientalism, Religion and Politics in England and Its Empire, 1648–1715* (Cambridge, 2015).
[109] Mark Goldie, 'The Theory of Religious Intolerance in Restoration England', in Ole Peter Grell, Jonathan Israel, and Nicholas Tyacke (eds), *From Persecution to Toleration: The Glorious Revolution and Religion in England* (Oxford, 1991), pp. 331–68.
[110] Henry Dodwell, *A Reply to Mr Baxter's Pretended Confutation* (London, 1681), p. 192.
[111] Bulman, *Anglican Enlightenment*, pp. 245–76.

neither fully-fledged Jacobites nor convinced nonjurors. They were committed to the dominant ecclesiological views of the Restoration. They conceived of the Church of England as a distinct society governed by sacerdotal priests. They baulked at associational and voluntarist Christian revival, favouring traditional forms of ecclesiastical discipline.[112]

Issues like the occasional conformity and Convocation controversies resulted in angry high-church charges of 'the church in danger'.[113] In raising this cry, men like Sacheverell took themselves to be defending the sacral status of the Church of England against those who, they believed, hoped to recast the Church as an institution either of the civil state or civil society. Their defence of the Church had roots in fears that freethinkers and deists were pillaging patristics and church history for schismatic purposes. They were sensible of the Roman Catholic accusation that Protestants were inherently disunited and prone to chaos. Tory slogans during the general election of 1710, for instance, included the following: 'No Rump Parliament', 'No Forty-Eight', 'No Presbyterian Rebellion', and 'Save the Queen's White Neck'.[114]

The plight of Tory high-churchmanship is that it suffered history being written by the victors. It was difficult to conceive of the Church of England as a holy catholic society blessed with spiritual autonomy once secular political action had removed its supreme governor during the Revolution. The catholicity of the church was hard to reconcile with the national character of its establishment. Apostolic *jure divino* justifications for sacerdotal priests confronted the magisterial argument that church government sat within the purview of the civil magistrate. If Christ had handed the keys of heaven to the priesthood of all believers, it became increasingly difficult to argue that he had handed the power of discipline to the spiritual rulers of the church. But, as the Tractarian revival and Oxford movement during the nineteenth century demonstrate, there was nothing inevitable about any victory of one mode of divinity against the others.[115]

A key feature of high-churchmanship was its willingness to engage with other modes of divinity on such issues as clerical pastoralism and learned ministry. High churchmen forced divines who engaged with ideas of civil religion onto the same territory. The claims that the church had once been a separate society and its priests retained sacerdotal status were central to Warburton's *The Alliance*

---

112 Sirota, *Christian Monitors*, pp. 14–17, 23–32.
113 Brent Sirota, 'The Occasional Conformity Controversy, Moderation and the Anglican Critique of Modernity, 1700–1714', *HJ*, 57:1 (2014), pp. 81–105.
114 W. A. Speck, *Tory and Whig: The Struggle in the Constituencies, 1701–1715* (London, 1970); Joseph Hone, *Literature and Party Politics at the Accession of Queen Anne* (Oxford, 2017), ch. 5.
115 Peter Nockles, *The Oxford Movement in Context* (Cambridge, 1994), pp. 44–103; B. W. Young, '"Knock-Kneed Giants": Victorian Representations of Eighteenth-Century Thought', in Jane Garnett and Colin Matthew (eds), *Revival and Religion since 1700: Essays for John Walsh* (London, 1993), pp. 79–93; *The Victorian Eighteenth Century* (Oxford, 2007), pp. 70–102.

of Church and State (1736) and the arguments of 'church Whigs' like Gibson. In his *Codex Juris Ecclesiastici Anglicani* (1713), Gibson examined the rights and duties of Anglican priests as well as the articles, canons, and constitution of the Church of England to show that, while priests retained sacerdotal status, their authority lay under the royal supremacy.[116] Although the ecclesiological claims of Warburton and Gibson were different, partly because Warburton's arguments were so idiosyncratic, both divines shared the goal of reconciling Anglican clergymen, so hostile to supremacy of the state over the church during the opening decades of the eighteenth century, with the Erastian realities of the Hanoverian order.

To discuss themes of learned and pastoral ministry alongside such questions as voluntarism and latitude is to step into ecclesiastical history. The eighteenth-century Church of England has repeatedly stood accused of somnolence. During the twentieth century, this accusation was a corollary of the outdated supposition that a decline in religious controversy attended the 'the growth of political stability'.[117] It was once common to suppose that eighteenth-century Anglican churchmen preferred port and plum pudding over pious principles. Hogarthian histories, redolent of *The Sleeping Congregation* of 1736 (Figure 1), paint the worldly picture of a venal clergy.[118]

However, such conclusions buy into the terms of nineteenth-century critics of the Hanoverian church. Tractarian revivalists, Victorian high churchmen, and evangelicals each had motives for writing an eighteenth-century history of spiritual indifference. The debate about the state of the eighteenth-century church will continue among social and ecclesiastical historians. Issues like pluralism, building maintenance, and spirituality will be balanced against such new challenges as urbanisation, industrialisation, and Methodism.[119] To pursue theories of civil religion in eighteenth-century England is to encounter an idealised portrait of learned and pastoral ministry. It was a portrait painted by laymen and clergymen concerned with the spiritual mission of the church and its relationship with the civil state.

---

[116] Norman Sykes, *Edmund Gibson, Bishop of London, 1669–1748: A Study in Politics and Religion in the Eighteenth Century* (London, 1926); Stephen Taylor, '"Dr. Codex" and the Whig "Pope": Edmund Gibson, Bishop of Lincoln and London, 1716–1748', in R. W. Davis (ed.), *Lords of Parliament: Studies, 1714–1914* (Stanford, 1995), pp. 9–28.
[117] See J. H. Plumb, *The Growth of Political Stability in England, 1675–1725* (London, 1967).
[118] Roy Porter, *English Society in the Eighteenth Century* (Harmondsworth, 1982), p. 191. For Hogarth, see Ronald Paulson, *Hogarth's Harlot: Sacred Parody in Enlightenment England* (Baltimore and London, 2003).
[119] F. C. Mather, 'Georgian Churchmanship Reconsidered: Some Variations in Anglican Public Worship, 1714–1830', *JEH*, 36:2 (1985), pp. 255–83; Peter Virgin, *The Church in an Age of Negligence* (Cambridge, 1989); Walsh, Haydon, and Taylor (eds), *Church of England*; W. M. Jacob, *The Clerical Profession in the Long Eighteenth Century* (Oxford, 2007); Sara Slinn, *The Education of the Anglican Clergy, 1780–1839* (Woodbridge, 2017).

Figure 1. William Hogarth, *The Sleeping Congregation* (1736). Image number 00136475001. © Trustees of the British Museum

Civil religion and the Enlightenment in England

Ideas of civil religion formed an important but neglected theme of the Enlightenment in England. Civil religionists believed priestly power had so disturbed the civil peace that it needed to be brought to heel. They also concerned themselves with reconciling religious pluralism and public religion.[120] The seventeenth-century wars of religion provided the occasion for intellectuals to grapple with religion and political life, maintaining a civil order free from religious zeal and turned towards worldly improvement.[121] Enlightened thinkers were developing a riposte, traced in the French context by Carl Becker, to Augustine's ridicule of Cicero's immortal commonwealth and civil theology of worldly citizens in book 22 of the fifth-century *The City of God against the Pagans*.[122]

The tendency of Enlightenment scholarship is to focus purely on the inward beliefs of thinkers.[123] When historians and literary scholars confront sceptics or atheists who upheld the established religion, it is easiest to explain the tension by arguing that elite irreligionists realised the need to use religion to keep the poor and vulgar governable.[124] Machiavellian conceptions of the political utility of the pious fraud converged with patrician conservatism. Undoubtedly, there existed a distinction between esoteric and exoteric philosophy. Some regions of the cultural world of the Enlightenment in England were imbued with elite exclusivism. However, this study will dwell remarkably little on questions of belief or unbelief. Whatever their inward thoughts, civil religionists held a principled commitment to the public religion bequeathed by the Reformation. They believed the Reformation had afforded the same liberty to the deist or sceptic as it had to the Dissenter or heterodox Anglican. Their world had been bequeathed by the struggles of Christian reform. Their civil order had emerged from the wars of religion. Historians might be attracted by the idea of smug unbelievers sniggering from within the comfort of the cabinet and the secrecy of the lodge. But Enlightened thinkers in England overwhelmingly believed that public religion was a feature of civilised society.

Such was the assessment of Alexis de Tocqueville in reflecting on the *ancien régime* and causes of the French Revolution. England had had its fair share of

---

[120] Jonathan Sheehan, 'Enlightenment, Religion, and the Enigma of Secularization: A Review Essay', *American Historical Review*, 108:4 (2003), pp. 1061–80; *The Enlightenment Bible: Translation, Scholarship, Culture* (Princeton, 2005), pp. xii–xiii; Justin Champion, 'Godless Politics: Hobbes and Public Religion', in William J. Bulman and Robert G. Ingram (eds), *God in the Enlightenment* (Oxford, 2016), pp. 42–62.
[121] Dan Edelstein, *The Enlightenment: A Genealogy* (Chicago, 2010), pp. 13, 125.
[122] Carl Becker, *The Heavenly City of the Eighteenth-Century Philosophers* (2nd edn, New Haven and London, 2003, orig. 1932).
[123] David Berman, *A History of Atheism in Britain from Hobbes to Russell* (London, 1988); Hunter and Wootton (eds), *Atheism*; Wayne Hudson, Diego Lucci, and Jeffrey R. Wigelsworth (eds), *Atheism and Deism Revalued: Heterodox Religious Identities in Britain, 1650–1800* (Farnham, 2014).
[124] Sarah Ellenzweig, *The Fringes of Belief: English Literature, Ancient Heresy, and the Politics of Freethinking, 1660–1760* (Stanford, 2008).

irreligion. It was 'Bolingbroke who taught Voltaire'. But irreligionists never took their philosophies to the conclusions of French *libertinage érudit* because they 'had something to fear from a revolution'. They 'hastened to come to the aid of the established beliefs'. Political parties 'found it in their interest to unite their cause with that of the Church'. Bolingbroke became 'the ally of the bishops'. Whatever 'the defects of its establishment and the abuses of all sorts which worked within it', elites revered the Church of England. So, 'like a politician', did Hume. But this was more than mere pragmatism. Religion, Tocqueville continued, 'is useful for the stability of the law and the good order of society'. Further, 'a civilised society, but above all a free society, cannot subsist without religion'. Respect for religion was 'the greatest guarantee of the stability of the state and the security of individuals'.[125]

The concern with religion improperly construed expressed itself in opposition to priestly power and barbarous enthusiasm. It is wise to recall the instruction of J. C. D. Clark to study the ways in which, between the Restoration and Catholic emancipation, England retained features of the *ancien régime* and confessional society including Tory and high-church ideologies of divine right monarchy and episcopacy.[126] Clark overstated his controversial arguments. His portrayal of the Church of England as a monolithic institution of *jure divino* Tory high-church-manship belied the many currents of reform that throve within it. His insistence that reform and 'radicalism' emerged only from Protestant Dissent neglected those possibilities within the establishment. But Clark provided a useful corrective to liberal and *marxisant* obsessions with locating the origins of secular modernity.

The questions of the religious character of the state and the role of clergymen dominated the century.[127] The cry of 'church in danger' echoed for decades in the occasional conformity controversy, against the repeal of the Tory Occasional Conformity Act (1711) in 1719, and in the Bangorian controversy following the incendiary sermon by Hoadly to George I entitled *The Nature of the Kingdom of Christ* (1717). The cry carried into Robert Walpole's much-satirised relationship with Gibson and their support for the Quaker's Tithe Bill and the Mortmain Act during the 1730s. In *The Pillars of Priestcraft and Orthodoxy Shaken* (1752), the Dissenter Richard Baron raised 'everlasting reasons for opposing all priests,

---

[125] Alexis de Tocqueville, *The Old Regime and the Revolution*, eds François Furet and Françoise Mélonio, trans. Alan S. Kahan (2 vols, Chicago and London, 1998), vol. 1, p. 206.
[126] J. C. D. Clark, *English Society, 1660–1832* (2nd edn, Cambridge, 2000); *Revolution and Rebellion: State and Society in England in the Seventeenth and Eighteenth Centuries* (Cambridge, 1986); 'On Hitting the Buffers: The Historiography of England's Ancien Regime: A Response', *Past & Present*, 117:1 (1987), pp. 195–207; *The Language of Liberty: Political Discourse and Social Dynamics in the Anglo-American World* (Cambridge, 1994); 'Secularization and Modernization: The Failure of a "Grand Narrative"', *HJ*, 55:1 (2012), pp. 161–94. But see Joanna Innes, 'Jonathan Clark, Social History, and England's "Ancien Regime"', *Past & Present*, 115:1 (1987), pp. 165–200.
[127] Philip Connell, *Secular Chains: Poetry and the Politics of Religion from Milton to Pope* (Oxford, 2016), pp. 54, 136, 162, 240, 242.

and an unanswerable argument against all their claims of power and authority'. He aimed to emancipate 'the minds of men, and to free them from those chains in which they have been long held to the great disgrace of both reason and Christianity'.[128] Gibbon argued that the 'public establishment of Christianity may be considered as one of those important and domestic revolutions which excite the most lively curiosity, and afford the most valuable instruction'. The 'ecclesiastical institutions' of Constantine's reign 'are still connected by an indissoluble chain, with the opinions, the passions, and the interests of the present generation'.[129]

The Enlightenment in England was not the same as the militantly anticlerical Enlightenment in France.[130] There was neither *un parti des philosophes* nor a civil religion of a deistical supreme being akin to that of Maximilien Robespierre. As Pocock wrote, 'an ox sits upon the tongue' when articulating 'the phrase "the English Enlightenment"'.[131] But this should not be to confuse the nature of English anticlericalism and civil religion. As Roy Porter argued, the Enlightenment 'throve in England *within* piety'.[132] Its exponents insisted that they were not simply defending right religion in general but Christianity in particular and above all. Pocock and B. W. Young have shown that the Enlightenment in England was 'conservative and in several ways clerical'.[133] This study expands the brief suggestion of Pocock that historians might understand

> the process of enlightenment in England as the slow but steady transformation of Anglicanism into a civil religion, which presented the King as a sacred figure only because he was the head of all civil society, and

---

[128] Richard Baron, *The Pillars of Priestcraft and Orthodoxy Shaken* (4 vols, London, 1752), vol. 1, pp. iii, vi.
[129] *DF*, vol. 1, p. 725.
[130] Peter Gay, *The Enlightenment: An Interpretation* (2 vols, London, 1966–9); Robert Darnton, 'In Search of the Enlightenment: Recent Attempts to Create a Social History of Ideas', *JMH*, 43:1 (1971), pp. 113–32; 'The Case for the Enlightenment: George Washington's False Teeth', in *George Washington's False Teeth: An Unconventional Guide to the Eighteenth Century* (New York and London, 2003), pp. 3–24.
[131] J. G. A. Pocock, 'Post-Puritan England and the Problem of the Enlightenment', in Perez Zagorin (ed.), *Culture and Politics from Puritanism to the Enlightenment* (Berkeley, 1980), pp. 91–111, at p. 91.
[132] Roy Porter, 'The Enlightenment in England', in Roy Porter and Mikuláš Teich (eds), *The Enlightenment in National Context* (Cambridge, 1981), pp. 1–18, at pp. 6–8; *Enlightenment: Britain and the Creation of the Modern World* (London, 2000), p. 99; James Bradley, 'The Changing Shape of Religious Ideas in Enlightened England', in Alister Chapman, John Coffey, and Brad S. Gregory (eds), *Seeing Things Their Way: Intellectual History and the Return of Religion* (Notre Dame, IN, 2009), pp. 175–201.
[133] J. G. A. Pocock, 'Clergy and Commerce: The Conservative Enlightenment in England', in R. J. Ajello (ed.), *L'Età dei Lumi: Studi Storici sul Settecento Europeo in Onore di Franco Venturi* (Naples, 1985), pp. 523–68, at p. 528; *Barbarism and Religion* (6 vols, Cambridge, 1999–2015); B. W. Young, *Religion and Enlightenment in Eighteenth-Century England: Theological Debate from Locke to Burke* (Oxford, 1998); 'Religious History and the Eighteenth-Century Historian', *HJ*, 43:3 (2000), pp. 849–68; 'John Jortin, Ecclesiastical History, and the Christian Republic of Letters', *HJ*, 55:4 (2012), pp. 961–81, at p. 973.

society as embodying the sacred so effectively that it needed no representative of God to head it.[134]

In this process, Anglicans syncretised the holy spirit with the structures of society to undermine the enthusiastic claim that the spirit could infuse the godly few.

The contributions of Pocock and Young sit alongside a larger movement to show how the Enlightenment emerged within rational, Socinian, and Protestant forms of Christianity.[135] In England, the Enlightenment had roots in the long Reformation and, specifically, the reformed polemic against priests.[136] Weapons like *imperium in imperio* and *praemunire* had been used against the papacy in the medieval church. They were turned against Roman Catholic priests during the Henrician Reformation, intolerant Anglicans during the late seventeenth century, and closed priesthoods during the Enlightenment. Throughout the eighteenth century, the Anglican vogue for moderation, forming an Arminian middle way between Roman Catholicism and Calvinist enthusiasm, represented the first full example of religious Enlightenment. Instituted by clergymen like Warburton and ranging from low- to high-church ecclesiology, the religious Enlightenment in England was 'an ethos or disposition' that embraced Lockean philosophy and Newtonian science.[137]

The conservative and clerical variations of the Enlightenment in England did not possess a monopoly on civil religion. It was also a feature of Enlightened Dissent.[138] It developed the reformed assumption that the mission of the state was the overthrow of the popish Antichrist and attacked the remnants of popery in English Protestantism, including the Trinity.[139] But eighteenth-century Dissent shed the tendency of its forebears to slip into a rule of saints, often dropping the Calvinist insistence on grace. Enlightened Dissenters believed worldly Christianity, though improving, was not yet theologically pure. Away from the

---

134 Pocock, 'Clergy and Commerce', p. 534.
135 Hugh Trevor-Roper, 'The Religious Origins of the Enlightenment', in *Religion, the Reformation and Social Change* (London, 1967), pp. 193–236; Sheridan Gilley, 'Christianity and Enlightenment', *History of European Ideas*, 1:2 (1981), pp. 103–121; James Bradley and Dale van Kley (eds), *Religion and Politics in Enlightenment Europe* (Notre Dame, IN, 2001); David Sorkin, *'A Wise, Enlightened and Reliable Piety': The Religious Enlightenment in Central and Western Europe, 1689–1789* (Southampton, 2002); S. J. Barnett, *The Enlightenment and Religion: The Myths of Modernity* (Manchester, 2003); Mark Curran, *Atheism, Religion and Enlightenment in Pre-Revolutionary Europe* (Woodbridge, 2012).
136 S. J. Barnett, *Idol Temples and Crafty Priests: The Origins of Enlightenment Anticlericalism* (Basingstoke, 1999).
137 David Sorkin, *The Religious Enlightenment: Protestants, Jews, and Catholics from London to Vienna* (Princeton, 2008), pp. 8–9, 23–65.
138 Franco Venturi, *Utopia and Reform in the Enlightenment* (Cambridge, 1971), p. 132; Knud Haakonssen (ed.), *Enlightenment and Religion: Rational Dissent in Eighteenth-Century Britain* (Cambridge, 1996).
139 Lamont, *Godly Rule*; Peter Toon (ed.), *Puritans, the Millennium and the Future of Israel: Puritan Eschatology, 1600–1660* (Cambridge and London, 1970); E. L. Tuveson, *Millennium and Utopia* (Gloucester, MA, 1972); Christianson, *Reformers and Babylon*; Firth, *Apocalyptic Tradition*.

radical fringes, they conceded the need for a public religion under the state even though they supposed that Christ could be the church's only lawgiver. Richard Price once remarked that at the time of the establishment of the Church of England, 'the nation was but emerging from Popery'. Was it possible, he asked, that the establishment 'should be entirely agreeable to the purity of the Christian doctrine' and that 'it should want no review in order to secure its safety, and adapt it to a more improved and enlightened age'?[140] For figures like Priestley, civil religion lay among the congregations of Dissenters who elected their learned and pastoral ministers while coexisting with the Church of England.

Although the subjects of this book are civil religion and the Enlightenment in England, one chapter is dedicated to Hume. Pocock has discussed Hume's self-perception as a 'North Briton' and Colin Kidd has reminded historians of the value of studying Scotland within an 'Anglo-British' framework.[141] This is not the occasion for a full-scale exploration of theories of civil religion in the Scottish Enlightenment.[142] The Presbyterian Reformation produced the Scottish Kirk, which, as a national church devoid of episcopacy, developed a different character from the established and episcopal Church of England. Hume's civil religion not only throws relief onto the English dimension but suggests Scottish points of departure. Hume, the sceptic, represents a vital case study in both the English and Scottish contexts of a thinker who upheld the magisterial Anglican and elder-elective Presbyterian Reformations for reasons beyond a tactical desire to keep the poor governable.

The scholarship of civil religion

Having related civil religion with the Enlightenment in England, it is possible to appreciate the problem of Rousseau. Prompted by earlier formulations in Machiavelli and Hobbes, Rousseau has provided the standard by which historians and political theorists define civil religion. In this guise, civil religion has become the tool of the politician seeking to keep a populace governable. Following the Second World War, this definition resulted in the association of civil religion with modern totalitarianism. Scholars looked back to the influence of Rousseau on Robespierre and the Terror. They often added G. W. F. Hegel by his sanctification of the Prussian state. The ideology of blind submission to the state, civil religion either reversed the modern insight of the separation of

---

[140] Richard Price, *Political Writings*, ed. D. O. Thomas (Cambridge, 1991), p. 10.
[141] J. G. A. Pocock, 'Hume and the American Revolution: The Dying Thoughts of a North Briton', in *Virtue, Commerce, and History: Essays on Political Thought and History, Chiefly in the Eighteenth Century* (Cambridge, 1985), pp. 125–41; Colin Kidd, *Subverting Scotland's Past: Scottish Whig Historians and the Creation of an Anglo-British Identity, 1689–c.1830* (Cambridge, 1993).
[142] Colin Kidd, 'Constructing a Civil Religion: Scots Presbyterians and the Eighteenth-Century British State', in J. Kirk (ed.), *The Scottish Churches and the Union Parliament, 1707–1999* (Edinburgh, 2001), pp. 1–21. I am grateful to Mark Goldie for providing unpublished material relating to civil religion in the Scottish Enlightenment.

church and state or it ignored the Augustinian claim that humans in the earthly city were not perfectible.[143]

In social and political theory, the secularisation thesis has lent weight to the standard definition of civil religion. The development of the social science of religion itself had roots in atheism.[144] Sociologists indebted to Emile Durkheim and Max Weber saw the decline of religion as emblematic of the transition from traditional to modern society. The disenchantment of the world replaced magic and superstition with science, reason, and scepticism. Durkheim, having consulted Rousseau, left open the possibility of a secular civil religion built around patriotism and based on sociology conceived as the science of morality.[145] Secularisation theorists have drawn the liberal conclusions that religion would inevitably decline, become separated from secular political authority, and 'privatise' to inward belief.[146]

Encouraged by Jürgen Habermas, the idea of the 'post-secular' has generated new avenues of research into the history of civil religion.[147] The post-secular turn has begun to alert intellectual historians to the secular assumptions of the discipline.[148] The prominence of public religion, especially evangelical Protestantism and fundamentalist Islam, and problems of integration and pluralism in multicultural society have made scholars wary of suggestions that religion could be 'privatised' or that it was bound to decline irretrievably, however much differentiation has occurred between secular and religious spheres.[149] In America,

---

[143] Karl Popper, *The Open Society and Its Enemies* (2 vols, London, 1945); J. L. Talmon, *The Origins of Totalitarian Democracy* (London, 1952); Robert Tucker, *Philosophy and Myth in Karl Marx* (Cambridge, 1961), p. 31. See, more recently, Ronald Beiner, *Civil Religion: A Dialogue in the History of Political Philosophy* (Cambridge, 2011).

[144] Talcott Parsons, 'The Theoretical Development of the Sociology of Religion', *JHI*, 5:2 (1944), pp. 176–90; Rodney Stark, 'Atheism, Faith, and the Social Scientific Study of Religion', *Journal of Contemporary Religion*, 14:1 (1999), pp. 41–62.

[145] Ruth A. Wallace, 'Emile Durkheim and the Civil Religion Concept', *Review of Religious Research*, 18:3 (1977), pp. 287–90; Marcela Christi, 'Durkheim's Political Sociology: Civil Religion, Nationalism and Globalisation', in Annika Hvithamar, Margit Warburg, and Brian Jacobsen (eds), *Holy Nations and Global Identities: Civil Religion, Nationalism and Globalisation* (Leiden, 2009), pp. 47–78.

[146] Bryan Wilson, *Religion in Secular Society* (London, 1966); Peter Berger, *The Sacred Canopy* (Garden City, NJ, 1967); Thomas Luckmann, *The Invisible Religion: The Problem of Religion in Modern Society* (New York, 1967).

[147] Jürgen Habermas and Eduardo Hendieta, *Religion and Rationality: Essays on Reason, God and Modernity* (Cambridge, 2002); Jürgen Habermas and Joseph Ratzinger, *Dialectics of Secularization: On Reason and Religion* (San Francisco, 2006); Jürgen Habermas, 'Religion in the Public Sphere', *European Journal of Philosophy*, 14:1 (2006), pp. 1–25; 'Notes on Post-Secular Society', *New Perspectives Quarterly*, 25:4 (2008), pp. 17–29; Philip S. Gorski, David Kyuman Kim, John Torpey, and Jonathan VanAntwerpen (eds), *The Post-Secular in Question: Religion in Contemporary Society* (New York and London, 2012).

[148] Michael Allen Gillespie, *The Theological Origins of Modernity* (Chicago, 2008); Chapman, Coffey, and Gregory (eds.), *Seeing Things Their Way*.

[149] Peter Berger, *The Desecularization of the World: Resurgent Religion and World Politics* (Washington, DC, 1999); Eduardo Mendieta and Jonathan VanAntwerpen (eds), *The Power of Religion in the Public Sphere* (New York, 2011).

there has been a strong overlap between post-secular scholarship and research into civil religion, showing that American republicanism emerged partly from the Calvinist idea of a covenanted community.[150] Since the secularisation thesis has relied on an impression of the Enlightenment in its most irreligious and secularising moods, it is necessary to study how Enlightened thinkers sought to reconcile rational and civilised religion with the state and civil society.[151] Even the most inwardly sceptical Hanoverian civil religionist argued that religion was a natural and inevitable feature of humanity. It was not simply that public arrangements needed to cope with religious belief. It was also that private belief and public worship were intrinsic aspects of political society.

In British historical scholarship, Goldie has briefly outlined concepts of civil religion in eighteenth-century England.[152] But Goldie's main interest has been the seventeenth century, especially Harrington, and 'neo-Harringtonians', like Henry Neville, who reformulated Harrington's republican and congregationalist civil religion for the temper of the Restoration through the magisterial crown-in-parliament.[153] Goldie revealed how, during the 1690s, the likes of Sir Robert Howard and William Stephens transformed Harrington's concept of 'priestcraft' into Whig anticlericalism.[154] Similarly, Locke remains a striking candidate for civil religion in arguing for a tolerant public religion based on Christian primitivism.[155] But to pursue civil religion during the eighteenth century is to encounter a different temper than those of Interregnum republicans, Restoration Whigs, and Revolution anticlericals. Just as the Enlightenment in England could have Tory moods, felt by Bolingbroke and the young Gibbon, English civil religionists could have Tory inclinations.

Bulman has recently demonstrated that the seventeenth-century roots of civil religion lay not simply among Whigs and low churchmen. All modes of Restoration Anglican divinity developed concepts of civil religion to generate civil peace after the Interregnum. The object was a variety of Christianity that promoted civilisation, morality, worldly improvement, political stability, and virtuous subjecthood. Civil religion belonged as much to Lancelot Addison, sacerdotal Anglican father of the Whig doyen Joseph, in conceiving of the church

---

[150] Robert N. Bellah, *The Broken Covenant: American Civil Religion in Time of Trial* (2nd edn, Chicago and London, 1975); Philip Gorski, *American Covenant: A History of Civil Religion from the Puritans to the Present* (Princeton, 2017).

[151] José Casanova, *Public Religions in the Modern World* (Chicago and London, 1994), pp. 30–2.

[152] Mark Goldie, 'Civil Religion and the English Enlightenment', in Gordon Schochet (ed.), *Politics, Politeness, and Patriotism* (Washington, DC, 1993), pp. 31–46.

[153] Goldie, 'Civil Religion of James Harrington', pp. 221–2.

[154] Goldie, 'Priestcraft and the Birth of Whiggism'.

[155] Mark Goldie, 'John Locke and Anglican Royalism', *Political Studies*, 31:1 (1983), pp. 61–85. See also Theodore J. Koontz, 'Religion and Political Cohesion: John Locke and Jean Jacques Rousseau', *Journal of Church and State*, 23:1 (1981), pp. 950–115; John Marshall, *John Locke, Toleration and Early Enlightenment Culture* (Cambridge, 2006), p. 517; A. L. Herold, '"The Chief Characteristic Mark of the True Church": John Locke's Theology of Toleration and His Case for Civil Religion', *Review of Politics*, 76:2 (2014), pp. 195–221.

as a distinct society blessed with *jure divino* priesthood and the alliance between princes and priests to form the state and defend civil society.[156] Similarly, during the eighteenth century, sacerdotal justifications of clerical authority, usually strongly associated with partisan high-church Toryism, underpinned the idea, propounded by Warburton, of the church as a distinct society that had entered into an alliance with the state.

Some historians have revealed more 'radical' versions of civil religion in early Hanoverian England. Taking its cue from Margaret Jacob, a motivation for this research is to locate a revolt against Christianity that anticipated the Enlightenment in France, casting English intellectual history at the turn of the eighteenth century as a battle between priests and freethinkers centred around the deist controversy.[157] A popular candidate for such a civil religion is Toland for his republicanism, materialism, and pantheism.[158] Henry Stubbe is another.[159] However, such 'radical' theories of civil religion were not mainstream. Theories of civil religion congenial to the magisterial Reformation will be the focus of this study. Themes here presented accord with the civil religion of a less 'radical' Toland, presented by Robert Sullivan and East, before Toland's public position evolved towards Spinozism and pantheism.[160] Despite, or, perhaps, due to, his idiosyncrasies, Toland has been the focus of a great deal of scholarship. Since there was a large cast of other theorists of civil religion, Toland need not feature here.

Pursuing civil religion

Enlightened intellectuals in England believed the Church of England could be transformed into a civil religion. They attempted to render the established church fully as a public institution of the state, placing its priests under the *jure humano* authority of the civil sovereign and adapting the Thirty-Nine Articles into a civil profession of faith. The ministers of the Church of England, at once claiming

---

[156] Bulman, *Anglican Enlightenment*, pp. 8, 141–5, 285–90; 'Introduction: Enlightenment for the Culture Wars', in Bulman and Ingram (eds), *God in the Enlightenment*, pp. 1–41, at pp. 24–5.
[157] Justin Champion, *Pillars of Priestcraft Shaken: The Church of England and Its Enemies, 1660–1730* (Cambridge, 1992), pp. 22, 186–91, 192–222. See also Margaret C. Jacob, *The Radical Enlightenment: Pantheists, Freemasons, and Republicans* (London, 1981); *Living the Enlightenment: Freemasonry and Politics in Eighteenth-Century Europe* (New York, 1991).
[158] Justin Champion, *Republican Learning: John Toland and the Crisis of Christian Culture, 1696–1722* (Manchester and New York, 2003), pp. 9, 167–89; Jonathan Israel, *Radical Enlightenment: Philosophy and the Making of Modernity, 1650–1750* (Oxford, 2001), p. 613. For Israel's 'moderate Enlightenment', see *Enlightenment Contested: Philosophy, Modernity, and the Emancipation of Man, 1670–1752* (Oxford, 2006).
[159] James R. Jacob, *Henry Stubbe, Radical Protestantism and the Early Enlightenment* (Cambridge, 1983).
[160] Robert E. Sullivan, *John Toland and the Deist Controversy: A Study in Adaptions* (Cambridge, MA, 1982), pp. 22–6, 142, 173–4, 184–5, 226; East, *Radicalization of Cicero*, pp. 210–16.

catholic apostolicity and the sole power to interpret revealed truth while recognising the imperfection of their articles of faith, were to preach the gospel message of Christ and prioritise pious living in this world over theological wrangling about the nature of the world to come. The civil religion of eighteenth-century England was one of shared rituals of public worship because its ministers were fallible humans who interpreted imperfectly the nature of the divine being. By observing the external worship of the Church of England, Hanoverian intellectuals hoped to fashion a modern civil religion in a Christian commonwealth.

This book presents a series of case studies to illustrate this argument. The studies include Shaftesbury, Trenchard, Gordon, Bolingbroke, Hume, and Gibbon. They also encompass Anglican churchmen, including Gibson, Warburton, Middleton, Blackburne, and Law, as well as several Enlightened Dissenters such as Priestley and Price. Revealing the varieties of civil religion in Hanoverian England, the case studies are neither exhaustive of the thinkers concerned nor equivalent to a full excavation. Since it is primarily an intellectual history of the idea of civil religion, this book does not focus on the impact of anticlericalism or civil religion in parliament. Further research might include William Hay MP, author of *An Essay on Civil Government* (1728) and *Religio Philosophi: Or, the Principles of Morality and Christianity* (1753), and Sir Richard Cocks MP and his *The Church of England Secur'd* (1722). Another possibility might be the Dissenting campaign, during the 1730s, to remove the Test and Corporation Acts during which the appearance of the Dissenting newspaper, *The Old Whig* (1735–8), provoked the Erastian arguments of *The Occasional Paper*.[161]

English civil religion might also be better understood in relation to legal anticlericalism. The common law mind tended toward Erastian hostility to the ecclesiastical courts and the jurisdictional pretensions of the Church of England. Sir Michael Foster, who would become a judge of the king's bench, refuted Gibson's clericalism in the *Codex* in *An Examination of the Scheme of Church Power* (1735). The Lord Chief Justice, Philip Yorke, earl of Hardwicke, ruled in '*Middleton* versus *Crofts*' (1736) that, since the Reformation, the Church of England lacked the power to make canons that bound the laity.[162] In the seventeenth- and eighteenth-century veneration for the Saxons lay a variety of anti-papal ancient constitutionalism in which Erastians lauded Saxon kings for holding the curia in check.[163]

---

[161] Andrew Thompson, 'Popery, Politics, and Private Judgement in Early Hanoverian Britain', *HJ*, 45:2 (2002), pp. 333–56; 'Contesting the Test Acts: Dissent, Parliament and the Public in the 1730s', *PH*, 24:1 (2005), pp. 58–70; James Bradley, 'The Public, Parliament and the Protestant Dissenting Deputies, 1732–1740', *PH*, 24:1 (2005), pp. 71–90.
[162] George R. Bush, 'Dr Codex Silenced: *Middleton* v *Crofts* Revisited', *Journal of Legal History*, 24:1 (2007), pp. 23–58.
[163] R. J. Smith, *The Gothic Bequest: Medieval Institutions in British Thought, 1688–1863* (Cambridge, 1987); Gabriel Glickman, *The English Catholic Community, 1688–1745: Politics, Culture and Ideology* (Woodbridge, 2009), pp. 209–15.

The limits of a study of this nature demand selectivity. The case studies involve figures associated with scepticism, deism, low- and high-church Anglicanism, and Protestant Dissent. Alongside the varieties of civil religion, they illustrate the central and uniting themes. They also provide various test cases for the central contention that the generation of a Christian civil religion was more concerned with public regulation of religion than inward belief. For the religious sceptic or deist, issues such as the Trinity could be accepted as matters of faith for so long as they did not endanger civil peace or the state.[164] For the Protestant Dissenter, the imperfect doctrines of the church establishment need not imply its abolition since they reflected the imperfect state of religious knowledge among Christians. For low-church Anglicans, the church establishment prioritised latitude to include as many sincere Christians within its fold as possible. Especially during the subscription controversy, the concern with sincerity led to opposition to the requirement for some professions to subscribe to the Thirty-Nine Articles. Rather than imply abolition of the church establishment, opposition to subscription reinforced the need for the Church of England to comprehend all sincere Protestants within the Christian commonwealth.

Since a repeated insistence of this study will be the importance of prioritising ecclesiology over theology and, in turn, public faith over private consciences, the methodology will involve different approaches towards published writings and private manuscripts or correspondence. In public, theorists of civil religion, especially when harbouring sceptical or deistical moods, concerned themselves with the church establishment. Their private writings often contain more heterodox or controversial opinions. Elite respect for popular belief in the Ciceronian mould or the distinction between esoteric and exoteric philosophy help to account for the difference between public and private writings. Sometimes, as in Bolingbroke's decision to publish his philosophical writings posthumously, caution about the public's reception influenced a thinker's attitude. As in the case of Gibbon's *Decline and Fall* or Hume's *Dialogues concerning Natural Religion* (1779), public discussion of Christian history occasioned major controversy and secured a reputation for irreligion. Yet Bolingbroke, Hume, and Gibbon each claimed that their arguments need not shake the fundamentals of Christianity. To appreciate their claims, it is necessary first to construct their conception of the public role of religion.

By proceeding through case studies, the methodology also reveals that English theories of civil religion were contingent and evolved over time. Throughout the eighteenth century, partisan distinctions of Whig and Tory never mapped clearly onto church distinctions of 'low and high', and the relationship between them weakened as the century wore on. In the age of Shaftesbury, Trenchard,

---

[164] Paul Lym, *Mystery Unveiled: The Crisis of the Trinity in Early Modern England* (Oxford, 2012); Brent Sirota, 'The Trinitarian Crisis in Church and State: Religious Controversy and the Making of the Post-Revolutionary Church of England, 1687–1701', *JBS*, 52:1 (2013), pp. 26–54.

and Gordon, Whig anticlericalism confronted Tory cries of 'church in danger'. Party identities were strong at moments like the Convocation controversy, the Sacheverell trial, the Tory revival under Queen Anne, the Jacobite rebellions, and the Bangorian controversy. Although it would be erroneous to label the eighteenth-century Church of England as the Tory party at prayer, the civil religion of Shaftesbury, Trenchard, and Gordon belonged to a world in which the majority of Anglican priests seemed committed to divine right priesthood and monarchy with many tending towards Jacobitism. Anglican priests seemed to put the security of the Hanoverian state at risk.

But the character of anticlericalism shifted over time. Whereas, in the aftermath of the Revolution, it was far from obvious that churchmen should support the Whigs, the construction of a church–Whig alliance, especially by Gibson and Walpole, over the course of the 1730s, 1740s, and 1750s blunted the edges of Whig anticlericalism and rendered the Church of England more at ease with the Revolution settlement. Generational shift encouraged this process. The civil religion of Bolingbroke and Hume, conceptualised with the likes of Gibson and Warburton in view, was antagonistic to overly clerical defences of Erastianism. After his accession in 1760, developing a trend that had begun under the Pelhams during the 1740s and 1750s, George III attempted to be a patriot king for all the people and took apart the Whig coalition that had dominated the reigns of the first two Hanoverian monarchs. The ecclesiological and doctrinal keynotes of civil religion prior to the reign of George III evolved as new issues emerged in religious politics. During the 1770s and 1780s, new debates about church reform focused on the issue of subscription.

Further, as the eighteenth century wore on, it became easier to reconcile religious pluralism with the Church of England. After the final defeat of Jacobitism in 1745 and despite events like the Gordon riots (1780), the need to integrate Catholicism within the political and imperial system began to assert itself. The acquisition of Quebec and integration of Ireland were central contexts in the growing demand for Catholic emancipation from the 1770s until 1829. Similarly, despite the failure of the repeal campaigns of the 1730s, the growing respectability of Protestant Dissent led to the subscription campaign of the 1770s and the routine passage of indemnity acts.[165] The case studies close with a study of civil religion and Enlightened divinity among Anglicans and Dissenters. During the 1790s, the respectability of Dissent collapsed in the reaction to the French Revolution and the rise of Napoleon. Whatever their differences on the truths of Christianity, it was a moment when Gibbon found himself at one with Edmund Burke. It was also a moment when Samuel Taylor Coleridge, with whom this book concludes, turned from civil religion in its Unitarian and congregational iterations towards the Church of England.

---

[165] K. R. M. Short, 'The English Indemnity Acts, 1726–1867', *Church History*, 42:3 (1973), pp. 366–76.

The case studies subdivide into analyses of individual thinkers and thematic chapters. Chapter 1 studies Shaftesbury. Trenchard and Gordon are the subjects of Chapter 2. Chapter 3 focuses on Bolingbroke and his engagement with Warburton. Chapter 4 turns to Hume and his Anglo-British contexts. Chapter 5 studies Gibbon and his engagement with Middleton. Chapter 6 discusses Anglican clergymen who were engaged in political and religious reform during the late eighteenth century, especially Law and Blackburne, and developed civil religion using Anglican comprehension. It considers Protestant Dissenters, above all Priestley and Price, who conceived of a civil religion along Unitarian and congregational lines. The Conclusion explores the response of Coleridge to eighteenth-century civil religion in his attempt to prepare the national church for an age of Roman Catholic emancipation.

1

Building Athens from Jerusalem: Anthony Ashley Cooper, Third Earl of Shaftesbury

The Revolution in church and state

Shaftesbury tends to be understood as a deist and protagonist of Enlightenment proto-secularism. The inclination of modern scholarship is to fit Shaftesbury into a history of the origins of liberalism and to count him among the forebears of the separation between religion and politics.[1] Israel, for instance, associated Shaftesbury with the 'radical Enlightenment' alongside Toland, Tindal, Charles Blount, Anthony Collins, and Bernard Mandeville.[2] Shaftesbury's support for a national church has usually been exculpated as the tactic of a prudent elite who buttressed social order with theological sanction irrespective of his view of its truth.[3] Such histories privilege Shaftesbury's hostility towards sacerdotal priesthoods over the positive role that he imagined for Christian clergymen in civilised society. They foreground the extensive history of priestcraft in the 'Miscellaneous Reflections' that appended Shaftesbury's major work *Characteristics of Men, Manners, Opinions, Times* (1711).[4] They downplay his inward professions of Protestant allegiance and dutiful attendance at his parish church.[5] Where Shaftesbury has been associated with civil religion, it has been in its most deistical and secularising forms.[6]

---

[1] Stanley Green, *Shaftesbury's Philosophy of Religion and Ethics: A Study in Enthusiasm* (Athens, OH, 1967), p. 119.
[2] Israel, *Radical Enlightenment*, pp. 68, 116, 625–6, 709; *Enlightenment Contested*, pp. 346, 348.
[3] Alfred Owen Aldridge, 'Shaftesbury and the Deist Manifesto', *Transactions of the American Philosophical Society*, new ser., 41:2 (1951), pp. 297–382, at pp. 297–8; Green, *Shaftesbury's Philosophy*, p. 105.
[4] *Characteristics*, pp. 357–65, 371–3, 377–9.
[5] See Anthony Ashley Cooper, fourth earl of Shaftesbury, 'A Sketch of the Life of the Third Earl of Shaftesbury by His Son, the Fourth Earl', in Benjamin Rand (ed.), *The Life, Unpublished Letters, and Philosophical Regimen of Anthony, Earl of Shaftesbury* (London, 1900), pp. xvii–xxxi, at p. xvii; *Characteristics*, p. 471.
[6] Champion, *Pillars of Priestcraft Shaken*, pp. 23, 229, 233; Beiner, *Civil Religion*, p. 2, n. 2.

Similarly, Shaftesbury has been classified as a 'radical' Whig.[7] He has been associated with such thinkers as Toland, Molesworth, Trenchard, Gordon, Walter Moyle, and Andrew Fletcher. In politics, these men were suspicious of the fiscal-military state and the court's wish, during the late 1690s, to maintain a standing army in peacetime. In Pocock's formulation, they were 'civic humanists' defending the autonomous freeholder-citizen in the country against the courtly forces of junto Whiggism championed by John, Lord Somers.[8] Although republican politics need not have implied irreligion, there is a tendency to suppose that these themes coexisted in Shaftesbury's circle. Linked with Anglo-Dutch intellectual circles in a 'republic of letters' and 'radical' Enlightenment, this mode of Whiggism is considered fully anticlerical and deistical.[9]

The result of each of these associations has been the neglect of the primary context in which Shaftesbury produced *Characteristics*. He must be situated within the contemporary debate about the church-state relationship in the aftermath of the Revolution of 1688–9. He was interjecting in the political rivalries and paper wars raging between the developing 'high- and low-church' parties. He was defending a unique settlement in which the established church acquiesced to a degree of statutory toleration. Many of his arguments in private correspondence and published writings were aimed at the rulers of post-Revolutionary England. He was close to such men as Somers, with whom he corresponded regularly and exchanged manuscript editions of his work.[10] Somers was the anonymous addressee of Shaftesbury's *A Letter Concerning Enthusiasm to my Lord ****** (1707). In 1698 Shaftesbury wrote a preface for his own edition of the sermons of the Restoration Cambridge divine Benjamin Whichcote.[11] There is also a relationship between Shaftesbury's religious writing and the complex plates published with the first edition of *Characteristics*.[12]

To understand Shaftesbury's civil religion fully, therefore, it is necessary to prioritise his ecclesiology over the intractable question of his inward belief. Shaftesbury aimed to transform the Church of England into a civil religion by defending the church-state relationship established by the Revolution of 1688–9 in the face of its Tory and high-church detractors. He conformed outwardly with

---

[7] Caroline Robbins, *The Eighteenth-Century Commonwealthman* (Cambridge, MA, 1959), pp. 56, 88–95, 128–33; Robert Voitle, *The Third Earl of Shaftesbury, 1671–1713* (Baton Rouge and London, 1984), p. 109; Blair Worden, 'Introduction', in Edmund Ludlow, *A Voyce from the Watch Tower, Part V: 1660–1662*, ed. Blair Worden (Camden Fourth Series, vol. 21, London, 1978), pp. 1–80, at pp. 39–46; David Hayton, 'The "Country" Interest and the Party System', in Clyve Jones (ed.), *Party and Management in Parliament, 1660–1784* (New York, 1984), pp. 37–85, at pp. 44, 52; Israel, *Enlightenment Contested*, p. 348.
[8] J. G. A. Pocock, *The Machiavellian Moment: Florentine Political Thought and the Atlantic Republican Tradition* (Cambridge, 1975), p. 15.
[9] Jacob, *Radical Enlightenment*, p. 149.
[10] Anthony Ashley Cooper, third earl of Shaftesbury, to John, Lord Somers, 26 May 1710, in Rand (ed.), *Life*, pp. 420–1.
[11] Benjamin Whichcote, *Select Sermons* (London, 1698).
[12] Felix Paknadel, 'Shaftesbury's Illustrations of *Characteristics*', *Journal of the Warburg and Courtauld Institutes*, 37 (1974), pp. 290–312.

the catholic and apostolic claims of the Church of England and argued that its clergymen should preach gospel Christianity only. The heterodox sentiments that he expressed in private correspondence and personal manuscript works composed during his several reclusive periods of repose must be understood in relation to his public writings on the question of government in church and state.

The novel strength of the Revolutionary settlement, argued Shaftesbury, was that it guaranteed inward freedom of thought while regulating outward worship to express belonging within the Christian commonwealth of Whig England. His defence of the national established church was not one of a prudent ruler seeking to support social hierarchy while sniggering within the privacy of the lodge. It was one of a writer in the reformed Christian tradition. Roman Catholics could not be true citizens of the commonwealth as they gave themselves to the yoke of popish priests. Roman Catholic priests were 'spiritual conquerors' whose superstitions, bearing no resemblance to the primitive gospel, had enabled 'priestly government' and 'independency on the civil magistrate'. Shaftesbury's project was to continue stripping away those accretions that had enabled the popish 'political model and subservient system of divinity'. Secular control over the church establishment would restrict clergymen to their proper function. They would maintain the 'external worship' and 'outward forms' mandated by the civil magistrate in accordance with the gospel.[13] The dictates of 'abundant charity and brotherly love', not 'steel, fire, gibbets, rods', would be the themes of 'religious pastors'.[14] Clergymen were to be learned in the scriptures to guide their flocks and prevent the commonwealth from backsliding into superstition and enthusiasm.

Shaftesbury believed himself to stand alongside 'just conformists to the lawful church' in support of the royal supremacy.[15] He reminded defenders of the idea of a distinct Anglican society that the 'letters patent' of the godly prince provided 'commission' for ministers.[16] The claim to priestly superiority on religiously exclusive grounds represented mere imposture and rested on 'wilful ignorance and blind idolatry for having taken opinions upon trust and consecrated ... certain idol-notions'.[17] Sacerdotalism would be replaced by two key priestly capacities. First, ministers would act as the learned *primus inter pares* of the priesthood of all believers. The universities would train clergymen, who would approach the Bible rationally and in Erasmian spirit without the aid of scholastic nonsenses, 'those Riddles of the School-Men'.[18] Ministers would be educated in the languages of scripture. They would analyse with scepticism

---

[13] *Characteristics*, pp. 377–9.
[14] Ibid., p. 387.
[15] Ibid., p. 471.
[16] Ibid., p. 481.
[17] Ibid., p. 29.
[18] Shaftesbury to Michael Ainsworth, 24 Feb. 1706, in Anthony Ashley Cooper, third earl of Shaftesbury, *Several Letters Written by a Noble Lord to a Young Man at the University* (London, 1716), p. 3.

the heated debates of church councils. Second, clergymen would be pastoral and worldly. They would not obsess about the irrelevant metaphysics of another world but prepare their flocks for it by means of good conduct in the current one. They would guide individuals in rationally and independently reading scripture. These learned and pastoral themes recurred frequently in Shaftesbury's correspondence with Michael Ainsworth, the undergraduate and future clergyman at University College, Oxford, to whom Shaftesbury served as patron. Shaftesbury warned Ainsworth that 'steadiness in honesty, good principles, moderation, and true Christianity' were now set 'at defiance by the far greater part and numbers of that body of clergy called the Church of England, who no more esteem themselves a Protestant church'.[19]

Shaftesbury's religious writings were a contribution to the Whig low-church dispute with Tory high-churchmanship. Lawrence Klein has demonstrated that Shaftesbury perceived his project in *Characteristics* as a partisan effort to defend the Revolution settlement. Klein cast Shaftesbury's project as primarily cultural: an effort to align the Whigs with ideals of civility, sociability, and politeness against Tory fears of toleration for the descendants of puritans and king-killers. His cultural project was comparable with that of Addison and Steele in *The Spectator*.[20] Enclosing a manuscript copy of the *Characteristics* in a letter to Somers, Shaftesbury explained his project by reference to the Tory and high-church party. He recounted how 'their sovereignty in arts and sciences, their presidents in letters, their alma maters and academies, have been acknowledged and taken for granted'. However, Shaftesbury continued, though they had 'treated the poor Presbyterians as impolite, unformed, without rival literature or manners', they might be 'somewhat moved to find themselves treated in the same way, not as corrupters of merely of morals and public principles, but as the very reverse or antipodes to good breeding, scholarship, behaviour, sense, and manners'.[21]

Whigs took the vitality of high-church ecclesiology as evidence that the Reformation was insecure and priestcraft remained within the established church. The thinker to whom Whigs owed the concept of priestcraft to describe the means with which priests sought spiritual power and political domination was Harrington. It is a well-established claim that Shaftesbury was a neo-Harringtonian thinker, one of a group of Whigs who reinterpreted Harrington's Interregnum political thought in a monarchical context. Klein has shown that Shaftesbury's Whiggish project in *Characteristics* can be situated within the neo-Harringtonian 'civic mode' in which a free self-governing community led by public virtue overcame the threats to liberty posed by the court, nobility, and

---

[19] Shaftesbury to Ainsworth, 11 May 1711, in Rand (ed.), *Life*, p. 434.
[20] Lawrence E. Klein, 'Shaftesbury, Politeness and the Politics of Religion', in Phillipson and Skinner (eds), *Political Discourse in Early Modern Britain*, pp. 283–301, at p. 283; *Shaftesbury and the Culture of Politeness: Moral Discourse and Cultural Politics in Early Eighteenth-Century England* (Cambridge, 1994), pp. 1–14, 20–1, 121–53.
[21] Shaftesbury to Somers, 30 March 1711, in Rand (ed.), *Life*, p. 432.

church.[22] Yet the coordinates of neo-Harringtonianism have been understood as primarily secular, determined by autonomy, liberty, and virtue. To secure Revolution principles, Shaftesbury is perceived as transforming Harrington's republic of armed freeholder-citizens into a commonwealth of discoursing gentlemen. Whereas Harrington's key safeguard against tyranny was an armed militia, Shaftesbury's was polite manners. Yet in the Christian commonwealth of Whig England, the parish clergyman was as much a public officeholder as the Justice of the Peace and the overseer of the poor. Klein further argued that Shaftesbury's religious writings sought to replace ecclesiastical domination in public discourse with gentlemanly cultural norms.[23] But Shaftesbury's project was as much about religion and ecclesiology as culture. The removal of fire-and-brimstone rhetoric from the public sphere was part of Shaftesbury's vision of polite society. But this did not imply the removal of clerical discourse. Rightly oriented, learned and pastoral clergymen played a role in polite culture.

To generate such a vision, Shaftesbury needed to identify the problem. In *Oceana* and later pamphlets, Harrington provided a formulation to demonstrate that the distribution of power necessarily followed the distribution of property.[24] Since this was no different for matters spiritual, it followed that priestcraft was not a purely Christian phenomenon. It was an intrinsic feature of any society in which priests operated beyond the control of the civil power. Both Harrington and Shaftesbury wrote histories of priestcraft that began in ancient Egypt and continued into the post-Reformation church. It was, Shaftesbury wrote, in Egypt, 'the motherland of superstition', that 'first religion grew unsociable'.[25] The hereditary caste of Egyptian priests developed a private interest in the creation of false superstitions on which depended lay contributions of land and wealth. As the priesthood expanded, more numerous became the artifices. Egyptian priestcraft exemplified the Harringtonian insight that 'dominion must naturally follow property'. Shaftesbury concluded that, 'according to political arithmetic, in every nation whatsoever ... *the quantity of superstition ... will in proportion nearly answer the number of priests, diviners, soothsayers, prophets, or such who gain their livelihood or receive advantages of officiating in religious affairs*'. The power of the Egyptian priesthood became so great that it threatened the monarchy. It was not surprising that 'we should find the property and power of the Egyptian priesthood in ancient days arrived to such a height as in a manner to have swallowed up the state and monarchy'.[26]

The dangers of Egyptian priestcraft related not only to sovereignty. Shaftesbury noted how the logic of Egyptian religion led to violence and persecution. As the 'proportion of so many laymen to each priest grew every day less and less, so

---

[22] Klein, 'Shaftesbury, Politeness and the Politics of Religion', pp. 287–8.
[23] Ibid., pp. 284–5.
[24] James Harrington, *The Political Works of James Harrington*, ed. J. G. A. Pocock (Cambridge, 1977), pp. 602, 762.
[25] *Characteristics*, p. 357.
[26] Ibid., pp. 358–60.

the wants and necessities of each priest must grow more and more'. Increasingly belligerent priests forced the civil magistrate to resign 'his title or share of right in things sacred'. The civil magistrate 'could no longer govern as he pleased in these affairs or check the growing number of these professors'. The priests were not content with scholarly study or tending the flocks. Nor were they dependent on the revenues of secular taxation for their livelihood. Their wealth and power turned on their ability to 'heighten the zeal of worshippers'. Priests needed to 'foment their emulation, prefer worship to worship, faith to faith and turn the spirit of enthusiasm to the side of sacred horror, religious antipathy and mutual discord between worshippers'. Priests gave the lie of exclusive religious knowledge, terrifying the gulled poor into a Manichean world of truth and error, and 'provinces and nations were divided by the most contrary rites and customs which could be devised in order to create the strongest aversion possible'.[27]

Shaftesbury's analysis of the political threat of the priesthood revealed how neo-Harringtonian politics lent themselves to a Protestant conception of correct church-state relations. Shaftesbury followed Harrington in identifying the Egyptian model of priestcraft as the basis for all later corrupt forms of priestliness and recounted how it had found its way into the Christian world. Harrington's history of the power of the church equated to a history of its wealth and landholdings. Since the times of the early church, priests had used their spiritual power over the laity to generate false superstitions and dupe them into obeisance.[28] By such means, they aggrandised material wealth and threatened the sovereignty of the secular ruler. This history of Roman Catholic superstition and priestly usurpation had continued into the last days of the pre-Reformation church.[29] Harrington's analysis brought a powerful new dimension to bear on standard Protestant histories of the Reformation. Alongside wresting spiritual dominion from the dark forces of popery, Harrington also believed that Henry VIII subjected the Church of England materially to the powers of the state. The dissolution of the monasteries and release of ecclesiastical lands to lay holders undermined the economic base of the church's political power.[30]

Similarly, Shaftesbury traced the Egyptian model of priestcraft into Roman Catholicism. 'The infection spreads' to modern times and 'nations now profane one to another war fiercer and, in religion's cause, forget humanity'.[31] Making use of John Spencer's *De Legibus Hebraeorum Ritualibus et Earum Rationibus* (1685), Shaftesbury explained how the ancient Hebrews had imitated Egyptian priestcraft. But, writing of the 'servile dependency of the whole Hebrew race on the Egyptian nation', Shaftesbury revealed how Enlightened scepticism about ancient superstition could slide into anti-Hebraism. Shaftesbury's condemnation of the ancient Hebrews showed how English civil religion might take an uncivil

---

[27] Ibid., p. 364.
[28] Harrington, *Political Works*, pp. 386, 845.
[29] Ibid., pp. 372, 537.
[30] Ibid., pp. 405–6, 606–7.
[31] *Characteristics*, p. 315.

face. In discussing the exodus of the Jews from Egypt, Shaftesbury used Tacitus' *Histories*, which had relied on Egyptian rather than Jewish sources, as well as Justin Martyr in claiming that the Jews had not voluntarily left Egypt against the wishes of the pharaoh but had rather been expelled for their leprosy and scabies. Referring to 'the stubborn habit and stupid humour of this people', Shaftesbury claimed that even as they were being 'conducted by visible divinity, supplied and fed from Heaven and supported by continual miracles', it was 'with the utmost difficulty they could be withheld from returning again' to the Egyptian tyranny. Joseph and Moses had been schooled in the art of Egyptian priestcraft, the latter instituting it in Hebraic law.[32]

The infection of priestcraft passed to the Magi priests of the Zoroastrians in Persia, who, upon the death of Emperor Cambyses in 521 BC, usurped the throne and reigned until they were removed by Darius I.[33] It reached Ethiopia and Mesopotamia. It was the eventual fate of the religion of pagan Rome. In a standard Protestant allusion to the corruptions of the pre-Reformation Christian church, Shaftesbury recalled how the pagan priests of ancient Rome maintained their dominion by means of 'the retaining laws or statutes of mortmain'. They were 'left in this manner as a bottomless gulf and devouring receptacle of land and treasure'. Imperial conquest spread Christian priestcraft across the Empire in a 'universal tyranny and oppression over mankind'.[34]

This analysis left little room for the idea of Constantine as a godly Christian *imperator*. His conversion bequeathed the priestcraft that had plagued late Roman paganism to Christianity. Early Christian priests ensured that the 'Roman emperors, as they grew more barbarous, grew so much the more superstitious'. The 'lands and revenues as well as the numbers of the heathen priests grew daily'. Due to the 'convert-emperor', the 'heathen church lands, with an increase of power, became transferred to the Christian clergy', which was corrupted 'by such riches and authority'.[35] The history of the early church, above all its councils, was the history of the continuing corruption of true religion and the domination of priests over the secular power. Shaftesbury observed how 'ably the Roman Christian and once catholic church, by the assistance of their converted emperors, proceeded in the establishment of their growing hierarchy'.[36]

Popish creeds, formularies, and vestments were taken directly from the corrupted religion of the late Roman pagans. Christian buildings with their 'external proportions, magnificence of structures, ceremonies, processions, choirs and those other harmonies' continued to 'captivate the eye and ear'. Christians 'displayed religion in a yet more gorgeous habit of temples, statues, paintings, vestments, copes, mitres, purple and the cathedral pomp'. Every

---

[32] Ibid., pp. 361–3.
[33] Ibid., pp. 362–3.
[34] Ibid., pp. 372–3.
[35] Ibid.
[36] Ibid., p. 377.

structure and edifice distracted the laity from true worship. Each creed and ritual perverted the gospel. The dominance of priests represented the inversion of the right relationship between humankind and God. Although the Roman Catholic Church 'cannot but appear in some respect august and venerable', its priests 'are the spiritual conquerors who, like the first Caesars, from small beginnings established the foundations of an almost universal monarchy'.[37]

A function of the church's growing strength in ancient Rome was its success in uniting theology with philosophy. The 'schools of the ancient philosophers, which had been long in their decline, came now to be dissolved and their sophistic teachers became ecclesiastical instructors'. Thus 'the unnatural union of religion and philosophy' was complete and 'the monstrous product of this match', scholasticism, 'appeared soon in the world'.[38] The Roman Catholic Church never forgot how to comprehend the 'seeming contrarieties of human passion' into their models of divinity and politics.[39] True Christians attempted to resist false religion. The Reformation, when scholasticism was identified as the ideology of spiritual tyranny, marked the first successful attempt to beat back the power of popery. The Erasmian impulses of later reformers combined with their Erastian programmes to restore true religion by the right church-state relationship. The secular magistrate handed the keys of heaven from the priests to the priesthood of all believers. The power of the sword would keep Christian ministers in their place as investigators of the scriptures. Thus Shaftesbury might have chosen to conclude his neo-Harringtonian history of priestcraft.

Reformed ecclesiology in the Christian commonwealth

But Shaftesbury believed popish priestcraft still to exist in Whig England. If Shaftesbury was adapting neo-Harringtonianism to Revolution principles to provide for an independent community governed by public virtue, his project had ecclesiastical implications. In secular politics, civic virtue shifted from the independence of the armed freeholder-citizen to the polite and sociable discourse of the liberty-loving Whig gentleman. Notwithstanding his longstanding associations with court Whigs like Somers, Shaftesbury agonised about the threats of corruption and dependence to virtue and the common good. He feared that 'some of our noble countrymen, who come with high advantage and a worthy character into the public', could fall victim to the venality of '[e]quipages, titles, precedencies, staffs, ribbons, and other such glittering ware' that 'are taken in exchange for inward merit, honour and a character'.[40] If the once-virtuous Whig ruler fell to corruption, the disapprobation and raillery of the polite gentlemanly classes were the salve. For, 'till our gentleman is become wholly prostitute and

---

[37] Ibid., pp. 377–8.
[38] Ibid., p. 373.
[39] Ibid., p. 377.
[40] *Characteristics*, p. 410.

shameless', explained Shaftesbury, 'he must in good policy avoid those to whom he lies so much exposed and shun that commerce and familiarity which was once his chief delight'.[41]

In parish, county, and parliament, virtuous officeholders were the agents of the Whig commonwealth. Meanwhile, clergymen were the public officeholders of its church. The sacerdotal principles of Tory high-churchmanship represented the religious dimension of the same threat posed by over-weaning nobility and royal absolutism. Shaftesbury saw a direct relationship between being 'a noted friend to liberty in Church and State'.[42] He sought to attack those 'new pretenders' of the bishop of Rome with their 'petty tyrannies and mimical polities'. As in confronting the dangers of secular tyranny, the raillery of polite gentlemen would guard against spiritual tyranny. The gravity of superstitious impostors would fall in the face of the 'wit and humour' that 'are corroborative of religion and promotive of true faith'. Despite 'the dark complexion and sour humour of some religious teachers', Shaftesbury continued, 'we may be justly said to have, in the main, a witty and good-humoured religion'.[43] The civility and politeness that would mark the Whig commonwealth would mean that 'imposture has no privilege'. Neither 'the power of a nobility, nor the awfulness of a church' would prevent the pursuit of liberty.[44]

Imposture would fall not only by gentlemanly culture but also by the ecclesiology of the reformed state. Anglican priests might arrogantly affect to legitimacy by claims of apostolic inheritance and sacerdotal power. They 'strive to give themselves the same air of independency on the civil magistrate' as Roman Catholic priests.[45] But the first shots against imposture were fired during the sixteenth century. In a letter to Somers, Shaftesbury praised 'our good Reformers of early times'.[46] Agents of popery 'raise the highest ridicule in the eyes of those who have real discernment and can distinguish originals from copies'.[47] The theme of securing the Reformation against high-churchmanship recurred in Shaftesbury's correspondence with Ainsworth. Shaftesbury was concerned that Ainsworth's attendance at Oxford in preparation for his ordination would corrupt his Christianity. He warned Ainsworth to 'avoid the Conceit and Pride, which is almost naturally inherent to the Function and Calling you are about to undertake'. He should never think of himself 'in the Presence of another, *That you are holier than he*'.[48]

The legitimacy of the ministry derived entirely from the sovereign magisterial state. Ainsworth would benefit from paying less attention to patristics

---

[41] Ibid., p. 412.
[42] Ibid., p. 411.
[43] Ibid., pp. 379–80.
[44] Ibid., p. 7.
[45] Ibid., p. 379.
[46] Shaftesbury to Somers, 26 May 1710, in Rand (ed.), *Life*, p. 420.
[47] *Characteristics*, p. 379.
[48] Shaftesbury to Ainsworth, 30 Dec. 1709, in Shaftesbury, *Several Letters*, p. 43.

and the debates of church councils than to the secular laws governing a church created by human hands. Since the Henrician Reformation, modern clergy relied on a 'modester title to express their voluntary negotiation between us and Heaven'. It was 'not immediately from God himself, but through the magistrate' that clergymen were appointed above the laity. The magisterial Reformation had left priests with 'legal charter and character, legal titles and precedencies, legal habits, coats of arms, colours, badges'. Clergymen should 'consider that a thousand badges or liveries by men merely can never be sufficient to entitle them to the same authority as theirs who bore the immediate testimony and miraculous signs of power from above'.[49] The apostles might have enjoyed divine commission and shown their spiritual superiority by wielding miracles. But for the claim that this commission had been inherited there was no scriptural sanction.

As part of his Erastian defence of the superiority of the civil magistrate, Shaftesbury made direct reference to the magisterial theme of the godly prince. Shaftesbury taunted his opponents to demonstrate their divine legitimacy: 'where shall we find this commission to have lain? How often divided, even in one and the same species of claimants? What party are they among moderns who, by virtue and of any immediate testimonial from Heaven, are thus entitled? Where are the letters patent? The credentials?' It was 'by the prince or sovereign power here on earth, that these gentlemen agents are appointed, distinguished and set over us'.[50] All 'the Preheminence, Wealth, or Pension, which you receive, or expect to receive', he explained to Ainsworth, 'by Help of this assum'd Character, is from the Publick, whence both the Authority and Profit is derived; and on which it legally depends'.[51]

Shaftesbury defended his arguments by reference to contemporary low-church and Whig scholarship on the church-state relationship. Although Shaftesbury had his differences with Tindal in questions of philosophy, for he believed Tindal to share the moral egoism of Hobbes, he praised 'Dr. Tindal's principles ... as to church government'.[52] Another intellectual resource was Bishop Burnet, in whose diocese was Shaftesbury's estate. Burnet was recommended reading for Ainsworth. The seminarian should prioritise Burnet's *An Exposition of the Thirty-Nine Articles of the Church of England* (1699). 'None can better explain the Sense of the Church, than one, who is the greatest Pillar of it since the first Founders', Shaftesbury maintained. Burnet was 'one, who best explain'd and asserted the Reformation it self', and who 'was chiefly instrumental in saving it from Popery before and at the Revolution'.[53] Shaftesbury was encouraged that

---

[49] *Characteristics*, pp. 480–1.
[50] Ibid.
[51] Shaftesbury to Ainsworth, 30 Dec. 1709, in Shaftesbury, *Several Letters*, p. 44.
[52] Shaftesbury to Ainsworth, 3 June 1709, in ibid., pp. 38–9. See Dmitri Levitin, 'Matthew Tindal's Rights of the Christian Church (1706) and the Church-State Relationship', *HJ*, 54:3 (2011), pp. 717–40.
[53] Shaftesbury to Ainsworth, 5 May 1709, in Shaftesbury, *Several Letters*, p. 34.

Ainsworth, upon leaving Oxford, came to enjoy the bishop's favour. Now 'the time is come that you are to receive full orders', it was fortuitous that it should come from 'the hand of our worthy, great, excellent Bishop'.[54]

It was in a similar ecclesiological mode that Shaftesbury was primarily receiving Harrington. Shaftesbury explained early in *Characteristics* that a 'notable author of our nation' had defended the idea of a national church. Harrington had aimed to reconstruct the insight of 'ancient policy' that 'a people should have a "public leading" in religion'.[55] He advised Ainsworth that Harrington was 'most sincere to Virtue and Religion, and even to the Interest of our Church'. Shaftesbury complained that 'many of our Modern Assertors of Toleration have seemed to leave us destitute of what he calls *a Publick Leading*, or *Ministry*; which Notion he [Harrington] treats as mere Enthusiasm, or horrid Irreligion'. These intriguing sentences show that, for theorists of civil religion, toleration and the national church were compatible. Shaftesbury explained that 'in truth, Religion cannot be left thus to shift for itself, without Care and Countenance of the Magistrate'.[56] To deny 'the magistrate a worship or take away a national church is as mere enthusiasm as the notion which sets up persecution'. The public role of the church establishment was to provide for external worship in the civil commonwealth while maintaining the Protestant commitment to toleration. 'Why', asked Shaftesbury, 'should there not be public walks as well as private gardens. Why not public libraries as well as private education and home tutors?'[57] A benign national establishment whose clerical agents were to discourage superstition and enthusiasm would encourage morality, piety, and peace.

Much of this vision rested on a distinction between public piety and private introspection. Shaftesbury argued by means of analogy that it would be difficult 'if religion, as by law established, were not allowed the same privilege as heraldry'. Gentlemen commonly agreed that 'particular persons may design or paint, in their private capacity, after what manner they think fit, but they must blazon only as the public directs'.[58] Stanley Grean suggested that Shaftesbury put this claim ironically.[59] However, once it is understood within the framework of Shaftesbury's distinction between esoteric and exoteric philosophy, its meaning becomes clear. Shaftesbury repeated the point by means of another analogy in writing that 'Naturalists may, in their separate and distinct capacity, inquire as they think fit into the real existence and natural truth of things, but they must by no means dispute the authorized forms'.[60] External worship was a crucial expression of belonging within the Christian commonwealth.

---

54 Shaftesbury to Ainsworth, 11 May 1711, in Rand (ed.), *Life*, p. 434.
55 *Characteristics*, p. 11.
56 Shaftesbury to Ainsworth, 5 May 1709, in Shaftesbury, *Several Letters*, p. 36.
57 *Characteristics*, p. 11.
58 Ibid., p. 161.
59 Grean, *Shaftesbury's Philosophy*, pp. 117–18.
60 *Characteristics*, p. 61.

Scholarship, pastoralia, and politeness

An intrinsic aspect of a public leading in religion was Christian ministry. The national established church would rely on a learned clergy steeped in polite and gentlemanly learning. A *sine qua non* would be the primacy of philosophy in the secular sphere, thereby undoing the success of scholastics in uniting theological sophistry with philosophy. Shaftesbury lamented how philosophy 'is no longer active in the world nor can hardly, with any advantage, be brought upon the public stage'. Modern society has 'immured her, poor lady, in colleges and cells'.[61] Philosophy belonged to worldly gentlemen. Since it was 'the study of happiness', Shaftesbury asked, 'must not everyone, in some manner or other, either skilfully or unskilfully philosophize?'[62]

Happiness was the remit of this world. The study of the next world belonged to clergymen and, rightly oriented, they would properly serve the lay believer in preparing for it. Theology was the remit of clergymen. 'Christian theology, the birth, procedure, generation and personal distinction of the Divinity' were 'mysteries only to be determined by the initiated or ordained, to whom the State has assigned the guardianship and promulgation of the divine oracles'.[63] These 'lawful superiors' were tasked with the exploration of scripture and it was the duty of lay believers to worship outwardly in accordance with their interpretations. Clergymen rightly 'teach us what we are to own and perform in worship' and 'we are dutiful in complying with them'.[64]

Shaftesbury's conception of learned ministry implied concern for the universities. John Gascoigne has demonstrated how a combination of Newtonian science and Anglicanism was achieved in some Cambridge colleges during the seventeenth and eighteenth centuries.[65] Crucial aspects of this curriculum included a commitment to study the scriptures alone and to treat with scepticism the interpretations of church councils and scholastics. Shaftesbury believed the goal of the next generation of clergymen should be to purge the church of schoolmen who, 'in the last Ages of the Church, found an effectual Way to destroy Religion by Philosophy, and render Reason and Philosophy ridiculous, under what Garb they had put in it'.[66] Philological training was essential. He recommended an understanding of pagan literature, including philosophy, poetry, plays, and comedies, to appreciate the linguistic and historical circumstances in which scripture had been composed.[67] Knowledge of ancient Greek aided understanding of the New Testament and the Septuagint version of the Hebrew Bible. The '*Greek* Language' was one of 'the *Foundations of*

---

[61] Ibid., p. 232.
[62] Ibid., p. 336.
[63] Ibid., p. 160.
[64] Ibid., p. 301.
[65] Gascoigne, *Cambridge in the Age of the Enlightenment*.
[66] Shaftesbury to Ainsworth, 24 Feb. 1706, in Shaftesbury, *Several Letters*, p. 3.
[67] *Characteristics*, pp. 438–9.

Learning, and the Source and Fountain of those Lights we have, whether in *Morality* or *Divinity*'.[68]

The supreme difficulties of theological interpretation required learned preachers. Otherwise, the layman might find recourse in mechanic preachers. Clerical learning had a practical and worldly use. It was not simply Christ's injunction to propagate Christianity around the world, but it was the entire purpose for which the secular civil magistrate appointed ministers of the gospel. The role of the clergy extended far beyond conceptions of prudent statecraft. A church establishment might render a people governable, Shaftesbury argued, but the nightmare of a Hobbesian covenant showed the dangers of political ministry. He was concerned that clerical preaching in some countries 'has not been appropriated to Spirituals' and 'a great part of those Divine Exhortations have had something in common with the Policies of the World, and the Affairs of Government'. Politically-motivated preaching concerned Shaftesbury because 'it must be own'd that *Preaching* it self will be so much the less apt to make any happy Revolution in Manners, as it has at any time been serviceable to Revolutions in State, or to the support of any other Interest than that of Christ's Kingdom'. Among the writers to whom Shaftesbury apportioned blame for 'Building a Political Christianity' stood Hobbes, who 'has done but very ill Service in the Moral World'. However much 'other parts of Philosophy may be obliged to him, *Ethicks* will appear to have no great share in the Obligation'.[69] Clergymen were endowed by the state because it was the function of the godly commonwealth to pursue the promise of the primitive gospel. They were not the tool of the statesman.

The clergy would prioritise their pastoral and pedagogical duties. Shaftesbury invoked William Davenant's epic poem *Gondibert* (1651), lamenting that the poet 'never dreamt of a time when the very countenance of moderation should be out of fashion with the gentlemen of this order'.[70] Once clergymen embraced their responsibility to act as virtuous exemplars, lay believers might justifiably place their faith in the interpretations and teachings of their spiritual guides. The layman 'is no critic nor competently learned in these originals'. It was plain that 'he can have no original judgement of his own but must rely still on the opinion of those who have opportunity to examine such matters, and whom he takes to be the unbiased and disinterested judges of these religious narratives'. The faith of the average believer 'is not in ancient facts or persons, nor in the ancient writ of primitive recorders, nor in the successive collators or conservators of these records'. Rather, 'his confidence and trust must be in those modern men, or societies of men, to whom the public or he himself ascribes the judgment of these records and commits the determination of sacred writ and genuine story'.[71]

---

[68] Shaftesbury to Ainsworth, 28 Jan. 1709, in Shaftesbury, *Several Letters*, p. 20.
[69] Anthony Ashley Cooper, third earl of Shaftesbury, 'Preface', in Whichcote, *Select Sermons*, p. xxiv.
[70] *Characteristics*, p. 482.
[71] Ibid., pp. 369–70.

As Shaftesbury explained to Somers in 1705, the national church must prevent those 'unhappy bigots, breaking out of the common road of religion, [who] are entangled in by-paths and deeper in the briars than before'.[72]

Pedagogical ministry involved preaching the primitive basics. Through the simple moral lessons of gospel Christianity, the clergy might cultivate virtue. In the preface to his edition of sermons by Whichcote, Shaftesbury claimed that Christianity was 'a Religion so full of all good Precepts, and so enforcing with respect to all the Duties of Morality, and Justice' that 'our Amazement ought rather to be; how Men, with such a Religion' should lead lives of 'Malice, Hatred, or Division'.[73] Another exemplar of pastoral churchmanship was Burnet, who was 'now the truest example of *Laborious*, *Primitive*, *Pious*, and *Learned Episcopacy*'.[74] Alongside Shaftesbury's emphasis on scripture stood his classicising impulse. Whig England was to revive the achievement of ancient Greece where priestcraft had not triumphed. Shaftesbury wished to design the 'modern world' on the 'ancient model' of the Greeks in politics, culture, and religion. Much like the Greeks, Shaftesbury aspired to descend from 'the higher regions of divinity' to 'plain honest morals'.[75] Religion would be geared not towards the pursuit of mysteries. Virtue, friendship, and honesty stood alongside religion, piety, adoration, and 'a generous surrender of [the] mind to whatever happens from that supreme cause or order of things'.[76]

To secure learned and pastoral ministry, theology needed to be mediated by politeness. Theological propositions were to be put to the test in the context of good-humoured raillery. Theological debate was intrinsic to Shaftesbury's plea in *Characteristics* 'for sociability, complacency and good humour in religion'.[77] As Shaftesbury wrote, 'there can be no rational belief but where comparison is allowed, examination permitted and a sincere toleration established'. If a belief were 'in any measure consonant to truth and reason', it would 'find as much favour in the eyes of mankind as truth and reason need desire'.[78] Once again, the importance of distinguishing between inward introspection and public piety mattered in ensuring the integrity of the divine oracles and their interpreters. In a letter to the printer John Darby in 1702, Shaftesbury thus commended Pierre Bayle: 'Whatever his opinions might be, either in politics or philosophy (for no two ever disagreed more in these than he and I), yet we lived and corresponded as entire friends.' Shaftesbury felt the need to 'do him the justice to say that whatever he might be in speculation, he was in practice one of the best Christians, and almost the only man I ever knew who, professing philosophy, loved truly

---

[72] Shaftesbury to Somers, 20 Oct. 1705, in Rand (ed.), *Life*, p. 338.
[73] Shaftesbury, 'Preface', in Whichcote, *Select Sermons*, sig. A3.
[74] Shaftesbury to Ainsworth, 5 May 1709, in Shaftesbury, *Several Letters*, p. 34.
[75] *Characteristics*, p. 21.
[76] Ibid., p. 433.
[77] Ibid., p. 385.
[78] Ibid., p. 383.

as a philosopher; with that innocence, virtue and temperance, humility, and contempt of the world and interest which might be called exemplary'.[79]

Toleration and the passions

Shaftesbury's national church was therefore tolerant. His vision was a conscious development of defences of toleration among seventeenth-century divines, especially those at Cambridge. The writings of Jeremy Taylor, bishop of Down and Connor during the Restoration, were 'in the front of this order of authors'.[80] He advised Ainsworth to pay particular attention to Chillingworth and his *The Religion of Protestants a Safe Way to Salvation* (1637), which had become a central text in defending *sola scriptura* divinity. 'CHILLINGWORTH *against Popery*', Shaftesbury intoned, 'is sufficient Reading for you, and will teach you the best Manner of that Polemick Divinity'.[81] Shaftesbury lauded Whichcote for his 'happy Temper, and God-like Disposition, which he labour'd to inspire'.[82] He praised the 'pious and learned' Cudworth.[83] Henry More was 'a learned and good man'.[84]

These writers recommended themselves by balancing the polarities of spiritual liberty and the vernacular availability of the Bible with the stability afforded by an established church. Such was the example of John Tillotson, archbishop of Canterbury, who, in his *Rule of Faith* (1666), accepted that scripture would always be interpreted differently, since all men and institutions were 'plainly fallible and subject to error and mistake'. Protestants should instead emphasise the spiritual basics common to all. Tillotson 'shows plainly how great a shame it is for us Protestants at least ... to disallow difference of opinions and forbid private examinations and search into matters of ancient record and Scriptural tradition'.[85]

A facet of Shaftesbury's praise for tolerationist modes of Restoration and post-Revolutionary Anglican divinity was their concern for moderation. The Church of England continued to position itself as a *via media* between the superstition of the Roman Catholic Church and the enthusiasm of Calvinist Geneva. 'Our Bishops and Dignify'd Church-men, (the most worthily and justly Dignify'd of any in any Age,)', Shaftesbury explained to Ainsworth, 'are, as they ever were, inclinable to Moderation in the high *Calvinistick* Points'. They were also 'inclinable to Moderation in other Points'. The essential theme was that 'THEY are for Toleration, *inviolable Toleration*'. Opponents of such moderation in the Tory and high-church party 'despise the Gentleness of their Lord and

---

[79] Shaftesbury to John Darby, 2 Feb. 1706, in Rand (ed.), *Life*, p. 385.
[80] *Characteristics*, p. 476.
[81] Shaftesbury to Ainsworth, 5 May 1709, in Shaftesbury, *Several Letters*, p. 34.
[82] Shaftesbury, 'Preface', in Whichcote, *Select Sermons*, p. xxxi.
[83] *Characteristics*, p. 264.
[84] Shaftesbury to Ainsworth, 30 Dec. 1709, in Shaftesbury, *Several Letters*, p. 43.
[85] *Characteristics*, pp. 479, 477. See John Tillotson, *The Works of the Most Reverend Dr. John Tillotson* (London, 1707), p. 677.

Master' as well as 'the sweet mild Government of our QUEEN'. Their religion was 'that abominable Blasphemous Representative of Church Power, attended with the worst of Temporal Governments, as we see it in Perfection of each Kind in FRANCE'.[86]

Shaftesbury believed that religion and its corruptions of superstition and enthusiasm were each natural passions. The motion of the passion of religion, 'when unguided and left wholly to itself, is in its nature turbulent'. Once 'the reins are let loose', the mind 'as far as it is able to act or think in such a state, approves the riot and justifies the wild effects by the supposed sacredness of the cause'.[87] Borrowing from Cicero, Shaftesbury identified 'superstition or ill custom' as the condition in which men forgot their natural benevolence.[88] It was the achievement of priestcraft to mispresent the divinity, for 'the ill character of a god does injury to the affections of men and disturbs and impairs the natural sense of right and wrong'.[89] Shaftesbury owed the identification of enthusiasm as a natural passion in particular to Cambridge divines like Whichcote and More.[90] He claimed his arguments were far 'from degrading enthusiasm or disclaiming it in himself that he looks on this passion, simply considered, as the most natural, and its object as the justest, in the world'.[91] But he believed enthusiasm needed to be restrained so that it did not produce tumultuous consequences. While it did not approve of its theology or ecclesiology, the Church of England would tolerate Protestant Dissent and the priesthood would act as a vanguard against the enthusiastic potential of millennial and apocalyptic thought.

It is worth further considering how Shaftesbury identified religion and its subversions as natural passions. It throws more light onto his religious neo-Harringtonianism. Shaftesbury claimed to follow Harrington in announcing that he sought to understand government through the 'scheme of the passions'.[92] By the regulation of 'this moral kind of architecture' would emerge a stable commonwealth.[93] The health of the body politic needed to be ordered by study of its 'inward anatomy'.[94] Virtue was a 'noble enthusiasm justly directed and regulated by that high standard' which the citizen 'supposes in the nature of things'.[95] A public spirit 'can come only from a social feeling or sense of partnership with humankind'. Thus 'morality and good government go together', since there was 'no real love of virtue without the knowledge of public good'.[96]

---

[86] Shaftesbury to Ainsworth, 24 Feb. 1706, in Shaftesbury, *Several Letters*, pp. 6–7.
[87] *Characteristics*, pp. 355–6.
[88] Ibid., p. 175. For Shaftesbury's Ciceronianism, see Stuart-Buttle, *From Moral Theology to Moral Philosophy*, ch. 2.
[89] Ibid., pp. 181–2.
[90] See Heyd, *'Be Sober and Reasonable'*, pp. 214–27.
[91] *Characteristics*, p. 353.
[92] Ibid., p. 54.
[93] Ibid., p. 215.
[94] Ibid., p. 194.
[95] Ibid., p. 353.
[96] Ibid., p. 50.

Shaftesbury believed men acted according to their passions and that reason was necessary to control these impulses. Reason defended the 'moral fortress' of the mind from 'fancy'.[97] Reason governed the mind and imagination and aided the development of 'right opinion' in the appreciation of philosophical goods by restricting the passions.[98] It was the inability to regulate these impulses that led to superstition and enthusiasm. By reflecting rationally, man would come to appreciate that he 'is not only born to virtue, friendship, honesty and faith but to religion, piety, adoration and a generous surrender of his mind to whatever happens from that supreme cause or order of things, which he acknowledges entirely just and perfect'.[99] A national church was necessary to direct passions in the pursuit of virtue and the common good. Clergymen would inculcate the natural passion of religion but not those of superstition and enthusiasm. They must work with the civil magistrate 'by making virtue to be apparently the interest of everyone, so as to remove all prejudices against it, create a fair reception for it and lead men into that path which afterwards they cannot easily quit'.[100]

The arrival of the Camisards, a group of Calvinist millenarians fleeing the French wars of religion provoked by the revocation of the edict of Nantes in 1685, provided Shaftesbury with the opportunity to demonstrate not only the danger of enthusiasm but also how it ought properly to be treated.[101] Shaftesbury reminded those who sought to quell the Camisards that enthusiasm when confronted with persecution and uniformity could quickly evolve into 'gravity', 'harsh adversity', and false claims of authority.[102] The solution to enthusiasm should not be persecution. Shaftesbury condemned the 'fierce unsociable way of modern zealots' in the Tory high-church party. Those 'starched, gruff gentlemen who guard religion as bullies do a mistress' gave the modern believer 'a very indifferent opinion of their lady's merit and their own wit' because they allowed it neither to be 'inspected by others nor care themselves to examine in a fair light'.[103] The passion of enthusiasm required a salve rather than an irritant. To apply 'a serious remedy and bring the sword or fasces as a cure must make the case more melancholy and increase the very cause of the distemper'. The magistrate must procure 'a gentler hand'. His tools must not be 'caustics, incisions and amputations' but 'the softest balms'. The magistrate ought to deploy 'cheerful

---

[97] Ibid., p. 237.
[98] Ibid., p. 422.
[99] Ibid., p. 433.
[100] Ibid., p. 186.
[101] Laborie, *Enlightening Enthusiasm*, pp. 166–93. See also Hillel Schwartz, *Knaves, Fools, Madmen and That Subtile Effluvium: A Study of the Opposition to the French Prophets in England, 1706–1710* (Gainesville, FL, 1978); *The French Prophets: The History of a Millenarian Group in Eighteenth-Century England* (Berkeley and Los Angeles, 1980); Jane Shaw, *Miracles in Enlightenment England* (New Haven and London, 2006).
[102] *Characteristics*, p. 32.
[103] Ibid., p. 246.

ways' to regulate 'fancy and speculation' as well as 'men's apprehensions and religious belief or fears'.[104]

To defend his vision of the Christian commonwealth, Shaftesbury couched Protestant ideas of toleration in classicism. The ancient Greeks provided a model of toleration for superstition and enthusiasm. It was not only 'the visionaries and enthusiasts of all kinds' who were tolerated. It was also 'philosophy [which] had as free a course and was permitted as a balance against superstition'. Some philosophical sects like 'the Pythagorean and latter Platonic' had 'joined in with the superstition and enthusiasm of the times' but others, including 'the Epicurean, the Academic and others', deployed 'the force of wit and raillery against it'. Thus 'reason had fair play' and 'learning and science flourished'. Because 'superstition and enthusiasm were mildly treated', they were never given the pretext to rage 'to that degree as to occasion bloodshed, wars, persecutions and devastations in the world'.[105]

It is noteworthy that Shaftesbury so lauded ancient Greece and early republican Rome for their toleration of philosophy. It is by returning to the question of toleration for philosophers that it becomes possible to appreciate fully the reasons for Shaftesbury's principled commitment to the reformed church-state. Shaftesbury equated the passion of religion with the true religion of primitive Christianity. The gospel message was the basis upon which the genius of the ancient Greeks could be reconstructed in modern times. The virtues of primitive Christianity were ideals that anybody, irrespective of inward belief, could rationally uphold. Thus, Shaftesbury's reader was introduced to the instance of a debate in 'The Moralists' that involved 'a gentleman of some rank, one who was generally esteemed to carry a sufficient caution and reserve in religious subjects of discourse as well as an apparent deference to religion and, in particular, to the national and established church', who was also to make the case for 'an open and free vindication not only of freethinking but free professing and discoursing in matters relating to religion and faith'.[106] In his preface to the sermons of Whichcote, Shaftesbury explicitly distinguished his position from those who judged 'not only *the Institution of Preaching*, but even the *Gospel* it self, and *our Holy Religion* to be a Fraud'.[107] The expression of freethought need never threaten true religion because no freethinker could rationally disagree with the practical message of Jesus Christ.

Shaftesbury believed that the two enemies of liberty of thought and freedom of conscience, superstition and enthusiasm, were also enemies of true religion and primitive Christianity. Freethinkers as much as Protestant Dissenters might recall that it was to the consequences of Christian reform that they owed their spiritual liberty. It was in the shared social practice of external worship inside

[104] Ibid., pp. 10–11
[105] Ibid., p. 11.
[106] Ibid., p. 472.
[107] Shaftesbury, 'Preface', in Whichcote, *Select Sermons*, unpaginated.

the national church that they expressed their citizenship within the Christian commonwealth of Whig England. They owed the same 'steady orthodoxy, resignation and entire submission to the truly Christian and catholic doctrines of our Holy Church as by law established' that Shaftesbury believed himself to manifest for principled reasons.[108] Instead of criticising Christianity *tout court*, Shaftesbury was constructing a modern civil religion inspired by the wisdom of the ancient paganism in Greece and Rome but founded in true religion conceived as primitive Christianity. His ecclesiological materials were those of Christian reform, especially the magisterial Reformation. In syncretising classicism and Protestantism to develop civilised, polite, and enlightened society, Shaftesbury provided for a civil religion with a Christian foundation.

[108] *Characteristics*, p. 471.

2

The Politics of Priestcraft: John Trenchard and Thomas Gordon

The bishop of Bangor's scheme

A central problem of interpretation in church-state relations during the eighteenth century is the legacy of Locke. Lockean theories of toleration tend to be taken as anticipations of the liberal separation between church and state.[1] Trenchard and Gordon stand at the centre of this problem because they are seen as key transmitters of the 'commonwealth' political theory that connected the 'British revolutions' of 1649, 1688, and 1776 through their two series of weekly essays, *The Independent Whig* (1720–1) and *Cato's Letters* (1720–3).[2] *The Independent Whig* appeared in America as early as 1724 and was printed as late as 1816. It featured in the Enlightenment in France by the militant hand of Baron d'Holbach in 1767.[3] Americanists, in particular, have categorised Trenchard and Gordon rather nebulously as 'libertarians' by their amalgamation of 'Lockeanism' with 'radical' Whiggery.[4] This categorisation takes Trenchard and Gordon's opposition to Tory political thought and high-church ecclesiology to imply a total distrust for all clergymen.

While the separationist reading of Locke, by its prolepsis, risks neglecting his relationships with Restoration and Revolution ecclesiology, Trenchard and Gordon show the difficulties in appreciating how an Erastian defence of the royal supremacy over the church proceeded with toleration. Andrew Thompson

---

[1] For valuable assessments of the relationship between natural law and toleration, see Jon Parkin and Timothy Stanton (eds), *Natural Law and Toleration in the Early Enlightenment* (Oxford, 2013); Timothy Stanton, 'Locke and the Fable of Liberalism', *HJ*, 61:3 (2018), pp. 597–622.
[2] Robbins, *Eighteenth-Century Commonwealthman*, pp. 111–13; Bernard Bailyn, *The Ideological Origins of the American Revolution* (Cambridge, MA, 1967), pp. 35–7, 44, 53; Pocock, *Machiavellian Moment*, pp. 467–77.
[3] Ronald Hamowy, 'Cato's Letters, John Locke, and the Republican Paradigm', *HPT*, 11:2 (1990), pp. 273–94, at pp. 293–4.
[4] Marie McMahon, *The Radical Whigs, John Trenchard and Thomas Gordon: Libertarian Loyalists to the New House of Hanover* (Lanham, MD, 1990), pp. 3, 205; Hamowy, 'Cato's Letters', pp. 289, 292.

has suggested that it is 'unclear what Trenchard and Gordon's views on the relationship between church and state were' because they seemed 'equivocal as to whether the best form of church-state relations was that of an Erastian supremacy of the state over the church or a Lockean division'.[5] By understanding Trenchard and Gordon's ecclesiastical writings on their own terms and not in exclusive relation to Locke, it will become clear that their position was the former. As Whigs and low churchmen feared that the Revolution settlement of 1689 was at risk from priestly aspirations toward asserting the independence of the Church of England from the crown-in-parliament, Trenchard and Gordon launched their defence of civil religion. They argued that the clergymen of the Church were public officeholders of the civil state responsible for preaching the reformed religion according to its articles of faith in order to contribute to the peace of English society.

Trenchard was a Whig politician. In 1722, he was elected Member of Parliament for Taunton. He was a member of those circles of 'country' Whiggism in which Shaftesbury mingled and, in 1697, penned, with Moyle, *An Argument, Shewing that a Standing Army is Inconsistent with a Free Government*. In 1698, he wrote *A Short History of Standing Armies in England*. His first publication on matters of religion came with *The Natural History of Superstition* (1709). Gordon was a Scottish Whig who became Trenchard's amanuensis. He published two pamphlets on religious matters at the outset of the controversy caused by Bishop Hoadly and his sermon, *The Nature of the Kingdom, or Church, of Christ* (1717). One was *A Modest Plea for Parson Alberoni* (1717), ironically subtitled 'a short but unanswerable defence of priestcraft'. The other was *An Apology for the Danger of the Church* (1719), which parodied Tory high-churchmanship. In 1722, Gordon penned a preface for a translation from the French Huguenot exile and jurist Jean Barbeyrac, who had sought refuge in Germany, entitled *The Spirit of Ecclesiastics in all Ages*. He produced a translation of Tacitus in 1728 and the works of Sallust in 1744.

Between 1720 and 1723, Trenchard and Gordon penned their two series of essays at the height of the Bangorian controversy and the South Sea crisis.[6] In the case of *The Independent Whig*, Gordon wrote twenty-two issues whereas Trenchard contributed eighteen issues and three were written by both men. An unidentified individual, who simply signed the issues 'C', authored a further ten. David Berman has suggested that Collins was the third contributor.[7] However, this suggestion rests upon primarily circumstantial evidence inferred from Collins's publishing history and accusations by non-contemporary opponents of *The Independent Whig* that Collins was involved in its production.[8] The association

---

5 Thompson, 'Popery, Politics, and Private Judgement', pp. 352–3, 355.
6 Starkie, *Church of England*, pp. 129, 132.
7 David Berman, 'Anthony Collins's Essays in the *Independent Whig*', *Journal of the History of Philosophy*, 13:4 (1975), pp. 463–9.
8 See Samuel Johnson, *A Letter to Mr. Jonathan Dickinson* (Boston, 1747); Philip Skelton, *Ophiomaches, or Deism Revealed* (London, 1749).

with Collins lends support to the otherwise unsustainable suggestion that Trenchard and Gordon were radically opposed to any form of priestliness. The following analysis assumes that the identity of the third author remains unresolved.

Trenchard and Gordon were theorists of civil religion. They supported the magisterial church-state relationship produced by the Henrician Reformation because it balanced the expression of belonging within the Christian commonwealth of Whig England by regulated external worship with the Protestant defence of inward freedom of conscience. They believed toleration and Erastianism were mutually compatible and developed Protestant criticisms of sacerdotal priestliness in opposition to Tory high-churchmanship. Only a national established church could restrain priestcraft by dis-incentivising the fabrication of superstitions through offering clergymen a secure living and using pastoral exemplars to preach the basic morality of the primitive gospel. Clergymen would also act as the vanguards against the enthusiasm of the seventeenth-century wars of religion. Trenchard and Gordon's defence of the church-state relationship owed a great deal to the long Reformation, but they also blended it with classicism. They hoped to reconstruct for Christian modernity the insights of ancient Roman paganism by creating a civil religion which served the ends of civilised and prosperous living in this world. By such means, the Christian would become the patriot. Champion has related Trenchard and Gordon's 'civil theology' with Harrington, Molesworth, Moyle, and Toland.[9] But Champion's emphasis on the republican character of such proposals has, in the case of Trenchard and Gordon, neglected its Anglican dimensions. Their commitment was to the superiority of the civil state in matters spiritual in general. But they specifically defended the magisterial church-state relationship bequeathed by the Henrician Reformation.

The syncretism between Christian reform and classicism was also a feature of Trenchard and Gordon's religious neo-Harringtonianism.[10] Study of early Hanoverian politics remains dominated by the secular application of neo-Harringtonian thought.[11] The key contexts remain the standing army controversy, the political threat posed by Jacobitism, the South Sea crisis and its aftermath during the 1720s, and the rise of Sir Robert Walpole. But the civic analysis of corruption, virtue, and service for the public good applied as much to religious politics as the secular sphere. Clergymen were as much public officeholders of the commonwealth as the minister of the crown. They were agents of the civil state and their effort at moral reformation belonged to the same campaign against corruption launched by Trenchard and Gordon during the South Sea crisis.

---

[9] Champion, *Pillars of Priestcraft Shaken*, pp. 170–95, 218–19.
[10] But see Annie Mitchell, 'Character of an Independent Whig – "Cato" and Bernard Mandeville', *History of European Ideas*, 29:3 (2003), pp. 291–311; 'A Liberal Republican Cato', *American Journal of Political Science*, 48:3 (2004), pp. 588–603.
[11] M. M. Goldsmith, 'Liberty, Virtue, and the Rule of Law, 1689–1770', in David Wootton (ed.), *Republicanism, Liberty, and Commercial Society* (Stanford, 1994), pp. 197–232, at pp. 203–11.

The Bangorian controversy generated a broader moment of crisis for English Whigs. It is now a familiar refrain that the Revolution did not result in the triumph of 'latitudinarian' low-churchmanship.[12] Trenchard and Gordon felt the need to refute Tory and high-church sacerdotal Anglicanism during the 1720s because they believed there was an ongoing conspiracy to reverse the Toleration Act and Hanoverian succession. In a pamphlet of 1718, Gordon attacked annual sermons preached in the martyred memory of Charles I. Instead of an 'Occasion of Seriousness and Humiliation' that might have reminded the laity of the dangers of enthusiasm, the sermons were 'an Annual Remembrance of a National Calamity' to encourage 'an abhorrence of the Means which brought it about' and draw an obvious analogy with resistance to James II.[13] Having lamented that the clergy had so 'Spirited up' the 'Commonality', Gordon resolved that he and Trenchard must appeal to the same commonality through popular prose.[14]

Trenchard and Gordon supported the anticlerical programme of the ministry led by James, Viscount Stanhope, and Charles Spencer, third earl of Sunderland, between 1717 and 1721. The Stanhope-Sunderland ministry suspended Convocation in March 1717 and reversed the reforms of the Queen Anne Tories by repealing the Schism and Occasional Conformity Acts in 1719.[15] Fearful of the ongoing threat of high-church Toryism, Trenchard and Gordon accepted proposals usually associated with court Whigs such as the Septennial Act of 1716 to stave off the election of Tory MPs. The Stanhope-Sunderland ministry was short-lived and unusually combative. It preceded Walpole's more concessive stance in church matters by forming alliances with powerful Whig churchmen including Gibson and William Wake, archbishop of Canterbury. Trenchard and Gordon's pamphlets and essays represented attempts to sway public opinion, especially during the months following the discovery, in April 1722, of the plot conceived by Atterbury to restore the Stuart line. They entreated Walpole to punish corrupt malefactors by taking a firm line against those involved in the South Sea crisis and in religious politics by reducing priestly power within safe bounds for the Christian commonwealth.

The pamphleteering of Trenchard and Gordon must also be understood within the context of early eighteenth-century metropolitan life. Their primary audience was London society in coffee-houses and clubs. In 1719, Trenchard and Gordon met at the Grecian Coffee House, Devereux Court, where they probably conceived *The Independent Whig*. Their works represented direct interventions in public debate, seeking to influence opinion and sway parliamentary votes. Their world was the same world of sociability and witty public discourse

---

[12] Champion, *Pillars of Priestcraft Shaken*, p. 15, n. 47.
[13] Thomas Gordon, *A Political Dissertation upon Bull-Baiting and Evening Lectures. With Occasional Meditations on the 30th of January* (London, 1718), pp. 3–4.
[14] Ibid., p. 22.
[15] G. M. Townend, 'Religious Radicalism and Conservatism in the Whig Party under George I: The Repeal of the Occasional Conformity and Schism Acts', *PH*, 7:1 (1988), pp. 24–44.

in which the claims of churchmen as much as politicians were to be put to the test of reason. As with Shaftesbury, Addison, and Steele, sociable politeness was to replace sanctimonious prelacy. Trenchard and Gordon took true religion as a yardstick against which to measure priestcraft and produce a positive vision for polite, learned, and pastoral clergymen.

Natural religion and its subversion

Trenchard and Gordon defined true religion as a simple and natural phenomenon. Plainly understood by all, religion in its truest sense did not require sacerdotal priests as each man was his own minister. The third, anonymous, author of *The Independent Whig* similarly claimed that 'Religion, or the Worship of a Deity, is natural to Man'.[16] Gospel Christianity was the apex of natural religion. In *Cato's Letters*, striking the anti-Hebraic notes of much eighteenth-century civil religion, Trenchard argued that Christ 'plainly intended to reduce men to natural religion, which was corrupted and defaced by the numerous superstitions of the Jews, and by the absurd idolatries of the Gentiles'. True Christianity consisted 'only in worshipping one god, and in doing good to men'. It lacked 'priests, sacrifices, and ceremonies'.[17] Gordon concurred that true Christianity was the golden rule. The 'moral duties of religion' included 'general peace, and unlimited charity, publick spirit, equity, forbearance, and good deeds to all men'. This morality was simple and easily comprehensible.[18] Trenchard and Gordon wrote jointly in *The Independent Whig* that 'The Kingdom of Heaven is said to be revealed to Babes and Sucklings ... easily learned and known, by those who make use of their natural Faculties, and uncorrupted Reason'.[19]

All that was required by the Old Testament, Gordon asserted, was that the lay believer 'fear God, and keep his Commandments'. The New Testament simply dictated the belief that 'Jesus Christ is come in the Flesh'. Whomsoever could 'prove his Obedience and Faith, by these two plain Duties, fulfils the Law and the Gospel'. If passages in scripture were unclear or debatable, 'a new Inspiration will be necessary to reduce them to Certainty'. Until then, he who hoped 'to put a Construction upon such Passages in Scripture, and injoins us to believe his Interpretation', cannot demand 'Submission to the Word of God, but to his own Authority and Imagination'.[20] The gospel laid down the requirements of Christianity. All else were things indifferent and voluntary human constructions.

The convergence of natural religion with primitive Christianity also carried civic republican dimensions. Roman paganism had been a religion of virtuous citizens whose simple piety lay in living well in this world in preparation

---

[16] *IW*, vol. 2, p. 97.
[17] *CL*, vol. 2, p. 940.
[18] Ibid., vol. 1, pp. 463–4.
[19] *IW*, vol. 1, p. 57.
[20] Ibid., pp. 23–4.

for rewards in the next life. Religion was to consist 'in doing good Actions', explained Gordon. Socrates, Plato, Cato, and Brutus were 'excellent Persons' who followed the 'simple Dictates of human Reason' and did not need 'Creeds and Fathers'. Modern Christianity would imitate virtuous paganism by consisting only in 'Living well' as testament that 'we believe well'.[21] True religion was conducive to 'publick spirit'. Piety was 'the highest virtue' because it enjoined 'one man's care for many, and the concern of every man for all'.[22] Religion was necessary for good government and 'no History or Voyages give us an Account of any Country, in any manner civilized, without Religion, as well as Priests or Ministers'.[23] It was the function of religion 'to propagate every divine truth' and 'to enforce every social and civil duty'.[24] The genius of Roman religion, Gordon argued, was to inspire love of country, virtue, and honour, rendering the 'public good' and 'the glory of the State' the highest 'end of all'.[25]

The arguments of Barbeyrac related to this analysis of the social and political roles of religion. Barbeyrac had argued that religion, by means of the threat of divine injunction, supported morality by acting upon the passion of fear and by driving human interest.[26] Trenchard and Gordon agreed that 'Morality is Natural Religion, which prompts us to do Good to all Men, and to all Men alike'. Morality 'is social Virtue, or rather the Mother of all social Virtues', since it 'wishes and promotes unlimited and universal Happiness to the whole World'.[27] But people might not always follow the dictates of morality due to the dominance of their passions. It was 'the Business of the Christian Religion, to recover to human Nature those Virtues, which were either lost or lessened by the Fall of Adam'. As Gordon later wrote, 'the Appetites and Passions of Men being too powerful for Reason, and the Law of Nature', religion had to be instituted to provide 'Sanctions and Restraints' to the virtuous and vicious.[28]

However, untrammelled priestliness quickly corrupted natural religion. Trenchard and Gordon's account of the origins of priestcraft was deeply neo-Harringtonian. Constructing human behaviour and society in terms of interests and passions, Gordon wrote that the clerical class in any society had an 'Interest' in the fabrication of superstition and the putative ability to enforce conformity. Priests had 'usurped this Privilege wholly to themselves' and 'it has wonderfully answered their great Ends of Power and Wealth'.[29] Realising that the laity was not always guided by pure reason, priests came to understand

---

[21] Ibid., pp. 224–6.
[22] *CL*, vol. 1, p. 251.
[23] *IW*, vol. 2, p. 97.
[24] Publius Cornelius Tacitus, *The Works of Tacitus*, ed. Thomas Gordon (2nd edn, 4 vols, London, 1737), vol. 3, p. 226.
[25] Ibid., p. 245.
[26] Jean Barbeyrac, *The Spirit of the Ecclesiasticks in all Sects and Ages*, ed. Thomas Gordon (London, 1722), pp. 3–4, 5–8, 13–15.
[27] *IW*, vol. 1, pp. xli–xlii.
[28] Ibid., vol. 2, pp. 73–4.
[29] Ibid., vol. 1, p. 229.

that the only way 'of dealing with mankind, is to deal with their passions'. It was a general maxim that the 'first elements, or knowledge of politicks, is the knowledge of the passions'.[30] Without reason and understanding to guide the passions, laymen were vulnerable to false religion.

Even the dominance of the secular power in spirituals had failed to quell superstition and priestcraft. Gordon wrote in the second number of *The Independent Whig* that the clergy, 'like other Militia, were raised and paid for protecting Mankind from their Spiritual Enemy'. Employed by the secular power to encourage pious worship, clerics 'soon made use of the Sword put into their Hands against their Masters, and set up for themselves'. Although 'the whole End of their Institution was to make Men wiser and better', by taking advantage of the natural ignorance of laymen, clerics taught 'blind Obedience' only to their own caste. Superstition was 'an inseparable Creature of their Power' as false doctrines, theologies, and mysteries entrenched clerical tyranny.[31]

In ancient times, priestcraft had been an innovation of Hebrews and pagans. Glossing Barbeyrac's translation of Samuel Pufendorf's *De Jure Naturae et Gentium* (1672), Trenchard and Gordon lamented in *The Independent Whig* how 'the Pagan, the Jewish, and too many Christian Priests, have all ever agreed in concealing, disguising, mangling, calumniating, and opposing the eternal Principles of Morality, or Natural Religion'. Through false superstitions, ceremonies, metaphysics, and dominion, priests had created 'a Religion of the Body, or a Religion of the Imagination, or a Religion of Shew, Profit and Terror'.[32] Pagan and Jewish priestcraft had provided the basis for Roman Catholic worship. In *Cato's Letters*, Trenchard provided an account of the 'the absurdities of the Romish Church' using the exegetical commentaries of the low-church and Whiggish dean of Norwich, Humphrey Prideaux.[33] Following Prideaux, Trenchard argued that Christian priestcraft 'is copied from the religion of Zoroaster and the Persian Magi' instituted during the reign of Darius I. Zoroaster's priests were said to be divinely instituted and secured by hereditary membership. They stood independent of civil power with large revenues in lands. Above all other priests stood the 'Archimagus, or arch-priest, who was the same as the high-priest amongst the Jews, or the Pope now amongst the Romanists'. Zoroaster had even 'borrowed a great part of his new religion from the Jews', including doctrines such as the immortality of the soul. The litany of superstitions derived by Roman Catholics from the Magi included candle-burning and pilgrimage.[34]

Like Shaftesbury, Trenchard and Gordon defined superstition as a natural phenomenon. In his *Natural History of Superstition*, Trenchard invoked the psychological arguments of Robert Burton, Méric Casaubon, and Henry More in

---

[30] *CL*, vol. 2, pp. 47–8.
[31] *IW*, vol. 1, p. 12.
[32] Ibid., p. xliii.
[33] *CL*, vol. 2, p. 939.
[34] Ibid., pp. 941–5.

his proposition that there was a universal and natural propensity to superstition among humans. There was 'something innate in our Constitution' that 'made us easily to be susceptible of wrong Impressions, subject to panic Fears, and prone to Superstition and Error'.[35] Nature, 'in many Circumstances, seems to work by a sort of secret Magic, and by ways unaccountable to us'.[36] If and when people were ignorant of the operation of nature, their passions overcame their reason and disposed them 'to mistake the Phantasms and Images of our own Brains'.[37] Clergymen, rightly oriented, needed to return laymen to 'the natural Calm and Serenity of their Minds' to limit the natural propensity to superstition.[38]

Enthusiasm was also a natural phenomenon.[39] It was 'a strong and impetuous Motion, or extraordinary and transcendant Ardor, Fervency or Pregnancy of the Soul, Spirits or Brain, which is vulgarly thought to be supernatural'.[40] Similarly, it was naturally contagious. Making reference to Newtonian science, Trenchard argued that 'Every thing in Nature is in constant Motion, and perpetually emitting Effluviums and minute Particles of its Substance, which operate upon, and strike other Bodies'.[41] Enthusiasm was a medical and physiological phenomenon, since 'the poisonous and melancholy Vapours streaming from an enthusiast, cause Distraction and Raving as well as the Bite of a Mad Dog'. Miasmic clouds spread the natural vapours emitting from the enthusiast. Some religious sects, such as the Quakers, had learned how to take advantage of these effluvia by harnessing them in worship. Citing George Keith, who had notoriously denounced the Quakers before joining the Anglican fold, and his pamphlet *The Magic of Quakerism; Or the Chief Mysteries of Quakerism Laid Open* (1707), Trenchard claimed that some Quakers 'have arrived to a great Proficiency in this natural Magnetism, or Magic, having by a watchful and accurate Observation of these mutual Effluxes and Emanations'.[42]

The politics of the Restoration and Revolution had been driven in part by superstition and enthusiasm. Trenchard and Gordon, living in the aftermath of the wars of religion, agonised over the political consequences of false religion. The enthusiast 'longs to feast and riot upon human Sacrifices, turn Cities and Nations into Shambles, and destroy with Fire and Sword such who dare thwart his Frenzy'. True religion, however, 'improves the Faculties, exhilarates the Spirits, makes the Mind calm and serene, renders us useful to Society, and

---

[35] John Trenchard, 'The Natural History of Superstition', in John Trenchard and Thomas Gordon, *A Collection of Tracts* (2 vols, London, 1751), vol. 1, p. 380.
[36] Ibid., p. 388.
[37] Ibid., p. 381.
[38] Ibid., p. 384.
[39] Matthew Day, 'The Sacred Contagion: John Trenchard, Natural History, and the Effluvial Politics of Religion', *History of Religions*, 50:2 (2010), pp. 144–61.
[40] Trenchard, 'Natural History of Superstition', in Trenchard and Gordon, *Collection of Tracts*, vol. 1, p. 400.
[41] Ibid., p. 385.
[42] Ibid., pp. 390–1.

most active in the Affairs of the World'.[43] Fearful of religious zeal, Trenchard warned against 'the Impostures of pretended Prophets, the Frauds of Priests, and the Dreams and Visions of Enthusiasts for heavenly Revelations, and our own Infirmities and panic Fears for divine Impulses'.[44] Enthusiastic preachers, those 'Pulpit *Fire-Brands*', '*Incendiaries*', and '*Pulpit-Blazers*', targeted the 'Ignorant' multitude in hope that it would be 'blown up into those Flames'.[45] Trenchard and Gordon both wrote in *The Independent Whig* that 'there are such Seeds of Superstition in human Nature, that all our Prudence and Caution will be little enough to prevent even Adoration to their Persons'.[46] Religion in its true and false forms was a natural phenomenon. But there was every reason to believe the false religions of superstition and enthusiasm were rife in Hanoverian England.

Anglican priestcraft

Priestcraft and superstition were as much problems among Protestants as ancient pagans and Roman Catholics. Praising Tillotson's fight against Anglican priestcraft, Trenchard and Gordon complained in *The Independent Whig* that the laity were caught in irrelevant 'Disputes about Religion with most Sets of Ecclesiastics'. Scholastic metaphysics continued to disrupt the perfect morality of the gospel whereas true Christianity was 'most easy and intelligible in itself, and adapted to the meanest Capacities'. False Christianity was 'a Metaphysical Science, made up of useless Subtleties, and insignificant Distinctions'.[47] Patristics were also a problem. True religion was felt inwardly and did not rely on 'Councils and Fathers'.[48] Barbeyrac had shown 'the Absurdities and Ravings of those Reverend old Gentlemen, whom we call the Fathers'.[49]

Patristics had been the enemy of the right relationship between church and state. Relying on Prideaux, Gordon cited the example of Saint Jerome who 'derives Episcopal Power from the Instigation of the Devil, which is also an impudent Reflection upon our Orthodox Church'. Saint Basil, who had been involved in constructing the Nicene creed, arrogantly 'challenged the Emperor, his Liege Lord, to fight him'. Saint Ambrose 'bullied Theodosius, the Lord's Anointed', and 'refused to admit his Imperial Majesty to partake of the Lord's Body, till he had made his humble Submission'.[50] The dispute between Ambrose and Theodosius had been the basis of a classic debate in Reformation Europe due to Ambrose's excommunication of the emperor. These examples show

---

43 Ibid., pp. 403, 384.
44 Ibid., p. 380.
45 Gordon, *Political Dissertation*, pp. 12–17.
46 *IW*, vol. 1, p. 19.
47 Ibid., pp. 55–6.
48 Ibid., p. 242.
49 Ibid., p. xliii.
50 Ibid., p. 244.

that Trenchard and Gordon believed Constantine and his successors were not paragons of godly kingship but quislings of Nicene episcopal power.

Superstitious priests in Protestant England were the modern imitators of these early corrupters. Trenchard and Gordon believed the problem of Anglican priestcraft had swelled under Stuart rule. A feature of Stuart priestcraft had been the compact struck between the clerical order and civil tyrants. In *Cato's Letters*, Trenchard addressed the laity and asked it to consider 'all the reigns since Queen Elizabeth's time to the Revolution' as reigns that 'oppressed you, and that Revolution that saved you'. The compact between Stuart tyrants and priests forced laymen 'to give up your persons, your consciences, and your fortunes, to the pleasure and lust of the prince'. By this compact, priests were guilty of *praemunire*. In 1610, priests persuaded James I to appoint three bishops to re-ordain the Scottish presbytery who, in turn, consecrated ten further bishops in Scotland. Trenchard recounted the advance of 'popish principles' in the Church of England under James I and Charles I, including seizing power of the keys to heaven and preaching doctrines like indelible clerical character, uninterrupted succession, and divine right of kings and bishops.[51] Under Charles II, priests never preached 'against the terrible excesses, the arbitrary imprisonments, the legal murders, and violation of property'.[52]

The reign of James II provided Trenchard and Gordon with the occasion to mock the internal inconsistencies of the Anglican insistence on *jure divino* monarchy. They accused priests of supporting James II by consecrating 'all his usurpations, his armies, and dispensing power' before turning against him when he provided royal indulgence to Protestant Dissent. Priests hypocritically supported the Whig opposition by endorsing the resistance theory that they had for so long harangued in the pulpit. It was ironic that priests rebelled 'upon their principles' but 'have been damning you and the nation for that resistance ever since'. Wavering clerical loyalty demonstrated the double standard, since, if 'a popish tyrant plunders and oppresses you, you neither can nor ought to have any remedy', but 'if he touch but a tithe-pig or surplice of theirs, their heel is ready to be lifted up against him'.[53]

Trenchard and Gordon attacked two further elements of Anglican priestcraft. One was the unreformed universities. Another was the charity school movement. Trenchard argued in *Cato's Letters* that the principles of the country's nobility and gentry were 'debauched in our universities' at the same time as 'those of our common people in our charity-schools, who are taught, as soon as they can speak, to blabber out *High Church* and *Ormond*', referring to the Jacobite James Butler, second duke of Ormond.[54] In *The Character of an Independent Whig* (1720), Gordon complained of 'a Popish, Impious and Rebellious Spirit' that

---

[51] *CL*, vol. 2, pp. 882–4.
[52] Ibid., p. 887.
[53] Ibid., p. 888.
[54] Ibid., p. 920.

'reigns at Oxford' where 'Disaffection is promoted' and 'open and black Perjury is justified'.[55] The magisterial Reformation had afforded means of reform but the 'Universities seem to dread no such Things as a Visitation'. Meanwhile 'the Corruption of our Seminaries' led to the spread of 'their disaffected Spawn in too many Parishes'.[56]

Charity schools were a feature of the wider reformation of manners movement that had emerged during the 1690s. The charity school movement had been launched by Archbishop Thomas Tenison to provide shelter, apprenticeships, and Anglican education to needy boys. But the schools had fallen victim to party dispute. Whigs like Mandeville feared that charity schools had become the seedbed of high-church and Tory disaffection.[57] Trenchard and Gordon noted that the schools themselves had been founded by 'pious men, many of them dissenters', in the face of Tory high-flying accusations that the reformation of manners movement was undermining the traditional disciplinary apparatus of the Church of England. However, high churchmen quickly realised the value of the schools in training loyal adherents. The schools now 'decoy superstitious and factious men out of their shops and their business, and old doting women out of their infirmaries, to hear too often seditious harangues upon the power of the clergy'. Lectures and instructions had become 'inconsistent with our present establishment of church and state'.[58]

Whigs and low churchmen had been complacent about the problem. They had ignored early calls from the likes of Tenison and Burnet to concern themselves with the inculcation of sound principles in lay and clerical education. In *Cato's Letters*, Trenchard complained that one reason Toryism, Jacobitism, and high-churchmanship continued to enjoy popular support was that, following the Glorious Revolution, nothing 'was ever done to rectify or regulate the education of youth, the source of all our other evils'. Schools of literature 'were suffered to continue under the direction of the enemies to all sound literature and publick virtue'. Opposed to liberty, high churchmen sent 'glowing hot from the universities' a new generation to preach against the Revolution.[59] As Trenchard later commented in opposition to charity schools, a 'free government must subsist upon the affections of the people' but 'if those affections be perpetually debauched' and 'if the education of youth be altogether inconsistent with the nature of it', free government would inevitably fall to tyranny.[60] An energetic defence of the pastoral and educational power of the Whig church order was urgent.

---

[55] Thomas Gordon, 'The Character of an Independent Whig', in Trenchard and Gordon, *Collection of Tracts*, vol. 1, p. 317.
[56] Ibid., p. 319.
[57] Bernard Mandeville, 'An Essay on Charity, and Charity-Schools', in *The Fable of the Bees: Or Private Vices, Publick Benefits* (2 vols, London, 1732), vol. 1, pp. 284, 309, 310. See M. G. Jones, *The Charity School Movement* (London, 1964), pp. 112–14.
[58] *CL*, vol. 2, pp. 918–20.
[59] Ibid., vol. 1, p. 145.
[60] Ibid., vol. 2, p. 921.

The national establishment

Such a defence first required a restatement of Whig ecclesiology and Revolution principles in church and state. Trenchard and Gordon married these themes with religious neo-Harringtonianism. Working with a standard Harringtonian principle, Trenchard wrote in *Cato's Letters* that 'it is most certain, that the first principle of all power is property; and every man will have his share of it in proportion as he enjoys property'. The 'balance of property' determined the balance of political power and 'the great secret in politicks is, nicely to watch and observe this fluctuation and change of natural power, and to adjust the political to it'.[61] Trenchard rehearsed the two great processes, first identified by Harrington, that altered property and politics in England. First, Henry VII strengthened the economic and political position of the lower orders to undermine the position of the nobility. Second, Henry VIII, 'by seizing the revenues of the ecclesiasticks ... and dispersing those estates amongst the people, made that balance much heavier'.[62] The result of these two shifts was the imbalance of power away from the nobility and church.

Trenchard believed that the declining independence of the church had determined the course of seventeenth-century politics. Royal policy came to rely on the doctrinal content of preaching rather than the political power of the church. James I, lacking Elizabeth's political moderation and harbouring absolutist dreams, took 'the assistance of the governing clergy (who hoped by his means to recover what they lost by the Reformation) to regain a power, by pulpit-haranguing and distinctions'. The campaign to regain absolutist power made James's reign 'a perpetual struggle between himself and his Parliaments' and 'by such conduct he sowed the seeds of that fatal and bloody Civil War'. The civil wars left Charles II with 'all the exterior advantages requisite to enslave a people', including a nation weary of the 'sound of liberty', a nobility alienated by sequestrations, and a clergy 'provoked by the loss of their dignities and revenues'.[63]

But there was more than religious neo-Harringtonianism at play in Trenchard and Gordon's analysis of the church-state relationship. There was also the Erastianism of the superiority of the temporal power over spirituals. In a message for the lower house of Convocation after it had censured Hoadly, Trenchard and Gordon reminded clerics that 'the Gospel has not given you one Foot of Land, or one Shilling of Money'. Instead, 'Your Church is a Creature of the Constitution, you are Creatures of the Law'. Further, 'you must evidently belye Divine Right, if you pretend to derive from thence, what all the World sees you owe to secular Bounty'.[64] Gordon praised Erastus for dismissing 'all these Squabbles of the Clergy about their own Power' and showing 'that none of them

---

[61] Ibid., pp. 607, 608, 610.
[62] Ibid., pp. 610–11.
[63] Ibid.
[64] *IW*, vol. 1, pp. xxv–xxvi.

had any Right to what they almost all claimed'. Erastus demonstrated 'from Reason and Scripture, that every State had the same Authority of modelling their Ecclesiastical as Civil Government'.[65] Of course, this interpretation represented a gloss on Erastus's position, since he had simply opposed excessive use of the power of excommunication against sixteenth-century Heidelberg.

Tory and high-church attempts to revive sacerdotal priestliness threatened the Reformation itself. The 'whole Reformation was built' upon the principle that 'Protestant States modelled their Ecclesiastical Polity according to their own Inclinations or Interests'. It was 'the last Degree of Priestly Insolence for a Body of Men to call themselves the only true Churchmen'. It was ironic, Gordon mocked, that high churchmen should resist the fundamental principles of the Reformation 'at the same time that they deny, and every-where exclaim against, the fundamental and essential Article which distinguishes it from most other Churches, and particularly from Presbytery'. In a rhetorical gesture that equated Tory high-churchmanship with Presbyterians for their pretensions to *jure divino* authority, Gordon claimed that 'the Calvinists are more Orthodox than the Churchmen themselves'.[66]

Invoking the name of Thomas Cranmer, Trenchard and Gordon argued that ordination should be 'no more than a Civil Appointment to an Ecclesiastical Office'. The 'Apostles had no Ambition, Jurisdiction, Dignities, or Revenues, to which they could be Successors'. Paraphrasing Hoadly's sermon in 1717, Trenchard and Gordon reminded churchmen that 'our Saviour himself declares, that *his Kingdom is not of this World*'.[67] Unlike modern divines, the apostles were 'inspired, had the Gift of working Miracles, could bestow the Holy Ghost, had the Discernment of Spirits'. They were 'proper Judges of the Fitness of Men for the Ministry, and could confer that Fitness'.[68] There was no scriptural evidence that these privileges had passed down to modern churchmen.

Within these Erastian themes sounded magisterial English notes. Trenchard dedicated a paper of *The Independent Whig* to the subject: 'The church proved a creature of the civil power, by acts of parliament, and the oaths of the clergy'.[69] He praised a 'bold and honest Physician (whose Name was Erastus)', who argued 'that the Gospel gave no Pre-eminence or Authority to Christians over one another'. Erastus showed that 'it was only a Matter of Prudence and Convenience to appoint particular Persons to officiate for the rest, with proper Rewards and Encouragements'.[70] At the time of the Henrician Reformation, the clergy 'threw themselves upon the King's Mercy, acknowledging his Supremacy in the fullest and most significant Words'.[71] Trenchard recited the litany of

---

[65] Ibid., p. 100.
[66] Ibid., p. 101.
[67] Ibid., p. 48.
[68] Ibid., p. 60.
[69] Ibid, p. 98.
[70] Ibid., pp. 100–1.
[71] Ibid., pp. 101–2.

parliamentary acts, royal constitutions, canons, and ordinances that had been enacted. These included royal power to call Convocation, appointment of the episcopate, and restriction of *praemunire*.[72] He listed Edwardian ecclesiastical reforms, such as the enactment of the Book of Common Prayer, and those of the Elizabethan era, including, most importantly, the oath of supremacy.[73]

A loud note was sounded for the godly prince. Trenchard and Gordon offered a yardstick against which to measure supreme governors of the Church of England. In *Cato's Letters*, Trenchard praised Elizabeth I 'who was resolved to be truly what she was called, Head of the Church', and 'kept her priests in a just and becoming subordination, and would not suffer them to meddle with or prate about her government'. Stuart kingship fell predictably short. Trenchard described James I as 'a weak prince' under whom 'many of the leading clergy advanced all the vilest tenets of popery'. Charles I, 'a bigot by nature as well as education', given that he had once prepared to enter the priesthood, conspired in Laudian popery. Trenchard dwelled upon the appointment of Richard Montagu to the bishopric of Chichester, despite being accused of popery by parliament, and Laud's hounding of John Bastwick for publishing two treatises attacking the Roman Catholic ceremonial.[74] Charles II was a crypto-papist who pursued 'the barefaced encouragement of popery, and the persecution of Protestants'. Cultivating a sense of an international Protestant brotherhood, Trenchard attacked Charles's dealings with Louis XIV as an attempt to 'destroy the only state in the world that could be then called the bulwark of liberty and the Protestant religion' through 'unjust wars with the United Provinces'.[75]

The Revolution represented a reassertion of the magisterial principle of the crown-in-parliament. William III and his successors left Englishmen 'protected and secure in standing laws' with 'full enjoyment of your consciences'.[76] By granting liberty of conscience to Protestant Dissenters, William demonstrated to the clergy that 'he would not be a blind tool to a priestly faction, but would equally protect all his subjects who were faithful to him'. Yet Revolution principles in religion were not secure. Queen Anne had fallen 'into the hands of a few desperate traitors' who 'put France into a condition again to enslave Europe' and aimed 'to place a popish traitor, an attainted fugitive, upon the throne of these kingdom'.[77] It was not difficult to decipher the identity of these desperate traitors: Robert Harley, earl of Oxford, and Bolingbroke.

There is further evidence of Trenchard and Gordon's Whiggish insistence on the magisterial authority of the crown-in-parliament. Trenchard claimed in *Cato's Letters* that churchmen hoped 'that some favourable opportunities might happen to get away the regale [prerogatives of royalty] from the crown'. But

---

[72] Ibid., pp. 102–4.
[73] Ibid., pp. 104–7.
[74] *CL*, vol. 2, pp. 883–5.
[75] Ibid., p. 887.
[76] Ibid.
[77] Ibid., pp. 888–9.

'we never had a prince whom they could entirely govern, or who would not be governed at all by them, but they have laid claim to it, and attempted it'. What made the difference, 'what stood always in their way, and made all their designs impracticable, was the power of Parliament, and the liberties of the people, who preserved the prerogative of the crown to preserve themselves'. Churchmen 'laboured to make the prince absolute' because it was 'easier to flatter, mislead, or bargain with one man (and often a weak one) than to deceive a whole people, and make them conspire against themselves'.[78] It is too often supposed that clashes between absolute and limited monarchy in early modern thought were based on secular terms. Trenchard's use of ideas of Christian reform demonstrates that religious concerns stood at the crux of early modern arguments against royal absolutism.

The equation of godly kingship with the crown-in-parliament related to Whig resistance theory. As Gordon wrote in *Cato's Letters*, 'To obey a prince, who does himself obey the laws, is confessed on all hands to be loyalty'. It was only 'ungodly pedants' who believed that loyalty 'also consists in the very contrary, and in obeying a wicked prince', who, 'though he be an enemy to God, is the vicegerent of God'.[79] Since the magisterial Reformation had been enacted by the king-in-parliament, a monarch opting to act without or against the will of parliament transgressed the principles of godly English monarchy. Trenchard argued in *Cato's Letters* that the 'constitution of our Church is excellently well adapted to our civil government', since bishops were held to account by the House of Lords and the inferior clergy by the House of Commons. Crucially, 'all are subject to the legislative power mediately, and immediately to the crown' which retained the power to appoint chief ecclesiastical officers.[80] The Revolution meant that the monarch, 'by act of Parliament, as well as interest and education, will be of the established Church'.[81]

It is, therefore, important to distinguish the civil religion of Trenchard and Gordon from that of Hobbes. As Rose has argued, Hobbesian Erastianism sought to make the sovereign a priestly sacerdotal king, contravening the standard Erastian defence of royal supremacy on jurisdictional and legal grounds.[82] The defence of a tolerant national establishment set the authors of *The Independent Whig* against Hobbes's argument that, as they rendered it, 'the Civil Magistrate of every Country is the Legislator in Matters of Religion'. They disagreed with Hobbes that the king's 'Subjects ought to obey him therein' and that, 'if they do not, they should be compelled by Force to profess that Religion which he injoins'. Such a position destroyed 'God's Dominion, by subverting his Authority and Laws, and by making a God of the Magistrate'. It rooted 'out all

---

[78] Ibid., p. 900.
[79] Ibid., vol. 1, p. 255.
[80] Ibid., vol. 2, p. 588.
[81] Ibid., p. 591.
[82] Rose, *Godly Kingship*, p. 204.

Religion, by taking away Mens Right to follow their Consciences therein' which 'constitutes the very Essence of Religion'.[83]

The role of clergymen

In Trenchard and Gordon's civil religion, clergymen were to be more than the mere officers of a prudent sovereign to keep the laity obeisant. The role of Christian ministers stretched deep into the history of Christian reform. Above all, clergymen were to be pastoral. The clerical 'Office is evidently adapted to promote the Welfare of Human Nature, to propagate its Peace and Prosperity in this World, as well as its eternal Felicity in the next'. As such, 'it is the Interest of all Men to honour it; and none but a Madman will condemn and ridicule what has a manifest Tendency to the Security and Happiness of all Mankind'.[84] Clergymen 'have the Possession and Direction of our Fears'. They 'are admitted in Health and Sickness' and, every Sunday, 'they have the sole Opportunity of gaining our Esteem by worthy and useful Instructions, and all the Week by their good Lives'. They had the power to 'educate us whilst young, influence us in our middle Age, govern us in our Dotage, and we neither live nor die without them'. Such a body of men, 'so constituted and endowed, so privileged and posted, are capable of being most useful and beneficent to Society, if their Actions be suitable to their Professions'.[85]

In classical notes of civic republicanism, Gordon wrote in his commentary in *The Works of Tacitus* that 'a parochial Clergy are of infinite use, where they take pains by their example and instructions to mend the hearts of the people, where they teach them to love God, and their Neighbour, and Virtue, and their Country, and to hate no man'.[86] Champion argued that this passage presents republican recognition of the 'useful propagandistic role of the clergy' in harnessing piety for the political order.[87] By this reading, Gordon connects English republicanism with anti-Christian freethinking, which perceived Anglicanism as inherently priest-ridden.[88] However, it would be more fruitful to understand the passage as a republican defence of Christian primitivism in the context of England's long Reformation.

Further evidence of the syncretism between Christian reform and civic republicanism lies in Trenchard and Gordon's political economy. Priests, free from secular control, were slaves of passion, economically unproductive, and incapable of providing a virtuous example of Christian citizenship. Gordon satirised a 'Clergyman, who is drunk on Saturday, will but, with an ill Grace,

---

[83] *IW*, vol. 2, pp. 112–13.
[84] Ibid., vol. 1, p. 18.
[85] Ibid., p. 19.
[86] Tacitus, *Works*, ed. Gordon, vol. 3, p. 221.
[87] Champion, *Pillars of Priestcraft Shaken*, p. 7, n. 23.
[88] Ibid., pp. 7, 15, 20, 24, 224, 234–5.

talk of his Dignity and Embassadorship on Sunday'.[89] Honouring priests by donations impoverished the laity because 'the people dare not work to support their families, but must contribute, out of the little which remains, to pay their oppressors for preaching them out of their wits'.[90] Invoking the theme of the Protestant grand tour, Gordon cited Burnet who 'tells us, in his Letters of Travels, that the Priests of Italy have found out a Secret to make Men miserable' through the supposedly godly practice of fasting.[91] Conversely, prudent living in this world served the public good. Furthermore, true religion cultivated good citizens. Clergymen were 'absolutely necessary to the Peace and Happiness of Society' in the same way as ancient Roman consuls who 'had an Officer attending their Triumphal Chariots'.[92] It was the genius of the early Roman republic to institute public priests to inculcate 'the raising and recommending of Public Spirit, so necessary to the prosperity of every Country, and even to the preservation of all'.[93]

Trenchard and Gordon's clergy would also be pedagogical. Gordon argued in his edition of Tacitus that it 'becomes the wisdom of all Governors so to fashion and regulate the public Teachers' and to remind these teachers that they were 'the Creatures of the State, appointed by the civil Power to a religious office'. This was 'the wisdom of England at the Reformation' as clergymen swore loyalty to the crown and to deny any independent power from the secular arm.[94] The apostles were the highest example of public teaching. Even though they enjoyed 'no power, no revenues, nor even the countenance of authority', their 'reverence and success flowed from their heavenly doctrine and behaviour'. Clergymen ought to imitate the apostles and make it their business to urge the gospel 'upon the consciences of men, to improve them in practical holiness, to purify their lives in this world, and thence fit them for another'.[95]

In *The Independent Whig*, Gordon rehearsed the pedagogical responsibilities of the clergy. The multitude could misunderstand elements of scripture, which, though 'given us from Heaven to be Light unto our Feet', was 'dark and insufficient without human Aid and Explication'.[96] It was 'absurd' that clergymen should involve the flock in rarefied metaphysical debates when the key precepts of Christianity were so clear. Recalling the famous passage of Locke in *The Reasonableness of Christianity* (1695), Gordon argued that nobody should 'send Cookmaids and Day-labourers to study Aristotle and Suarez' or 'to rake into the Jargon of the Schools'.[97] Clergymen must 'press the Reading

---

[89] *IW*, vol. 1, p. 20.
[90] *CL*, vol. 2, p. 799.
[91] *IW*, vol. 1, p. 232.
[92] Ibid., p. 28.
[93] Tacitus, *Works*, ed. Gordon, vol. 3, p. 245.
[94] Ibid., p. 224.
[95] Ibid., pp. 226–7.
[96] *IW*, vol. 1, p. 39.
[97] Ibid., p. 26.

of the Scripture upon their Hearers' and 'inculcate the plain Precepts of Faith and Morality contained in it'. They should 'demonstrate the Goodness of God to Men by proving, that he has laid down to us in plain Words, every Duty which he requires of us, either to himself, our Neighbour, or ourselves'. They should execute those duties of the Christian religion dictated by the word of God as 'necessary to be performed by single Persons in the several Churches or Societies of Christians'.[98] Those duties included reading scripture, public prayers, and administering the sacraments.

Toleration and enthusiasm

The clergy must further maintain the Toleration Act. Trenchard and Gordon sought to relate political with religious liberty by arguing that political liberty could only thrive where there also existed liberty of conscience. Civil tyranny was almost invariably supported by false religion, since true religion encouraged spiritual exploration. Neither 'the Christian religion, nor natural religion, nor any thing else that ought to be called religion, can subsist under tyrannical governments', for 'such governments are fertile in superstition, in wild whimsies, delusive phantoms, and ridiculous dreams' all designed 'to terrify the human soul, degrade its dignity, deface its beauty, and fetter it with slavish and unmanly ears'. In tones echoing Shaftesbury, religion under civil tyranny was the 'proper object of fraud, grimace, and imposition' governed by 'gloomy impostors'.[99]

In *Cato's Letters*, Gordon rehearsed the worst excesses of Stuart tyranny, arguing that there could never be 'a more provoking, impudent, shocking, and blasphemous position, than to assert all this group of horrors, or the author of them, to be of God's appointment', for 'God must be belied, his creatures must be fettered, frightened, deceived, and starved'.[100] Everything 'dear and desirable to society must result from a state of liberty', including not only 'property and life' but 'conscience and the faculties of the soul'. Religion, 'in order to do good, must be left entirely free', lest it become the tool of usurping priests and civil tyrants. False religion was the otherworldly metaphysics of superstitious impostors who seek to 'preach up self-denial, to preach against the world, and to claim successorship to the poor, wandering, holy and disinterested Apostles'.[101]

A tolerant national establishment was necessary to provide a moderate corrective to enthusiasm. Toleration for Protestant Dissent should not be confused with approval. Gordon believed Calvinism was equally as dangerous as Roman Catholicism or Islam in its enforcement of intolerant orthodoxy, since 'Affliction and misery, oppression and imposture, are as bad in Christendom as in Turkey, in Holland as in Rome'.[102] When repressed by the ecclesiastical and

---

[98] Ibid., pp. 28–9.
[99] *CL*, vol. 1, p. 462.
[100] Ibid., pp. 439–40.
[101] Tacitus, *Works*, ed. Gordon, vol. 3, p. 6.
[102] *CL*, vol. 2, pp. 907–8.

civil powers, Protestant sectarianism became enthusiasm. Trenchard repeated the themes of his *Natural History* in *Cato's Letters* by arguing that enthusiasm was a natural and contagious phenomenon that needed careful treatment. Discussing such examples as the sixteenth-century Spanish Hermits, the Alumbrados, the Illuminati, the seventeenth-century Italian Quietists, and the Camisards in London, Trenchard wrote of the best means to treat such enthusiastic believers.[103] A moderate option of public worship would show these men that they are not 'princes, prophets, or messengers from heaven' and would provide a corrective for mechanic preachers.[104]

As part of their defence of toleration, Trenchard and Gordon tried to demonstrate that Protestant Dissent posed no threat to the Church of England. In *Cato's Letters*, Trenchard expressed his puzzlement that 'some men of good understanding and unquestionable integrity apprehend the danger to the legal constitution of the Church'. The Independents, Anabaptists, and Quakers, the latter lacking a clergy altogether, were each opposed to ecclesiastical establishments and refused to vie for such power. They desired 'nothing but liberty of conscience, and do not envy other preferments which they cannot enjoy themselves'.[105]

Presbyterians had historically not cared to be described as Dissenters because their expulsion from the Church of England during the early 1660s had been forcible and they continued to defend the idea of a national church. Still, Trenchard dealt with them as the perpetual targets of Tory and high-church ire. He conceded that the 'Presbyterians are candidates for church-dominion; and without doubt their priests have hawks' eyes at the church preferments'. But he believed their small number and recent schism into Subscribers and Nonsubscribers rendered them too weak to challenge the Anglican establishment.[106] In 1717 the Irish Presbyterian divine John Abernathy refused to minister to a congregation in Dublin to which he had been assigned. His refusal was taken as treason, challenging the authority of the ecclesiastical courts. The Presbyterians divided into those Nonsubscribers who supported Abernathy and those Subscribers who sided with the Presbyterian synod. In 1726, he and his supporters were ejected from the Irish Presbyterian church.

Trenchard and Gordon invoked models of Restoration and post-Revolutionary divinity to defend their anti-enthusiastic pastoralism. *The Independent Whig* remonstrated with high churchmen for 'constantly charging others with Atheism' who simply sought to allow inward liberty of conscience. Among the victims of such clerical attacks were 'the most learned, best, and most religious Men, as Cudworth, Tillotson, and Locke'.[107] The paper also made use of 'Mr. Chillingworth' and his *Rule of Faith* set in opposition to the arguments of John

---

[103] Ibid., p. 856.
[104] Ibid., p. 859.
[105] Ibid.
[106] Ibid.
[107] *IW*, vol. 2, p. 140.

Bramhall, bishop of Armagh, in defending *sola scriptura* Christianity.[108] Gordon argued that Locke, 'One of the greatest Men of the last Age', had shown the need to reform the universities for the prevention of priestcraft.[109] With Locke, Trenchard argued in *Cato's Letters* that 'Every man's religion is his own; nor can the religion of any man, of what nature or figure soever, be the religion of another man, unless he also chooses it; which action utterly excludes all force, power, or government.' Religion was a 'relation between God and our own souls only, and consists in a disposition of mind to obey the will of our great Creator, in the manner which we think most acceptable to him'. Civil authority played no legitimate role in this relation other than protecting it from invasion.[110]

Another key figure was Hoadly. In one pamphlet of 1720, Gordon situated his intervention at the centre of the Bangorian controversy. Declaring his opposition to 'High Flying Tenets', which led to 'the severest Misery, even brutish Ignorance, abject Slavery, Poverty and Wickedness', Gordon equated 'an Army of aspiring Ecclesiasticks' with the opponents of the Reformation who believed 'Dominion is the Word, Servitude the Duty, and Damnation the Penalty'. In defence of 'Reason and the Gospel' Gordon aligned himself with 'the Bishop of Bangor, a Champion for Truth'.[111] In *The Independent Whig*, Gordon continued that it was 'as impious as unjust to deny an unlimited Toleration to all Dissenters whatsoever, who own the Laws, and our civil Form of Government'. In explicitly Bangorian terms, Gordon claimed that Dissenters were legitimate in justifying their religious opinions 'by Sincerity'. In any event, 'even where that is wanting, God alone is able to judge, and alone has a Right to punish'.[112] That these works were composed as an explicit defence of the Bangorian position suggests that it risks prolepsis to read into Hoadly's position the seeds of disestablishmentarianism.[113]

Trenchard and Gordon have often been characterised as deists because of the intense anticlericalism of their pamphlets, especially during the Bangorian controversy.[114] But to focus on their inward faith is to misunderstand those motivations that shaped their writings on the public role of religion. Irrespective of their views of the normative truths of Christianity, they believed it could be rendered a civil religion by equating gospel primitivism with natural religion.

---

[108] Ibid., p. 52.
[109] Ibid., p. 95.
[110] *CL*, vol. 1, p. 414.
[111] Thomas Gordon, 'Considerations Offered upon the Approaching Peace, and upon the Importance of Gibraltar to the British Empire, being the Second Part of the Independent Whig', in Trenchard and Gordon, *Collection of Tracts*, vol. 1, pp. 270–1.
[112] *IW*, vol. 2, pp. 88–9.
[113] Starkie, *Church of England*, pp. 3, 17, 189–90.
[114] McMahon, *Radical Whigs*, p. 159; Jacob, *Radical Enlightenment*, pp. 151–2; Schwartz, *Knaves, Fools, Madmen and That Subtile Effluvium*, p. 53; Heyd, *'Be Sober and Reasonable'*, p. 210, n. 58; Berman, 'Anthony Collins's Essays', p. 464; Peter Harrison, *'Religion' and the Religions in the English Enlightenment* (Cambridge, 2002), p. 125; Stark, 'Atheism, Faith, and the Social Scientific Study of Religion', p. 49.

True religion was simple, clear, and readily comprehensible. It consisted solely in the outward exercise of the golden rule. The soteriological relationship between the lay Protestant believer and God was both exclusive and based entirely on the personal characteristic of sincerity. Trenchard and Gordon relied on the legal and ecclesiastical framework of the magisterial Reformation. More broadly, their Erastianism allowed them to develop a positive defence for pastoral clergymen in Hanoverian England and they drew from Whig and low-church modes of divinity to defend their arguments. Their Christian reform also had a civic voice as they cast Christianity as the modern version of the Roman pagan achievement of rendering religion worldly. Trenchard and Gordon hoped to serve the ends of virtuous, prosperous, and civilised living in this world by turning the priest into the patriot. Christian ministers were to inculcate right religion and, in so doing, they formed good citizens for this world in anticipation of the next.

3

The Church-State Alliance:
Henry St John, Viscount Bolingbroke, and William Warburton

The opposition to Walpole

Bolingbroke defies easy classification. A would-be leader of the Tory high-flyers, he served in Queen Anne's Tory ministries from 1702 until her death in 1714 before supporting the failed Jacobite succession in 1715.[1] He joined the Old Pretender and served as his secretary of state in 1715–16. He returned to England in 1723 from exile in Paris thanks to a qualified pardon from parliament, which excluded him from the House of Lords. The pen being forced upon him, Bolingbroke spent the 1720s and 1730s attempting to unite a disparate collection of Whig and Tory opponents to the ministries of Walpole on a 'country' platform through the political journal *The Craftsman*.[2] During the 1730s, Bolingbroke became associated with the 'patriot' opposition to Walpole and the alternative court surrounding Frederick, Prince of Wales.[3] Bolingbroke's campaign synthesised, in civic and ancient constitutional voice, Whig and Tory political languages. He wrote of England's mixed and balanced constitution, government in the service of the common good, and the ancient balance between monarchy and parliament. Such themes comprised the 'spirit of liberty' that was 'authorized by the voice of the country'.[4]

Despite Bolingbroke's kaleidoscopic political identities, his religious writings were those of a theorist of civil religion. He sought to defend the Erastian supremacy of the crown-in-parliament over the Church of England from the encroachment of powerful bishops such as Gibson and the clericalist defences of the Church of England of Warburton. Bolingbroke displayed outward conformity to the Thirty-Nine Articles. The Church of England was an institution of the civil

---

[1] Henry St John was elevated to the House of Lords as Viscount Bolingbroke in July 1712. For the sake of clarity, this chapter will refer to him as Bolingbroke throughout.
[2] The pardon from George I and parliament barred Bolingbroke from returning to the House of Lords.
[3] Christine Gerrard, *The Patriot Opposition to Walpole* (Oxford, 1994).
[4] Henry St John, Viscount Bolingbroke, *Political Writings*, ed. David Armitage (Cambridge, 1997), p. 37.

state, subject to its governance. Bolingbroke always supported the ecclesiastical settlement of the Revolution and insisted upon the Anglican character of the church-state relationship. He was adamant that the monarch must profess the same Anglican religion as the nation and he defended the royal supremacy of the crown-in-parliament.

In his posthumous philosophical publications, he conceived of natural religion in which rational individuals exercised understanding of the supreme being through empirical observation of nature, and equated it with primitive Christianity. He attacked priestcraft, by which priestly power relied on the economic and spiritual exploitation of a superstitious laity, and feared enthusiasm. An Erastian writing in the reformed Christian tradition, Bolingbroke relied on the godly prince as a bulwark against priestly usurpation and sanctified the state as the sole guarantor of true religion. He also conceived of a positive public role for clergymen in the vanguard against superstition and enthusiasm. Although he believed the Thirty-Nine Articles of the Church of England did not equate with the precepts of gospel Christianity, he hoped that the national church would be further purged of superstition in time. He outwardly observed its articles of faith because he believed reverence for the public faith sanctified belonging within the Christian commonwealth of Hanoverian England.

Although Bolingbroke's religious thought has not been studied seriously for over half a century, he has occasionally been associated with civil religion.[5] However, this association has been too strongly motivated by fascination with Bolingbroke's deism. He is supposed to have propounded a Machiavellian conception of the political utility of religion due to his antipathy for historical Christianity.[6] Neglected has been Bolingbroke's debt to the legal and ecclesiastical scholarship of the long Reformation and his insistence that the Church of England could profess natural religion using Christian primitive principles. He judged a church establishment beneficial for the social and political order, but he also believed it was vital for the spiritual flourishing of individual lay Protestants. Whatever the precise nature of Bolingbroke's own views on religion, he maintained a principled commitment to the idea of a Christian civil religion.

Obvious objections to this line of argument relate to Bolingbroke's political career. Although that which follows may appear digressive, it repays first dispensing with these problems. In 1702–3, Bolingbroke sponsored the Occasional Conformity Bill to prohibit the practice and, in 1714, he introduced

---

[5] Earlier scholarship includes Leslie Stephen, *History of English Thought in the Eighteenth Century* (2 vols, London, 1881); Norman Torrey, *Voltaire and the English Deists* (New Haven, 1930); D. G. James, *The Life of Reason: Hobbes, Locke, Bolingbroke* (London, 1949); Walter Mackintosh Merrill, *From Statesman to Philosopher: A Study in Bolingbroke's Deism* (London, 1949).

[6] H. T. Dickinson, *Bolingbroke* (London, 1970), pp. xi, 164. See also Alfred Owen Aldridge, 'Shaftesbury and Bolingbroke', *Philological Quarterly*, 31:1 (1952), pp. 1–16, at pp. 14, 20; Bernard Cottret (ed.), *Bolingbroke's Political Writings: The Conservative Enlightenment* (London and New York, 1997), p. 8.

the Schism Bill to undermine Dissenting education and academies. He was manoeuvring to court high churchmen in his campaign for the Tory leadership. The *de facto* Tory leader, Harley, who became Queen Anne's first lord of the treasury between 1710 and 1714, had attended a Dissenting academy and was suspected to be sympathetic to Nonconformists.[7] Speaking in favour of the Schism Bill in 1714, Bolingbroke pointedly argued that 'it was a Bill of the last importance, since it concerns the security of the Church of England, which is the best and firmest support of the monarchy'.[8] Bolingbroke engaged in religious questions on just two occasions in twelve years. He did so when his stock was low among high churchmen who had never resolved the tensions generated by choosing between the exclusivity of the Church of England and a Roman Catholic king whose prerogative powers had undermined it.

Bolingbroke also needed to compensate for his own religious skeletons. His stepmother hailed from a French-Swiss Huguenot family. His grandmother appears to have had puritan inclinations and was reputedly patroness to such Nonconformist ministers as Daniel Burgess and Thomas Manton. In a letter to Jonathan Swift in 1721, Bolingbroke indicated that Manton had influenced his education:

> I resolve, since I am this morning in the humour of scribbling, to make my letter at least as long as one of your sermons, and if you do not mend my next shall be as long as one of Dr Manton's, who taught my youth to yawn, and prepar'd me to be an High church man, that I might never hear him read, nor read him more.[9]

It was also rumoured that Bolingbroke had attended a Dissenting academy. During the debates on the Schism Bill, the Whig MP Nicholas Lechmere alluded to Bolingbroke, 'who had been bred among schismatics', but was, 'or, at least pretended to be, [among] the strongest supporters of the established church'. Thomas, marquess of Wharton, quipped that 'persons who had been educated in dissenting academies ... appear the most forward in suppressing them'.[10] Bolingbroke's rakish personal life and antipathy for orthodox Christianity cast further doubt upon his suitability for the highest of offices.[11] In *A Journal to Stella* (written between 1710 and 1713), Swift supposed that Bolingbroke conformed occasionally to qualify for office. Like 'several rakes', it was not 'for piety, but employments; according to Act of Parliament'.[12]

---

[7] Robert Harley was raised to the peerage as earl of Oxford in 1711.
[8] *Debates and Speeches in Both Houses of Parliament concerning the Schism-Bill* (London, 1715), p. 6.
[9] Bolingbroke to Jonathan Swift, 28 July 1721, in Harold Williams (ed.), *The Correspondence of Jonathan Swift* (5 vols, Oxford, 1963–5), vol. 2, p. 398.
[10] William Cobbett (ed.), *The Parliamentary History of England* (36 vols, London, 1806–20), vol. 6, pp. 1351–2.
[11] Dickinson, *Bolingbroke*, p. 119.
[12] Jonathan Swift, *The Works of Jonathan Swift*, ed. Walter Scott (19 vols, Edinburgh, 1814), vol. 2, p. 415.

After 1715, Bolingbroke claimed that his attitude towards the church-state relationship had been broadly consistent with Revolution principles. He never manifested support for *jure divino* monarchy or episcopacy. In his communications with the Old Pretender he attempted in vain to persuade him to convert to Anglicanism. As Bolingbroke recalled in his apologia, *A Letter to Sir William Wyndham* (1717), 'We of the laity had nothing more to do than to lay in our claim, that we could never submit to be governed by a prince who was not of the religion of our country.' The Pretender's Roman Catholic faith was founded neither 'on the love of virtue and the detestation of vice' nor 'on a sense of that obedience which is due to the will of the Supreme Being; and a sense of those obligations which creatures formed to live in a mutual dependence on one another lie under'. James was only capable of 'blind submission to the church of Rome, and a strict adherence to all the terms of that communion'. There was 'on him no tincture of the religion of a prince'.[13] Bolingbroke was rehearsing the standard Christian reformist claim that a godly Roman Catholic prince was oxymoronic, since he would return the laity to priestly and civil tyranny.

It is sometimes supposed that Walpole and his bishops constructed an ecclesiastical consensus that, if it did not resolve it, assuaged the religious drama of the post-Revolutionary years.[14] But there was renewed agitation during the 1730s over the repeal of the Test and Corporation Acts with Dissenters petitioning parliament during its 1732–3 session. The toleration debate occasioned the controversy that followed the sermon preached by Francis Hare, ministerialist bishop of Chichester, on King Charles Day in 1732.[15] Hare opposed repeal using commonplace attacks on regicidal puritans. A pro-toleration element of the court seized on the sermon to discredit his position by casting him as a crypto-Jacobite.[16] There was a protracted and high-profile controversy surrounding the attempt, defeated by Gibson, to appoint Thomas Rundle, long suspected of heterodoxy, to the see of Gloucester in 1733. There were efforts to push the Tithe Bill (1731), Church Rates and Repairs Bill (1733), Ecclesiastical Courts Bills (1733 and 1734), Quakers Tithe Bill (1736), and Mortmain Bill (1736) through parliament, although only the last of these reached the statute book.[17] The fear that it might provoke latent religious tensions was a major reason for the failure to implement church reform during the mid-eighteenth century.[18]

---

[13] Henry St John, Viscount Bolingbroke, *The Works of Lord Bolingbroke* (4 vols, London, 1844), vol. 1, pp. 168–9.
[14] Harvey C. Mansfield Jr, *Statesmanship and Party Government: A Study of Burke and Bolingbroke* (London, 1965), p. 42; Holmes, *Trial of Dr Sacheverell*, pp. 275–6.
[15] Andrew Lacey, *The Cult of King Charles the Martyr* (Woodbridge, 2003).
[16] Colley, *In Defiance of Oligarchy*, pp. 104–15.
[17] Stephen Taylor, 'Sir Robert Walpole, the Church of England, and the Quakers Tithe Bill of 1736', *HJ*, 28:1 (1985), pp. 51–77; 'Whigs, Tories and Anticlericalism: Ecclesiastical Courts Legislation in 1733', *PH*, 19:3 (2000), pp. 329–55.
[18] Stephen Taylor, 'Whigs, Bishops and America: The Politics of Church Reform in Mid-Eighteenth-Century England', *HJ*, 36:2 (1993), pp. 331–56. See also Stephen Taylor, 'Church and State in England in the Mid-Eighteenth Century: The Newcastle Years 1742–62'

It is equally misleading to suppose that the anti-ministerialists were ideologically cohesive.[19] Bolingbroke steered a middle course between dissident Whigs who believed the king's ministers were undermining the Revolution and Tories who cared little for Revolution principles. Bolingbroke first needed to renounce his high-flying and Jacobite past. In his *Dissertation upon Parties* (1733), he recalled that, whereas post-Revolutionary Whigs had been the party of the 'power and majesty of the people, an original contract, the authority and independency of Parliament, liberty, resistance, exclusion, abdication, deposition', Queen Anne Tories had been committed to 'Divine hereditary, indefeasible right, lineal succession, passive-obedience, prerogative, non-resistance, slavery, nay and sometimes popery too'.[20]

The party labels of Whiggism and Toryism, he argued, had emerged during the exclusion crisis. Partisan identification with other issues, including the relationship between parliament and crown, Dissent, the Church of England, and Roman Catholicism, then turned upon the question of exclusion. But when James II opted for both arbitrary civil rule and prerogative toleration, he united Whigs and Tories. The Revolution balanced the need to defend the Church through the Test and Corporation Acts with toleration of inward consciences.[21] There was no need to relieve Dissenters still further because the penal laws 'have not been these many years a terror'. Those laws which 'were designed to hinder the propagation of their principles, and those which shut the door of all public preferment, even to such amongst them as conformed occasionally', were also repealed. Yet those politicians, like himself, who 'have been reputed their enemies', he emphasised, 'and who have acted as such on several occasions, acknowledge their error'.[22]

Bolingbroke thereby hoped to persuade the public that religious dividing lines were no longer significant. The 'polemical skill of [Charles] Leslie' and the 'antique erudition of [Hilkiah] Bedford', both nonjuring divines and defenders of patriarchalist monarchy, represented nothing more than 'those old shackles of false law, false reason, and false gospel'.[23] The mainstay of Bolingbroke's opposition to Walpole instead rested upon country suspicion of the alliance between the Whig ministry and the 'monied interest' created by the fiscal-military state.[24] The opposition repeatedly claimed to be acting in the name of patriotism, attacking the ministry on the more obvious issues of the land forces

---

(PhD thesis, University of Cambridge, 1987). I am grateful to Professor Taylor for providing me with unpublished materials relating to the relationship between religion and politics between 1714 and 1760.
[19] See Alexander Pettit, *Illusory Consensus: Bolingbroke and the Polemical Response to Walpole, 1730–1737* (London, 1997).
[20] Bolingbroke, *Political Writings*, p. 5.
[21] Ibid., p. 37.
[22] Ibid., pp. 6–7.
[23] Ibid.
[24] John Brewer, *The Sinews of Power: War, Money, and the English State, 1688–1783* (Cambridge, MA, 1990).

and control of the House of Commons by place and patronage.²⁵ Bolingbroke accused Walpole of overturning the Revolution settlement and 'the civil faith of the old Whigs'.²⁶

Occasionally, Bolingbroke could unite dissident Whigs and old Tories by attacking those Whig bishops who, Bolingbroke claimed, kept Walpole in place. On several occasions, Walpole relied on the support of 'church Whigs' to shore up his parliamentary majorities.²⁷ Bolingbroke hoped not to 'suffer the arch slyness of G— ... the dogmatical dryness of H— ... or the sousing superstition of S—' as they attempted 'to slip new shackles on us, which are inconsistent with the constituent principles of our establishment'.²⁸ The trio of Whig bishops to whom Bolingbroke referred were Gibson, now known as 'Walpole's pope', Hare, Walpole's tutor at Cambridge and author of *Church Authority Vindicated* (1713) and *Scripture Vindicated from the Misrepresentation of the Bishop of Bangor* (1721), and Thomas Sherlock, school-friend to Walpole, successor to Gibson as bishop of London, and another antagonist of Hoadly.

Bolingbroke launched *The Craftsman* with the dissident Whig, William Pulteney, in December 1726. Appearing on Mondays and Wednesdays, it soon underwent major change and became the *Country Journal: Or, the Craftsman* in May 1727.²⁹ Bolingbroke acknowledged his authorship of forty-four contributions, although Simon Varey has suggested that he authored many more.³⁰ The journal carried some of those works for which Bolingbroke has become most renowned, including *Remarks on the History of England* (running from 13 June 1730 to 22 May 1731) and the *Dissertation* (running from 27 October 1733 to 26 January 1734). Following the defeat of the opposition in the general election of 1734, Bolingbroke abandoned *The Craftsman* and again retired to France where he seems to have composed the essay *On the Spirit of Patriotism* in 1736 before it was published in 1749. Perhaps Bolingbroke's most famous work, *The Idea of a Patriot King*, was composed in 1738 after his return to England. The former work was addressed to Henry Hyde, Viscount Cornbury, one of the aristocratic 'boy patriots' elected in 1734. The latter work seems to have been connected with the circle around Prince Frederick at Leicester House.

---

25 Quentin Skinner, 'The Principles and Practice of Opposition: The Case of Bolingbroke versus Walpole', in Neil McKendrick (ed.), *Historical Perspectives: Studies in English Thought and Society in Honour of J. H. Plumb* (London, 1974), pp. 93–128, at pp. 99–100. For Bolingbroke's attitude towards party, see Max Skjönsberg, 'Lord Bolingbroke's Theory of Party and Opposition', *HJ*, 59:4 (2016), pp. 947–73.
26 Bolingbroke, *Political Writings*, p. 8.
27 Cobbett (ed.), *Parliamentary History*, vol. 8, pp. 789, 841, 882, 992, 1177–9; vol. 9, p. 336.
28 Bolingbroke, *Political Writings*, p. 10.
29 Simon Varey, 'Introduction', in Henry St John, Viscount Bolingbroke, *Contributions to the Craftsman*, ed. Simon Varey (Oxford, 1982), pp. xiii–xv; M. R. A. Harris, 'Figures Relating to the Printing and Distribution of the *Craftsman* 1726 to 1730', *Bulletin of the Institute of Historical Research*, 43:108 (1970), pp. 233–42.
30 *The Last Will and Testament of the Late Rt. Hon. Henry St. John, Lord Viscount Bolingbroke* (London, 1752), pp. 8–9.

Over the course of his life, following exile to France and his investigations into religion during the 1720s and 1730s, Bolingbroke composed extensive philosophical works which he never published. He revised most of these philosophical writings during the years following the death of Wyndham in 1740 and the fall of Walpole in 1742. They were published in 1754, three years after Bolingbroke's death, upon Bolingbroke's instructions to his literary executor, David Mallet.[31] The longest of these works, *Letters or Essays addressed to Alexander Pope*, was composed in dialogue form with the Roman Catholic poet, and Bolingbroke chose to dedicate it to Pope after their extensive conversations between 1725 and 1735.[32] He gathered together remaining fragments and minutes of essays. Mallet published Bolingbroke's *Letters on the Study and Use of History*, written in Chanteloup between 1735 and 1738, *Reflections upon Exile*, and *Of the Use of Retirement and Study* in March 1752. In 1753, Mallet followed up with a volume containing such works as *A Letter to Sir William Wyndham* and *Reflections on the Present State of the Nation*. In 1754, Mallet produced the collected works.

Natural religion and priestcraft

Having dispensed with the complexities of Bolingbroke's career, it is now possible to pursue his civil religion. Bolingbroke's conception of civil religion rested on the claim that natural religion was morally equivalent to primitive Christianity. He argued that there were sufficient proofs in nature for the existence of one infinitely wise and powerful supreme being, the first intelligent cause of all things, to be uncovered purely by the exercise of reason, observation, and experiment. In *The Substance of Some Letters Written Originally in French, about the Year 1720, to M. de Pouilly*, Bolingbroke argued that natural phenomena provided sufficient evidence for the 'existence of an all-perfect, self-existent being, the source of all existence, invisible and incomprehensible'.[33] These proofs were revealed not only by divine intervention but also by nature and reason. Bolingbroke crisply summarised his position in one of his essays to Pope in *Concerning Authority in Matters of Religion*. Natural theology 'rests on better foundation than authority of any kind, and the duties of natural religion, and the sins against it, are held out to us by the constitution of our nature, and by daily experience, in characters so visible, that he who runs may read them'. The religion of nature, 'and therefore the God of nature, is simple and plain', since it 'tells us nothing which our reason is unable to comprehend'. Natural religion and reason always agreed because 'they are always the same, and the whole economy of God's dispensations to man is of a piece'.[34]

---

[31] Ibid., especially pp. 8–10.
[32] Bolingbroke, *Works*, vol. 4, p. 111.
[33] Ibid., vol. 2, p. 464.
[34] Ibid., vol. 3, pp. 380–1.

Such a deistical conception of natural religion might render implausible the suggestion that Bolingbroke was a principled supporter of Christianity. But Bolingbroke insisted that gospel Christianity represented the apex of natural religion. In *Concerning Authority in Matters of Religion*, he defended 'the articles of belief, which Christ himself exacted by what he said, and by what he did'. The 'system of religion, which Christ published, and his evangelists recorded is a complete system to all the purposes of true religion, natural and revealed'.[35] Even the deistical aristocrat might rationally endorse the primitive gospel and make it a basis from which to lead a moral and religious life.

Because it was plain and simple, natural religion was available to all by exercise of reason. In *Concerning Authority in Matters of Religion*, Bolingbroke stated: 'I am a rational creature, and am therefore obliged to judge for myself in all those cases where reason alone is the judge; the judge of the thing itself; for even in the others, reason is the judge of the authority.' The idea of a sacerdotal priestly hierarchy distinct from the laity carried no rational or scriptural justification. The 'divine, or the philosopher, may intend to deceive us'. Clergymen had no sacerdotal power by some privilege to witness the 'sublime objects of divine philosophy' because 'God has dealt more equally with his human creatures'. The 'all-wise God' rendered the universe so that 'every man is, by his nature, capable of acquiring certain and sufficient knowledge of those things which are the most important to him'.[36]

However, natural religion had been corrupted over many centuries. Bolingbroke accused Saint Paul of being the first to destroy Christian purity by grafting pagan doctrines onto scripture. The doctrines of the immortality of the soul, the Trinity, and future rewards and punishments were all corruptly sourced from the ancient Egyptians and Greeks. Paul added his own inventions including predestination and passive obedience. As Bolingbroke wrote to Swift, priestly Christianity became 'a lofty & pompous structure erected close to the humble & plain building of Natural Religion'.[37] Christ's articles of belief 'have been lengthened immeasurably, and we may add both unnecessarily and presumptuously by others since his time'.[38] Another key source of spiritual corruption was Platonism. It had become the basis for the artificial theology of orthodox Christianity by replacing rational proofs with metaphysics. Bolingbroke complained how natural philosophy 'made little progress among the Greeks and the Romans'.[39] He singled out Aristotle, partly because of his influence over scholasticism, as 'that usurper & Tyrant'. In a letter to Wyndham dated 16 June 1740, Bolingbroke recommended Locke's *An Essay concerning*

---

[35] Ibid., p. 418.
[36] Ibid., p. 376.
[37] Bolingbroke to Swift, 12 Sept. 1724, in *Correspondence of Swift*, vol. 3, p. 27.
[38] Bolingbroke, *Works*, vol. 3, p. 418.
[39] Ibid., vol. 2, p. 495.

Human Understanding (1689) and Francis Bacon's *Novum Organum* (1620) to Wyndham's son to counteract 'Greek Dialectics'.[40]

Bolingbroke's attack on orthodox Christianity was fully deist. He rejected the doctrine of particular providence and replaced it with general providence. Revelation was simply another superstition fabricated by priests to suppress the exercise of individual rationality. Clerics sought 'to maintain the insufficiency of human reason, though God thought it so sufficient', and they boasted 'the necessity of a revelation that might supply the defects of reason'. By rendering natural moral law mysterious and decipherable only with 'a profound knowledge of theology', the priestly order could advance its own power.[41] Religion founded on revelation was mere priestcraft. Such religions 'grow voluminous and mysterious, oppose belief to knowledge, and when they cannot stand a reasonable examination, escape from reason by assuming that they are above it'.[42]

This deistical onslaught involved deep suspicion of the provenance of scripture. Bolingbroke applied sceptical principles of historical study to scripture, treating the accepted holy texts as temporal products of human acts. Responding to Barbeyrac's translation of sermons by Tillotson, Bolingbroke condemned the 'gross defects, and palpable falsehoods, in almost every page of the Scriptures, and the whole tenor of them is such as no man, who acknowledges a Supreme, All-perfect Being, can believe it to be his word'. He could not believe the claim that 'the Pentateuch, and the other books of the Old Testament, were written under a divine influence, and have any right to be called the word of God'.[43] He observed that 'history has been purposely and systematically falsified in all ages, and that partiality and prejudice have occasioned both voluntary and involuntary errors even in the best'. The greatest culprit was 'ecclesiastical authority [which] had led the way to this corruption in all ages, and all religions'. Even though Christianity was founded in truth, 'yet what numberless fables have been invented to raise, to embellish, and to support these structures according to the interest and taste of the several architects?'[44]

Like Shaftesbury, Bolingbroke's condemnation of the origins of Christian superstition had anti-Hebraic shades. The laws of Moses should not be considered as 'means of preserving monotheism, and the purity of worship, in opposition to polytheism and superstition', since they were derived from 'a multitude and ceremonies, founded in the superstitions of Egypt'.[45] Bolingbroke claimed that there was no evidence for Moses' authorship of the Pentateuch.[46]

---

[40] Bolingbroke to Sir William Wyndham, 16 June 1740, in Adrian Lashmore-Davies (ed.), *The Unpublished Letters of Henry St John, First Viscount Bolingbroke* (5 vols, London, 2013), vol. 5, p. 255.
[41] Bolingbroke, *Works*, vol. 3, p. 402.
[42] Ibid., p. 381.
[43] Ibid., p. 32.
[44] Ibid., vol. 2, p. 213.
[45] Ibid., vol. 3, p. 37.
[46] Ibid., vol. 2, p. 495.

Following Hobbes and Spinoza, Bolingbroke also argued that there was no evidence that the Old Testament Jews merited special divine anointment.[47] The 'law of the Jews' might have 'exacted from the all the duties necessary to maintain peace and good order among themselves', he commented. But, 'if this be a mark of divinity, the laws, which rapparees and banditti establish in their societies have the same'. The 'whole tenor of the Jewish laws, took them out of all moral obligations to the rest of mankind'. The claim that God had chosen them generated 'a legal injustice and cruelty in their whole conduct' that was 'pressed upon them by their priests and their prophets'.[48]

Priestcraft was, therefore, a phenomenon that drew inspiration from 'the propagation of error in natural theology, as it descended from the Egyptians and other nations to the Greeks' and was institutionalised by Paul. It followed that priestcraft was not a purely Christian phenomenon, for 'the great principle that maintained all the corruptions of natural religion, was that of priestcraft'. It was a product of the union between philosophy and theology. In priest-ridden religions, philosophers and priests 'were the same persons'. Even when 'they assumed their distinct characters, the priests were too powerful, and the people too bigotted, to hope for any reformation'. Any rational opposition to superstition was simply and successfully condemned as atheism. The consequence was that 'the whole scheme of religion was applied then, as it is in many countries, Christian and others, still, to the advantage of those who has the conduct of it'.[49]

The imbalance between the civil and ecclesiastical power was a consequence of superstitious priestcraft. In Christian societies, 'the constitution of the Christian church, by which the peace of the world was laid, in the first ages of Christianity', was now 'at the mercy of an order of men, who indulge their passions, and find their account several ways in disturbing it'. Since its establishment by Constantine, true Christianity had fallen victim to episcopal treachery. Even though there were 'some few good and learned but not infallible men' within the body of the fourth-century clergy, they were for the most part 'ignorant, contentious, and profligate'. Church councils were 'riotous assemblies, governed by intrigue, and celebrated with noise, confusion, and the greatest indecency'.[50] The council of Nicaea was a site of 'several superstitious sports'.[51] The state of the church did not improve in later ages of the Roman Empire, for, 'as learning and knowledge decreased in the latter empire, the imposition of ecclesiastical authority grew up'. Both 'the power and discipline' of the church became 'as independent of the civil authority' as its 'doctrines'.[52]

The power of the church proved so great that it survived the fall of the Roman Empire. It bequeathed the corrupt church-state relationship to medieval popery.

---

[47] Ibid., p. 508.
[48] Ibid., vol. 3, p. 27.
[49] Ibid., pp. 237–9.
[50] Ibid., vol. 4, p. 25.
[51] Ibid., vol. 3, p. 505.
[52] Ibid., vol. 4, p. 25.

'Christianity had not been established many centuries in the West, before a claim to universal property was set foot in favor of the faithful, that is of Christians', and the bishop of Rome claimed 'universal empire, not only over the religious, but over all civil societies'.[53] Roman Catholic priests developed 'what has been seen very often since among the clergy, a sort of holy ambition' which 'proved as strong a motive in the hearts of good men transported by a mistaken zeal for the church, whose cause they confounded with the cause of religion'.[54] Lay believers were duped by false superstitions and mysteries which shrouded natural religion 'to advance, under pious pretences, the grandeur, wealth, and dominion of the religions over the civil society'. Priests 'established a church as independent on the state'. But such popery remained a danger in reformed societies. Bemoaning how the doctrine of the Trinity was enshrined in the Thirty-Nine Articles of the Church of England, Bolingbroke commented in *Concerning Matters of Authority in Religion* that 'the church has been in every age an hydra, such a monster as the poets feign with many heads', and that the 'scene of Christianity has been always a scene of dissension, of hatred, of persecution, and of blood'.[55]

The alliance between church and state

It was at this juncture that Bolingbroke took aim at Warburton and his *Alliance between Church and State*. Warburton had begun life as a scholarly parochial clergyman whose literary fame and theological prowess led to his appointment, in 1740, as chaplain to Prince Frederick and, later, to George II as well as to a presence in the European republic of letters.[56] Warburton first courted notoriety when he defended the disputed Christian orthodoxy of Pope, a mutual friend of Warburton and Bolingbroke, in Pope's *Essay on Man* (1734).[57] Warburton secured his reputation as a defender of orthodox Christianity by critical works against Hume and Bolingbroke.[58] Warburton wrote the *Alliance* in an attempt to reconcile theories of civil religion with sacerdotal priesthoods, producing further amended editions in 1741, 1748, and 1766. He believed his conception of the church-state relationship was a deliberate compromise between popish

---

[53] Ibid., vol. 3, p. 492.
[54] Ibid., vol. 4, p. 27.
[55] Ibid., pp. 24–5.
[56] For earlier scholarship, see A. W. Evans, *Warburton and the Warburtonians: A Study in Some Eighteenth-Century Controversies* (London, 1932); Robert M. Ryley, *William Warburton* (Boston, MA, 1984). See also Frank Manuel, *The Eighteenth Century Confronts the Gods* (Cambridge, MA, 1959), p. 122; Clifton Cherpeck, 'Warburton and the *Encyclopédie*', *Comparative Literature*, 7 (1955), pp. 226–39; J. H. Brumfitt, *Voltaire and Warburton* (Geneva, 1961), pp. 43–4.
[57] William Warburton, *A Vindication of Mr. Pope's* Essay on Man (London, 1739); *A Critical and Philosophical Commentary on Mr. Pope's* Essay on Man (London, 1742). See also George Sherburn (ed.), *The Correspondence of Alexander Pope* (5 vols, Oxford, 1956), vol. 4, pp. 402, 488–520.
[58] William Warburton, *A View of Lord Bolingbroke's Philosophy* (3 vols, London, 1754–6); *Remarks on Mr. David Hume's* Essay on the Natural History of Religion (London, 1757).

principles that rendered 'the State a creature of the Church' and Erastian ones that left 'the Church a Creature of the State'. His argument was also with 'the PRESBYTERIAN [who] would regulate the State on Church Ideas; the HOBBEIST, the Church, on Reasons of State: And, to compleat the Farce, the QUAKER [who] abolishes the very Being of a Church; and the MENNONITE [Anabaptist] [who] suppresses the Office of the Civil Magistrate'.[59]

As Stephen Taylor has shown, the *Alliance* was idiosyncratic and unrepresentative of contemporary defences of a church establishment.[60] By his attempt to reconcile a Lockean interpretation of the origins of secular government with a sacerdotal defence of the established church, Warburton struck at the heart of eighteenth-century party politics. He believed that church and state had originally been two separate societies but were compacted together in a grand contract for the Christian well-being of the laity and security of the state. Both church and state were originally '*Sovereign, and independent on the other*', but the governors of the church later ceded this independence in a '*free Convention*' with the state.[61] The contract was to be found 'in the same *Archive* with the famous ORIGINAL COMPACT between Magistrate and People'.[62] It formed '*a politic League and Alliance for mutual Support and Defence*'. The church establishment would 'APPLY ITS UTMOST INFLUENCE IN THE SERVICE OF THE STATE'. The state would 'SUPPORT AND PROTECT THE CHURCH'.[63] The terms of the contract between church and state stipulated that the function of the civil magistrate was the protection of the 'TEMPORAL LIBERTY AND PROPERTY OF MAN'.[64] It was also the inculcation of morality insofar as it affected civil tranquillity. This morality involved 'three fundamental Principles of Natural Religion', including the existence, being, and providence of God and the natural difference between good and evil. Such precepts, expressed in primitive Christianity, formed 'the very Foundation and Bond of Civil Policy'.[65]

Accepting, therefore, standard defences among civil religionists for the political and social utility of the church, Warburton then attempted to secure ecclesiological compromise by reconciling sacerdotal Anglican priests with the superiority of the civil magistrate. The church establishment retained its

---

[59] William Warburton, *The Alliance between Church and State* (4th edn, London, 1766), p. 28. For interpretations of Warburton within Enlightened divinity, see Young, *Religion and Enlightenment*, pp. 171–212; Robert G. Ingram, 'William Warburton, Divine Action, and Enlightened Christianity', in William Gibson and Robert G. Ingram (eds), *Religious Identities in Britain, 1660–1832* (Burlington, VT, 2005), pp. 97–117; *Reformation without End*, chs 14–17.

[60] Stephen Taylor, 'William Warburton and the Alliance of Church and State', *JEH*, 43:2 (1992), pp. 271–86. See also R. W. Greaves, 'The Working of an Alliance: A Comment on Warburton', in G. V. Bennett and J. D. Walsh (eds), *Essays in Modern English Church History: In Memory of Norman Sykes* (Oxford, 1966), pp. 163–80.

[61] Warburton, *Alliance*, p. 85.

[62] Ibid., p. 203.

[63] Ibid., pp. 85, 112.

[64] Ibid., p. 30.

[65] Ibid., p. 36.

divine right over doctrine and discipline. Questions of faith stood beyond the remit of the secular powers. Instead, they belonged to the church as 'CHRIST'S KINGDOM' on earth. It was a society of 'divine appointment', at first 'declared Sovereign'. The free convention between church and state stipulated that the church establishment would receive maintenance for its ministers through tithing, ecclesiastical jurisdiction over doctrinal discipline including the reformation of manners, and the right to sit in the legislature. The church would receive protection from external violence including a test act. In return, the state secured recognition of its sovereignty.[66] Thus, Warburton gave a tacit nod to anti-sacerdotal arguments. He claimed that his vision of the church-state relationship would prevent the 'Evil' that the church as an independent society might wreak over the state. He averred how 'coercive Power introduces an *Imperium in Imperio*'.[67]

Warburton was defending the novel Revolution settlement by which the Test Act secured the superiority of the Church of England while its ministers acquiesced to the Toleration Act. It was the duty of the magistrate to provide succour and support for true religion consistent with the Protestant principle of liberty of conscience. An 'ESTABLISHED RELIGION AND A TEST-LAW' were built upon 'THE FUNDAMENTAL PRINCIPLES OF THE LAW OF NATURE AND NATIONS'.[68] Equally, in 1763, Warburton argued that the 'most just of all Public Laws, the Law of TOLERATION ... is certainly of DIVINE ORIGINAL'.[69] In religiously plural society, a test act was necessary to secure the commitment made by the state to defend the church establishment. By protecting the establishment, the civil magistrate allowed the public faith to act as a moral sanctifier of the social and political order. Established religions taught the moral and social virtues but Christianity, by its primitive precepts, was the most useful to the state. Within Christianity, Warburton argued, 'public Utility and Truth do coincide'.[70]

In language remarkably close to lay theorists of civil religion, Warburton wrote of the importance of shared rituals of external worship in the Christian commonwealth. We 'must have *our Meditations on the Divine Nature* drawn out into ARTICLES OF FAITH; and *our Meditations on the several Relations in which we stand towards Him* digested into suitable and correspondent ACTS OF RELIGIOUS WORSHIP'. Both must be 'professed and performed in COMMON'.[71] A public ministry, learned and pastoral, served public utility by searching for truth to procure '*the Favour of God*' and to '*advance and improve our own intellectual Nature*'.[72] To defend the role of the Church of England in intellectual and social life, Warburton drew on classic authorities of eighteenth-century

---

[66] Ibid., p. 216.
[67] Ibid., p. 74.
[68] Ibid., p. 3.
[69] William Warburton, *The Doctrine of Grace* (London, 1763), pp. 189–90.
[70] Warburton, *Alliance*, p. 347.
[71] Ibid., p. 57.
[72] Ibid., p. 52.

latitudinarianism. In his posthumous pamphlet, *Directions for the Study of Philosophy*, written around 1769, Warburton especially recommended for clergymen 'the daily and long continued use' of Locke's *Essay concerning Human Understanding* in order 'to think justly'. Also important were Cudworth, Stillingfleet, Chillingworth, Hooker, Taylor, Burnet, and Samuel Clarke.[73]

Similarly, the object of public ministry was to combat the two evils of superstition and enthusiasm. The civil magistrate must support 'public Officers and Ministers' who needed, in turn, to 'act by some *common Policy*'. Those men 'set aside for this Office' should 'preside in, direct, and superintend the *Ritual of Worship*, lest any thing childish, profane, or superstitious should (as it certainly would, if left to every one's Fancy) obtrude itself into *religious Service*'. Likewise, 'Meditations, not tempered with these outward Acts, are apt … to fly out into *Enthusiasm*'. In tones recalling the plain style of Restoration and early eighteenth-century preaching favoured by the likes of Burnet, Warburton insisted that the public rituals of worship must be readily comprehensible for the poor. The 'greatest Care therefore is to be taken, that the *solemn Acts of Religion* be preserved *simple*, *decent*, and *significative*'.[74] By unexpected means, Warburton produced a vision of the public role of the Church of England that appeared remarkably similar to those of theorists of civil religion who refused to lend credence to the idea of sacerdotal priestly authority.

Although idiosyncratic, Warburton's ecclesiology shared with that of Gibson the goal of reconciling sacerdotal Anglicanism with the jurisdictional superiority of the secular state. Gibson's approach relied instead on more conventional scholarship on canon law. In his *Codex*, Gibson studied the legal, juridical, and ecclesiastical documents of the Reformation. He argued that the royal supremacy did not automatically involve jurisdiction over questions of doctrine and faith. The terms of the royal supremacy banished popish usurpation of temporal power, but they still respected the '*Divine Right*' of the Church of England 'to the Exercise of Spiritual Disciplin'. The bishops held 'a general Authority from the *Word of God*, to exercise Disciplin in the Church'. Meanwhile the godly prince was the ultimate source of all temporal power, acting 'as Supreme and Sovereign in the State' and 'as Supreme Head of the Church'.[75] The '*External Administration*' of the Church came 'from the *Crown* and in Subordination to the *Royal Supremacy*'. Much like Warburton, Gibson calibrated his argument against Tory high churchmen who would render the church a complete '*Creature of the State*'.[76]

Despite maintaining a conception of sacerdotal priestliness, Gibson also believed in learned and pastoral ministry to fight superstition and enthusiasm. In

---

[73] William Warburton, *The Works of the Right Reverend William Warburton* (12 vols, London, 1811), vol. 10, pp. 357, 358–60, 363, 365, 366, 368, 371, 373.
[74] Warburton, *Alliance*, p. 59.
[75] Edmund Gibson, *Codex Juris Ecclesiastici Anglicani* (2 vols, London, 1713), vol. 1, pp. xvii–xviii.
[76] Ibid., pp. 18–19.

1737, Gibson published *Some Considerations upon Pluralities, Non-Residence and Salaries of Curates* in which he justified pluralities for those who were 'very well worthy for their learning' and held at least a Master of the Arts. He reminded his audience that 'a well-meaning zeal might not always be attended with cool and sedate thinking'.[77] As bishop of London, Gibson composed a series of 'pastoral letters' beginning in 1728. The letters stood in the tradition of Tillotson's circular letter of 1692 to the bishops and Burnet's *Discourse of the Pastoral Care*. Gibson hoped to compose 'some few rules, which were very short and easy and which, being frequently perused and duly attended to, might be a means … to preserve sincere and unprejudiced Christians from those dangerous infections'.[78]

During the Dissenting campaign to repeal the Test Act during the 1730s, Gibson reminded the public that 'the mistaken or affected Zeal of Obstinacy, and Enthusiasm' had 'produced such a Number of horrible, destructive Events, throughout all Christendom'. This had been 'the very Case of England, during the Fanatic Times'. Against enthusiasm 'there seems to be no Defence, but that of supporting one established Form of Doctrine and Discipline, leaving the rest to a bare Liberty of Conscience'.[79] He insisted that 'the strength and clearness of the evidences of Christianity with the advantages and excellencies of the Gospel institution' were sufficient props to civil order.[80] A public ministry was necessary to prevent backsliding into the puritan frenzies of the seventeenth century.

Warburton and Gibson engaged with lay concepts of civil religion by attempting to strike a middle course between Tory high churchmen and Erastians who denied priests a mediating power. But Bolingbroke, who believed the earthly church was entirely a creation of the state, believed Warburton's clericalism had gone too far. The idea of 'a formal alliance between the church and the state, as between two independent distinct powers, is a very groundless and whimsical notion'. If there had been any alliances, Bolingbroke rehearsed the standard Protestant line that princes throughout history had continually struck tyrannous agreements with ecclesiastics. A 'fraudulent or silent compact between princes and priests became very real, as soon as an ecclesiastical order was established'. Absolutist princes agreed 'to reverence the divine right of the clergy', provided the priests, 'in return, made use of their influence over consciences to establish an opinion of a divine right in them'.[81] In his essays to Pope, Bolingbroke noted that that 'paradoxical acquaintance of yours', Warburton, had assumed the original independence of the two institutions. Warburton neglected that the state must concede greater legitimacy to the ecclesiastical body, since the church's legitimacy was 'derived from a greater authority than her own'. The 'supposed

---

[77] Edmund Gibson, *Some Considerations upon Pluralities, Non-Residence and Salaries of Curates* (London, 1737), p. 10.
[78] Edmund Gibson, *The Bishop of London's Pastoral Letter* (London, 1728), p. 4.
[79] Edmund Gibson, *The Dispute Adjusted* (Dublin, 1733), pp. 15–16.
[80] Edmund Gibson, *The Bishop of London's Second Pastoral Letter* (London, 1730), p. 75.
[81] Bolingbroke, *Works*, vol. 4, p. 28.

terms of union' would be construed as 'concessions of the religious society to the civil, for the sake of order and peace', rather than 'grants of the civil to the religious society'.[82]

By attacking the compact between arbitrary princes and tyrannical ecclesiastics, Bolingbroke was safely on Whig territory. In a contribution to *The Craftsman* in September 1734, he described how arbitrary princes, 'are reduced to maintain an Opinion, which draws after it great Danger, and is the strongest Invitation to the Attempts of their ambitious Subjects'. The supposition 'that Princes are in Themselves SACRED, when once They mount the Throne, though the Means, by which They rose to it, were ever so flagitious'. Bolingbroke noted how ancient princes had claimed sacerdotal authority in order to legitimise their rulership. Those princes, 'particularly the heathen Emperors, used to *deify* Themselves, with a View of obliging the People, from a religious Reverence, to submit patiently to their Extravagances'. Modern *jure divino* monarchies were 'but Copies of this Original, and calculated to the same Views'. Fortunately, 'the People have been wise enough, in these Kingdoms, to explode such dangerous and iniquitous Superstitions'.[83]

But the relationship between superstition and tyranny extended further than modern princes. In the opening edition of *The Craftsman* in December 1726, the author likened the techniques used by priests to develop their ecclesiastical tyranny to the craft used by Walpole and the ministerialists to support their civil tyranny. The author aimed 'to lay open the frauds, abuses and secret iniquities of all professions' and their 'pernicious mixtures of craft, and several scandalous prostitutions'. He noted how the 'same malignant contagion has infected the other learned faculties and polite professions'. It 'crept into the camp as well as the court' and 'prevailed in the church as well as in the state'.[84] In January 1736, Bolingbroke wrote a letter to his brother-in-law in anticipation of the *Idea of a Patriot King* in which he likened ministerialist practitioners of craft to the priests of Baal:

> Whatever happens, it will be a comfort to me that I have had the opportunity before my death of contributing to revive the true spirit of Constitution in Great Britain ... The victim may be saved even though the same butcherly priests should continue to administer our political Rites. Or, who knows? a zealous high priest may arise, and these priests of Baal may be hewed in pieces.[85]

It is sometimes supposed that Bolingbroke's attack on 'craft' was primarily secular and anti-ministerialist in character.[86] But such a reading risks separating

---

[82] Ibid., vol. 3, pp. 489–90.
[83] Bolingbroke, *Contributions to the* Craftsman, pp. 172–3.
[84] Caleb d'Anvers, *The Craftsman*, 1 (5 Dec. 1726).
[85] Bolingbroke to his brother-in-law, 25 Jan. 1736, reprinted in Walter Sichel, *Bolingbroke and His Times: The Sequel* (New York, 1968), pp. 545–6.
[86] Isaac Kramnick, *Bolingbroke and His Circle: The Politics of Nostalgia in the Age of*

'craft' from 'priestcraft'. There was a strong reformed ecclesiological current within Bolingbroke's definition of the crafts by which tyranny was imposed. *The Craftsman* was written and signed by the pseudonymous Caleb D'Anvers, a choice of name that indicated more than just loyalty to Revolution principles and the Hanoverian succession. The name Anvers, French for Antwerp, indicated loyalty to the cause of the Holy Roman Empire, under which Antwerp was then ruled, and opposition to the Jacobites. The name Caleb was taken from the Old Testament son of Jephynneh, one of the leaders of the Israelites sent into the promised land as a scout. The biblical choice of name is instructive: having slain the priests of Baal, Hanoverian England was to be a new Israel governed by true religion.

Civil and ecclesiastical polity

Given the strong deistical tendency of Bolingbroke's religious writings, he might appear an unlikely candidate for a Christian civil religion rooted in reverence for the Church of England and its unreformed articles of faith. However, Bolingbroke's defence of an established church was based on standard propositions in the traditions of Erastianism and Christian reform. His suspicions about the doctrine of the Trinity and the authorship of scripture implied reform to the Church of England. But, until the state of Christian theological opinion had progressed, Bolingbroke still believed in respecting the church establishment. His was a Ciceronian *religio* without *superstitio* and he relied upon the distinction between esoteric and exoteric philosophy to conceive of aristocratic rulership involving prudent respect for popular belief. Nevertheless, he believed even an impure Church of England replete with superstitious doctrines like the Trinity could form the basis for Christian civil religion.

In defending his vision of the church-state relationship, Bolingbroke drew from standard episodes in the history of Christian reform. The establishment of the Christian church under Constantine created the occasion for a godly Christian *imperator*, which was missed due to episcopal power. After Constantine, princes 'might have made themselves heads of the church, defenders of the faith, and, next under God and his Son Christ Jesus, supreme moderators and governors in all matters, ecclesiastical and civil, without being priests'. On some occasions, Constantine and his successors had taken 'airs of supremacy'. But because they had failed to preserve 'a steady exercise of the pontifical power over ecclesiastical affairs and ecclesiastical persons in the Christian church, the exercise of it devolved of course on the bishops'.[87] Roman emperors should have been able to keep 'the whole power over ecclesiastical as well as civil affairs in their own hands, and have applied the former to preserve order and discipline, to prevent

---

Walpole (London, 1968), pp. 19–20; Skinner, 'Principles and Practice of Opposition', pp. 95, 113–21.
[87] Bolingbroke, *Works*, vol. 3, pp. 503–4.

abuse and corruption in the Christian, as it had been their prerogative and their duty to apply it in the heathen church'. Such a supremacy of the civil state was 'natural' and 'reasonable'.[88]

The battle to secure the right relationship between church and state as well as true religion had recurred since the Constantinean establishment. In *Concerning Authority in Matters of Religion*, Bolingbroke condemned 'Constantine's grant to Sylvester' as a forgery 'preserved in that grand repertoire of forgeries, the records of the Roman church'.[89] The battle between *imperium* and *sacerdos* recurred anew as 'the Guelphs and Ghibellines were not more animated against each other at any time, than the Tories and Whigs at this'. Even the French, 'good papists as they are', remained unconvinced by the supposed grant to Sylvester 'and the quarrel between Philip le Bel and Boniface the Eighth may be said to subsist even now'. Bolingbroke was citing the fourteenth-century clash between the French monarchy and the papacy that had occasioned the *Defensor Pacis* (1324) and *Defensor Minor* (*c*. 1342) of Marsilius. Bolingbroke observed that those 'who have shook off the Roman yoke entirely, admit still less of this ecclesiastical code' because Protestants 'reject every thing in it that is not conformable to the law of the state, and to the doctrines of the church, which this law has established'. In Hoadlyite tones, he concluded this passage by observing that 'Christ's kingdom is not of this world'.[90]

By taking control of the ecclesiastical power for the first time, those godly Protestant princes who led the Reformation had defeated the popish concept of *imperium in imperio* and begun to create the institutional conditions for the flourishing of true religion. It is common to conceptualise Bolingbroke's idea of a patriot king as a product of his deism.[91] This approach casts the patriot king as a prince of superlative virtue who bestrode the natural order according to the general providence of the supreme being. The patriot king stood atop the balanced and mixed constitution and exercised the highest duties in the natural moral order. Those were 'the duties of a king to his country'.[92]

However, the idea of patriot kingship owed as much to the tradition of Christian reform as deism. In *Concerning Authority in Matters of Religion*, Bolingbroke denied the Roman Catholic doctrine that 'the avowed ends of religious, and the real ends of civil societies, are so distinct as to require distinct powers, and a mutual independence'. According to the basic moral dictates of natural religion and primitive Christianity, the salvation of souls was an end of civil government. If 'to abstain from evil, and to do good works, be means of salvation', it followed that 'the means of salvation are objects of civil government'. It behove the godly prince to govern accordingly. 'It is the duty of

---

[88] Ibid., p. 502.
[89] Ibid., p. 491.
[90] Bolingbroke, *Political Writings*, p. 51.
[91] Mansfield, *Statesmanship and Party Government*, p. 42; Smith, *Georgian Monarchy*, p. 21.
[92] Bolingbroke, *Political Writings*, p. 217.

princes and magistrates', Bolingbroke argued, 'to promote a strict observation to the law of nature, of private and public morality, and to make those who live in subjection to them good men, in order to make them good citizens.'[93] Virtue and morality fell within the Christian duties of the godly prince. Princes and magistrates punished transgressions of positive law as the reproduction of the law of nature but also provided 'rewards and encouragement to virtue' as 'the surest way, not only to reform the outward behaviour, but to create a habitual disposition to the practice of religion'.[94] Such a position should also be read as a civic republican exhortation for the peace and public good of the commonwealth.[95]

Bolingbroke also measured the godliness of England's princes. He praised Henry VIII as a king who destroyed the pope's power 'in his dominions' and gave 'several incurable wounds' to the church's ownership of land that had provided the economic basis for its spiritual tyranny.[96] In 'this eager pursuit after ecclesiastical liberty', 'letters patent, under the great seal, were made necessary to determine the articles of faith, which men were to believe fully, and the doctrines, rites and ceremonies, which they were to observe and practice under several penalties'.[97] Elizabeth I represented the apotheosis of the godly monarch. She supported the 'oppressed people' of the Netherlands and favoured Henry III and IV of France against the house of Lorraine as well as the French Protestants against the Medici.[98] Although, Bolingbroke conceded, the court of high commission might have had extraordinary power, 'the steadiness of the queen, in maintaining this part of the prerogative' and 'the great moderation of the bishops in these early days of the reformation' meant that its jurisdiction was exercised prudently.[99] Elizabeth produced a moderate ecclesiastical settlement, midway between Rome and Geneva, which 'farther still from pushing any sort of men, puritans, and even papists, into despair', aimed at equipoise. She maintained the Protestant principle of freedom of conscience even when 'the bull of Pius Quintus, and the rebellion, and other attempts, consequent upon it, obliged her to procure new laws'. She wisely 'distinguished "papists in conscience from papists in faction"'.[100] Conversely, James I and Charles I were ungodly kings, having broken the compact between king and people by their absolutism.[101]

Accompanying Bolingbroke's account of the godly prince was a neo-Harringtonian conceptualisation of property and power. Bolingbroke believed secular reforms to noble land ownership under Henry VII and the sale of church lands under Henry VIII provided the basis for the political developments of the

---

[93] Bolingbroke, *Works*, vol. 3, p. 487.
[94] Ibid., pp. 487–8.
[95] See Kramnick, *Bolingbroke and His Circle*, pp. 104–5.
[96] Henry St John, Viscount Bolingbroke, *Historical Writings*, ed. Isaac Kramnick (Chicago and London, 1972), p. 221.
[97] Ibid., pp. 223–4.
[98] Ibid., p. 242.
[99] Ibid., p. 246.
[100] Ibid., p. 248.
[101] Ibid., pp. 291–6, 330–9.

seventeenth century. In the centuries between the decline of Saxon liberty during the Norman Conquest and the Henrician revolution in property, the commons 'had not property enough to have any share in this power' and 'the sole check which could be opposed to the encroachments of the crown was the power of the barons and of the clergy'. However, the church and the nobility often had opposing interests 'so that they were not only very incapable of forming a secure barrier to liberty, but their power became terrible and dangerous to the crown itself'. Nobility and church could both encroach 'on the prince's authority, whilst they resisted his encroachments, real or pretended, on their own privileges'. Under 'the plausible veil of law, or gospel', private ambition 'had a greater share than public liberty in their contests'.[102]

Erastian ecclesiology and neo-Harringtonianism coincided in the context of the legal and ecclesiastical framework of the long Reformation. When the church-state relationship had been subverted, Bolingbroke had shown that its agents – the priests – were superstitious, powerful, and destabilising. They peddled false religion and used otherworldly metaphysics for corrupt worldly ends. They wrongly took their legitimacy as divine. They falsely claimed a privileged mediating relationship with God. As Warburton noted, Bolingbroke joined up with Shaftesbury, Trenchard, and Gordon in seeking to remove any remnant of sacerdotal authority from priests.[103] The true legitimacy of clergymen lay elsewhere. Since Christ's kingdom was not of this world, ecclesiastical polity was merely a subset of temporal power. In England, it was the royal supremacy of the crown-in-parliament that set the clergy above the laity and their appointment was on the basis of Christian primitivism. The established church must teach 'genuine Christianity', which was 'contained in the gospels'. It was 'the word of God; it requires, therefore, our veneration, and a strict conformity to it'. The established church must not preach 'traditional Christianity ... which passes for the genuine, and which we all profess, is derived from the writings of fathers and doctors of the church, and from the decrees of councils'.[104]

Bolingbroke discussed the authority of the clergy in *Concerning Authority in Matters of Religion*. He explained to Pope that Christ appointed the apostles as great religious teachers and not as divinely-ordained messengers. The idea of apostolic succession was ridiculous. Christ 'sent out his apostles to teach and to baptise, and the utmost power he gave them, besides that of working miracles to convince and to convert, was to shake off the dust of their feet, and to protest against the infidelity of those, who refused to receive them and the gospel they published'. The apostles had a right of ordination over others 'to accompany and to succeed them in the same office, the office of teaching and baptising'. The apostles 'could give no more power than they received'.[105] Clergymen

---

[102] Ibid., p. 234.
[103] Warburton, *Works*, vol. 12, p. 115.
[104] Bolingbroke, *Works*, vol. 4, p. 109.
[105] Ibid., vol. 3, p. 491.

were appointed by human authority in order to minister the simple precepts of primitive Christianity. In all ages, clergymen must 'teach the duties of natural religion with evangelical simplicity as Christ himself did in his sermon on the mount and elsewhere'.[106]

In so doing, clergymen would defend the Protestant principle of the priesthood of all believers. By their ministry, 'they might have enabled every one to be his own casuist, and have made good men as well as Christians', enlarging 'the kingdom of God'.[107] The clergy must only act by example and the civil power might choose to co-opt them into the civil state. An established clergy 'might co-operate with the civil magistrate very usefully no doubt'. They would do so 'by exhortations and reproofs, whereof they are seldom sparing, and much more by example, which can alone give efficacy to the former, and which is not, however, very frequently employed'. Clergymen were 'assistants to the civil magistrate, in concert with him, and in subordination to him'.[108] It was the role of true Christianity to prepare believers for the next life by means of good conduct in this one. Clergymen created moral and virtuous men whose precepts accorded with the interest of the civil state.

Bolingbroke discussed the role of the clergy anecdotally in a contribution to *The Craftsman* in 1729. Referring to instances when 'venal Abuses were to grow in the *Senate* and the *Administration*', Bolingbroke wrote of a gentleman who, on his death-bed, wished to perform a generous act that might outlive him, perhaps giving to a charity or providing an allowance to a schoolmaster to instruct impoverished boys. The finances were left to a group of trustees including a country clergyman, 'a bold, troublesome, over-bearing Creature, always creating Animosities and Divisions; and a common *Barreter* [litigant] in his Country'. By threatening the other trustees, the clergyman 'got the whole to himself, and accordingly made a *Political Use* of it' by employing an ignorant woman to instruct the boys from whom he would then receive an allowance. To inflate his power, 'and because he would be more fashionable and get all he could, no Boy was permitted to receive the Benefit of his Charity, who did not first shake him handsomly by the Palm'.[109] The state endowed clergymen to be spiritual guides and preach the public faith. Clergymen were officeholders of the civil state and their corruption was equally as dangerous for the public good as the craft of the ministerialist.

In generating a vision of Christian civil religion, Bolingbroke hoped to generate good citizens. A true Christian believer was also a patriot as he placed the interests of this world as the end of his moral life. It has sometimes been supposed that Bolingbroke's deism was wholly anticlerical and that he believed religion, in a Machiavellian sense, was a social and political

---

[106] Ibid., p. 402.
[107] Ibid.
[108] Ibid., p. 488.
[109] Bolingbroke, *Contributions to the* Craftsman, pp. 97–8.

instrument.[110] Bolingbroke invoked Machiavelli's name when he discussed the success of the ancient civil religions in forming good citizens. In his *History of England*, Bolingbroke paraphrased Machiavelli's *Discourses* when he discussed how the 'grandeur and felicity' of the Roman republic owed a great deal to the religious settlement of Numa.[111] Bolingbroke also praised the ancient 'Egyptian wisdom' in their religious and civil institutions as well as the following 'philosophical legislators': Zoroaster and Zamolxis, Minos, Charondas, Numa, Pythagoras, and Moses. They each instituted the doctrines of revelation and future rewards and punishments over cloudy and credulous peoples. Such doctrines, however superstitious, were 'a proper expedient to enforce obedience to the political regimen'.[112]

But Bolingbroke's conception of civil religion was more specifically Christian. It rested on a principled commitment to the precepts of Christian reform on primitivist principles. This line of argument is so central in relating Bolingbroke's deism with his commitment to the reformed Christian commonwealth that it is worth dwelling upon it a little further. 'To make government effectual to all the good purposes of it', Bolingbroke wrote in *Concerning Authority in Matters of Religion*, 'there must be a religion'. It must be a national religion with established clergymen maintained 'in reputation and reverence' so that 'all other religions or sects must be kept too low to become the rivals of it'. A 'religious order subject to the civil magistrate, and subservient to the civil power', was one of the 'first principles of good policy'.[113] These were universal truths for all states. But it was 'eminently true of Christianity in particular'. There was 'no religion ever appeared in the world, whose natural tendency was so much directed to promote the peace and happiness of mankind'.[114]

Toleration, tests, and rulers

In Bolingbroke's vision, the civil religion of Hanoverian England was the modern Christian perfection of the success of the ancient pagan civil faiths. To be revered, the established faith required the acquiescence even of those who failed to concur with its articles of faith: Dissenters and freethinkers. They must support the national church by conceding the need for a test act in public office and for regulated public worship in the Christian commonwealth. By way of return, the agents of the Church of England would defend inward freedom of conscience by the Protestant commitment to the primitive gospel. Bolingbroke's civil religion was infused with Protestant spiritual individualism. He believed his policy could be pursued 'not only without persecution but without the

---

[110] Dickinson, *Bolingbroke*, pp. 164–5; Kramnick, *Bolingbroke and His Circle*, p. 104.
[111] Bolingbroke, *Works*, vol. 1, p. 292.
[112] Ibid., vol. 3, p. 223.
[113] Ibid., vol. 4, p. 108.
[114] Ibid., vol. 3, p. 396.

invasion of any one right which men can justly claim under the freest and most equitable government'.[115]

It was not simply prudent but also an expression of its Protestantism for the Church of England to tolerate Dissent. In the first letter of the *Dissertation*, Bolingbroke apologised for those, including himself, who had supported harsh treatment of Dissent. 'Experience hath removed prejudice' and 'indulgence hath done what severity never could'.[116] In *Concerning Matters of Authority in Religion*, Bolingbroke observed that the Reformation had unleashed disorder, war, and massacre by 'the several ridiculous and mad sects, to the rise of which this reformation gave occasion'.[117] It was neither politic nor legitimate to impose uniformity on sectarians even though they had betrayed natural religion and primitive Christianity by their frenzy. A benevolent, pastoral, and pedagogical established church might teach basic moral precepts in such a way as to prevent the rise of sects. An established church was needed because reason was not 'given to all alike, and being very imperfectly given to those who possess the greatest share, our wisdom and our happiness are very imperfect likewise'.[118]

There was a comprehensive impulse within Bolingbroke's line of argument. He believed Englishmen were 'now in the true and only road, which can possibly lead to a perfect reconciliation among Protestants'. This road would end in 'the abolition of all their differences; or to terms of difference so little essential, as to deserve none of distinction'. To achieve perfect reconciliation, the principles of the Christian gospel must be followed, above all, 'mutual good will', because these 'happy ends ... never can be obtained by force'. To attempt to enforce religious uniformity would prompt a return to the religious trauma of the seventeenth century. Force 'may support a rivalship and erect even counter-establishments' and 'by the same means, our ancient disputes will be revived'. Then, paraphrasing the high-church cries of the early eighteenth century, Bolingbroke claimed that 'the Church will be thought really in danger'.[119] Once all differences among Protestants had been resolved by improvements in Christian understanding, it would become possible for the church to reform and comprehend all sincere believers.

Until that stage, however, Bolingbroke supported the Test Act. Since the established church was a public institution of the civil state, its officeholders must profess the same religion as the state. Human law 'may and ought to exclude these men from power in the state, kings especially, who profess a private conscience repugnant to the public conscience of the state'. Such individuals could not be allowed to use their power 'the more to propagate their own schemes of religion, to strengthen their own party and to recommend their particular notions about ecclesiastical government, which cannot be done

---

[115] Ibid., vol. 4, pp. 108–9.
[116] Bolingbroke, *Political Writings*, p. 7.
[117] Bolingbroke, *Works*, vol. 1, p. 105.
[118] Ibid., p. 212.
[119] Bolingbroke, *Political Writings*, p. 7.

without manifest danger to the public peace'.[120] Such impositions had been the violent experience of the seventeenth century. The state was justified in maintaining toleration for inward consciences and a test act to preserve its peace and liberty.

A critical reader of Bolingbroke might have recalled his earlier support for the Occasional Conformity and Schism Bills. In *A Letter to Sir William Wyndham*, Bolingbroke argued that the bills were consistent with the principles of freedom of conscience and Erastian governance of the established church. 'I verily think that the persecution of dissenters entered into no man's head', Bolingbroke explained. Certainly, one motivation was party interest. The Tories hoped that the Whigs' 'sting would be taken away'. Although the bills had had partisan objectives, Bolingbroke believed them neither unreasonable nor unjust. The good of society required that 'no person should be deprived of the protection of the government on account of his opinions in religious matters', but 'it does not follow from hence that men ought to be trusted in any degree with the preservation of the establishment, who must, to be consistent with their principles, endeavor the subversion of what is established'. Dissenters still did not profess true religion and no government could 'connive at the propagating of these prejudices'. The 'evil effect' of sectarianism 'is without remedy, and may therefore deserve indulgence'. But it merited no more.[121]

Bolingbroke's tolerant religious establishment also rested on a Ciceronian appeal to the common good. The method for resolving religious difference was first to resolve civil disputes. Bolingbroke accused clergymen of every denomination of using superstition as a means to threaten civil peace: 'It is a certain truth, that our religious and civil contests have mutually, and almost alternately, raised and fomented each other.' Bolingbroke also noted how 'Churchmen and Dissenters have sometimes differed, and sometimes thought, or been made to think, that they differed, at least, as much about civil as religious matters'.[122] Adapting Cicero in *De Amicitia*, Bolingbroke wrote that to feel the same way about the commonwealth was the basis for unity in private and public relations.[123] He accepted that Dissenters historically sided with Whiggism 'and they want no apology for doing so'. Dissenters supported that party with whose principles they concurred, and they never acted as 'a sect, or a faction' that sought to undermine civil authority by pursuing 'an interest distinct from the interest of the whole'. It befitted the Dissenters, Bolingbroke concluded, to support the nation and the Country party 'and their country will owe them all the acknowledgements, which are due from good and grateful citizens of the same commonwealth'.[124]

---

[120] Bolingbroke, *Works*, vol. 4, p. 109.
[121] Ibid., vol. 1, pp. 115–16.
[122] Bolingbroke, *Political Writings*, p. 7.
[123] Cicero, *De Senectute, de Amicitia, de Divinatione*, p. 145. The passage was taken from *De Amicitia*, X.33: 'vel ut de re publica non idem sentitur' (trans. 'the parties to it did not entertain the same political views').
[124] Bolingbroke, *Political Writings*, p. 8.

Just as the Protestant Dissenter must hold the national establishment in due reverence as a sincere member of the Christian commonwealth, so too must the freethinker. Bolingbroke wrote in his essays to Pope how, among people 'immersed in ignorance and superstition, there arose in ancient days, as there have since, some men of more genius than the common herd'. These men had 'better means of observing nature themselves, and more leisure for the investigation of truth, and for the improvement of knowledge'.[125] While the promise of primitive Christianity was the liberty of all consciences, Bolingbroke did not suppose that this promise entailed intellectual equality. Since it was 'much harder to examine and judge, than to take up opinions on trust', 'the greatest part of the world borrows, from others, those [opinions] which they entertain concerning all the affairs of life and death'.[126]

Even if he did not need to borrow opinions from others, the freethinker must maintain a principled commitment to the Protestant church-state relationship in Hanoverian England. It was not simply that it kept the commonality governable. It was also that Christian reform was the basis on which the elite freethinker could pursue his inward thoughts as securely as the heterodox Anglican or Protestant Dissenter. Bolingbroke believed the articles of faith of the Church of England were corrupt. But Bolingbroke claimed to Pope that his country parson would justifiably admonish him for 'going through the journey of life without opening the eyes of my mind, and employing my intellectual sight'. It would not be justified, 'like those of your [Catholic] church, to remain in voluntary blindness'. Nor would it be right, 'like those of ours [Anglican], to let him see for me, though my eyes are open, though my faculties of vision are at least as good as his, and though I have all the objects of sight before my eyes that he has before his'.[127] The role of the ruler in Hanoverian England was outwardly to observe the remaining superstitions of the Church of England until its articles of faith had been reformed back to primitive Christianity.

There were further Ciceronian dimensions within this argument. Bolingbroke's *On the Spirit of Patriotism* (1737) called for the British aristocracy to reform the nation by serving the country in defence of the common good. Addressed to Cornbury, the essay followed Cicero in arguing that service to the nation was the highest duty and that the responsibility to serve inhered in proportion to one's position in the commonwealth. The greatest responsibility fell to the aristocracy 'who are born to instruct, to guide, and to preserve'.[128] Such men understood that 'the influence of reason is slow and calm, that of passions sudden and violent'.[129] Patriotic aristocrats supported the godly king in serving the common good in the Christian commonwealth in accordance with the natural order.

---

[125] Bolingbroke, *Works*, vol. 3, p. 222.
[126] Ibid., vol. 1, pp. 182–3.
[127] Ibid., vol. 3, p. 376.
[128] Bolingbroke, *Political Writings*, p. 193.
[129] Bolingbroke, *Works*, vol. 3, p. 224.

This classicising disposition reflected the priorities and style of the patriot opposition to Walpole. It is worth comparing, for instance, Bolingbroke's arguments with the work of the 'Anglo-Scot' poet and playwright, James Thomson, whose mutual friends included Mallet and Pope.[130] During the early 1730s, inspired in part by his grand tour, Thomson composed the poem *Liberty* (1735–6), although it would not be until 1740 that he would make the acquaintance of Sir George Lyttleton and Prince Frederick to become fully associated with the patriot Whigs. Taking as its themes the civic republican motifs of liberty, luxury, virtue, and corruption, the poem divides into five parts, comparing liberty in ancient and modern Italy, ancient Greece, ancient Rome, and Britain. In his fifth, closing, part, the poet addresses the goddess of liberty on the matter of modern liberty and its prospects in Great Britain. Tracing the death of liberty in ancient Rome before celebrating its revival in Britain, the poem opens by the author considering, as might the grand tourist, 'a vast Monument, once-glorious *Rome*'. While contemplating the ruins of Rome, the author was interrupted by 'the fair majestic POWER // Of LIBERTY', 'her bright Temples bound with *British* Oak'.[131]

Later in the poem, the poet laments how 'SCHOLASTIC DISCORD', 'CLERIC PRIDE', 'HOLY SLANDER', and 'PERSECUTING ZEAL' had extinguished the spirit of liberty.[132] 'Idiot SUPERSTITION' and 'ten thousand Monkish Forms' had charmed or scared 'the Simple into Slaves', poisoning reason and spreading ignorance.[133] The allusion to the Church of Rome was obvious. But modern Britain enjoyed 'RELIGION, rational, and free'.[134] The poem closes by the author condemning 'false designing Men' in an allusion both secular and religious. But, thanks to Britain's patriots, such as Richard Boyle, earl of Burlington, '*Kings* and *Senates fit*, the *Palace* see! // The *Temple* breathing a religious Awe'.[135] Much like Bolingbroke's public writings, Thomson's *Liberty* was a patriot celebration of the Revolution settlement in church and state tied with a warning of the priestcraft that might emerge from the close relationship between priests like Gibson and ministers like Walpole.

Not all of Bolingbroke's analysis of religion went public during his lifetime. He was never willing to publish his philosophical works. He had always believed it was the duty of the aristocratic elite to maintain the peace and stability of civil society. He retained a principled commitment to the reformed church-state relationship as a means of securing toleration and freedom of conscience for all

---

[130] See Mary Jane W. Scott, *James Thomson, Anglo-Scot* (Athens, GA, 1988); James Sambrook, *James Thomson, 1700–1748: A Life* (Oxford, 1991), especially pp. 39, 372, 377, 429.
[131] James Thomson, 'Liberty, A Poem', in James Sambrook (ed.), *Liberty, the Castle of Indolence, and Other Poems* (Oxford, 1986), I: 18, 25–6, 29.
[132] Ibid., IV: 59, 62, 64, 66.
[133] Ibid., IV: 76–7, 79.
[134] Ibid., IV: 561.
[135] Ibid., V: 577, 691–2.

members of the Christian commonwealth – whether Anglican, freethinker, or Dissenter. In a letter to Swift in September 1724, Bolingbroke wrote:

> the term Esprit fort, in English free thinker, is according to my observation, usually apply'd to Men whom I look upon to be the Pests of Society, because their endeavours are directed to losen the bands of it, & to take att least one curb out of the mouth of that wild Beast Man when it would be well if he was check'd by half a score others.[136]

In his *Letters or Essays addressed to Alexander Pope*, Bolingbroke made it clear that he never aimed to undermine the institution of the church. Rather, he wished to purify it. 'Truth and falsehood, knowledge and ignorance, revelations of the Creator, inventions of the creature, dictates of reason, sallies of enthusiasm,' explained Bolingbroke, 'have been blended so long together in our systems of theology, that it may be thought dangerous to separate them; lest by attacking some parts of these systems we should shake the whole.'[137] In correspondence with the Lord Chancellor, Hardwicke, in 1744, Bolingbroke insisted that he had no dispute with 'evangelical religion'.[138]

Bolingbroke's respect for the possibility of Christian civil religion, despite his deism, can be inferred by contrasting his response to Warburton's *Alliance* with that of Rousseau in *The Social Contract*. Rousseau believed Warburton had mistakenly supposed that 'among us politics and religion have a common object'.[139] Worse, Warburton wrongheadedly took Christianity, of all the religions, as the 'strongest support' for the body politic. By contrast, Rousseau argued that 'the Christian law is at bottom more harmful than useful to a strong constitution of the State'.[140] In later editions of the *Alliance*, Warburton responded in kind by arguing that Rousseau mistakenly tarred reformed churches like the Church of England with the same brush as the Church of Rome. Writing of 'the *slavish spirit of Christianity*', Warburton claimed, 'instead of the *spirit of Christianity*', Rousseau 'has given us the *spirit of Popery*'.[141] Conversely, Bolingbroke's problem with Warburton's ecclesiology had been that it had supposed the church ever to have been an independent society with sacerdotal status. Bolingbroke's position was neither that the ends of religion and politics were mutually incompatible, nor that Christianity could not form the basis for a state. However, Warburton claimed that Bolingbroke pretended to 'a great regard to religion in general' while taking 'every opportunity of declaiming publickly against that system of religion, or at least against

---

[136] Bolingbroke to Swift, 12 Sept. 1724, in *Correspondence of Swift*, vol. 3, p. 27.
[137] Bolingbroke, *Works*, vol. 3, p. 53.
[138] Bolingbroke to Philip Yorke, Earl of Hardwicke, 12 Nov. 1744, in P. C. Yorke (ed.), *The Life and Correspondence of Philip Yorke, Earl of Hardwicke* (3 vols, Cambridge, 1913), vol. 1, pp. 367–8.
[139] Rousseau, *Social Contract*, p. 72.
[140] Ibid., p. 146.
[141] Bolingbroke, *Works*, vol. 7, p. 207.

that Church-Establishment, which is received in Britain'.[142] At least Rousseau had been public about his deism.

But such an interpretation of Bolingbroke would do great violence to his religious and ecclesiological thought, especially his public intention to purify rather than shake the entire system of the church. He was critical of those doctrines of artificial theology that he deemed extraneous to true religion, above all the doctrines of the Trinity, sacerdotal priesthood, and revelation. Bolingbroke's true religion was a natural religion to be uncovered by the exercise of human reason and which was replicated by primitive Christianity expressed in the gospel. Until the Church of England came to reform its articles of faith back to primitive purity, it was prudent for gentlemen to respect the remaining superstitions in its articles of faith. Bolingbroke's ecclesiological thought was infused with Christian reform. He identified the godly prince as the defender of the lay Protestant believer against superstitious priestcraft. He argued that an established church was necessary to institute the plain and simple natural religion of the gospel and prevent the laity from tripping into turbulent sects. Since primitive Christianity taught only the virtues of moral benevolence, its establishment also proved beneficial to maintaining the peace of the commonwealth. In Bolingbroke's civil religion, the clergy was to be governed using the legal and ecclesiastical framework of the magisterial Reformation, since civil authority enabled the lay Protestant believer to exercise their own rational and spiritual capacities. Their Christianity was civil because true religion was worldly.

---

[142] Warburton, *View of Lord Bolingbroke's Philosophy*, vol. 3, p. 56.

4

The Civil Faith of Common Sense: David Hume

True and false religion

It might sound oddly dissonant to hear the name 'Hume' uttered alongside the term 'civil religion'. A great deal of ink has been spilled in favour of the view that the man once upbraided as 'the fattest hog of Epicurus's stye' and 'the see-saw sceptic of the remotest North' looked forward to the end of religious belief and, in particular, Christianity.[1] It has even been argued that Hume denied the possibility of a civil religion altogether.[2] These interpretations rely entirely on Hume's attacks on religion in general and conclude that he believed all religion could prove only deleterious to human happiness and society. They are also concerned primarily with Hume's religious identity and whether he qualified as a modern pagan, deist, atheist, agnostic, sceptic, or irreligionist in general.[3] However, to focus purely on Hume's inward religion, or lack thereof, is to miss much of the point. Hume wagged his pen against all the

---

[1] Major John Cartwright, *American Independence* (London, 1775), p. xii.
[2] J. B. Schneewind, *The Invention of Autonomy: A History of Modern Political Philosophy* (Cambridge, 1998), pp. 354–5; Beiner, *Civil Religion*, pp. 229–36. Frederick Whelan, noting Hume's acquiescence with church establishments, argued rightly that Hume did not endorse a Machiavellian or Rousseauian religion of the *patrie*. But these were only two strains of civil religion. See Frederick G. Whelan, *Hume and Machiavelli: Political Realism and Liberal Thought* (Lanham, MD, 2004), pp. 13–14, 155.
[3] For Hume as the paragon of Peter Gay's 'modern paganism', see *Enlightenment*, vol. 1, pp. 401–19. For Hume as a deist, see J. C. A. Gaskin, 'Hume's Attenuated Deism', *Archiv für Geschichte der Philosophie*, 65:2 (1983), pp. 160–73; *Hume's Philosophy of Religion* (2nd edn, Basingstoke, 1988), pp. 219–29. For Hume as an irreligious opponent of all religion, see Donald T. Siebert, *The Moral Animus of David Hume* (Newark, DE, 1990); Keith Yandell, *Hume's 'Inexplicable Mystery': His Views on Religion* (Philadelphia, 1990); Adam Potkay, 'Hume's "Supplement to Gulliver": The Medieval Volumes of the *History of England*', *Eighteenth-Century Life*, 25:2 (2001), pp. 32–46; Mark Webb, 'The Argument of the *Natural History*', *HS*, 17:2 (1991), pp. 141–59; Terence Penelhum, *Themes in Hume: The Self, the Will, Religion* (Oxford, 2003), pp. 177–260; Paul Russell, *The Riddle of Hume's Treatise: Skepticism, Naturalism, and Irreligion* (Oxford, 2008); Thomas Holden, *Spectres of False Divinity: Hume's Moral Atheism* (Oxford, 2010). See also Shane Andre, 'Was Hume an Atheist?', *HS*, 19:1 (1993), pp. 141–66; James Noxon, 'Hume's Agnosticism', in V. C. Chappell (ed.), *Hume: A Collection of Critical Essays* (New York, 1966), pp. 361–83.

negative features of religion as he understood them: priestcraft, superstition, enthusiasm, intolerance, hypocrisy, bigotry, and civil strife. By analysing what Hume perceived to be wrong with religion, it becomes possible to demonstrate his positive vision for it. He rendered the Churches of England and Scotland as civil religions in their respective contexts against powerful Anglican priests and *jure divino* Presbyterianism. Their ministers were to preach the civil faith of their states.

A substantial strand of scholarship has noted Hume's willingness to adjust himself to established religion.[4] It is common to point to Hume's interest in the civil religions of the ancient pagan world in which religion had a worldly orientation and was governed by priests who were tolerant and content to allow philosophers their intellectual freedom.[5] Nevertheless, nobody has yet argued that Hume developed a civil religion. A useful point of departure is to borrow the insight of students of the philosophy of religion that Hume distinguished between 'true religion' and 'false religion' and that he did so for more than just tactical reasons.[6] A note of caution is necessary, since much of this scholarship is concerned with whether Hume meant true religion in a normative sense and how it might relate to his own religious identity. Instead, the analysis below focuses on the role played by Hume's distinction between true and false religion in his conception of civil religion. To speak here of Hume's idea of true religion is to speak of proper religion. This takes Hume's personal beliefs out of the immediate focus and reveals how ideas of church government played a fundamental role in his conception of political society.

---

[4] Forbes, *Hume's Philosophical Politics*, pp. 214–16; Ryu Susato, 'Taming "the Tyranny of Priests": Hume's Advocacy of Religious Establishments', *JHI*, 73:2 (2012), pp. 273–93; James A. Harris, *Hume: An Intellectual Biography* (Cambridge, 2015), p. 22.

[5] See Donald W. Livingston, *Hume's Philosophy of Common Life* (Chicago and London, 1984), p. 331; 'Hume's Historical Conception of Liberty', in Nicholas Capaldi and Donald W. Livingston (eds), *Liberty in Hume's History of England* (Dordrecht, 1990), pp. 105–53, at pp. 142–3; Thomas W. Merrill, *Hume and the Politics of the Enlightenment* (New York, 2015), p. 144.

[6] See Nicholas Capaldi, 'Hume's Philosophy of Religion: God without Ethics', *IJPR*, 1:4 (1970), pp. 233–40; Livingston, *Hume's Philosophy of Common Life*, pp. 311–13, 329–34; 'Hume's Conception of "True Religion"', in Antony Flew, Donald W. Livingston, George I. Mavrodes, and David Fate Norton (eds), *Hume's Philosophy of Religion: The Sixth James Montgomery Hester Seminar* (Winston-Salem, NC, 1986), pp. 33–73; *Philosophical Melancholy and Delirium: Hume's Pathology of Philosophy* (Chicago, 1998), p. 76; John Immerwahr, 'Hume's Aesthetic Theism', *HS*, 22:2 (1996), pp. 225–338; Timothy M. Costelloe, '"In Every Civilized Community": Hume on Belief and the Demise of Religion', *IJPR*, 55:3 (2004), pp. 171–85; Lorne Falkenstein, 'Hume on "Genuine", "True", and "Rational" Religion', *Eighteenth Century Thought*, 4 (2009), pp. 171–201; Willem Lemmens, '"Beyond the Calm Sunshine of the Mind": Hume on Religion and Morality', *Aufklärung und Kritik*, 37 (2011), pp. 214–50; Don Garrett, 'What's True about Hume's "True Religion"?', *JSP*, 10:2 (2012), pp. 199–220; Ryan Patrick Hanley, 'Hume's Critique and Defense of Religion', in Christopher Nadon (ed.), *Enlightenment and Secularism: Essays on the Mobilization of Reason* (Lanham, MD, 2013), pp. 89–101; André C. Willis, *Toward a Humean True Religion: Genuine Moderate Hope, Practical Morality* (University Park, PA, 2014); 'The Potential Value of Hume's "Religion"', *JSP*, 13:1 (2015), pp. 1–15.

The analysis will begin with Hume's attack on religion and his reasons for it. He objected to the phenomena of superstition, that set of false beliefs fabricated by crafty priests to advance their political and economic interests, and enthusiasm, that fanatical behaviour of the misguided religious believer. He observed the bigotry and hypocrisy of false religionists throughout history and agonised over the destabilising potential of religion when not properly reconciled with the political interests of society. Superstition led to the subversion of secular relations and enthusiasm was the product of religion improperly regulated. Hume went to such lengths to attack false religion because he understood religious sentiment to be a feature of human nature and he believed true religion was reconcilable with civilised society. Further, he argued that it was an integral part of a flourishing society. To that end, it was essential there should be a church establishment. But the establishment must be reformed. He argued that the history of Christianity since its earliest days had been the history of superstition, priestcraft, and imposture. The victory of corrupt Christianity had been achieved by its establishment under Constantine and the history of the Roman Catholic Church was the history of Christian reformers resisting such corruption. Since the Reformation, this history had become the history of a church establishment continuing the struggle against superstition while providing a vanguard against enthusiasm.

The Reformation played a crucial role in Hume's analysis of modern politics. It had provided the civil state with the means to control priests and set them in their proper capacity as clergymen. They were to be parochial functionaries and pedagogical teachers of the traditional tales of Christianity as much as they were to be learned men steeped in the disciplines of philology, history, and fine letters. They would elevate the mind to consider, calmly and relying on the mild and moderate passions, the ultimate cause of the universe while appreciating the limits of human understanding. There would be no grandiose truth-claims bolstered with fabricated domains of theological philosophy like metaphysics and scholasticism. True religion would prioritise the knowable morality of common life, which Hume claimed to have systematised using his science of man, over and above unprovable postulations about the life beyond this world. Hume's civil religion would recover the insights of the ancients, prior to the corruptions of post-Nicene Christianity, when philosophers were free and priests tolerant. It would be a modern Ciceronian *religio* stripped of *superstitio*.

Evidence of Hume's civil religion ranges across his correspondence and printed works. Many of his writings on religion, like other subjects, underwent frequent revision and redrafting with the evolution of circumstance, especially his changing relationship with the Scottish Presbyterian clergy. The analysis below is not a general exposition of Hume's writings on religion, but an examination of his conception of civil religion within them. The morality that Hume hoped would be instituted by true religionists can be found in his works of moral philosophy. These are his *Treatise of Human Nature* (1739–40), in which he first laid out his science of man, *An Enquiry concerning Human Understanding* (1748), which restated many positions discussed in the *Treatise*, and *An Enquiry concerning the Principles of Morals* (1751). His ecclesiological thought can be recovered using his essays on morals, politics, and literature, the first of which appeared in 1742, which were routinely revised until his death in 1776, and his *History of England* (1754–62). His justifications for his conception of the church-state relationship were also laid out in his two works that examined the phenomenon of religion in human nature. The first of these texts was *The Natural History of Religion*, first published as part of *Four Dissertations* in 1757, in which he provided a naturalist history of the causes and nature of religious belief.[7] The second text was the posthumous *Dialogues concerning Natural Religion* in which Hume recounted a fictionalised debate between three men, Demea, Philo, and Cleanthes, over the nature of God's existence.

Superstition and enthusiasm

Hume's prescription for the church-state relationship can only be understood in light of his analysis of what he believed to have gone wrong with religion. He developed this theme in opening his essay 'Of Superstition and Enthusiasm' by claiming that *'the corruption of the best things produces the worst'*. Nowhere was this clearer than 'by the pernicious effects of *superstition* and *enthusiasm*', those 'two species of false religion' and 'corruptions of true religion'.[8] Historians tend to characterise the essay as an original intervention in the eighteenth-century British debate about the nature of religious belief.[9] Yet the essay rehearsed similar distinctions drawn between superstition and enthusiasm, as well as the social and political consequences of both phenomena, laid out, among others, by Shaftesbury, whose *Characteristics* Hume had read avidly.[10]

Superstition, Hume argued, was a phenomenon that 'steals in gradually and insensibly'. It 'renders men tame and submissive; is acceptable to the magistrate, and seems inoffensive to the people'. It had led to compacts between rulers and priests as during the many centuries between the establishment of Christianity by Constantine and the Protestant Reformation. In superstitious political societies, 'the priest, having firmly established his authority, becomes the tyrant and disturber of human society, by his endless contentions, persecutions, and religious wars'. Priestcraft was the consequence of superstition and, by means of spiritual and economic aggrandisement, priests achieved their tyrannical dominance. Their rule was one of intolerance, false beliefs, and persecution. 'How smoothly', Hume asked his reader, 'did the ROMISH church

---

[7] Richard Serjeantson, 'Hume's *Natural History of Religion* (1757) and the Demise of Modern Eusebianism', in John Robertson and Sarah Mortimer (eds), *The Intellectual Consequences of Religious Heterodoxy, 1600–1750* (Leiden, 2012), pp. 267–95.
[8] David Hume, 'Of Superstition and Enthusiasm', in *Essays Moral, Political, and Literary*, ed. E. F. Miller (Indianapolis, 1985), p. 73.
[9] Nicholas Phillipson, *David Hume: The Philosopher as Historian* (revised edn, New Haven and London, 2012), p. 66. See also J. G. A. Pocock, 'Superstition and Enthusiasm in Gibbon's History of Religion', *Eighteenth-Century Life*, 8:1 (1982), pp. 83–94.
[10] Harris, *Hume*, pp. 44–9, 51–7.

advance in her acquisition of power? But into what dismal convulsions did she throw all EUROPE, in order to maintain it?'[11]

Hume provided a clear explanation for the source of such superstition in the *Enquiry concerning Human Understanding*. In Christian society, superstition resulted from the union of philosophy with theology. Priestly imposture represented the dominance of philosophical Christianity in secular politics. The problem was that religionists sought to make normative truth-claims about the origins and operation of the universe which could be proved neither rationally nor empirically. Human reason attempted to reconcile complex phenomena into a series of general causes but 'as to the causes of these general causes, we should in vain attempt their discovery'. These 'ultimate springs and principles are totally shut up from human curiosity and enquiry'.[12] The attempt to understand them and justify this knowledge with elaborate systems of philosophy had created superstition. Bigotry was the offspring of this kind of philosophy, 'who, after allying with superstition, separates himself entirely from the interest of his parent, and becomes her most inveterate enemy and persecutor'.[13]

In the ancient world, philosophers had lived in 'great harmony with the established superstition' by respecting it outwardly in external worship but engaging inwardly in free thought.[14] Religion enjoyed 'very little influence on common life'. Men attended the temple and 'the gods left the rest of their conduct to themselves, and were little pleased or offended with those virtues or vices, which only affected the peace and happiness of human society'. Common life was 'the business of philosophy alone'. Philosophy regulated 'men's ordinary behaviour and deportment'.[15] But the fusion of modern religion with philosophy meant the '[s]peculative dogmas of religion' had become 'occasions of such furious dispute'.[16] In the modern age, philosophy 'has no such extensive influence'. It was confined 'mostly to speculations in the closet; in the same manner, as the ancient religion was limited to sacrifices in the temple'. Its place 'is now supplied by the modern religion, which inspects our whole conduct, and prescribes an universal rule to our actions, to our words, to our very thoughts and inclinations'.[17]

Such philosophical bigotry became most dangerous when shared by the vulgar. Superstition, argued Hume in his *Natural History*, was a 'popular theology'. Its adherents shared a penchant for 'absurdity and contradiction'.[18] They sought to make ideas seem more sacred by rendering them ever more

---

[11] Hume, 'Of Superstition and Enthusiasm', p. 77.
[12] David Hume, *An Enquiry concerning Human Understanding*, ed. Tom L. Beauchamp (Oxford, 1999), p. 112.
[13] Ibid., p. 188.
[14] Ibid.
[15] David Hume, *An Enquiry concerning the Principles of Morals*, ed. Tom L. Beauchamp (Oxford, 1998), pp. 197–8.
[16] Hume, *Human Understanding*, p. 188.
[17] Hume, *Principles of Morals*, p. 198.
[18] *DNHR*, p. 166.

incomprehensible. They denigrated common sense and rational thought in the service of false religion. They created a '*systematical, scholastic*' religion which was more likely to prosper than the '*traditional, mythological religion*' of the ancient world because it wielded an iron grip over humankind through the idea of an omnipotent and vengeful god represented in an 'immoral and unamiable light'.[19] The monotheism of Christianity had sunk the human mind into 'the lowest submission and abasement'. It represented 'the monkish virtues of mortification, penance, humility, and passive suffering, as the only qualities which are acceptable' to God.[20] By its metaphysical wrangling, it prioritised God's power over his benevolence. It rendered fear more significant than virtue. It made everyday morality vicious.

The deleterious impact of the union of philosophy and theology was most obvious in Roman Catholic society. The 'ROMAN *christian*, or *catholic* church had spread itself over the civilized world', he explained, 'and had engrossed all the learning of the times'. Its superstition had led to priestcraft and, with it, the subversion of all secular relations. The Roman Catholic Church became 'really one large state within itself', a phrase that recalled the charges of *praemunire* and *imperium in imperio*. Worse, the 'PERIPATETIC philosophy was alone admitted into all the schools, to the utter depravation of every other kind of learning'.[21] Hume explained the point further in 'Of the Protestant Succession'. Roman Catholicism was accompanied with 'its natural attendants of inquisitors, and stakes, and gibbets', making it 'less tolerating' than Protestantism. By failing to divide 'the sacerdotal from the regal office', it was 'prejudicial to any state'.[22]

Superstition subverted every natural human instinct as well as misrepresenting the God of Christianity. In the *History of England*, Hume recounted the sack of Jerusalem by the Crusaders who 'put the numerous garrison and inhabitants to the sword without distinction'. No 'age or sex was spared' and 'infants on the breast were pierced by the same blow with their mothers, who implored for mercy'. Men who had been promised quarter 'were butchered in cold blood by those ferocious conquerors' and the streets of Jerusalem were 'covered with dead bodies'. Meanwhile 'the triumphant warriors, after every enemy was subdued and slaughtered, immediately turned themselves, with the sentiments of humiliation and contrition, towards the holy sepulchre'. These soldiers wept and sung anthems 'to their Saviour, who had there purchased their salvation by his death and agony'.[23] But they wept no tears for their victims.

Here was religion ripped from all moral sentiment. It ignored suffering and subdued sympathy. It placed the approbation of a capricious and vengeful deity over the fellow-feeling of men. Hume developed the idea that false religion subverted human nature in his essay 'Of the Standard of Taste'. More often than

---

[19] Ibid., pp. 176, 190.
[20] Ibid., p. 163.
[21] David Hume, 'Of the Rise and Progress of the Arts and Sciences', in *Essays*, p. 121.
[22] David Hume, 'Of the Protestant Succession', in ibid., p. 510.
[23] *HE*, vol. 1, p. 250.

not in works of religious art, Hume explained, the 'same good sense, that directs men in the ordinary occurrences of life, is not hearkened to in religious matters, which are supposed to be placed altogether above the cognizance of human reason'. But '*bigotry* and *superstition*' so confound 'the sentiments of morality, and alter the boundaries of vice and virtue' to be neither morally agreeable and useful nor enjoyable. Hume singled out the Roman Catholic Church for using art to represent 'violent hatred' and 'divine wrath and vengeance'.[24]

As well as superstition, Hume reserved ire for the false religion of enthusiasm. Whereas superstition lent itself to priestly power, enthusiasm lent itself to popular power. This had been shown by 'the *anabaptists* in GERMANY, the *camisars* in FRANCE, the *levellers* and other fanatics in ENGLAND, and the *covenanters* in SCOTLAND'. Enthusiasm was 'founded on strong spirits, and a presumptuous boldness of character'. It naturally 'begets the most extreme resolutions', especially 'after it rises to that height as to inspire the deluded fanatic with the opinion of divine illuminations, and with a contempt for the common rules of reason, morality, and prudence'. Enthusiasm produced 'the most cruel disorders in human society'. Yet its fury 'is like that of thunder and tempest, which exhaust themselves in a little time, and leave the air more calm and serene than before'. Once they had exhausted themselves, erstwhile fanatics 'sink into the greatest remissness and coolness in sacred matters'.[25] It is reasonable to imagine Hume here casting eighteenth-century society as the calm that had emerged following the enthusiasm of the seventeenth-century wars of religion.

It was also by their political consequences that Hume took such interest in the phenomena of superstition and enthusiasm. Superstition had been the product of the subversion of secular relations and the triumph of the ecclesiastical over the civil power. But enthusiasm was the consequence of religion when removed from all social control. Hume's maxim was that '*superstition is an enemy to civil liberty, and enthusiasm a friend to it*'. Superstition 'groans under the dominion of priests' whereas enthusiasm 'is destructive of all ecclesiastical power'. Enthusiasm, 'being the infirmity of bold and ambitious tempers, is naturally accompanied with a spirit of liberty' whereas superstition, 'on the contrary, renders men tame and abject, and fits them for slavery'.[26] These distinctions helped to account for the modern English party system. The leaders of the Whigs 'have either been *deists* or profest *latitudinarians* in their principles' so that they were 'friends to toleration, and indifferent to any particular sect of *christians*'. Sectaries, 'who have all a strong tincture of enthusiasm, have always, without exception, concurred with that party, in defence of civil liberty'. Conversely, the 'resemblance in their superstitions long united the high-church *Tories*, and the *Roman catholics*, in support of prerogative and kingly power'.[27]

---

[24] David Hume, 'Of the Standard of Taste', in *Essays*, p. 247.
[25] Hume, 'Of Superstition and Enthusiasm', p. 77.
[26] Ibid., p. 78.
[27] Ibid., p. 79.

The final aspect of false religion that pertains to Hume's civil religion was his analysis of its origins in human nature. Superstition and enthusiasm were products of natural passions. The sources of superstition were 'weakness, fear, melancholy, together with ignorance'. The sources of enthusiasm were 'hope, pride, presumption, a warm imagination, together with ignorance'. Both were products of violent passions. Superstition resulted from the mind of man being 'subject to certain unaccountable terrors and apprehensions, proceeding either from the unhappy situation of private or public affairs, from ill health, from a gloomy and melancholic disposition, or from the occurrence of all these circumstances'.[28] Enthusiasm was the result of the mind of man being 'subject to an unaccountable elevation and presumption, arising from prosperous success, from luxuriant health, from strong spirits, or from a bold and confident disposition'.[29] As he explained in the *Natural History*, 'Our natural terrors present the notion of a devilish and malicious deity'. Conversely, our 'propensity to adulation leads us to acknowledge an excellent and divine' one. Men's early images of the deity were built from the passions of hope and fear. Every 'image of vengeance, severity, cruelty, and malice must occur' and augments 'the ghastliness and horror, which oppresses the amazed religionist'. A 'panic having once seized the mind, the active fancy still farther multiplies the objects of terror'.[30]

Religion was, therefore, a product of the passions, especially hope and fear. These passions were not instinctual but the results of the reflection of the mind on the natural order. The 'first religious principles must be secondary', Hume explained at the start of the *Natural History*, 'such as may easily be perverted by various accidents and causes, and whose operation too, in some cases, by an extraordinary concurrence of circumstances, be altogether prevented'.[31] The first ideas of religion 'arose not from a contemplation of the works of nature, but from a concern with regard to the events of life, and from the incessant hopes and fears which actuate the human mind'.[32] Hume's analysis of religion was similar to those of Shaftesbury and Trenchard, although Hume refused to accept the idea of a natural religion. All three identified the phenomenon of religion with human passions and, therefore, understood it to be a feature of human nature.[33] Hume argued at the close of the *Natural History* that it was a 'noble privilege' of 'human reason to attain the knowledge of the supreme Being' and, 'from the visible works of nature, be enabled to infer so sublime a principle as its supreme Creator'. But the 'religious principles, which have, in fact, prevailed in the world' were simply 'sick men's dreams'.[34] Hume hoped to construct true

---

[28] Ibid., p. 73.
[29] Ibid., p. 74.
[30] *DNHR*, pp. 176–7.
[31] Ibid., p. 134.
[32] Ibid., p. 139.
[33] Harrison, *'Religion' and the Religions*, pp. 125–6, 169–72.
[34] *DNHR*, p. 184.

religion and the noble privilege that pertained to it on different passions. To do so, he first required the correct ordering of church-state relations.

The church establishment

The means with which to purge false religion from political society were, in Hume's analysis, afforded by the Protestant Reformation. The forms of Reformation that had emerged in England and Scotland had been different, but their effects were similar. In England, it was a magisterial Reformation that allowed church reformers to begin to purge the corruptions of Roman Catholic priestcraft. The 'acknowledgement of the king's supremacy introduced there a great simplicity in government', Hume explained in the *History of England*, 'by uniting the spiritual with the civil power, and preventing disputes about limits, which never could be exactly determined between the contending jurisdictions'. A way opened 'for checking the exorbitancies of superstition, and breaking those shackles, by which all human reason, policy, and industry had so long been encumbered'. Due to the royal supremacy, the prince, unlike the Roman pontiff, had no interest in nourishing the 'excessive growth' of the spiritual power and, 'except when blinded by his own ignorance or bigotry, would be sure to restrain it within tolerable limits, and prevent its abuses'.[35] The result was an effort to reverse the imposture and subversion of secular relations achieved by Roman Catholic superstition.

The union of civil and ecclesiastical power would prevent the rise of superstition because the established clergy would be controlled by the magistrate. Hume made a mischievous but significant reference to the Erastian character of a reformed clergy in the *Treatise*. Discussing the practice of promising, he observed how "'tis one of the most mysterious and incomprehensible operations that can possibly be imagin'd' and compared it with transubstantiation and holy orders. He added a footnote to clarify that, by these religious doctrines, he meant 'so far, as holy orders are suppos'd to produce the *indelible character*'. In other respects, 'they are only a legal qualification'. Hume had no objection to the legal character of holy orders. He objected to sacerdotal priesthoods in which 'a certain form of words, along with a certain intention, changes entirely the nature of an external object, and even of a human creature'. Sacerdotalism and transubstantiation were 'monstrous doctrines' and 'mere priestly innovations'. They had 'no public interest in view'.[36]

As an historian, Hume was narrating attempts by Christian reformers to purge superstition. In the *History of England*, he praised the constitution of the Anglo-Saxons because 'the Wittenagemot enacted statutes which regulated the ecclesiastical as well as civil government' and 'those dangerous principles, by

---

[35] *HE*, vol. 3, p. 207.
[36] David Hume, *A Treatise of Human Nature*, eds David Fate Norton and Mary J. Norton (Oxford, 2000), pp. 336–7.

which the church is totally severed from the state', were unknown to them.[37] Later in the *History*, he inferred from the clash between Henry II and Becket that the 'union of the civil and ecclesiastical power serves extremely, in every civilized government, to the maintenance of peace and order'. It prevented 'those mutual incroachments, which, as there can be no ultimate judge between them, are often attended with the most dangerous consequences'.[38] Hume's argument belonged to a commonplace view that the Anglo-Saxon church and laity had been incorporated into the same structures without any autonomy for the ecclesiastical hierarchy.[39] Henry II's problem was that the age before him had seen 'the progress of ecclesiastical usurpations' both 'in England, as well as in other catholic countries', which had not been resisted by the civil magistrate. Matters had now come to a head as a 'sovereign of the greatest abilities was now on the throne' and a 'prelate of the most inflexible and intrepid character was possessed of the primacy'.[40]

In discussing events like the church-state battles of the twelfth century, Hume was tilling the same soil as scholars and historians of Christian reform. He was locating civil stability in the suppression of the principle of *imperium in imperio*. Much like other students of Christian reform, Hume combined this analysis with another focused on the ancient civil religions. There is a faint echo in his essay 'Of Parties in General' of a standard eighteenth-century civic republican theme. 'Of all men', he proclaimed, 'that distinguish themselves by memorable atchievements, the first place of honour seems due to LEGISLATORS and founders of states, who transmit a system of laws and institutions to secure the peace, happiness, and liberty of future generations.' By the same token, the 'founders of sects and factions' were rightly 'detested and hated'.[41] Although it is easy to imagine the name Numa dancing upon the tip of Hume's pen, Hume did not provide any examples. Instead, he glossed his history of religion as a feature of human nature. Most ancient religions 'arose in the unknown ages of government, when men were as yet barbarous and uninstructed, and the prince, as well as peasant, were disposed to receive, with implicit faith, every pious tale and fiction, which was offered him'. It was convenient that the civil magistrate 'embraced the religion of the people, and entering cordially into the care of sacred matters, naturally acquired an authority in them, and united the ecclesiastical with the civil power'.[42] Hume endorsed the well-regulated pagan civil religions of the ancient world; they formed a model to which modern Christian societies might aspire.

Nevertheless, the order achieved by the ancient civil religions had been ruptured by the rise of Christianity. The new religion appeared 'while principles

---

[37] *HE*, vol. 1, p. 163.
[38] Ibid., p. 311.
[39] Smith, *Gothic Bequest*, pp. 29–30, 153–4, 178.
[40] *HE*, vol. 1, pp. 311–12.
[41] David Hume, 'Of Parties in General', in *Essays*, p. 54.
[42] Ibid., p. 61.

directly opposite to it were firmly established in the polite part of the world'. Since the civil magistrate in imperial Rome was unwilling to countenance Christianity, the apparatus of the secular power was not used to restrain the interested diligence of the priests who were 'allowed to engross all the authority in the new sect'.[43] Once Christianity became the established religion following the conversion of Constantine, 'the same principles of priestly government' continued and bequeathed to early Christianity 'a spirit of persecution, which has ever since been the poison of human society, and the source of the most inveterate factions in every government'. The authority of priests and original separation of civil and ecclesiastical power had contributed to render 'CHRISTENDOM the scene of religious wars and divisions'.[44]

There was a further significant way in which Christianity had subverted the genius of ancient civil religions. Religions that arose 'in ages totally ignorant and barbarous' consisted 'mostly of traditional tales and fictions, which may be different in every sect, without being contrary to each other'. Even when they were contrary, 'every one adheres to the tradition of his own sect, without much reasoning or disputation'.[45] These ancient religions were religions of common sense. They were the products of communal conventions and traditions which, over time, provided the scene for social life. These religions were not normative in content. They did not make universalist truth-claims. They were simply the popular superstitions by which people lived to soothe the violent passions – primarily hope and fear – caused by the uncertainty of life.

But Christianity was not like these ancient religions. It had appeared 'as philosophy was widely spread over the world' and 'the teachers of the new sect were obliged to form a system of speculative opinions'. Priests made philosophical claims and generated metaphysical systems. They had to 'divide, with some accuracy, their articles of faith; and to explain, comment, confute, and defend with all the subtilty of argument and science'.[46] Thence was generated a keenness to dispute and, as co-religionists disagreed, 'divisions and heresies'. Such disputes aided the priests in their policy of 'begetting a mutual hatred and antipathy among their deluded followers'. Religion was no longer a benign feature of human nature which soothed the psychological traumas of life. It no longer served the purposes of civil order. 'Sects of philosophy' in the ancient world 'were more zealous than parties of religion' because the latter were controlled by the ancient civil faiths. But modern religion had produced parties 'more furious and enraged than the most cruel factions that ever arose from interest and ambition'.[47]

Hume's line of argument, so far, seems to point towards a Machiavellian or Rousseauian civil religion which praised paganism over Christianity. But,

---

[43] Ibid.
[44] Ibid., p. 62.
[45] Ibid.
[46] Ibid.
[47] Ibid., p. 63.

for Hume, the Reformation allowed Christianity to become a modern version of the peaceful union of religion and politics that had prevailed in the ancient pagan world. It allowed priests to be restrained and restored their focus only to the morality of common life. Hume added weight to this argument by analysing the church-state relationship in terms of political economy.[48] In the *History of England*, there is a passage which rewards study in full. Hume called the passage a '*Digression concerning the ecclesiastical state*' and it occasioned an analytical interlude in Hume's history of the sixteenth century.[49] 'Most of the arts and professions in a state', he began, 'are of such a nature, that, while they promote the interest of society, they are also useful or agreeable to some individuals.' In this instance, the magistrate was wise not to interpose in a profession whose practitioners, 'finding their profits to rise by the favour of their customers, increase, as much as possible, their skill and industry'. Without any 'injudicious tampering', 'the commodity is always sure to be at all time nearly proportioned to the demand'.[50]

But there were other callings 'which, though useful and even necessary in a state, bring no particular advantage or pleasure to any individual' and the civil magistrate must 'alter its conduct with regard to the retainers of those professions'. Practitioners were to be given 'public encouragement in order to their subsistence' and the civil magistrate must 'provide against that negligence' to which those practitioners were subject by various expedients including 'by annexing peculiar honours to the profession, by establishing a long subordination of ranks and a strict dependance'. Examples of such professions included the finances, armies, fleets, and magistracy. Clergymen were another. The encouragement of churchmen could not be safely 'entrusted to the liberality of individuals, who are attached to their doctrines, and who find benefit or consolation from their spiritual ministry and assistance'. Their 'industry and vigilance' would not 'be whetted by such an additional motive' and 'their skill in the profession, as well as their address in governing the minds of the people' would not 'receive daily encrease, from their encreasing practice, study, and attention'. Every 'wise legislator will study to prevent', Hume concluded, 'this interested diligence of the clergy'.[51] Unwise legislators allowed individuals attached to dangerous superstitions to choose which preachers they wished to support with funds.

To this argument, Hume introduced his distinction between true and false religion. In every religion, 'except the true', the interested diligence of the clergy 'is highly pernicious'. Such interested diligence 'has even a natural tendency to pervert the true, by infusing into it a strong mixture of superstition, folly, and delusion'.[52] Each 'ghostly practitioner' would seek to appear more 'precious

---

[48] For political economy and Hume, see John Robertson, *The Case for the Enlightenment: Scotland and Naples, 1680–1760* (Cambridge, 2005), pp. 256–324.
[49] *HE*, vol. 3, p. 134.
[50] Ibid., p. 135.
[51] Ibid.
[52] Ibid., pp. 135–6.

and sacred in the eyes of the laity and will inspire them with the most violent abhorrence of all other sects, and continually endeavour, by some novelty, to excite the languid devotion of his audience'. Questions of truth, good morality, and decency were irrelevant to these practitioners of superstitious craft. Every tenet and doctrine would excite the violent passions, 'the disorderly affections of the human frame'. 'Customers will be drawn to each conventicle by new industry and address' as priests played upon the passionate credulity of the laity. By failing to interpose himself in the interested diligence of the priests, the civil magistrate would discover 'that he has dearly paid for his pretended frugality, in saving a fixed establishment for the priests'. It would be wiser to establish the priests and turn them into 'spiritual guides'. He would 'bribe their indolence, by assigning stated salaries to their profession, and rendering it superfluous for them to be farther active, than merely to prevent their flock from straying in quest of new pastures'.[53] Some urban centres had become sites of uneducated sermon-gadding laymen incentivising charismatic preachers. It would be dangerous to allow clergymen to rely on voluntary subscription in this context. The civil magistrate could reconcile religion with the stability of the civil state and the political interests of society by means of public establishment.

By distinguishing between true and false religion, Hume was adding the theme of political economy to the language of Christian reform. He built on this dualism by engaging in a specific attack on the Roman Catholic Church. Few ecclesiastical establishments 'have been fixed upon a worse foundation than that of the church of Rome' which had been among the 'more hurtful to the peace and happiness of mankind'. Roman Catholic priests' revenues, privileges, immunities, and powers rendered them capable of challenging the civil magistrate and they were able to encroach and usurp secular power. This threatened the correct structure of political power as the 'supreme head of the church was a foreign potentate, guided by interests, always different from those of the community, sometimes contrary to them'. It also reduced inward liberty as the dictates of religious uniformity, rites, and ceremonies meant 'all liberty of thought ran a manifest risque of being extinguished' and 'violent persecutions, or what was worse, a stupid and abject credulity', proliferated.[54]

It undermined the progress of commerce and, by it, the arts and refinement in manners. Due to 'the establishment of monasteries, many of the lowest vulgar were taken from the useful arts, and maintained in those receptacles of sloth and ignorance'.[55] Even though the church 'possessed large revenues', her leaders were 'not contented with her acquisitions' and 'retained a power of practising farther on the ignorance of mankind'. Each priest called upon 'the voluntary oblations of the faithful'. The result was an 'expensive and buthensome establishment' dominated by priests who 'trusted entirely to their own art and

---

[53] Ibid., p. 136.
[54] Ibid.
[55] Ibid.

invention for attaining a subsistence'. Nevertheless, Hume recognised the advantages brought by the Romish church. During barbarous times, ecclesiastical privileges 'had served as a cheque on the despotism of kings'. The union of all western churches under the pope had 'facilitated the intercourse of nations, and tended to bind all the parts of Europe'. In some degrees, at least, the church's pomp, opulence, and splendour in outward worship encouraged 'the fine arts, and began to diffuse a general elegance of taste, by uniting it with religion'.[56] But the failure of the civil magistrate to regulate properly the church's power had rendered those advantages void.

Hume was clearly committed to the church-state relationship bequeathed by the Protestant Reformation. Although Hume concurred with Machiavelli and Rousseau in endorsing the achievements of the ancient pagan civil religions, he nevertheless believed that these achievements could be reconstructed by the primacy of the civil magistrate over modern Christianity. By studying the history of the church-state relationship in the ancient and modern worlds, Hume hoped that the civil magistrate would be able to purge the false religion of superstition by means of prudent management of the political economy of priestcraft. In these senses, Hume was committed to the general ecclesiological themes of Christian reform. But, in two key ways, there was something more distinctively Scottish and Presbyterian in Hume's analysis of the union of the civil and ecclesiastical powers.

First, Hume retained an explicit preference for *jure humano* Presbyterian ecclesiology over the Anglican settlement. This was simply because Presbyterian church government, once purged of its *jure divino* pretensions, was more fully reformed and lent itself better to an Erastian model by removing all sacerdotal power from clerical office. In versions of his essay 'Of Superstition and Enthusiasm' between 1748 and 1768, Hume claimed that 'Modern Judaism and popery, (especially the latter)', were 'the most unphilosophical and absurd superstitions which have yet been known in the world'. They were 'the most enslaved by their priests'. The Church of England 'may justly be said to retain some mixture of Popish superstition' and 'partakes also, in its original constitution, of a propensity to priestly power and dominion; particularly in the respect it exacts to the sacerdotal character'. Although, 'according to the sentiments of that Church, the prayers of the priest must be accompanied with those of the laity; yet is he the mouth of the congregation, his person is sacred, and without his presence few would think their public devotions, or the sacraments, and other rites, acceptable to the divinity'.[57]

The Presbyterian model was a safer option. In his essay 'Idea of a Perfect Commonwealth', Hume responded to Harrington's *Oceana* with 'a form of government, to which I cannot, in theory, discover any considerable objection'. This form of government would involve a church-state settlement more

[56] Ibid., p. 137.
[57] Hume, 'Of Superstition and Enthusiasm', p. 619.

Scottish and Presbyterian than English and Anglican. In Oceanic mood, Hume divided Great Britain and Ireland into one hundred counties with each county containing one hundred parishes. There would be no magisterial Reformation and no episcopate. The parish church would be the centre of political activity as, each year, freeholders and householders subject to a property criterion would ballot to elect their county representative.[58] The county representatives would elect some of their number to a national senate each year. The senate would elect, by an intricate system of balloting, the following magistrates from among their number: 'a protector, who represents the dignity of the commonwealth, and presides in the senate', and 'two secretaries of state'. They would also elect 'a council of state, a council of religion and learning, a council of trade, a council of laws, a council of war, a council of the admiralty, each council consisting of five persons; together with six commissioners of the treasury and a first commissioner'.[59]

The officers of the national church would be officers of the civil state but would not risk the residual priestcraft that Hume believed to distinguish the Anglican model. The parishes in Hume's ideal commonwealth would be governed by 'rectors and ministers' appointed by the magistrates. The 'Presbyterian government is established' and 'the highest ecclesiastical court is an assembly or synod of all the presbyters of the county'. Even within this model, care would be taken to prevent priestly domination. From the ecclesiastical court the magistrate 'may take any cause ... and determine it themselves' and the magistrate 'may try, and depose or suspend any presbyter'.[60] As to 'the clergy and militia', the reasons for his prescriptions were obvious: 'Without the dependence of the clergy on the civil magistrates, and without a militia, it is in vain to think that any free government will ever have security or stability.'[61] In this essay, Hume was engaging in a particular political language not unlike Shaftesbury, Trenchard, and Gordon. His essay was not a manifesto for political reform but a development of the civic and neo-Harringtonian style.

The second way in which Hume's civil religion was distinctively Scottish and Presbyterian related to the different histories of the Reformation in England and Scotland. The magisterial variety of England's Reformation relied on the idea of the godly prince. But Hume had little time for the idea. Forbes revealed how Hume can be characterised as a 'sceptical Whig' since, while he was supportive of the Revolution of 1688, he was critical of peculiarly English Whig shibboleths like the idea of an ancient constitution.[62] These, in correspondence,

---

[58] David Hume, 'Idea of a Perfect Commonwealth', in *Essays*, p. 516.
[59] Ibid., p. 518.
[60] Ibid., p. 520.
[61] Ibid., p. 525.
[62] See Forbes, *Hume's Philosophical Politics*, pp. 125–92. See also John Robertson, 'Universal Monarchy and the Liberties of Europe: David Hume's Critique of an English Whig Doctrine', in Phillipson and Skinner (eds), *Political Discourse in Early Modern Britain*, pp. 349–73. For Hume's defence of the Revolution, see Nicholas Phillipson, 'Propriety, Property,

Hume called 'the plaguy Prejudices of Whiggism' and he described his essay 'Of the Protestant Succession' as one penned by 'a Whig, but a very sceptical one'.[63] In contradistinction to English theorists of civil religion, Hume argued that whether 'the supreme magistrate' who bestrode the civil and ecclesiastical powers 'receives the appellation of prince or prelate, is not material'. It was material that the magistrate 'prevents those gross impostures and bigotted persecutions, which, in all false religions, are the chief foundation of clerical authority'.[64] It was obvious that supposedly reformed princes could still be bigoted or superstitious. Henry VIII 'still valued himself maintaining the catholic doctrine', however much he had altered the ecclesiological structures of the church-state, and he guarded, 'by fire and sword, the imagined purity of his speculative principles'.[65]

Hume believed progress in English opinion over the course of the eighteenth century was further rendering the idea of the godly prince irrelevant. In his essay 'Whether the British Government Inclines More to Absolute Monarchy, or to a Republic', he explained that growing anticlericalism since the Revolution had undermined Protestant reverence for godly kingship. There had been 'a sudden and sensible change in the opinion of men within these last fifty years, by the progress of learning and of liberty'. Most people in Britain 'have divested themselves of all superstitious reverence to names and authority'. The result was that the 'clergy have much lost their credit' and their 'pretensions and doctrines have been ridiculed'. Most pertinently, the 'mere name of *king* commands little respect' and 'to talk of a king as GOD's vicegerent on earth, or to give him any of those magnificent titles, which formerly dazzled mankind, would but excite laughter'.[66]

Instead of godly kingship, Hume's analysis of the management of the church-state relationship was built around the themes of prudence and moderation. These, when displayed by rulers, would balance liberty, which was encouraged by enthusiasm, and authority, which was encouraged by superstition. 'In all governments', he declared at the close of his essay 'Of the Origin of Government', 'there is a perpetual intestine struggle, open or secret, between AUTHORITY and LIBERTY'. This was a struggle in which neither 'could ever absolutely prevail'.[67] It was not their godliness that distinguished England's most successful monarchs. In the *History of England*, he remarked that of all the European churches that underwent the Reformation 'no one

---

and Prudence: David Hume and the Defence of the Revolution', in Phillipson and Skinner (eds), *Political Discourse in Early Modern Britain*, pp. 302–20.
[63] David Hume to Gilbert Elliot of Minto, 12 March 1763, in J. Y. T. Greig (ed.), *The Letters of David Hume* (2 vols, Oxford, 1932), vol. 1, p. 379; Hume to Henry Home, 9 Feb. 1748, in ibid., p. 111.
[64] *HE*, vol. 1, p. 311.
[65] Ibid., vol. 3, p. 213.
[66] David Hume, 'Whether the British Government Inclines More to Absolute Monarchy, or to a Republic', in *Essays*, p. 51.
[67] David Hume, 'Of Civil Liberty', in ibid., p. 40.

proceeded with so much reason and moderation as the church of England'. This advantage was partly due to 'the interposition of the civil magistrate in this innovation' and partly 'from the gradual and slow steps, by which the reformation was conducted in that kingdom'. Those who oversaw the Reformation minimised rage and animosity against Roman Catholicism and fitted the Church of England to the character of the English people. The 'fabric of the secular hierarchy was maintained entire' while the 'ancient liturgy was preserved, so far as was thought consistent with the new principles'.[68] Ceremonies that had become venerable through usage were maintained in the name of order. The habits of the clergy were kept and no 'innovation was admitted merely from spite and opposition to the former usage'. The new religion, 'by mitigating the genius of ancient superstition, and rendering it more compatible with the peace and interests of society', helped to preserve 'that happy medium, which wise men have always sought, and which the people have so seldom been able to maintain'.[69]

Such a prudent and moderate ruler was Elizabeth I. She understood the need to combine a reformed religion with traditional external forms of worship. She realised that it was 'the external appearance, which is the chief circumstance with the people'.[70] She dealt with the religious character of the people as she found it and maintained a religious settlement suitable to it. She resisted the urgings of her more zealous reformers and avoided attempts to remove 'those forms and observances, which, without distracting men of more refined apprehensions, tend, in a very innocent manner, to allure, and amuse, and engage the vulgar'.[71]

Similarly, the history of Stuart kingship was less the history of ungodly princes than imprudent and immoderate ones. The parliaments of Charles I were populated by enthusiastic puritans imbued with 'the rigid tenets of that sect' and led by figures who could not 'enjoy any peace of mind; because obliged to hear prayers offered up to the Divinity, by a priest covered with a white linen vestment'.[72] The debates of the Commons were characterised by that 'enthusiastic fire, which afterwards set the whole nation in combustion'.[73] But Charles was unequal to the challenge with his attachment to royal absolutism and Laudianism. Hume reserved most venom for Laud who 'acquired so great an ascendant over Charles, and who led him, by the facility of his temper, into a conduct, which proved so fatal to himself and to his kingdoms'.[74] Laud exalted the relationship between the king and priests and allowed the latter to intrude 'on the royal rights the most incontestible; in order to exalt the hierarchy, and

[68] *HE*, vol. 4, p. 119.
[69] Ibid., p. 120.
[70] Ibid., p. 14.
[71] Ibid., pp. 122–3.
[72] Ibid., vol. 5, p. 159.
[73] Ibid., p. 213.
[74] Ibid., p. 223.

procure to their own order dominion and independence'.[75] Here was nothing other than priestcraft and the subversion of secular relations.

James II manifestly failed the test of moderate and prudent kingship. His 'refined policy' of trying to play 'one party against another' failed miserably. In offering indulgence by prerogative to Protestant Dissenters and Roman Catholics, his 'intentions were so obvious' that nobody believed his commitment to toleration.[76] His grandfather, James I, had been less obviously imprudent. He attempted 'the same stratagem which was practiced by Minos, Numa, and the most celebrated legislators of antiquity' in attempting to buttress his political authority with theological sanction in the form of divine right. But the times were not suited to this stratagem and James would have done better to maintain 'the sacred veil, which had hitherto covered the English constitution, and which threw obscurity upon it' in order to advance royal prerogative.[77]

Nevertheless, Hume insisted that stable, civilised, and flourishing society was only possible through the union of civil and ecclesiastical powers. He composed a draft preface for the second volume of the *History of England* which repays quotation in full. The 'proper office of religion is to reform men's lives, to purify their hearts, to inforce all moral duties, and to secure obedience to the laws and civil magistrate'. In performing 'these salutary purposes, its operations, tho' infinitely valuable, are secret and silent, and seldom come under the cognizance of history'. It was the 'adulterate species of it alone, which inflames faction, animates sedition, and prompts rebellion'. It 'distinguishes itself on the open theatre of the world, and is the great source of revolutions and public convulsions'. Due to the dominance of false religion, the historian 'has scarce occasion to mention any other kind of religion; and he may retain the highest regard for true piety, even while he excuses all the abuses of it'.[78] Hume later revised the passage and gave it to Cleanthes, the defender of natural monotheism in the *Dialogues*, who said to Philo, his interlocutor and the voice of scepticism, that the 'proper office of religion' was 'to regulate the heart of men, humanize their conduct, [and] infuse the spirit of temperance, order, and obedience'. Since 'its operation is silent, and only enforces the motives of morality and justice, it is in danger of being overlooked, and confounded with these other motives'. When it 'distinguishes itself, and acts as a separate principle over men, it has departed from its proper sphere, and has become only a cover to faction and ambition'.[79]

---

[75] Ibid., p. 228.
[76] Ibid., vol. 6, p. 482.
[77] Ibid., vol. 5, pp. 93–4.
[78] Ernest Campbell Mossner, *The Life of David Hume* (2nd edn, Oxford, 1980), pp. 306–7. The draft preface, reprinted by Mossner, can be found in a manuscript held at King's College, Cambridge.
[79] *DNHR*, p. 122. See Jennifer A. Herdt, *Religion and Faction in Hume's Moral Philosophy* (Cambridge, 1997).

Clergymen not priests

By his own admission, Hume's observations on the positive role of religion in political society were few and far between. When religion played its role properly, its operation was silent and need attract the attention neither of the politician nor the historian. Nevertheless, it is possible to reconstruct Hume's conception of religion in civilised society. Hume's views did not pass unnoticed by some of his Enlightened contemporaries. In his memoirs, Gibbon recalled that the French *philosophes* and *Encyclopédistes* could not support Hume's approach to religion. Writing of Jean le Rond d'Alembert, Denis Diderot, Claude Adrien Helvétius, and d'Holbach, Gibbon remembered that 'they laughed at the scepticism of Hume, preached the tenets of atheism with the bigotry of dogmatists, and damned all believers with ridicule and contempt'.[80] These men wished that Hume would be overtly irreligious. They abhorred his respect for church establishments and would not recognise his distinctions between true religion and its popular, vulgar, and false subversions. They hoped he would write his histories with a view to removing all the props for Christianity. For Helvétius, this was 'le plus beau projet du monde', and for Friedrich Melchoir, Baron von Grimm, it was 'un des plus importants services rendus à la philosophie'.[81] To Helvétius and the other *philosophes* Hume lacked 'a contempt of all religion' and, Hume recalled, 'they used to laugh at me for my narrow way of thinking'.[82]

One of the aspects of Hume's civil religion that surely most offended them was his insistence that clergymen could be learned. The proper office of clergymen, as Hume put it in the *Enquiry concerning Human Understanding*, was to join the 'wise and learned' to provide 'an everlasting check to all kinds of superstitious delusion'.[83] Their studies in ecclesiastical and profane history, philology, and scripture were to act as the bulwarks against popish superstition and imposture. They would reveal the corruptions that had bedevilled Christianity since its establishment and, in so doing, teach Christianity as a religion of common life. This was more than simple posturing. His support for the idea of learned clergymen was expressed practically in concern for the universities where he campaigned for Moderate clergymen of the Church of Scotland in their effort to generate a civilised religion of politeness and virtue. He took great interest, for instance, in the bid of the erstwhile clergyman Adam Ferguson to achieve the chair of natural philosophy at Edinburgh in 1759.[84] Ferguson was 'a Man of

---

[80] Edward Gibbon, *Memoirs of My Life*, ed. Betty Radice (London, 1984), p. 140. See also Michael Malherbe, 'Hume's Reception in France', in Peter Jones (ed.), *The Reception of David Hume in Europe* (London, 2005), pp. 34–97.
[81] Trans. 'the most beautiful project in the world' and 'one of the most important services rendered for philosophy'. See, for Helvétius, John Hill Burton (ed.), *Letters of Eminent Persons Addressed to David Hume* (Edinburgh, 1849), p. 13. For Grimm, Laurence L. Bongie, *David Hume: Prophet of the Counter-Revolution* (Oxford, 1965), p. 25.
[82] Hume to Sir John Pringle, 10 Feb. 1773, in *Letters*, vol. 2, p. 274.
[83] Hume, *Human Understanding*, p. 169.
[84] Hume to William Robertson, 29 May 1759, in Raymond Klibansky and Ernest C. Mossner

Sense, Knowledge, Taste, Elegance & Morals' who would be, Hume explained to his friend Gilbert Elliot, an ideal tutor to the son of John Stuart, earl of Bute.[85]

There was a particularly close bond between Hume and William Robertson. Robertson had feared that Hume's performance on the history of sixteenth-century Britain would outshine his own and asked, in vain, for Hume not to 'write this period'.[86] Hume suggested that they read each other's efforts and propose improvements before publication. Although Robertson would not accede, Hume promised to do his best to publicise Robertson's work. 'All the people whose Friendship or Judgement either of us value are Friends to both', he explained, '& will be pleas'd with the Success of both; as we will be with that of each other.'[87] In the English context, Hume also struck up positive relations with learned clergymen, including Richard Price, who had sent Hume a copy of his response to Hume's essay 'Of Miracles'. Hume contrasted the 'proper Decency and Good Manners' of their relationship with the 'Rancour and Animosity' and the 'illiberal Language' of the antitype of learned ministry, Warburton.[88]

Hume was attempting to generate a sociable religion of virtue, civility, and politeness. His was a cultural project against the superstitious priestliness and traditional Calvinism of the Popular party embodied by the spirit of the Covenanters. Hume associated, to this end, with the Moderate campaigns in the mid-century Church of Scotland.[89] Hume became joint-secretary of the Philosophical Society of Edinburgh. He was a founder-member of the Select Society, alongside Adam Smith, with the likes of Ferguson and John Home. From May 1751, Moderate ministers began to gather prior to the annual assembly of the Church of Scotland. Hume and Smith would attend with Robertson, Ferguson, Alexander Carlyle, John Home, Hugh Blair, Hugh Bannatine, and John Jardine. Carlyle later recorded that Hume 'took much to the company of the younger clergy', by which Carlyle meant the new generation of Moderates, 'not from a wish to bring them over to his opinions, for he never attempted to overturn any man's principles, but they best understood his notions, and could furnish him with literary conversation'. The Popular party, 'the zealots on the opposite side', had been outraged by these friendships.[90]

These close bonds within the world of the Scottish Moderates continued throughout Hume's life. In correspondence with Blair, Hume wrote of his 'debt to all my Friends in Letters' especially his 'great & enormous Debts to the Clergy'. Hume praised Robertson's distinction as an historian, Ferguson's 'Piety

---

(eds), *New Letters of David Hume* (Oxford, 1954), pp. 55–8.
[85] Hume to Elliot, 9 Aug. 1757, in *Letters*, vol. 1, p. 263.
[86] Hume to Robertson, 25 Jan. 1759, in ibid., p. 294.
[87] Hume to Robertson, 8 Feb. 1759, in *New Letters*, p. 46.
[88] Hume to [Richard Price], 18 March 1767, in ibid., p. 234.
[89] See Richard Sher, *Church and University in the Scottish Enlightenment: The Moderate Literati of Edinburgh* (Princeton, 1985), pp. 60, 65–72, 104, 207, 154–6, 236.
[90] Alexander Carlyle, *The Autobiography of Alexander Carlyle of Inveresk, 1722–1805*, ed. John Hill Burton (new edn, London and Edinburgh, 1910), pp. 288–9.

& Learning', and Blair's skills as a literary critic.[91] Hume's will would single out Blair, Ferguson, and John Home for their friendship.[92] During Hume's final days, John Home hastened to join him on journeys prescribed by the doctor between London and Bath.[93] On one occasion, Hume drafted a review, which he suppressed out of concern that their association with him would undermine the Moderates' reputation, of the clergyman Robert Henry's *History of Great Britain* (1773) in which Hume wrote of 'the *celebrated* Dr. Robertson'. 'It is happy', he continued, 'for the inhabitants of this metropolis, which has naturally a great influence on the country, that the same persons who can make such a figure in profane learning, are entrusted with the guidance of the people in their spiritual concerns.' This spirit was exemplified by Blair who equally combined 'Learning and Piety, Taste and Devotion, Philosophy and Faith'.[94]

Adherents of the Popular party received Hume and the Moderate clergy as allies in a campaign against them. In 1755, the Popular clergyman John Bonar of Cockpen penned *An Analysis of the Moral and Religious Sentiments contained in the Writings of Sopho, and David Hume, esq.* The essay targeted Sopho, or Henry Home, Lord Kames, and placed him under the banner of infidelity alongside the sceptic Hume in response to his *Essays on the Principles of Morality and Natural Religion* (1751). The general assembly of the Church of Scotland resolved unanimously to censure Hume and Kames for impious and immoral conduct.[95] A vigorous campaign by the Moderates was launched in defence of both men. The Popular party 'intend to give me over to Satan, which they think they have the power of doing', wrote Hume. 'My friends, however, prevailed, and my damnation is postponed for a twelvemonth.' Hume was particularly unimpressed by 'the godly, spiteful, pious, splenetic, charitable, unrelenting, meek, persecuting, Christian, inhuman, peace-making, furious' George Anderson, chaplain to Watson's hospital in Edinburgh.[96] During the general assembly of 1756, Hume gathered with Robertson, Carlyle, John Home, Jardine, Ferguson, William Wilkie, Elliot, and Patrick Murray, Lord Elibank, to plan their strategy against Anderson and the Popular campaign.[97]

Hume's clergy would not simply be learned. It would also be pastoral and pedagogical. Hume edited his essay 'Of Superstition and Enthusiasm' several times. But, in the editions spanning the period between 1748 and 1768, he kept a telling footnote which is worth citing in full: 'By *Priests*, I here mean only the pretenders to power and dominion, and to a superior sanctity of character,

---

91 Hume to Hugh Blair et al., 6 April 1765, in *Letters*, vol. 1, pp. 495–7.
92 See Mossner, *Life of David Hume*, pp. 591, 599.
93 See John Home, *A Sketch of the Character of Mr. Hume and Diary of a Journey from Morpeth to Bath*, ed. David Fate Norton (Edinburgh, 1976).
94 David Hume, 'Review of Robert Henry's *History of Great Britain*', in David Fate Norton and Richard H. Popkin (eds), *David Hume: Philosophical Historian* (Indianapolis, 1965), p. 388.
95 See Mossner, *Life of David Hume*, p. 343.
96 Hume to Allan Ramsay, [June 1755], in *Letters*, vol. 1, p. 224.
97 See Carlyle, *Autobiography*, pp. 323–4.

distinct from virtue and good morals.' These were 'very different from *clergymen*, who are set apart *by the laws*, to the care of sacred matters, and to the conducting our public devotions with greater decency and order'. There was 'no rank of men more to be respected than the latter'.[98] In the same essay, Hume had cast the phenomena of superstition and enthusiasm as the corruptions of true religion caused by the violent and immoderate passions. The role of the clergy was to appeal to the mild and moderate passions, encouraging sociable sentiments and the operation of sympathy among the laity. They would ground religion in virtue and good morals, teaching the traditional tales of Christianity with the humility to appreciate the limits of human understanding. It was, as Hume explained in the *Natural History*, 'the temperate and moderate' life that could stabilise secular relations. 'Any of the human affections may lead us into the notion of invisible, intelligent power', Hume explained. 'But if we examine our hearts, or observe what passes around us,' he continued, 'we shall find that men are much oftener thrown on their knees by the melancholy than by the agreeable passions.'[99]

There was a strongly Ciceronian dimension within this argument. It was the customary morality of common life that would form the virtues and vices and not the confected moral sentiments of superstition or enthusiasm. In 1776 James Boswell asked the dying Hume whether he had been religious during his childhood days. Hume replied that 'he used to read *The Whole Duty of Man*; that he made an abstract from the catalogue of vices at the end of it, and examined himself by this, leaving out murder and theft and much vices as he had no chance of committing, having no inclination to commit them'.[100] *The Whole Duty of Man* was a standard devotional text in high-church circles partly because it was distinctly anti-Calvinist. It is curious that Hume should have accessed the work.[101] In correspondence with Francis Hutcheson, Hume explained that he desired 'to take my catalogue of Virtues from *Cicero's Offices*, not from the *Whole Duty of Man*' because Ciceronian virtues carried the legitimation of common life.[102]

Pastorally, clergymen were to teach moral sentiments that were consistent with the natural and artificial virtues systematised in Hume's science of man. In the *History of England*, Hume repeated the argument first made in 'Of Superstition and Enthusiasm' that enthusiasm represented the violent subversion of the natural moral sentiments, the sympathetic operation of calm passions, which

---

[98] Hume, 'Of Superstition and Enthusiasm', p. 619.
[99] *DNHR*, pp. 184, 143.
[100] James Boswell, *Boswell in Extremes: 1776–1778*, eds Charles Mc. Weis and Frederick A. Pottle (London, 1971), p. 11.
[101] See Rivers, *Reason, Grace, and Sentiment*, vol. 1, pp. 22–3.
[102] Hume to Francis Hutcheson, 17 Sept. 1739, in *Letters*, vol. 1, p. 34. For the influence of Cicero on Hume, see Peter Jones, *Hume's Sentiments: Their Ciceronian and French Context* (Edinburgh, 1982); James Moore, 'Utility and Humanity: The Quest for the *Honestum* in Cicero, Hutcheson, and Hume', *Utilitas*, 14:3 (2002), pp. 365–86; Stuart-Buttle, *From Moral Theology to Moral Philosophy*, ch. 5.

marked human nature. Religious enthusiasm was caused by the 'melancholy with which the fear of death, torture, and persecution inspires the sectaries'. It held up the false prospect of eternal rewards to overcome 'the dread of temporal punishments'. The 'glory of martyrdom stimulates all the more furious zealots, especially the leaders and preachers'. Excited by 'violent animosity', men pass naturally 'from hating the persons of their tyrants, to a more violent abhorrence of their doctrines'. But, Hume concluded, a tolerant church establishment in which clergymen taught the basic precepts of morality meant that 'mutual hatred relaxes among the sectaries' and 'their attachment to their particular modes of religion decays'. The 'common occupations and pleasures of life succeed to the acrimony of disputation'.[103]

It is worth pursuing this theme further. Clergymen were to teach, explained Hume in the *Natural History*, 'the manly, steady virtue, which either preserves us from disastrous, melancholy accidents, or teaches us to bear them'. They were to preach devotion in line with sociability, politeness, and civility. They would enable men to control and enjoy 'such calm sunshine of the mind' in which the 'spectres of false divinity never make their appearance'.[104] Warmed under such light, the laity would make moral distinctions based on that which was useful and agreeable. They would not live in abject fear of a vengeful Christian God with his posthumous punishments. The clergy would become the modern Christian inheritors of the practices of the ancient pagan priests exemplified by Cicero. They would acknowledge the popular stories that were the functions of the natural appearance of religious belief. But they would not allow such superstitions to become fused with philosophy. Nor would they allow religion to grow unsocial by threatening the civil state or plunging sincere believers into barbarism. Their *religio* would be stripped of *superstitio*. As with the ancient civil religions, it was not the normative truth value of the civil faith that mattered for Hume. Rather, the civil religion needed to be moderate, civilised, and capable of calming superstition and enthusiasm.

This argument can also be read through the lens of political economy. Clergymen must preach that virtue and morality were reconcilable with luxury and commercial society. In his essay 'Of Luxury', which, after 1760, he renamed 'Of Refinement in the Arts', Hume defended the consumption of luxurious commodities as a practice that provided pleasure and encouraged sociability. It generated 'innocent gratification' and had further economic benefits as 'a kind of *storehouse* of labour'. It refined manners and polite society. There was 'an indissoluble chain' that connected '*industry, knowledge,* and *humanity*'. Calvinist asceticism was in Hume's sights. Luxury could be a vice when men forgot their duty and virtues like generosity. But 'no gratification, however sensual, can of itself be esteemed vicious', not least because

---

[103] *HE*, vol. 3, p. 433.
[104] *DNHR*, p. 182.

the operation of sympathy among humans allowed for moral approbation and disapprobation when luxury faded into vice.[105]

Further evidence of pastoral and pedagogical themes can be found within Hume's engagement with the Moderate Scottish clergy. Early in his career, he encountered William Leechman, who would become, from 1744, professor of divinity at Glasgow. In June 1743, Hume critiqued a sermon by Leechman on the nature, reasonableness, and advantages of prayer. Hume explained that he had 'read Mr Leechman's Sermon with a great deal of Pleasure, & think it a very good one'. It benefited from 'a very clear Manly expression' but Leechman 'does not consider his Ear enough, nor aim at a Style that may be smooth & harmonious; which, next to Perspicuity is the chief Ornament of Style'. Nevertheless, Hume thought Leechman pushed at the boundaries of true religion by placing such emphasis on prayer. 'Plato', Hume explained, 'says there are three kinds of Atheists. The first who deny a Deity, the second who deny his Providence, the third who assert, that he is influenc'd by Prayers or Sacrifices.' Leechman belonged in the third category. Hume objected to Leechman's emphasis on 'Devotion & Prayer' and 'to every thing we commonly call Religion, except the Practice of Morality, & the Assent of the Understanding to the Proposition *that God exists*'.[106]

The church establishment must also tolerate Dissent. Uniformity prevented progress and enlightenment. Persecution simply worsened grave enthusiasm and generated civil strife. In his *History of England*, Hume rehearsed the arguments in favour of toleration by discussing Cardinal Reginald Pole's campaign against Bishop Stephen Gardiner under Mary I. Hume argued that Pole was a man of 'learning, piety, and humanity'. Although he was 'very sincere in his religious principles', he had been suspected in Rome of lenience towards Lutheranism. Pole showed his 'moderation' by recommending 'a toleration of the heretical tenets'. Pole's defenders believed persecution and 'theological animosity, so fierce and violent', were 'the scandal of all religion'.[107]

No enterprise was more unfortunate than that of 'founding persecution upon policy, or endeavouring, for the sake of peace, to settle an entire uniformity of opinion, in questions which, of all others, are least subjected to the criterion of human reason'. Uniformity in belief might 'be owing at first to the stupid ignorance alone and barbarism of the people, who never indulge themselves in any speculation or enquiry', but that provided no expedient for 'banishing for ever all curiosity and all improvement in science and cultivation'. To aspire to the chimera of uniformity would expose people 'to all the abject terrors of superstition' and the magistrate 'to the endless encroachments of ecclesiastics'. It would render 'men so delicate, that they can never endure to hear of opposition; and they will some time pay dearly for that false tranquillity, in

---

[105] David Hume, 'Of Refinement in the Arts', in *Essays*, pp. 272, 271, 279.
[106] Hume to William Mure, [30 June 1743], in *New Letters*, pp. 10–13.
[107] *HE*, vol. 3, pp. 430–1.

which they have been so long indulged'. Once their principles were challenged, they would 'fly out into the most outrageous violence'. Persecution served 'to make men more obstinate in their persuasion, and to increase the number of their proselytes'.[108] It behove clergymen to cast a tolerant pose with religious heterodoxy. But there was another category of dissent with which clergymen needed to engage: the freethinker.

Clergymen and philosophers

Hume's civil religion complemented philosophy. He had gone to great lengths to identify superstition as the beastly product of the union of philosophy with theology. But religion, properly construed, concerned itself with the social relations of common life. It belonged to this world and it accepted its intellectual limits. All the 'philosophy, therefore, in the world, and all the religion, which is nothing but a species of philosophy, will never be able to carry us beyond the usual course of experience, or give us measures of conduct and behaviour different from those which are furnished by reflections on common life'.[109] It could not authoritatively make truth-claims about the origins and nature of the universe. If the philosophy of Hume's *Treatise* 'makes no addition to the arguments for religion', he believed he had 'at least the satisfaction to think it takes nothing from them, but that everything remains precisely as before'.[110] In considering such matters as the possibility of a world after this one, religion strayed into the realm of the speculative, the world of philosophy.

In this vein, Hume joined Rousseau in endorsing Machiavelli's famous condemnation of the otherworldliness of Christianity. In the *Discourses*, Machiavelli had argued that 'the peoples of ancient times were greater lovers of liberty than those of our own day'. Even though Christianity 'has shown us truth and the true path', it 'defined the supreme good as humility, abjection, and contempt of worldly things' whereas the ancient civil religions had 'located it in greatness of mind, strength of body, and in all the other things apt to make men the strongest'.[111] Hume referred to this passage in the *Natural History*. The doctrines of Roman Catholic Christianity with which Machiavelli had been acquainted, Hume concurred, 'which recommend only passive courage and suffering, had subdued the spirit of mankind, and had fitted them for slavery and subjection'. Machiavelli's observation, he continued, 'would certainly be just, were there not many other circumstances in human society which controul the genius and character of a religion'.[112] In the reformed church-state in Scotland and England that emerged during the decades following Machiavelli's death, it fell to the civil magistrate to determine those circumstances by the regulation of

---

[108] Ibid., pp. 432–3.
[109] Hume, *Human Understanding*, p. 197.
[110] Hume, *Treatise*, p. 164.
[111] Machiavelli, *Discourses*, pp. 158–9.
[112] *DNHR*, p. 164.

public religion. But Hume transformed the tone of Machiavellian civil religion from a civic defence of martial and active citizens serving the *grandezza* of the expansionary commonwealth into an Enlightened civil religion of politeness and sociability. Above all, argued Hume, 'the most genuine method of serving the divinity is by promoting the happiness of his creatures'.[113]

The activity of speculation belonged to philosophy. To flourish, philosophy needed 'entire liberty above all other privileges' in order that 'the free opposition of sentiments and argumentation' would proceed without the interposition of 'any creeds, confessions, or penal statutes'.[114] But philosophers must respect religion. In a particularly revealing letter in 1764, Hume wrote of the classical inspiration for philosophical prudence when discussing religious matters. 'It is putting too great a respect on the vulgar, and on their superstitions', he explained to James Edmonstoune, 'to pique one's self on sincerity with regard to them. Did ever one make it a point of honour to speak truth to children or madmen?' Hume continued that Xenophon had endorsed the Pythian oracle when it 'advised every one to worship the gods' for the good of the state. It was required by 'the common duties of society' and 'the ecclesiastical profession only adds a little more to an innocent dissimulation, or rather simulation, without which it is impossible to pass through the world'.[115] Religious tales were harmless when they were beliefs by which the commonality could live peacefully. In Ciceronian vein, officers of the state were prudent to entertain these tales because they were features of human nature and belonged to common life.

Hume attempted to live out the prudential and respectful distance between philosophers and clergymen. One such example occurred during the 1750s. In 1757 Hume wrote an open letter in which he defended John Home and his play *Douglas*. Hume noted 'the opposition, which prevails between us, with regard to many of our speculative tenets', since Home was attempting to create a rational version of natural religion based on the primitive gospel. But they both venerated 'liberty of thought' and maintained 'a mutual friendship and regard'.[116] Hume planned that the open letter should form the dedication in his *Four Dissertations*. James Harris has suggested that Hume intended to advance the Moderate cause by publishing the *Natural History* and the other essays alongside it.[117] But, on 20 January 1757, Hume instructed his publisher to remove the letter. He had shown it to some of his friends, 'Men of very good Sense, who were seiz'd with an Apprehension, that it wou'd hurt that Party in the Church, with which he [Home] had always been connected, and wou'd involve him, and them of Consequence, in the Suspicion of Infidelity'.[118] In the end, Hume decided that his Moderate

---

[113] Ibid., p. 181.
[114] Hume, *Human Understanding*, p. 187.
[115] Hume to Colonel James Edmonstoune, [April 1764], in *Letters*, vol. 1, p. 439.
[116] David Hume, 'To the Reverend Mr. Hume, Author of *Douglas*, a Tragedy', in Alice Edna Gipson, *John Home: A Study of His Life and Works* (Caldwell, ID, [1917]), pp. 88–9.
[117] Harris, *Hume*, pp. 355–64.
[118] Hume to Andrew Millar, 20 Jan. 1757, in *Letters*, vol. 1, pp. 239–40.

friends were overreacting and proceeded with publication. A similar example occurred while Hume was writing the *Treatise*. He wrote to Henry Home, the future Lord Kames, and explained that he had purged some thoughts concerning miracles from the text so as not to offend Joseph Butler, bishop of Bristol, when he came to read it. Hume had 'resolved not to be an enthusiast in philosophy, while I was blaming other enthusiasms'.[119]

However, there was more than simply Ciceronian prudence at stake. First, it is now clear that Hume believed it was to the Protestant Reformation that the philosopher owed his liberty as much as the Christian. Second, Hume saw in philosophy the basis upon which to construct true religion. Opening his essay 'Of Suicide', Hume claimed that one 'considerable advantage, that arises from philosophy, consists in the sovereign antidote, which it affords to superstition and false religion'.[120] In Part XII of the *Dialogues*, the sceptic, Philo, stated that among his 'unfeigned sentiments' was a 'veneration for true religion'. This stood alongside an 'abhorrence of vulgar superstitions' with their 'pernicious consequences on public affairs'. True religion was of 'the philosophical and rational kind'.[121] Philosophers and clergymen played complementary roles in constructing true religion. They were both agents in the generation of civil religion.

Philosophy chided religion when it made bold and superstitious claims just as religion chided philosophy when it risked tearing asunder the bonds of common life. Thomas Merrill has shown how Hume's philosophical project was to inform a polite, reading, gentlemanly culture that could mediate between religion and philosophy.[122] Hume's polite gentlemen, mild and moderate in their passions and sentiments, would occupy the same world as philosophers. They would remind philosophers of common life and avoid philosophical enthusiasm. During the 1730s, at least, Hume was optimistic that in England there were 'many honest gentlemen, who being always employ'd in their domestic affairs, or amusing themselves in common recreations, have carry'd their thoughts very little beyond those objects, which are every day expos'd to their senses'. These men 'I pretend not to make philosophers', Hume explained. Instead of 'refining them into philosophers, I wish we cou'd communicate to our founders of systems, a share of this gross earthly mixture'. They would temper 'those fiery particles' and 'a warm imagination' that took philosophy away from 'common practice and experience'.[123] Philosophical culture would exist peacefully within Christian society.

There were Baylean dimensions within this argument. John Robertson and James Harris have situated Hume in the context of the challenge set by Bayle

---

[119] Hume to Home, 2 Dec. 1737, in ibid., pp. 24–5.
[120] David Hume, 'Of Suicide', in *Essays*, p. 577.
[121] *DNHR*, pp. 121–2.
[122] See Merrill, *Hume and the Politics of the Enlightenment*, pp. 10–16, 22–9.
[123] Hume, *Treatise*, p. 177.

that a society of atheists was equally as plausible as a society of idolaters.[124] Part of Hume's project was to show that it was possible for philosophers to question the nature of the universal cause without disrupting morality and civil order. The Epicurean in the *Enquiry concerning Human Understanding* defended himself in front of the Athenians by stating that he opposed the 'religious philosophers' but not 'the tradition of your forefathers, and doctrine of your priests (in which I willingly acquiesce)', since 'philosophical disquisitions' need not undermine 'the foundations of society'.[125] Philosophers need simply realise that 'men reason not in the same manner' as they did, 'but draw many consequences from the belief of a divine Existence, and suppose that the Deity will inflict punishments on vice, and bestow rewards on virtue, beyond what appear in the ordinary course of nature'. Those who attacked tales of religion might be capable intellectuals. But they were not 'good citizens and politicians' because they 'free men from one restraint upon their passions, and make the infringement of the laws of equity and society, in one respect, more easy and secure'.[126]

It is in the mood provided by Hume, the philosopher, that conclusions may be drawn about Hume, the theorist of civil religion. Sher has warned against treating 'the brilliant but often idiosyncratic thought of David Hume as if it were the epitome of the age'.[127] In the field of civil religion in England and Scotland, Hume's thought was not representative. He was never willing to build the idea of true religion from normative claims in scripture. He never accepted the idea of natural religion inducted by reason and experience to which Scottish Moderates, Anglican latitudinarians, and deists proved amenable. Hume's civil religion was based upon the morality of virtue, sociability, and moderation inferred from his science of man. His use of the term 'true religion', signifying proper religion, involved the learned and pastoral teaching of the tales and traditions that a Ciceronian modern gentleman would respect in outward worship while giving no philosophical quarter to their truth-claims.

But to conclude that Hume was a pragmatic defender of the church-state relationship and its role in maintaining civil order and keeping the vulgar governable is to miss much of the point. In Hume's voluminous writings lay a commitment to the aspiration that Christian morality could be reconciled with civilised and polite society. Aside from the commonplace claim that Hume praised the ancient pagan civil religions, his reliance on the history of Christian reform provides evidence for Hume's commitment to a church order built within the civil state. His acceptance of religion as a feature of human nature went beyond a prudent philosopher offering prescriptions for managing religious sentiments. It represented a willingness to engage with Protestant,

---

[124] Robertson, *Case for the Enlightenment*, pp. 256–324; Harris, *Hume*, pp. 230–1. See also Alan Charles Kors, 'The French Context of Hume's Philosophical Theology', *HS*, 21:2 (1995), pp. 221–36.
[125] Hume, *Human Understanding*, p. 189.
[126] Ibid., p. 197.
[127] Sher, *Church and University*, p. 7.

especially Presbyterian, ecclesiology to purge the false religions of superstition and enthusiasm from political society. Irrespective of his own inward thoughts on religion, Hume recognised that philosophical freedom and the enlightenment and progress that attended it relied on the legacies of Christian reform.

5

The Legacy of Ancient Rome: Edward Gibbon and Conyers Middleton

The Church of England and the Antonines

In *Decline and Fall* and his other writings, Gibbon's conception of civil religion was as much pagan in focus as Christian. The relationship between religious belief and civil order underpinned Gibbon's analysis of ancient pagan society, Christian Rome, and modern Europe. He praised the worldliness and patriotism of Roman paganism as well as the moral perfection and spiritual purity of primitive Christianity. But he abjured corrupt religion, both pagan and Christian, and analysed it by distinguishing between superstition and enthusiasm.[1] To purge the world of corrupt religion, Gibbon hoped to regulate public religion through a church establishment. But his ecclesiology went far beyond pragmatic statements of the civil utility of an established faith. He hoped to maintain the status of the Church of England as the civil religion by defending its articles of faith. Its clergymen were public officeholders responsible for preaching the revealed faith in the reformed tradition. Gibbon's Church of England relied on the magisterial Reformation to remove sacerdotal priestliness from society. Clergymen would be learned in techniques of studying scripture, reversing the corruptions that were attached to Christianity during the centuries after Jesus Christ. Clergymen would also become pedagogical and pastoral, preaching a worldly morality based upon gospel Christianity, and providing public worship to undermine enthusiasm.

Traditionally, Gibbon has been associated with the Enlightenment conceived as 'the triumph of human reason' or 'the rise of modern paganism'.[2] Another strand of scholarship has cast Gibbon as, first, a Christian writer who, second,

---

[1] Pocock, 'Superstition and Enthusiasm'.
[2] See, for example, Harold L. Bond, *The Literary Art of Edward Gibbon* (Oxford, 1960), p. 160. Peter Gay described the contribution of Christianity to Gibbon's thought as 'modest and subterranean' in *Enlightenment*, vol. 1, p. 326. See also David Jordan, *Gibbon and His Roman Empire* (Urbana, 1971), p. 157.

defended the need for public worship.³ To focus primarily on Gibbon's inward faith is to obscure the role that he believed religion should play in society. Gibbon remained sceptical of the capacities of the human mind to comprehend the mysteries of the universe. Howsoever imperfect the articles of faith of the Church of England might have been, he did not believe they were perfectible in this world. Even if the elite philosopher or religionist doubted the veracity of the Thirty-Nine Articles, it behove them to respect the creed not simply as the lawful established religion but also to reinforce the beliefs of the laity, provided they did not endanger the safety and welfare of the civil state. Gibbon believed the intellectual liberty that marked his age was a direct product of the Protestant Reformation and its tendency to purge society of superstitious priestliness and frenzied enthusiasm. To suppose that Gibbon was a modern pagan who sneered ironically at the deluded vulgar from the comfort of his desk is to risk neglecting his belief that Christianity, on primitive principles, could be rendered a modern civil religion by means of the magisterial Reformation.

Pocock has briefly entertained the possibility that Gibbon was constructing a civil religion.[4] Curiously, Pocock did not pursue the theme in his marathon study of the European contexts for Gibbon.[5] Nevertheless, Pocock has demonstrated that, by choosing to begin *Decline and Fall* with the age of the Roman Antonine emperors, between the raising of Nerva to the principate by the assassins of Domitian in AD 96 and prior to the accession, in AD 161, of Commodus, whose misrule led to his strangling in AD 192, Gibbon idealised the religious settlement of that period.[6] By analysing the decline of paganism, Pocock's Gibbon acted as witness to the end of worldly religion, civic virtue, and patriotism. Thus, the role of religion in stabilising, destroying or reconstituting the fabric of civil society became a central concern of *Decline and Fall*.[7]

---

[3] Joseph Swain, *Edward Gibbon the Historian* (London, 1966), p. 65; Owen Chadwick, 'Gibbon and the Church Historians', in G. W. Bowersock, John Clive, and Stephen Graubard (eds), *Edward Gibbon and the Decline and Fall of the Roman Empire* (Cambridge, MA, 1977), pp. 219–31, at p. 221; Martin Price, '"The Dark and Implacable Genius of Superstition": An Aspect of Gibbon's Irony', in J. C. Hilson, M. M. B. Jones, and J. R. Watson (eds), *Augustan Worlds: Essays in Honour of A. R. Humphreys* (Leicester, 1978), pp. 241–59; David Dillon Smith, 'Gibbon in Church', *JEH*, 35:3 (1984), pp. 452–63; Paul Turnbull, 'The "Supposed Infidelity" of Edward Gibbon', *HJ*, 25:1 (1982), pp. 23–41; 'Gibbon and Pastor Allamand', *JRH*, 16:3 (1991), pp. 280–91; 'Gibbon's Exchange with Priestley', *BJECS*, 14:2 (1991), pp. 139–58.
[4] J. G. A. Pocock, 'Gibbon and the Primitive Church', in Stefan Collini, Richard Whatmore, and Brian Young (eds), *History, Religion, and Culture: British Intellectual History, 1750–1950* (Cambridge, 2000), pp. 48–68, at pp. 59–60; 'Between Machiavelli and Hume: Gibbon as Civic Humanist and Philosophical Historian', *Daedalus*, 105:3 (1976), pp. 152–69, at p. 153. See also Peter Ghosh, 'Gibbon's First Thoughts: Rome, Christianity and the *Essai sur l'Etude de la Littérature*, 1758–61', *Journal of Roman Studies*, 85 (1995), pp. 148–64.
[5] Pocock, *Barbarism and Religion*.
[6] Pocock, 'Superstition and Enthusiasm', p. 93; 'Gibbon's *Decline and Fall* and the World View of the Late Enlightenment', in *Virtue, Commerce, and History*, pp. 143–56.
[7] Pocock, 'Superstition and Enthusiasm', p. 83.

To understand how Gibbon hoped to construct Christian civil religion, it is necessary to rehearse his admiration for Roman paganism alongside his support for primitive Christianity. In pagan Rome, the 'ancient fabric' of religion created by the legendary second king of Rome, Numa, enjoyed the legitimacy of 'the opinions and habits of eleven hundred years'. Gibbon described a benign and tolerant religion of the state, whose officers served simultaneously in temporal and spiritual offices. Between the ages of Numa and the Christian emperor, Gratian, whose reign began in AD 367, thirty years after the death of Constantine, the majesty of priests 'attracted the admiration of the people'. Prior to the establishment of Christianity, the priestly order 'received, from consecrated lands, and the public revenue, an ample stipend, which liberally supported the splendour of the priesthood, and all the expences of the religious worship of the state'.[8] Even sceptics entertained the superstitions of the plebeians. Notwithstanding 'the fashionable irreligion of the Antonines', both 'the interests of the priests and the credulity of the people were sufficiently respected'.[9]

The pagan establishment remained worldly and civic. The 'service of the altar was not incompatible with the command of armies'. Romans, 'after their consulships and triumphs, aspired to the place of pontiff, or of augur'. The model represented the achievement of *religio* without *superstitio*, for 'the seats of Cicero and Pompey were filled, in the fourth century, by the most illustrious members of the senate' while 'the dignity of their birth reflected additional splendour on their sacerdotal character'.[10] The parallel with the eighteenth-century Church of England was obvious. It was not simply crucial that the priesthood should be properly respected by means of establishment. It was essential for those to whom latitude had been extended for philosophical and theological speculation that they revered the established religion irrespective of their inward thoughts about its doctrines.

Gibbon exemplified the strengths of the pagan establishment in the person of the senator, Quintus Aurelius Symmachus, who praised it for having 'reduced the world under my laws'. Its rites had 'repelled Hannibal from the city, and the Gauls from the Capitol'. Symmachus criticised the confiscation of church revenues because it risked undermining the externals of worship. Ceremonies might lose 'their force and energy, if they were no longer celebrated at the expence, as well as in the name, of the republic'. Symmachus was a tolerant sceptic who accepted that the 'great and incomprehensible *secret* of the universe' stood beyond human inquiry. Since religious mysteries could not be resolved by reason, they were matters of faith. Where 'reason cannot instruct, custom may be permitted to guide'. Every nation 'seems to consult the dictates of prudence, by a faithful attachment to those rites, and opinions, which have received the sanction of ages'.[11]

---

[8] *DF*, vol. 2, p. 73.
[9] Ibid., vol. 1, p. 58.
[10] Ibid., vol. 2, p. 73.
[11] Ibid., p. 75.

In addition to such men as Symmachus, Gibbon believed the age of the Antonines represented the height of Roman grandeur. If a man 'were called to fix the period in the history of the world, during which the condition of the human race was most happy and prosperous, he would, without hesitation, name that which elapsed from the death of Domitian to the accession of Commodus'.[12] After the age of the Antonines, paganism began to collapse. Philosophers and Roman elites had hitherto respected the superstitions of the poor and revered the instituted religion by keeping their speculations to themselves. In public, the 'philosophic part of mankind affected to treat with respect and decency the religious institutions of their country'. Their scepticism was private and politic; it simply elevated the faculties of the mind. However, for their more foolish peers, imprudent scepticism became the vogue. The 'fashion of incredulity' passed from the philosopher 'to the man of pleasure or business, from the noble to the plebeian, and from the master to the menial slave who waited at his table, and who eagerly listened to the freedom of his conversation'.[13] Roman civil religion collapsed through the spread of fashionable scepticism from elite to plebeian.

These might seem to be reflections of the modern pagan. However, Gibbon approved of another ancient model of religion. Prior to the progress of Christian superstition during the centuries following Jesus Christ and the first apostles, Gibbon wrote of 'the pure and perfect simplicity of the Christian model'.[14] The religion propagated by Christ was spiritually simple. It lacked religious mysteries, dogmas, superstition or enthusiasm. It presupposed an equality between religious believers and instituted no ecclesiological hierarchies. Although its focus was the prospect of rewards and punishments in the next world, primitive Christianity respected Rome's laws and church-state relationship. Gibbon admired 'the pure and holy precepts of the Gospel'.[15] In church government, 'the pure and spiritual worship of a Christian congregation' presumed a fundamental equality among its members.[16] Gibbon praised 'the purity of the Christian religion, the sanctity of its moral precepts, and the innocent as well as austere lives of the greater number of those, who during the first ages embraced the faith of the gospel'. It was a 'benevolent' doctrine and its adherents 'yielded the most passive obedience to the laws, though they declined the active cares of war and government'.[17] However, much like Roman paganism, corruption would come to despoil the new religion.

---

[12] Ibid., vol. 1, p. 103.
[13] Ibid., p. 498.
[14] Ibid., vol. 2, p. 92.
[15] Ibid., vol. 1, p. 523.
[16] Ibid., vol. 2, p. 96.
[17] Ibid., vol. 1, p. 514.

Corrupt Christianity

The ill fate of pagan civil religion had been occasioned by the spread of fashionable scepticism that undermined reverence for the customary beliefs of Roman society. But Gibbon gave different reasons for the corruption of primitive Christianity. In a standard Protestant argument, Gibbon believed corrupt Christianity had been caused by the reduction of the mind from pious contemplation of the universal cause to superstitious idolatry. The imagination 'eagerly embraced such inferior objects of adoration, as were more proportioned to its gross conceptions and imperfect faculties'. The 'sublime and simple theology of the primitive Christians' had been 'gradually corrupted' by the introduction of a 'popular mythology which tended to restore the reign of polytheism'.[18] Gibbon's remark is striking, since it was a commonplace Protestant criticism of Roman Catholicism that its collections of martyrs, saints, and shrines amounted to little more than superstitious polytheism.

Although the demise of paganism, an 'ancient and popular superstition', was a 'singular event in the history of the human mind', it bequeathed a legacy to Christianity.[19] Gibbon invoked the name of Middleton and his *Letter from Rome* (1729) in discussing how Roman emperors and the Christian hierarchy deliberately borrowed pagan rituals and practices to sanctify the new religion following its establishment by Constantine.[20] Middleton was a clergyman and Fellow of Trinity College, Cambridge, whose grand tour during the 1720s had occasioned his *Letter from Rome*. In travelling to Rome, Middleton had hoped 'to visit the genuine Remains and *venerable Reliques of Pagan Rome*' and to contemplate 'the greatest Men that ever lived'. He sought amusement 'with the Thoughts of taking a turn in those very Walks where Cicero and his Friend had held *their Philosophical Disputations*, or standing in that very Spot, where he had delivered some of his *famous Orations*'. Instead, Middleton encountered those sights linked with St Peter and was forced to spend his 'Time Abroad attending to ridiculous Fictions of this kind'.[21]

Over the course of the *Letter from Rome*, Middleton hoped to expose 'the true Spring and Source of those Impostures, which, under the Name of Religion,

---

[18] Ibid., vol. 2, pp. 95–6.
[19] Ibid., p. 71.
[20] Ibid., p. 97, n. 90. For Middleton, see Ted A. Campbell, 'John Wesley and Conyers Middleton on Divine Intervention in History', *Church History*, 55:1 (1986), pp. 39–49; Robert G. Ingram, '"The Weight of Historical Evidence": Conyers Middleton and the Eighteenth-Century Miracles Debate', in Robert D. Cornwall and William Gibson (eds), *Religion, Politics and Dissent, 1660–1832: Essays in Honour of James E. Bradley* (Farnham, 2010), pp. 85–109; Hugh Trevor-Roper, 'From Deism to History: Conyers Middleton', in Hugh Trevor-Roper, *History and the Enlightenment* (New Haven, 2010), pp. 71–119; B. W. Young, 'Conyers Middleton: The Historical Consequences of Orthodoxy', in Robertson and Mortimer (eds), *Intellectual Consequences of Religious Heterodoxy*, pp. 235–65, at p. 241; Ingram, *Reformation without End*, chs 6–9; Stuart-Buttle, *From Moral Theology to Moral Philosophy*, ch. 4.
[21] Conyers Middleton, *A Letter from Rome* (London, 1729), pp. 11–12.

have been forged and contrived from Time to Time for no other Purpose, than to oppress the Liberty, as well as engross, the Property of Mankind'.[22] In *A Free Inquiry into the Miraculous Powers* (1749), Middleton explained that he aspired to 'free the minds of men from an inveterate imposture, which, through a long succession of ages, has disgraced the religion of the Gospel, and tyrannized over the reason and senses of the Christian world'.[23] Part of this project was the exposure of the corrupt pagan superstitions that had passed to the early church. Pagan rites and worship once condemned by primitive Christians as superstitious and profane became the ceremonies and forms of the Roman Catholic Church. Those practices that wise Roman pagans like Seneca and Cicero had seen as mere folly, 'too gross even for *Ægyptian Idolatry* to swallow', had become 'the *principal Part of Worship*' and 'distinguishing *Article of Faith*'.[24] This corrupt religion stood in contrast with pure gospel Christianity.

Like Middleton, whose grand tour had occasioned the *Letter*, Gibbon had visited Rome as a youth and imagined the city's ancient past.[25] Gibbon described how Christians 'imitated the profane model which they were impatient to destroy'. They were 'insensibly subdued by the arts of their vanquished rivals'. They inherited the 'same uniform original spirit of superstition'. Roman rituals, including 'luminaries, garlands, frankincense, and libations of wine', were taken up. The 'Christian emperors condescended to accept the robe and ensigns, which were appropriated to the office of the supreme pontiff'.[26]

The infiltration of Roman paganism was not the only source of spiritual corruption. 'In the profession of Christianity,' Gibbon explained, 'the variety of national characters may be distinguished.' Whereas the 'natives of Syria and Egypt abandoned their lives to lazy and contemplative devotion', Romans 'aspired to the dominion of the world' and 'the wit of the lively and loquacious Greeks was consumed in the disputes of metaphysical theology'.[27] Each of these national characters had left their mark. But, much like Shaftesbury and Bolingbroke, whose reliance on Josephus and Tacitus for the history of the Hebrews Gibbon shared, Gibbon's account of the corruptions of early Christianity shaded into slights on the ancient Jewish nation.[28] The character of the Jewish worship had been the opposite of Roman civil religion. Gibbon contrasted the '*pacific system*' of Hadrian and the two Antonine emperors that led to forty-three years of peace

---

[22] Ibid., p. 3.
[23] Conyers Middleton, *A Free Inquiry into the Miraculous Powers, which are Supposed to have Subsisted in the Christian Church, from the Earliest Ages through Several Centuries* (London, 1749), p. xxxi.
[24] Middleton, *Letter from Rome*, p. 44.
[25] Gibbon, *Memoirs*, p. 146.
[26] *DF*, vol. 2, pp. 97, 86, 73.
[27] Ibid., vol. 3, p. 423.
[28] Ralph Lerner, 'Gibbon's Jewish Problem', in Ralph Lerner, *Naïve Readings: Reveilles Political and Philosophic* (Chicago, 2016), pp. 92–118. For Gibbon's use of Josephus and Tacitus in Jewish history, see his *Vindication. DF*, vol. 3, pp. 1116–24.

with 'the desperate fanaticism of the Jews'.[29] The Jews and their 'religious fury' destroyed the peace of the age with rebellion.[30]

Jewish insistence on their elect status, 'their lofty claim of superior sanctity', drove the superstition and intolerance of 'their unsocial religion'.[31] Christians learned the art of superstitious persecution from them. 'The inflexible, and, if we may use the expression, the intolerant zeal of the Christians, derived, it is true, from the Jewish religion,' Gibbon argued, 'but purified from the narrow and unsocial spirit, which, instead of inviting, had deterred the Gentiles from embracing the law of Moses.' Christians 'were all equally animated by the same exclusive zeal, and by the same abhorrence for idolatry which had distinguished the Jews from the other nations of the ancient world'.[32] The Jews and Christians formed 'a very important exception' to the religious toleration that attended '*the Union and internal Prosperity*' of the Antonine age.[33]

Alongside Roman and Jewish superstition, the importation of Greek philosophy had also subverted the pure and simple religion of the gospel. Christian mysteries were increasingly explained by reference to abstruse Platonism as Athens and Jerusalem became the same city. Irrelevant and trivial debates over the incarnation and the Trinity were 'alike scandalous to the church, alike pernicious to the state' because Christians 'were more solicitous to explore the nature, than to practise the laws, of their founder' over these unknowable mysteries.[34] The concern with Greek corruption aroused Gibbon's most infamous condemnation of the council of Nicaea when a dispute emerged over the divinity of Christ. He derided 'the furious contests which the differences of a single diphthong excited between the Homoousians and Homoiousians'.[35] Heresy had come to depend on one iota as the council favoured *homoousios*, meaning consubstantial, over *homoiousios*, denoting that Christ was of similar substance as God.

Much of Gibbon's ire was reserved for the Athanasian creed. He criticised those Christians, both Roman Catholic and reformed, who 'freely adopted the theology of the four, or the six first councils' and used the creed to pronounce 'the eternal damnation of all who did not believe the Catholic faith'.[36] The irony was that such contention was not necessary for Christian faith. These were Christian mysteries and were unknowable without revelation. Human reason 'by its unassisted strength is incapable of perceiving the mysteries of faith'.[37] In any event, such mysteries were not an essential of faith laid out in the gospel. Christ had achieved conversions from among the heathens 'in peace and piety'. But

---

[29] *DF*, vol. 1, pp. 37, 454.
[30] Ibid., p. 38, n. 27.
[31] Ibid., pp. 517–18.
[32] Ibid., pp. 447, 459.
[33] Ibid., pp. 57, n. 3, and 56.
[34] Ibid., vol. 2, p. 932.
[35] Ibid., vol. 1, p. 787.
[36] Ibid., vol. 3, p. 436.
[37] Ibid., vol. 1, p. 498.

the later spiritual conquerors of the Roman Catholic Church showed that 'the principle of discord was alive in their bosom'.[38]

Corrupt Christianity was also an otherworldly religion. The Roman state had not oriented the focus of primitive Christianity towards secular concerns even though primitive Christians had respected the civil laws of the Roman Empire and had not tried to create a separate society. As Christianity grew corrupt, Gibbon explained in *A Vindication of Some Passages in the Fifteenth and Sixteenth Chapters* (1779), the problem ran deeper. Prior to the accretion of Roman and Jewish superstition as well as Greek philosophy, the 'errors of the primitive Christians' were tactical rather than doctrinal. Primitive Christians imprudently 'exposed themselves to the reproaches of the Pagans', he claimed, 'by their obstinate refusal to take an active part in the civil administration, or military defence of the empire'.[39] By contrast, 'the Roman discipline was connected with the national superstition'. A solemn oath of fidelity was yearly given in the name of the gods and the emperor. Public sacrifices were daily performed in the camps.[40] Gibbon glossed the response of Ambrose, bishop of Milan, to pleas like those of Symmachus for the need for religion to strike a worldly pose. Ambrose asked 'with some contempt' why it was considered necessary 'to introduce an imaginary and invisible power as the cause of those victories, which were sufficiently explained by the valour and discipline of the legions'.[41]

Mystery and corruption made Christianity ever more otherworldly. Concern with the increasingly complex prospect of rewards and punishments in the next life involved withdrawal from civil life and, worse, asceticism. Gibbon's Romans mouthed the criticism of Machiavelli that Christianity had left men weak. The pagan Eunapius witnessed the replacement of 'those deities, who are conceived by the understanding' by men who were 'the meanest and most contemptible slaves'. Monks consecrated tombs 'as the objects of the veneration of the people'.[42] Christians descended to more ridiculous levels of superstition than pagans, as fictions were composed to legitimise sanctified relics, heroes fabricated for martyrdom, and basic standards of reason enervated. Eventually, 'something was still deemed wanting to the sanctity of a Christian church, till it had been consecrated by some portion of holy relics, which fixed and inflamed the devotion of the faithful'.[43]

Gibbon condemned the ascetic incivility of Christianity in a classic Protestant criticism of monasticism. Monks abused 'the rigid precepts of the gospel'. They were 'inspired by the savage enthusiasm which represented man as a criminal, and God as a tyrant'. Monastic practice relied on the false understanding of man

[38] Ibid., vol. 2, p. 932.
[39] Ibid., vol. 3, pp. 1162–3.
[40] Ibid., p. 1166.
[41] Ibid., vol. 2, p. 76.
[42] Ibid., p. 90.
[43] Ibid., p. 92.

in the earthly city as broken and corrupt.[44] Monasticism represented the depths to which barbarism might plunge. Monks destroyed 'the sensibility of both the mind and body'. A 'cruel, unfeeling temper has distinguished the monks of every age and country'. They were 'inflamed by religious hatred; and their merciless zeal has strenuously administered the holy office of the Inquisition'.[45] The faculties of the mind and their relationship with nature were now mistrusted and abused as 'every sensation that is offensive to man, was thought acceptable to God'.[46] Platonism had especially provided intellectual props for such corruption. Criticising the hyper-Platonist cult of denial of the physical and sensual based on the idea of the community of goods, Gibbon sardonically observed how a monk denied himself meat but might make a scholastic distinction to enable eating fowl 'as if birds, wild or domestic, had been less profane than the grosser animals of the field'.[47]

However, the otherworldliness of Christianity was not inevitable. The worldliness of its early professors became clear in its developing ecclesiastical hierarchies. Although Christians had been 'dead to the business and pleasures of the world', their 'love of action, which could never be entirely distinguished', soon found occupation in 'the government of the church' as a 'separate society, which attacked the established religion of the empire'. This separate society was obliged to adopt 'some form of internal policy'. It appointed 'a sufficient number of ministers, instrusted not only with the spiritual functions, but even with the temporal direction of the Christian commonwealth'.[48] The safety, honour, and aggrandisement of that society 'were productive, even in the most pious minds, of a spirit of patriotism'. Among church governors, the 'ambition of raising themselves or their friends to the honours and offices of the church' was disguised by 'the laudable intention of devoting to the public benefit, which, for that purpose only, it became their duty to solicit'. The 'ecclesiastical governors of the Christians' were instructed 'to unite the wisdom of the serpent with the innocence of the dove'. In the 'church as well as in the world', it was the attributes of 'eloquence and firmness', 'knowledge of mankind', and 'dexterity in business' that advanced ecclesiastical governors as they realised 'the turbulent passions of active life'.[49]

---

[44] Ibid., p. 411.
[45] Ibid., pp. 427–8.
[46] Ibid., p. 420.
[47] Ibid., p. 421. For Gibbon's claim that the primitive Christians, for a time, adopted a Platonist community of goods and sold 'those worldly possessions, which they despised', see ibid., vol. 1, pp. 490–1.
[48] Ibid., vol. 1, pp. 482–3.
[49] Ibid., p. 483.

Separate societies and sacerdotal power

The development of church hierarchies aroused the latent worldliness among Christians. But their concern with the realities of this life had resulted not in love of the Roman state but in the idea of the church as a separate society distinct from the civil state. This love subverted primitive principles. Gibbon quipped that modern 'hostile disputants' of Rome, Paris, Oxford, and Geneva had alike 'struggled to reduce the primitive and gospel model' to 'their own policy'. The few candid and impartial inquirers, like the German Lutheran ecclesiastical historian Johann Lorenz von Mosheim (1693–1755), argued that the apostles 'declined the office of legislation' for earthly church government. The apostles refused 'to exclude the Christians of a future age from the liberty of varying their forms of ecclesiastical government according to the changes of times and circumstances'.[50] The apostles recognised that Christ's kingdom was not of this world and did not hand down *jure divino* authority to future Christian ministers.

Gibbon relied not only on Mosheim but also on Hooker's *Ecclesiastical Polity* in describing apostolic ecclesiology. The apostolic model was adopted during the first century in Jerusalem, Ephesus, and Corinth. It was governed by 'faith and charity' and 'Independence and equality'. Primitive Christians had realised the need to regulate public worship. The 'public functions of religion' were 'solely intrusted to the established ministers of the church, the *bishops* and the *presbyters*'. Bishops inspected 'the faith and manners of the Christians who were committed to their pastoral care'. Since 'the most perfect equality of freedom requires the directing hand of a superior magistrate' and 'the order of public deliberations soon introduces the office of a president', primitive Christians instituted an 'honourable and perpetual magistracy'.[51] The jurisdiction of bishops consisted in maintaining the administration, sacraments, and discipline of the church, superintending religious ceremonies, consecrating ministers, managing the public funds of the church, and judging doctrinal disputes. These powers were exercised according to the advice of a college of presbyters with 'the consent and approbation of the assembly of Christians'. The first bishops were *primus inter pares* and 'the honourable servants of a free people'. Such was 'the mild and equal constitution by which the Christians were governed more than an hundred years after the death of the apostles'.[52]

But this simple system of *jure humano* appointments based on the equality of Christian believers was eventually subverted by a corrupt hierarchy using fabricated *jure divino* claims to authority. Invoking the authority of Mosheim and Ezekiel, Freiherr von Spanheim, the Swiss philologist and theologian, Gibbon noted that the progress of ecclesiastical authority 'gave birth to the memorable distinction of the laity and of the clergy, which had been unknown to the Greeks and Romans'. In its truest appellation, the distinction separated 'the body of the

---

[50] Ibid.
[51] Ibid., p. 484.
[52] Ibid., pp. 484–5.

Christian people' from 'the chosen portion that had been set apart for the service of religion'. That portion formed 'a celebrated order of men'. But the Christian hierarchy went much further. The clergy disturbed 'the peace of the infant church' by uniting 'their zeal and activity' with their 'love of power' in order 'to enlarge the limits of the Christian empire'. To secure their ascendancy, they acquired 'the two most efficacious instruments of government': the prospect of 'rewards and punishments'.[53]

Soon the 'lofty title of Bishop began to raise itself' even though the 'pious and humble' presbyters who first received the episcopal title 'would probably have rejected, the power and pomp which now encircles the tiara of the Roman pontiff, or the mitre of a German prelate'.[54] The opportunity for bishops to aggrandise themselves came with the convenience of uniting widespread and diverse Christian communities. As Mosheim had explained, the institution of provincial synods comprising bishops and senior presbyters, observed still by 'a listening multitude', fused the 'separate and independent' republics of Christians by canonical decrees into a greater union, 'a great fœderative republic' and a catholic church.[55] As the councils superseded particular churches in legislative authority, the bishops began to gain 'a much larger share of executive and arbitrary power'. They started 'to attack, with united vigour, the original rights of their clergy and people'.[56]

By the third century, the language of 'command' had replaced that of 'exhortation'. The 'earthly claim to a transitory dominion' of princes and magistrates was overshadowed by the corrupt doctrine of *jure divino* episcopacy. Bishops had become 'the vicegerents of Christ, the successors of the apostles, and the mystic substitutes of the high priest of the Mosaic law'. Their 'exclusive privilege of conferring the sacerdotal character' invaded 'the freedom both of clerical and of popular elections'. Thus were scattered 'the seeds of future usurpations'.[57] Where the lower clergy and laity resisted episcopal usurpation, 'their patriotism received the ignominious epithets of faction and schism'.[58]

Among the bishops, there also began a competition for pre-eminence. As the Christian community grew, provincial synods were notable for 'the difference of personal merit and reputation'. Ambitious bishops seized the 'lofty titles of Metropolitans and Primates' and began to usurp power from their episcopal brethren. They affected 'to display, in the most pompous terms, the temporal honours and advantages of the city' over which they presided; 'the numbers and opulence of the Christians who were subject over their pastoral care'; the 'saints and martyrs who had arisen among them'; and 'the purity with which they preserved the tradition of the faith, as it had been transmitted through a

---

[53] Ibid., p. 490.
[54] Ibid., pp. 484–5.
[55] Ibid., pp. 486–7.
[56] Ibid., p. 487.
[57] Ibid.
[58] Ibid., p. 488.

series of orthodox bishops from the apostle of the apostolic disciple, to whom the foundation of their church was ascribed'.[59]

Given every other cause 'of a civil or of an ecclesiastical nature', it was predictable that the bishop of Rome would come to dominate his episcopal brethren.[60] Instead of recalling the church government of the early apostles and primitive Christians at Antioch, Ephesus, and Corinth, the bishops of Rome began to assert that Saint Peter had been 'most eminent among the apostles', and 'very prudently claimed the inheritance of whatsoever prerogatives were attributed either to the person or to the office of St. Peter'.[61] They began to formulate doctrines of excommunication and penance as 'the most essential part of religion'. It quickly became 'much less dangerous for the disciples of Christ to neglect the observance of the moral duties, than to despise the censures and authority of their bishops'.[62] Petrine 'sacerdotal monarchy' had become the basis for papal supremacy.[63] During the 'ages of ignorance which followed the subversion of the Roman Empire in the West', bishops of Rome 'extended their dominion over the laity as well as clergy of the Latin church'.[64]

The practice of tithing aided the growth of sacerdotal power and papal dominion. Despite an early flirtation with the idea of a Platonist community of goods, primitive Christians had retained 'their patrimony ... legacies and inheritances [and] ... separate property by all the lawful means of trade and industry'. In the language of Christian political economy, Gibbon believed primitive Christianity had been compatible with worldly wealth. Of their incomes, Christians voluntarily gave a 'moderate proportion' to 'the ministers of the gospel'. During assemblies, 'every believer, according to the exigency of the occasion, and the measure of his wealth and piety, presented his voluntary offering for use of the common fund'.[65] But Christians in and around Rome, the metropole, 'were possessed of a very considerable wealth'. It was said that 'vessels of gold and silver were used in their religious worship' and 'many among their proselytes had sold their lands and houses to increase the public riches of the sect'. There the pursuit of worldly wellbeing had been destroyed by superstitious idolatry. The children of Christians in Rome 'found themselves beggars' because 'their parents had been saints'.[66]

Across Rome, laws, 'which were enacted with the same design as our statutes of mortmain', decreed that no landed property be given to any corporate body. However, Roman senators and emperors, such as Alexander Severus, had waived this prohibition within the city of Rome. By the end of the third century,

---

[59] Ibid.
[60] Ibid.
[61] Ibid., p. 489.
[62] Ibid., p. 496.
[63] Ibid., vol. 3, p. 109.
[64] Ibid., vol. 1, p. 580.
[65] Ibid., pp. 490–1.
[66] Ibid., p. 491.

substantial estates had been bestowed upon 'opulent churches' especially in the capital. Having seized control of its apparatus, bishops employed deacons solely 'in the management and distribution of the ecclesiastical revenue'. The 'evangelic perfection' of the early church and all 'moral virtue' were destroyed.[67]

As the Roman Empire collapsed, it bequeathed its corrupt ecclesiastical structure of popes and sacerdotal priests to the medieval world. It was through Pietro Giannone's *Civil History of Naples* (1723), Gibbon recalled in his memoirs, that he 'observed with a critical eye the progress and abuse of sacerdotal power, and the revolutions of Italy in the dark ages'.[68] In Germany, Gibbon argued in his essay, 'Outlines of the History of the World', the popes of the twelfth century 'prevailed against their ancient Sovereigns, the Emperors of Germany'. Henry IV was deprived of his dominions and Henry V, keen to avoid a similar fate, resigned the contested right of investiture in 1121. The 'Fictitious Donation of Constantine, and the Will of Matilda' were asserted by popes against the lower clergy and princes. Gibbon continued this account of papal domination through the war between Frederick I, Barbarossa, and Pope Alexander II.[69] To Innocent III Gibbon ascribed the loftiest pretensions. Although all Roman pontiffs reserved the title of a 'Universal Monarchy, Temporal and Spiritual; and maintained that all their inferior Powers, Emperors, Kings, Bishops, derived from the Chair of St Peter their delegated Authority', Innocent established the doctrine of transubstantiation and the Inquisition.[70]

Gibbon aligned himself with a mainstream critique of the domination of the bishop of Rome in seventeenth-century English Protestant and French Gallican polemic by emphasising the pope's deposing power against the last Merovingian king, Childeric III (*c*. 717–*c*. 754). Gibbon drew on the seventeenth-century French Jansenist, Jean de Launoy, and the ecclesiastical historians, Antoine Pagi and Noël Alexandre, in writing that the 'feeble' Childeric had overseen chaos and sedition during his reign. But the nobility was bound by an oath of fidelity that made his blood 'pure and sacred'. Pope Zachary acceded to their request to depose Childeric, who, 'a victim of public safety', was 'degraded, shaved, and confined in a monastery for the remainder of his days'.[71] Pepin, the first of the Carolingians who had conspired with Zachary, gained the throne. The 'mutual obligations of the popes and the Carolingian family' formed 'the important link of ancient and modern, of civil and ecclesiastical, history'. It was the apex of compacts between tyrannous bishops and their quisling kings. The Carolingians received 'a favourable occasion, a specious title, the wishes of the people, the prayers and intrigues of the clergy'.[72]

---

[67] Ibid., pp. 492–3.
[68] Gibbon, *Memoirs*, p. 201.
[69] Edward Gibbon, *The English Essays of Edward Gibbon*, ed. Patricia Craddock (Oxford, 1972), p. 165.
[70] Ibid., p. 176.
[71] *DF*, vol. 3, p. 110.
[72] Ibid., p. 109.

The battle against sacerdotal and papal tyranny was yet to be won. While studying in Lausanne as a youth, Gibbon began to engage in the Protestant history of Roman Catholic corruption and medieval Christian reform. His observations, taken together, form a Foxean impression of celebrating the antecedents of the Reformation. He discussed the rivalry between Pope Boniface VIII and Philip the Fair, which had provided one context for the *Defensor Pacis* of Marsilius. During the dispute, 'the greater part of the French Clergy remembered that they were subjects as well as Priests' and the crown was, 'in some degree, delivered from a servile dependence on a foreign Prelate'.[73] Gibbon studied the relationship between revenues and power in the early-medieval papacy.[74] He explored the Guelph-Ghibelline wars.[75] His early studies opened him to Sarpi, who 'was very favourably disposed for a Reformation in General, tho' he dissapprooved of the violent proceedings of many who bore that name'. In the dispute between the Venetian republic and Paul V during the early seventeenth century, Sarpi 'was well disposed for an entire rupture with the Church of Rome'.[76] The 'fabric of superstition' that upheld papal supremacy and 'might long have defied the feeble efforts of reason', Gibbon noted in *Decline and Fall*, would be assaulted by 'a crowd of daring fanatics, who, from the twelfth to the sixteenth century, assumed the popular character of reformers'. They resisted 'the empire' that the church of Rome had gained 'by fraud'.[77]

The Protestant Reformation represented the first successful attempt to rid Christianity of the superstitious and priestly accretions that had attended it since the rise of episcopal power in the Roman Empire. Gibbon's account of the Reformation took place in chapter 54 of *Decline and Fall* in which he briefly pursued his history of superstition and the church into the medieval period. He first noted 'the strong, though secret, discontent which armed the most pious Christians against the church of Rome'. Reformers confronted a 'despotic, oppressive, and odious' Roman Catholic hierarchy whose innovations had been 'rapid and scandalous'. The 'fearless enthusiasts' of the early Reformation brought to the ground 'the lofty fabric of superstition, from the abuse of indulgences to the intercession of the Virgin'. Those who might have been condemned to the monasteries and nunneries 'were restored to the liberty and labours of social life'. The hierarchy of saints, angels, and deities were 'stripped of their temporal power, and reduced to the enjoyment of celestial happiness'. Images and relics were removed and the 'credulity of the people' was no longer fed by miracles and visions.[78]

It was ironic that Gibbon argued that a Christian sect, known as the Paulicians, which had originated in the seventh century and whose dualism

[73] Gibbon, *English Essays*, p. 183.
[74] Ibid., pp. 17–18.
[75] Ibid., p. 20.
[76] Ibid., p. 24.
[77] *DF*, vol. 1, p. 580.
[78] Ibid., vol. 3, p. 434.

and Manicheanism relied on neo-Platonist theology, had led the opposition to ecclesiastical formalism. The success of the Paulicians during the eleventh and twelfth centuries occasioned the genesis of the Reformation. In 'the state, in the church, and even in the cloister', wrote Gibbon, 'a latent succession was preserved of the disciples of St. Paul; who protested against the tyranny of Rome, embraced the Bible as a rule of faith, and purified their creed from all the visions of the Gnostic theology'. The next group of church reformers was better known: 'The struggles of Wickliff in England, of Huss in Bohemia, were premature and ineffectual; but the names of Zuinglius, Luther, and Calvin, are pronounced with gratitude as the deliverers of nations.'[79]

The modern Antonines

Gibbon's fleeting mention of the sixteenth-century reformers allows attention to turn from the general theme of Christian reform to the specific history of the Church of England. Gibbon revered the magisterial Reformation that had prevailed since the 1530s as the godly prince subjected the church to a state establishment. Discussing the first volume of William Blackstone's *Commentaries on the Laws of England* (1765–9), Gibbon provided a Whiggish account of the contract between ruler and people. The duties of the king, 'implied by the original contract', had been 'more precisely laid out at the Revolution, and expressed in the Coronation Oath'. These duties including governing according to the law, executing justice with mercy, and maintaining the established religion.[80] The coronation oath after 1689 required the English monarch to 'maintain the laws of God, the true profession of the gospel and the protestant reformed religion established by law'.[81] Gibbon composed a summary of the constitution in church and state in magisterial terms. The monarch was 'supreme Head of the Church of England; which title is vested in him since the reign of Henry viii'. In this capacity, 'he convenes and dissolves Synods; rejects or confirms their constitutions, appoints Bishops and other dignitaries, and receives in his Court of Chancery appeals from all Ecclesiastical Courts'.[82] The king rightly received clerical first fruits and tenths 'which were formerly paid to the Pope'.[83]

Having established that 'the Ecclesiastical order is now very properly subjected to the Civil', Gibbon rehearsed how bishops were appointed. Although 'there is indeed the shadow of an election still left', it had been 'reduced to nothing by the ... powers of the crown'. Royal permission was needed to enable the chapter to proceed to election; it was always accompanied with a recommendation; no bishop may be 'consecrated without letters patent, directed to

---

[79] Ibid., p. 436.
[80] Gibbon, *English Essays*, p. 69.
[81] Williams (ed.), *Eighteenth-Century Constitution*, p. 38.
[82] Gibbon, *English Essays*, p. 71.
[83] Ibid., p. 73.

the Archbishop &c.'; and the bishop must 'receive his temporalities from the King; who by his election acquires a right of presenting, to whatever benefices, his was in possession of'. The king also regulated 'the most numerous part of the Clergy', among whom 'certainly the most useful are the parish priests'. They were divided into rectors or parsons and vicars. The rectors and parsons represented 'the *person* of the Church, and have a property for their lives in the parsonage tithes, glebe and all other dues'. The latter were only 'perpetual curattes, with a regular stipend, usually consisting of certain small tithes and a portion of the glebe; whilst the benefice it is annexed to the patron of the living, who becomes properly the Parson or Spiritual corporation'.[84]

The language of the godly Christian *imperator* in the magisterial Reformation represented the modern equivalent of the Numean religious settlement. While explaining the system of pagan worship established by Numa in *Decline and Fall*, Gibbon recalled how 'the KING of the SACRIFICES represented the person of Numa, and of his successors, in the religious functions, which could be performed only by royal hands'. Gibbon here performed an important move by couching the standard language of reformed godly kingship upon classical assumptions. Gibbon went on to explain that 'the authority, which the Roman priests had formerly obtained in the counsels of the republic, was gradually abolished by the establishment of the monarchy, and the removal of the seat of empire'. However, 'the dignity of their sacred character was still protected by the laws and manners of their country; and they still continued, more especially the college of pontiffs, to exercise in the capital, and sometimes in the provinces, the rights of their ecclesiastical and civil jurisdiction'.[85] Gibbon's ancient sources for his account of the Roman ecclesiastical hierarchy were Cicero, Livy, and Dionysius of Halicarnassus. Among the moderns stood Louis de Beaufort and 'the work of an English Whig, as well as a Roman antiquary': Moyle and his *Essay upon the Constitution of the Roman Government* (written *c*. 1699 and published in 1726).[86]

In the ancient and modern worlds, Gibbon supported an established public worship. He also envisioned a positive role for its clergymen. Their most important function was to be learned inquisitors of scripture, purging its superstitious appendages. They were to examine the 'scanty and suspicious materials of ecclesiastical history' to 'enable us to dispel the dark cloud that hangs over the first age of the church'. Clergymen were to be like Mosheim and Spanheim. They were to be trained in the philological and historical arts. As theologians, they might 'indulge the pleasing task of describing Religion as she descended from Heaven, arrayed in her native purity'. But, as historians, they must 'discover the inevitable mixture of error and corruption, which she contracted

---

[84] Ibid., p. 79.
[85] *DF*, vol. 2, p. 72.
[86] Ibid., p. 72, n. 3.

in a long residence upon earth, among a weak and degenerate race of beings'.[87] Learned clergymen served the ends of religion, since the 'extravagant tales' of superstitious Christianity debased 'the reason, the faith and the morals of the Christians', vitiated 'the faculties of the mind', and extinguished 'the hostile light of philosophy and science'.[88]

Gibbon's insistence that clergymen should be learned implied concern about the universities. The traveller who visited Oxford or Cambridge would be 'surprised and edified by the apparent order and tranquillity that prevail in the seats of the English muses'. The square cap and black gown were 'adapted to the civil and even clerical profession'; the 'degrees of learning and of age are externally distinguished'; and the fixed hours of the hall and chapel 'represent the discipline of a regular, and, as it were, a religious community'.[89] Gibbon praised Robert Lowth, bishop of Oxford then London and professor of poetry at Oxford, 'whose taste and erudition must reflect on the society in which they were formed', to paint the ideal of academic life. Lowth, claimed Gibbon, had benefited from 'a well-regulated course of useful discipline and studies, and in the agreeable and improving commerce of gentlemen and of scholars'. His studies had drawn no distinction between worldliness and scholarship. The atmosphere in which he studied was notable for 'emulation without envy, ambition without jealousy, contention without animosity'. There was a 'liberal pursuit of knowledge' and 'genuine freedom of thought'. He breathed the same air as 'the HOOKERS, the CHILLINGWORTHS, and the LOCKES'. He followed their 'benevolence and humanity'; their 'vast genius and comprehensive knowledge'. They 'always treated their adversaries with civility and respect' and they made 'candour, moderation, and liberal judgement as much the rule and law as the subject of their discourse'.[90]

Due, perhaps, to his own experience at Oxford, Gibbon could not share such a vision. He applauded 'the filial piety' displayed by Lowth even though it was 'impossible for me to imitate'. As much as Oxford would 'cheerfully renounce me for a son', he was 'willing to disclaim her for a mother'.[91] At Magdalen College, Gibbon had converted to Roman Catholicism.[92] Later in life, he partly blamed the Fellowship for its laxity in attending to his education. Instead of acting as an 'ecclesiastical school' that inculcated 'orthodox principles of religion', Gibbon claimed that he had been left to grope his 'way to the chapel and communion-table'. Uninstructed, blindness and idleness 'urged me to advance without armour into the dangerous mazes of controversy and at the

---

[87] Ibid., vol. 1, p. 446.
[88] Ibid., vol. 2, p. 428.
[89] Gibbon, *Memoirs*, p. 77.
[90] Ibid., p. 78.
[91] Ibid.
[92] Ibid., p. 89. See also David Womersley, 'Gibbon's Apostasy', *BJECS*, 11:1 (1988), pp. 51–70.

age of sixteen I bewildered myself into the errors of the Church of Rome'.[93] Possessed of 'skilful and diligent professors', he might have risen from 'translations to originals, from the Latin to the Greek classics, from dead languages to living science'.[94] The shelves of the library at Magdalen had groaned 'under the weight of Benedictine folios, of the editions of the fathers and the collections of the Middle Ages'. He likened the Fellows of the College to monks and, in the tradition of civic political economy, criticised how their otherworldliness led to idleness. Having 'supinely enjoyed the gifts of the founder' the days of the Fellows were filled 'by a series of uniform employments' in the chapel, hall, coffee-house, and common room until 'they retired, weary and self-satisfied, to a long slumber'.[95]

The universities also remained vulnerable to scholastic backsliding. They had been founded during 'a dark age of false and barbarous science' and remained 'tainted with the vices of their origin'. Their early function had been the education of priests and monks. Their government remained in clerical hands, 'an order of men whose manners are remote from the present world, and whose eyes are dazzled by the light of philosophy'. Their legal incorporation by papal and royal charters had granted them a monopoly in public education. Even by the eighteenth century, these 'venerable bodies are sufficiently old to partake of all the prejudices and infirmities of the age'. Gibbon doubted whether 'any reformation will be a voluntary act' and 'so deeply are they rooted in law and prejudice that even the omnipotence of Parliament would shrink from an enquiry into the state and abuses' of the universities.[96]

Reform was, however, possible at the level of the colleges. Gibbon praised William Markham, bishop of Gloucester, for improving the scholarly regimen at Christ Church by introducing a new course of classical and philosophical studies.[97] Recalling the language of political economy, Gibbon drew an analogy between the awarding of academic degrees and 'mechanic operations' by which apprentices gained a licence 'to practise his trade and mystery'. Academic distinction should celebrate 'manly and successful study' instead of pettifogging in the 'mysterious faculty of theology' in which 'the cloak of reason sits awkwardly on our fashionable divines'.[98]

Priestly superstition was not the only threat to civil religion. Enthusiasm was another form of corrupt religion against which the Church of England must stand guard. In Gibbon's own time, the spectre of enthusiasm reared its head during the Gordon riots, an anti-Catholic protest against the Papists Act (1778) for Catholic relief, in which 'forty thousand Puritans such as they might be in the

---

[93] Ibid., pp. 86–7.
[94] Ibid., p. 79.
[95] Ibid., p. 82.
[96] Ibid., p. 79.
[97] Ibid., p. 93.
[98] Ibid., p. 80.

time of Cromwell have started out of their graves'.⁹⁹ If Gibbon's understanding of enthusiasm harked back to the religious tumult of the Interregnum, his vision for clerical preaching recalled the plain style of the Restoration and early eighteenth century. Preaching should avoid all the 'prejudices and passions' of polemic divinity. Injunctions should aver the 'irrevocable obligation, to maintain and propagate his religious opinions' for 'the force of reason and eloquence'.¹⁰⁰

Much can be inferred about Gibbon's ideal parish clergy from his life as a gentleman in Buriton, Hampshire, where he regularly attended sermons. His custom, following the Lord's Prayer and psalm, was to refer to the sermon using his own edition of the Greek Bible. 'This method', he recorded in his journal in August 1762, 'I find both useful and agreeable and intend to keep it up whenever I go to church.'¹⁰¹ His journal reveals further comments on the performance of parochial clergymen. The Reverend Barton's exposition, Gibbon recorded on 18 July 1762, was 'good but too full of comparisons'.¹⁰²

Gibbon approved most of gospel preaching that aimed to reinforce moral duty by appeals to reason. Referring to the sermons of Dr John Foster, on 1 September 1763, Gibbon commented: 'Quel miracle. Un Theologien qui prefère la raison à la fois, et qui est plus effrayè du vice que de l'hérésie.'¹⁰³ While sojourning at Lausanne at the behest of his father following his ejection from Magdalen, Gibbon regularly attended sermons. One particular ceremonial sermon, the presentation of the *bailif* at the cathedral, presented Gibbon with another exemplar. On 1 December 1763, the minister Polier de Bottens preached of the duties of a ruler and people as well as discussing the rights of free men. Bottens displayed 'les talens d'un Orateur et les sentiments d'un Citoyen'. He knew how to speak of the duties of the sovereign and people as well as the willingness of free men to serve 'un prince et non point un tyran'. His sermon was replete with 'dignité, d'onction et de force'.¹⁰⁴ While staying in Paris in 1763, Gibbon heard the antitype of pastoral preaching. On 22 February, Gibbon listened to Jean François Copel, known as the 'Père Elysée', whose style had earned the approbation of Diderot. Copel's subject had been the uncertainty and inefficacy of giving penitence on the death-bed. Gibbon was most unimpressed to hear Copel cast God not as 'Père commun de toute la nature' but rather as 'Juge severe' and 'maitre impitoyable'. Preaching the anger and vengeance of God showed that Copel had 'beaucoup plus d'imagination que d'ame'.¹⁰⁵

---

⁹⁹ Gibbon to Dorothea Gibbon, Thursday 8 June 1780, in *Letters*, vol. 2, p. 243.
¹⁰⁰ *DF*, vol. 1, p. 875.
¹⁰¹ D. M. Low (ed.), *Gibbon's Journal to January 28th. 1763* (London, 1929), p. 94. See also pp. 106, 110, 179.
¹⁰² Ibid., p. 98.
¹⁰³ Trans. 'What a miracle. A theologian who prefers reason to faith, and who is more frightened of vice than heresy.' Edward Gibbon, *Le Journal de Gibbon à Lausanne, 17 août 1763–19 avril 1764*, ed. Georges Bonnard (Lausanne, 1945), p. 20, n. 3.
¹⁰⁴ Trans. 'the talents of an orator and the sentiments of a citizen ... a prince and certainly not a tyrant ... dignity, unction and strength'. Ibid., p. 161.
¹⁰⁵ Trans. 'a common father of all nature ... a severe judge ... a ruthless master ... much

Sermons should be plain and easily understood in motivating the basic morality of the gospel. They should inculcate the social virtues. Pomp and pageantry would not move Christian hearts. In one entry of his journal in August 1762, Gibbon wondered whether 'the philosophic method' of the English preacher was preferable to 'the Rhetoric of the French preachers'. The English method was certainly safer since it was 'difficult for a man to make himself ridiculous, who proposes only to deliver plain sense on a subject he has thoroughly studied'. But the English method risked slipping into 'the least pretensions towards the sublime, or the pathetic' that the listener must 'admire or laugh'. People in general were 'so well acquainted with our duty, that it is almost superfluous to convince us of it'. It was not the head 'that holds out', but the heart and, 'by a moving eloquence', it was possible 'to rouse the sleeping sentiments of the heart, & incite it to acts of virtue'. By a regular attendance of sermons in which eloquence and plain sense were deployed, clergymen might inculcate the habit of virtue and performance of good works.[106]

Toleration and gentlemen

A further aspect of the benign and pastoral orientation of the public religion was its commitment to toleration. Gibbon identified the history of tolerant reformed Christianity firmly with Erasmianism. Since the days of Luther and Calvin, he explained in *Decline and Fall*, 'a secret reformation has been silently working in the bosom of the reformed churches' as 'the disciples of Erasmus diffused a spirit of freedom and moderation'. While Erasmus was 'the father of rational theology', Erasmianism was carried forth by the Dutch Arminians, Hugo Grotius, Philipp van Limborch, and Jean Le Clerc. Gibbon lauded Limborch as 'moderate and judicious' for his Erasmian claim that 'any speculative truths were dearly purchased at the expence of practical virtue and publick peace'.[107] In England, he praised the rational theology of Chillingworth as well as 'the latitudinarians of Cambridge': Tillotson, Clarke, and Hoadly.[108] Although liberty of conscience 'has been claimed as a common benefit, an inalienable right', it was 'the free governments of Holland and England' that had instituted 'the practice of toleration'.[109]

Gibbon relied especially on Chillingworth and Bayle, both of whom had also youthfully converted to Roman Catholicism only to re-join the reformed fold. Chillingworth 'unravelled his mistakes, and delivered his mind from the yoke of authority and superstition'. He developed the creed that scripture was the

---

more imagination than spirit'. Edward Gibbon, *Miscellanea Gibboniana*, eds G. R. de Beer, Georges Bonnard, and Louis Jounod (Lausanne, 1952), pp. 96–7.
[106] Low (ed.), *Gibbon's Journal*, pp. 126–7.
[107] Ibid., pp. 87, 148–9.
[108] *DF*, vol. 3, p. 438 and n. 38.
[109] Ibid., pp. 438–9.

true religion and private reason the sole interpreter for Protestants.[110] Had Bayle decided to remain within the Roman Catholic Church and join the ecclesiastical profession, 'the genius and favour of such a proselyte might have aspired to wealth and honours'. Yet, 'the hypocrite would have found less happiness in the comforts of a benefice or the dignity of a mitre than he enjoyed at Rotterdam, in a private state of exile, indigence and freedom'.[111] Praising the *Dictionnaire Historique et Critique* (1697) as 'a vast repository of facts and opinions', Gibbon characterised Bayle as balancing the false religions 'in his sceptical scales'.[112] The 'philosopher of Rotterdam' condemned equally the persecution of Louis XIV as well as the 'republican maxims of the Calvinists, their vain prophecies, and the intolerant bigotry'.[113]

Truly reformed churches were tolerant because their clergymen realised that their articles of faith were not perfectible. Their doctrines stood beyond the reach of human intellect and were matters of faith. Most radically, Gibbon believed the Trinity was a matter of faith. The only scriptural justification for the doctrine, in 1 John 5:7, was 'condemned by the orthodox fathers, ancient versions, and authentic manuscripts'.[114] A related matter of faith was the divinity of Christ. Gibbon explained that Apollonius of Tyana, the Greek Pythagorean, had been born around the same time as Jesus Christ. Yet the former's life 'is related in so fabulous a manner by his disciples, that we are at a loss to discover whether he was a sage, an impostor, or a fanatic'.[115] The elevation of Christ to the level of a deity began in the Pauline epistles and church councils fraudulently misinterpreted the meaning of the term, 'God was manifested in the flesh', by replacing the word 'God' for the word 'who'. Yet the original reading was retained in the Latin and Syriac versions of the Bible while the reasoning remained in the Greek version and in the logic of the Latin fathers.[116]

It might be objected that, by these lines of argument, Gibbon was emptying civil religion of any discernibly Christian content. Of the early reformers, Gibbon wrote that the philosopher 'who calculates the degree of their merit and the value of their reformation will prudently ask from what articles of faith, *above* or *against* our reason, they have enfranchised the Christians'. Such an enfranchisement 'is doubtless a benefit so far as it may be compatible with truth and piety'. The philosopher would conclude that 'we shall rather be surprised by the timidity, than scandalised by the freedom of our first reformers'.[117] The early reformers kept the doctrines of original sin, redemption, grace, and predestination which 'have been strained from the epistles of St. Paul' and 'prepared

---

[110] Gibbon, *Memoirs*, p. 90.
[111] Ibid., p. 91.
[112] Ibid., p. 92.
[113] Ibid., p. 91.
[114] *DF*, vol. 2, pp. 441–2.
[115] Ibid., vol. 1, p. 315, n. 63.
[116] Ibid., vol. 2, p. 940.
[117] Ibid., vol. 3, p. 436.

by the fathers and schoolmen'.[118] In a footnote, Gibbon noted that under Edward VI 'our reformation was more bold and perfect', but still bemoaned how 'in the fundamental articles of the church of England, a strong and explicit declaration against the real presence was obliterated in the original copy, to please the people, or the Lutherans, or Queen Elizabeth'.[119]

However, to object that Gibbon was rushing to de-Christianise civil religion is to neglect Gibbon's insistence that the mysteries of Christianity were matters of faith beyond human reason. Further, as he had argued with regard to Roman paganism, Gibbon believed that custom sufficed in those areas left dark by human reason. As Young has shown, Gibbon opposed the tenets of freethinkers and atheists.[120] Gibbon could not 'approve the intolerant zeal of the philosophers and Encyclopaedists the friends of d'Olbach and Helvetius'.[121] Irrespective of Gibbon's inward thought about the normative truths of Christianity, he believed reverence for the established religion of Hanoverian England was a crucial expression of citizenship within it. In a section that was never included in his memoirs, Gibbon thus recalled his activities at his parish church. After his library, 'I must not forget an occasional place of weekly study: the parish Church which I frequented, commonly twice, every Sunday in conformity with the pious or decent custom of the family'. In the family's pew he kept an edition of the Septuagint Bible and the Greek testament. During the morning and evening services, he would consult the verse on which the sermon was based in the original text. Should he come across 'doubt, alas or objections that invincibly rushed into my head', he would later consult 'the learned expositors' at home.[122]

Gibbon's insistence that reverence for the reformed religion was the only means by which patriotic citizenship could truly be expressed is also clear in his youthful conversion back to Protestantism. After Oxford, Gibbon passed some years at Lausanne under the tutelage of Daniel Pavillard, a minister of the Swiss Reformed Church and honorary professor of civil history as well as librarian at the academy of Lausanne. Gibbon took seventeen months to re-join the Protestant fold. On Christmas Day 1754, he took the sacrament at the church of Lausanne and there resolved to suspend his 'religious enquiries, acquiescing with implicit belief in the tenets and mysteries which are adopted by the general consent of Catholics and Protestants'.[123] He wrote to his aunt Catherine Porten in February 1755, reporting that he had become 'a good Protestant'. Having been brought up 'with all the ideas of the Church of England', at first, he could

---

[118] Ibid., p. 437.
[119] Ibid., n. 33.
[120] B. W. Young, '"Scepticism in Excess": Gibbon and Eighteenth-Century Christianity', *HJ*, 41:1 (1998), pp. 179–99.
[121] Gibbon, *Memoirs*, p. 140.
[122] Edward Gibbon, *The Autobiographies of Edward Gibbon*, ed. John Murray (London, 1897), pp. 248–9.
[123] Gibbon, *Memoirs*, p. 98.

'scarce resolve to communion with Presbyterians' in Switzerland. He eventually decided that he could partake in Swiss Reformed services because 'whatever difference there may be between their churches & ours, in the government & discipline they still regard us as brethren and profess the same faith as us'.[124]

In later life, Gibbon believed it was crucial for elite sceptics to revere the established faith because its popular devotion was still insecure. Although the Reformation had resulted in a simpler worship, it remained 'to observe, whether such sublime simplicity be consistent with popular devotion'. Gibbon was unsure 'whether the vulgar, in the absence of all visible objects, will not be inflamed by enthusiasm, or insensibly subside in languor and indifference'. Sacerdotal priests had at least restrained 'the bigot from thinking as he pleases, and the slave from speaking as he thinks'.[125] It was dangerous for enthusiastic philosophers to take the licence to attack the public faith. Conversely, the threat of superstitious priestcraft remained strong. Although lay Christians were taught to acknowledge no law but scripture alone and no interpreter but their consciences, this 'freedom was the consequence, rather than the design, of the reformation'. The 'patriot reformers were ambitious of succeeding the tyrants whom they had dethroned'.[126] Citing Burnet's three-volume *The History of the Reformation of the Church of England* (1679–1753), Gibbon condemned 'the flames of Smithfield' and 'the zeal of Cranmer' in state persecution of Anabaptism. Unfortunately, the 'sense and humanity' of the young Edward VI 'were oppressed by the authority of the primate'.[127]

It is instructive, again, to compare Gibbon's Ciceronian caution in requiring the sceptical philosopher to respect the public worship with the arguments of the heterodox Cambridge clergyman, Middleton. In his three-volume *Life of Cicero* (1741), Middleton argued that Cicero had been an exemplar of 'natural' religion in contradistinction to the corrupted superstitions of Roman paganism. Cicero's religion was 'undoubtedly of *heavenly extraction*'.[128] Albeit he did so on the basis of probability rather than certainty, Cicero believed in God, general providence, and the doctrine of posthumous punishments and rewards.[129] Further, '*Cicero's porticos*' represented 'the seat of the most refined reason, wit, and learning'. Although the site of Cicero's living place had been replaced by the '*Monkish cloisters*' of a Dominican monastery, 'a nursery of superstition, bigotry, and enthusiasm', its ruins recalled a man whose writings, 'by spreading the light of reason and liberty thro' the world, have been one great instrument of obstructing their unwearied pains to enslave it'.[130]

---

[124] Gibbon to Porten, Feb. 1755, in *Letters*, vol. 1, p. 3.
[125] *DF*, vol. 3, p. 437.
[126] Ibid., p. 438.
[127] Ibid., n. 37.
[128] Conyers Middleton, *The History of the Life of Marcus Tullius Cicero* (3 vols, London, 1741), vol. 3, p. 349.
[129] Ibid., pp. 340–4.
[130] Ibid., vol. 1, pp. xxi–xxxii.

In his *Letter to Dr. Waterland* (1730), referring to Daniel Waterland, orthodox Master of Magdalene College, Cambridge, Middleton argued that his aim to reconcile Christian faith with the precepts of natural religion did not stand in tension with his support of the established church. Invoking Socrates, Seneca, and Cicero, Middleton claimed that heathen moralists, 'though they clearly saw the cheat and forgery of the *established Religion*, yet always persuade and recommend a submission to it'. They knew 'what mischief must needs befal the State by the subversion of constitutions so greatly reverenced by the people'.[131] Middleton recalled that, during his exile, Cicero decided to visit sacred sites in order to give himself 'an opportunity of shewing himself every where in a light, which naturally attracts the attention of the multitude, by testing a pious regard to the favourite superstitions and local religions of the Country'.[132]

Roman pagan observance served as a reminder that religion should usefully reinforce the moral and social virtues. In one section of the *Letter from Rome*, Middleton argued that ancient heroes 'were raised up into Gods, and received *Divine Honours* in Acknowledgement for some *signal Benefits* they had been the *Authors* of to Mankind'. By contrast, Roman Catholic saints were often 'never heard of, but in their own *Legends or Fabulous Histories*' and many owed 'all the Honours now paid them, to their *Vices* or their *Errors*'. The false heroes of Roman Catholicism simply raised 'Rebellion in Defence of *their Idol*' and threw 'whole Kingdoms into Convulsions for the Sake of some *gainful Imposture*'.[133]

Much like Gibbon, it might be argued that Middleton was stripping civil religion of any Christian content, simply preferring the ancient Roman civil faith over any iteration of Christianity. Ingram has argued that the truth of the civil religion did not matter to Middleton.[134] In the *Letter to Dr. Waterland*, Middleton seemed to suggest that the most important aspect of a public religion was that it reinforce the civil order. Middleton argued that there had never been 'a nation in the world, whose *publick Religion* was formed upon the *plan of Nature*, and instituted on the principles of *meer Reason*'. To succeed, religions needed a greater authority than empirical reason. All public religions had 'ever derived their Authority from the pretence of a *Divine Original*, and a *Revelation from Heaven*'.[135] This foundation was necessary to move the credulous multitude.

However, even if the content of the civil religion did not matter for Middleton, much like Gibbon and Hume, it mattered that the doctrines of Christianity were made civil. Christianity, Middleton argued, could not be 'treated as a *meer Imposture*; on a level only with the other *Impostures*'. Any attempt to subvert the civil status of Christianity was 'both *irrational* and *immoral*'. Christianity should be thought 'the *best of all other religions*; the best contrived to promote

---

[131] Conyers Middleton, *A Letter to Dr. Waterland* (London, 1731), p. 52.
[132] Middleton, *Life of Cicero*, vol. 2, p. 22.
[133] Middleton, *Letter from Rome*, p. 33.
[134] Ingram, *Reformation without End*, pp. 130–2.
[135] Middleton, *Letter to Dr. Waterland*, p. 50.

publick peace and the *good of society*.[136] To the objection that Middleton was a clergyman and could not sincerely profess the established faith, Middleton might conjure the example of Cicero, who, despite his doubts about augury and divination, believed divination *'was wisely retained for the sake of Government, and the influence it had on the peace of the Republick'*.[137] The distinction between esoteric and exoteric philosophy mattered as much to the heterodox clergyman as it did to the sceptical gentleman philosopher.

There are many similarities between the Ciceronian approach of Middleton and Gibbon in constructing a civil religion. Both men also wrote of the early corruption of Christianity in the age of the Roman Empire. Irrespective of their views of the doctrines of the Church of England and the spiritual content of a civil religion, both insisted on the need to transform Christianity into a civil religion. But, to return to Gibbon, there remains an objection that, in writing his history of the Roman Empire, he was rushing to de-Christianise the content of civil religion.

There is, perhaps, an incongruity between Gibbon's Ciceronian commitment to revering even imperfect established articles of faith and the nature of the fifteenth and sixteenth chapters of *Decline and Fall*. Gibbon's reputation as an atheist or deist owes a great deal to the immediate reception of those two chapters in which he offered secular reasons for the spread of primitive Christianity as opposed to a providential justification.[138] The secular causes were fivefold. First, the 'inflexible and … the intolerant zeal of the Christians' that had its origins in the Jewish religion. Second, the 'doctrine of a future life'. Third, 'the miraculous powers ascribed to the primitive church'. Fourth, the 'pure and austere morals of the Christians'. Fifth, the 'union and discipline of the Christian republic, which gradually formed an independent and increasing state in the heart of the Roman Empire'.[139]

Pocock has persuasively argued that the chapters were preliminary to Gibbon's main historical argument that properly began with the history of the council of Nicaea.[140] David Womersley has suggested that Gibbon's key motivation in writing the chapters, which Gibbon himself judged to be expendable from his history, was a desire for fame.[141] Nevertheless, there remains a tension between Gibbon's immediate reception and his own intentions. At the opening of chapter

---

[136] Ibid., p. 55.
[137] Ibid., pp. 52–3.
[138] See Myron C. Noonkester, 'Gibbon and the Clergy: Private Virtues, Public Vices', *Harvard Theological Quarterly*, 83:4 (1990), pp. 399–414; David Womersley (ed.), *Religious Scepticism: Contemporary Responses to Gibbon* (Bristol, 1997); *Gibbon and the 'Watchmen of the Holy City': The Historian and His Reputation, 1776–1815* (Oxford, 2002).
[139] *DF*, vol. 1, p. 447.
[140] J. G. A. Pocock, 'Edward Gibbon in History: Aspects of the Text in *The History of the Decline and Fall of the Roman Empire*', in Grethe B. Petersen (ed.), *The Tanner Lectures on Human Values*, vol. 11 (Salt Lake City, 1988), pp. 289–364, at p. 339. See also Pocock, 'Gibbon and the Primitive Church', p. 48.
[141] See David Womersley, 'Gibbon and the "Watchmen of the Holy City": Revision and

15, Gibbon argued that the 'great law of impartiality' required the historian 'to reveal the imperfections of the uninspired teachers and believers of the gospel' even though, 'to a careless observer, *their* faults may seem to cast a shade on the faith which they professed'.[142] It is likely that Gibbon did not believe his account of the secular reasons for the rise of Christianity should undermine any of the essentials of the Christian faith. In his guise as an elite of Hanoverian England, he felt safe to publish the fifteenth and sixteenth chapters without threatening the integrity of the public religion.

Smile, sigh, and subscribe

Each volume of *Decline and Fall* emerged from the press as the Church of England underwent the subscription controversy. Clergymen who doubted the veracity of the Thirty-Nine Articles, especially those relating to the Trinity, argued that they should not be required to subscribe to them to hold office within the Church of England. The 'volumes of controversy are overspread with cobwebs', Gibbon quipped in *Decline and Fall*, while the 'doctrine of a Protestant church is far removed from the knowledge or belief of its private members'. Meanwhile, 'the forms of orthodoxy, the articles of faith, are subscribed with a sigh or smile by the modern clergy'.[143] Gibbon was referring to those who subscribed despite their doubts about the Trinity, intimating that doubts about the veracity of its articles was no reason to seek to undermine the established faith.

The articles were imperfect human formularies and, where reason failed to instruct, custom was a legitimate guide. Opponents of subscription might have consulted the second chapter of *Decline and Fall*, in which Gibbon described the Antonine religious order. Although the patricians viewed 'with a smile of pity and indulgence the various errors of the vulgar', they 'diligently practised the ceremonies of their fathers [and] devoutly frequented the temples of the gods'. Sometimes they condescended 'to act a part in the theatre of superstition' and 'concealed the sentiments of an Atheist under the sacerdotal robes'. Rational men of such a temper 'were scarcely inclined to wrangle about their respective modes of faith and worship'.[144]

Since opponents of subscription were considering leaving the Church of England, Gibbon was charting a middle way between orthodoxy and Dissent. Opponents of subscription might learn from the Antonines that a universal spirit of toleration, including of the vulgar, needed to accompany the contemplation of the universal cause. The ecclesiastical policy of those emperors 'was happily seconded by the reflections of the enlightened, and by the habits of the superstitious, part of their subjects'. The various modes of worship were 'all considered

---

Religion in the *Decline and Fall*', in Rosamond McKitterick and Roland Quinault (eds), *Edward Gibbon and Empire* (Cambridge, 1997), pp. 190–216, at pp. 213–15.
[142] *DF*, vol. 1, p. 447.
[143] Ibid., vol. 3, p. 439.
[144] Ibid., vol. 1, p. 59.

by the people, as equally true; by the philosopher, as equally false; and by the magistrate, as equally useful'. Toleration resulted in 'not only mutual indulgence, but even religious concord'. Opponents of subscription needed to recall the limits of the human mind in deciphering mysteries of faith. Orthodox clergymen needed to remember that it was not their sacerdotal role to fabricate superstitions or engage in pointless metaphysical squabbles. Under the Antonines, the 'superstition of the people was not embittered by any mixture of theological rancour; nor was it confined by the chains of any speculative system'.[145]

Following the parliamentary defeat of a petition to relieve clergymen, lawyers, and physicians from the requirement to subscribe in 1762, Gibbon wrote to John Holroyd Baker, earl of Sheffield, celebrating 'the late Victory of our Dear Mamma the Church of England'. Her '71 rebellious sons' in the Commons who supported abolition had 'pretended to set aside her will on account of insanity'. Fortunately, she was saved by '217 worthy champions' led by Lord North, Edmund Burke, Hans Stanley, Charles Fox, Godfrey Clarke, and others. Even though the Church's saviours 'allowed the 39 Clauses of her Testament were absurd and unreasonable', they 'suffered the validity of it with infinite humour'.[146] Gibbon's letter seems remarkably similar to a passage in *Decline and Fall* in which he argued that the devotion of the poet or philosopher 'may be secretly nourished by prayer, meditation, and study', but the exercise of 'public worship appears to be the only solid foundation of the religious sentiments of the people, which derive their force from imitation and habit'. Should that worship be interrupted, it 'may consummate, in the period of a few years, the important work of a national revolution'. The 'memory of theological opinions cannot long be preserved, without the artificial helps of priests, of temples, and of books'.[147]

Dissenters seized upon the failure of the anti-subscription campaign as confirmation of their case against the popish nature of the Church of England. One such figure was Priestley. While discussing the anti-subscription campaign in *Decline and Fall*, Gibbon recommended 'to public animadversion' two passages in Priestley's *History of the Corruptions of Christianity* (1782), at the first of which, 'the priest', and, at the second, 'the magistrate, may tremble!'[148] The first passage discussed Priestley's providential Unitarianism. Following the Reformation, Priestley explained, divine providence had opened 'the minds of men by easy degrees'. The 'detection of one falsehood, prepares us for the detection of another, till before we are aware of it, we can find no trace the immense, and seemingly well compacted system'.[149] The second passage attacked on explicitly millenarian grounds the idea of an alliance between church and state as an impious proposition. But the relationship was so strong,

---

[145] Ibid., p. 56.
[146] Gibbon to Sheffield, 8 Feb. 1762, in *Letters*, vol. 1, p. 305.
[147] *DF*, vol. 2, p. 89.
[148] Ibid., vol. 3, p. 439, n. 42.
[149] Joseph Priestley, *An History of the Corruptions of Christianity* (2 vols, Birmingham, 1782), vol. 1, pp. 275–6.

intimated Priestley, that its destruction might only be precluded by the collapse of the civil power. Such a situation may be a calamity but, he asked, 'what convulsion in the political world ought to be a subject of lamentation, if it be attended with so desirable an event' as the second coming of Christ?[150]

In Priestley's arguments, Gibbon feared that puritan enthusiasm was donning a more respectable cloak. Gibbon reported, with some tint of irony, that 'the friends of Christianity are alarmed at the boundless impulse of enquiry and scepticism'. They were right to be so, since the secular order relied on an established faith. The 'pillars of revelation are shaken by those men who preserve the name without the substance of religion' and 'who indulge the licence without the temper of philosophy'.[151] Priestley was guilty of enthusiasm in both religion and philosophy. His dangerous arguments risked not simply undermining the public faith but the civil order that depended on it.

Gibbon had had form with Priestley. In December 1782, Priestley sent Gibbon his first volume of the *History of the Corruptions of Christianity*. Priestley supposed that Gibbon had accurately identified the main reason for the corruption of primitive Christianity as the church fathers' adoption of the Platonic distinction between matter and spirit. This had led to the mistaken conceptions of the soul as immaterial and eternal as well as of Christ being raised to equal status with God. Gibbon replied on 28 January 1783 that, unlike Priestley, Gibbon respected Christianity as the lawfully established faith. Priestley had mistakenly supposed that Gibbon wished to undo the very basis of the Christian commonwealth of Whig England. Gibbon warned Priestley that 'as long as you attach opinions which I have never maintained, or maintained principles which I have never denied you may safely exult in my silence'. Gibbon felt assured that the public would decide 'to whom the invidious name of *unbeliever* belongs': between 'the historian, who without interposing his own sentiments, has delivered a simple narrative of authentic facts' or the disputant who 'proudly rejects all natural proof of the immortality of the soul, overthrows (by circumscribing) the inspiration of the Evangelists and the Apostles, and condemns the religion of every Christian Nation as a fable less innocent, but not less absurd, than Mahomet's journey to the third heaven'.[152]

If the subscription controversy had been grist to the mill of Dissent, the arrival of the French Revolution stoked Gibbon's fears of enthusiasm yet further. In his memoirs, Gibbon commented on the panic and disorder spreading across France. The 'fanatic missionaries of sedition have scattered seeds of discontent in our cities and villages'. This compared favourably with Gibbon's England. He was fortunate to have been born 'in a free and enlightened country, in an honourable and wealthy family'.[153] In a letter to Sheffield in 1789, Gibbon bemoaned how revolutionary fervour meant the French priesthood was 'plundered in a Way

---

[150] Ibid., vol. 2, p. 484.
[151] *DF*, vol. 3, p. 439.
[152] Gibbon to Joseph Priestley, 28 Jan. 1783, in *Letters*, vol. 2, pp. 320–1.
[153] Gibbon, *Memoirs*, pp. 179–80.

which strikes at the root of all property'. Meanwhile, across the Channel, a group of Dissenters were still celebrating the Revolution as symbolic of human progress. In England, 'a set of wild Visionaries (like our Dr Price) ... gravely debate and dream about the establishment of a pure and perfect democracy'.[154]

It was an error to imitate the philosophic cabals of Parisian society in striking at the public faith that underpinned French civil order. Gibbon wrote with gently ironic approbation for Burke's *Reflections on the Revolution in France* (1791) in private correspondence: 'I admire his eloquence, I approve his politics, I adore his chivalry, and I can even forgive his superstition.' The 'primitive Church, which I have treated with some freedom, was itself, at that time, an innovation, and *I* was attached to the old Pagan establishment'.[155] Gibbon's sentiments are similar to a passage in his *Vindication*, in which he explained to his clerical opponents that 'the Pagan worship was a matter, not of *opinion*, but of *custom*'.[156] It mattered that custom had filled the territory left vacant by reason. However dissatisfied religious believers or philosophic sceptics in England might have been with their national worship, their gravest error was to neglect its importance in expressing citizenship. Gibbon instructively commented on Burke in his memoirs to great ironic effect. Gibbon could 'almost excuse his [Burke's] reverence for Church establishments'. He had sometimes 'thought of writing a dialogue of the dead, in which Lucian, Erasmus, and Voltaire should mutually acknowledge the danger of exposing an *old* superstition to the contempt of the blind and fanatic multitude'.[157]

Gibbon believed a Christian civil religion was intrinsic to building civilised and enlightened society. He argued that the Erasmian strands of the Reformation had begun to return Christians to pious contemplation of the universal cause without persecuting others over unverifiable mysteries of faith. Through the legacy of Erasmus and the latitudinarians, inward freedom of conscience had become balanced with an appreciation of the limits of the human intellect. The established faith restrained superstitious priestcraft and brought popular beliefs within the sphere of civil safety. A pastoral, pedagogical, and tolerant establishment prevented backsliding into enthusiasm. The Church of England was to revive the ancient achievement of serving worldly civic life and patriotic citizenship. It would reinforce public peace and wellbeing in this world in preparation for the prospect of punishments and rewards in the next world. Respect for the public religion was not simply advisable for the prudent statesman. It was a crucial expression of citizenship within the reformed Christian commonwealth of Hanoverian England. It behove the sceptical patrician, Protestant Dissenter, and heterodox Anglican to smile and condescend to the national faith. Priestley and his friends had failed to understand that civilisation, governed by the limits of human understanding, could hope for little more.

---

[154] Gibbon to John Baker Holroyd, earl of Sheffield, 15 Dec. 1789, in *Letters*, vol. 3, p. 184.
[155] Gibbon to Sheffield, 5 Feb. 1791, in ibid., p. 216.
[156] *DF*, vol. 3, p. 1158.
[157] Gibbon, *Memoirs*, p. 194.

6

Subscription, Reform, and Dissent: Civil Religion and Enlightened Divinity during the Late Eighteenth Century

Sincerity and the unreformed Church of England

During the late eighteenth century, two new concepts of civil religion came to challenge hitherto dominant Anglican versions. The first new concept remained Anglican, but its supporters were committed to a more comprehensive vision of an established church. Proponents of the second new concept rejected Anglicanism for a Dissenting vision of civil religion that, approaching the arrival of the millennium, would not require an established church. Both had much in common with earlier strands of civil religion. They celebrated the civil magistrate as the guarantor of Protestant spiritual liberty. Until the point of millennial perfection, proponents of both new concepts of civil religion remained committed to a church establishment in the Protestant nation against the dark forces of Roman Catholicism at home and abroad. The church establishment also upheld Christian morality in support of social order. Superstition and sacerdotal priests were to be prevented by the secular protections of the state in the Christian commonwealth. Committed to a *sola scriptura* approach, they aimed to construct anew the precepts of primitive Christianity. Learned ministers of the gospel would guide the laity in accessing the scriptures to maintain the relationship between the believer and God without sacerdotal mediation. Ministers were also pastoral and pedagogical to prevent backsliding into enthusiasm. Reason, science, and polite letters remained key signifiers of enlightened religion.

Such features remained constant. But the features that changed were the targets of the language of Protestant Reformation and spiritual enlightenment. A language once used to justify the Christian commonwealth of Whig England founded on the Revolution settlement of 1689 was now being redeployed, to varying extents, against that very order. Dissenters turned the touchstones of Anglican anti-Catholicism – corruption, priestcraft, and usurpation – into a manifesto for reform.[1] Proponents of both new concepts of civil religion sought a comprehensive vision of the church establishment. If the church was the whole nation at prayer, it should include the entire people without doctrinal speculation in matters of faith. The church establishment must institutionalise a common worship as the expression of a commonwealth founded upon gospel Christianity.

The first new concept of civil religion emerged during the subscription controversy between the 1760s and 1780s. Its exponents claimed to follow the principles of Anglican latitudinarianism to their fullest conclusions. Hanoverian latitudinarians had insisted that the established church should tolerate theological breadth among its followers. In the absence of enforceable conformity, clergymen would have to dwell on the essential doctrines, uniting all Protestants in external worship, and accept that the rest were merely *adiaphora*. The essentials had been laid out by Christ in the gospel. Further, the scientific study of nature on Newtonian principles was taken to confirm the creative ordering of God.[2] Latitudinarianism was a deliberate compromise. It sought to hold together Protestants whose doctrines and theologies were often in conflict. It distinguished between inward faith and outward loyalty. It required that disagreement with the articles and creeds of the established church be put aside in the interest of Protestant unity and civil order.

But the central problem confronting those seeking to reconcile heterodox beliefs with the Anglican establishment was the Protestant preoccupation with sincerity. By the 1760s, the development of 'rational' Christianity brought increasing pressure to bear on proponents of Anglican civil religion who had overwhelmingly emphasised latitude. Arguments for church reform came initially from within latitudinarian circles and its supporters sought to generate a comprehensive Protestant establishment with minimal doctrinal requirements. Attention fixed upon the practice at the universities of imposing subscription to the Thirty-Nine Articles on students. The articles relating to the doctrine of the Trinity proved most burdensome. Among Anglican latitudinarians who opposed the principle of subscription, the dominant conception of Hanoverian civil religion began to collapse under the weight of sincerity. The doctrines of some clergymen had slid so far into Socinianism or Unitarianism that, in opposition to Gibbon, they believed it would no longer suffice to sigh and smile to receive their livings.

There have been several histories of the subscription controversy in the context of eighteenth-century English debates about church reform. These histories have highlighted how the arguments in favour of abolition were couched in the language of ongoing Protestant Reformation as learned clergymen claimed to purge Christianity of its corruptions to return by means of *sola scriptura*

---

[1] James Bradley, 'Anti-Catholicism as Anglican Anticlericalism: Nonconformity and the Ideological Origins of Radical Disaffection', in Aston and Cragoe (eds), *Anticlericalism in Britain*, pp. 67–92.
[2] See Gascoigne, *Cambridge in the Age of the Enlightenment*.

principles back to the true religion of the gospel.³ Ideas of civil religion lay at the heart of the debate. Anglican opponents of subscription were defending an establishment with the classic hallmarks of eighteenth-century English civil religion, but which asserted the principle of comprehension. They believed the Church of England had to make good its reformed commitment to sincerity and unite all English Protestants against the dark forces of popery. Although latitudinarians accepted that churches were human and imperfect institutions, they were mistaken to deny access to the establishment to Protestants who were loyal to the Christian commonwealth but whose tender consciences led them to doubt sincerely its articles and creeds.

The campaign was led by a group of clergymen associated with the University of Cambridge. Edmund Law (1703–87) was master of Peterhouse from 1754 and became bishop of Carlisle in 1768. His long-time friend, Francis Blackburne (1705–87), produced the central publication for the anti-subscription movement: *The Confessional*. First published in 1767, it was expanded in 1770. Blackburne's work provided the occasion for a meeting at the Feathers Tavern in London in 1770 at which he drew up a petition calling for abolition of subscription. The petition was presented to the House of Commons in February 1772, but it enjoyed the support of only seventy-one MPs. In 1774, when another attempt was made, the petition was not even put to the vote.⁴ Following the failure of the petition, Blackburne refused any preferment that might require a fresh subscription, but both he and Law resolved to remain within the fold of the establishment.

They stayed with a rump of latitudinarian clergymen who continued to defend, from within the establishment, both standard and comprehensive Anglican conceptions of civil religion. Later Cambridge clergymen who would come to represent the survival of the latitudinarian tradition in its competing forms included Bishop Richard Watson (1737–1816), William Paley (1743–1805), Christopher Wyvill (1740–1822), and John Horne Tooke (1736–1812). But a group of reformers opted to secede from the Church of England altogether. About ten Anglican ministers left the Church; four for Unitarianism.⁵ John Jebb (1736–86), a Peterhouse associate of Bishop Law,

---

3 Martin Fitzpatrick, 'Rational Dissent in the Late Eighteenth Century with Particular Reference to the Growth of Toleration' (PhD thesis, University of Wales, 1982); 'Latitudinarianism at the Parting of the Ways'; Gascoigne, *Cambridge in the Age of the Enlightenment*, pp. 130–8; A. M. C. Waterman, 'A Cambridge "Via Media" in Late Georgian Anglicanism', *JEH*, 42:3 (1991), pp. 419–36; Young, *Religion and Enlightenment*, pp. 45–80; Bradley, 'Changing Shape of Religious Ideas in Enlightened England'.
4 G. M. Ditchfield, 'The Subscription Issue in British Parliamentary Politics, 1772–79', *PH*, 7:1 (1988), pp. 45–80; Joanna Innes, 'Parliament and Church Reform: Off and on the Agenda', in Gordon Pentland and Michael T. Davis (eds), *Property and Popular Politics: England and Scotland, 1760–1832* (Cambridge, 1989), pp. 39–57.
5 E. M. Wilbur, *A History of Unitarianism* (Cambridge, MA, 1952), p. 290. See John Jebb, *A Short State of the Reasons for a Late Resignation* (Cambridge, 1773); Theophilus Lindsey, *A Farewell Address to the Parishioners of Catterick* (London, 1774); *A Sermon Preached at the*

resigned his Fellowship for Unitarianism in 1775, having failed to reform the university's curriculum and examination system.[6] Theophilus Lindsey (1723–1808), Blackburne's son-in-law, found new livings at the first Unitarian chapel set up in London's Essex Street. It would be attended by Augustus Fitzroy, duke of Grafton, prime minister, and chancellor of the University of Cambridge, whose own secession from the established church followed years spent trying to reform it.[7] The Essex Street congregation would also count John Disney (1746–1816), another Peterhusian and son-in-law of Blackburne whom Bishop Law had chosen for a chaplain.

For those seceding from the establishment, a third variety of civil religion was available. Dissatisfaction with the apparent conservatism of the Church in maintaining articles and creeds composed during the sixteenth century prompted reformers to take civil religion in Unitarian and congregational directions. This variety of civil religion was a product of old Protestant Dissent. Its proponents criticised the Church of England for being unreformed and provided a vision of a civilised and polite Christian commonwealth which, upon the arrival of the millennium, would jettison an established church. Its vision of civil religion was not to be realised immediately; it was to be the product of continual enlightenment and spiritual improvement. Its millennial vision was one of gradual and progressive reform in which the second coming would result from human perfectibility. Until that point, Dissenting theorists of civil religion accepted the need for a tolerant church establishment to defend social order, embody the whole Protestant nation at prayer, and foster spiritual improvement by its learned and pastoral ministry.

The likes of Disney, Jebb, and Lindsey were aligning themselves with such figures as Priestley and Price. Priestley was a Unitarian theologian and clergyman whose polymath career produced works on natural philosophy, chemistry, education, and political theory. The reaction to the French Revolution during the 1790s brought great dangers to Priestley and forced him to flee to the United States of America where he became an associate of Benjamin Franklin. The interests of Price were equally as wide-ranging. A Welsh Nonconformist of a liberal Calvinist hue, his works covered moral philosophy, politics, finance, and mathematics. His ardent support for the cause of the American colonists during the 1770s gave him a reputation as a political as well as a religious reformer. His sermon to the Revolution Society on 5 November 1789 in support of the early stages of the French Revolution provided the occasion for the fulminations of Burke's *Reflections*.

Opening of the Chapel in Essex-House, Essex-Street (London, 1774); John Disney, *Reasons for Resigning the Rectory of Panton and Vicarage of Swinderby in Lincolnshire* (2nd edn, London, 1783).

[6] John Jebb, *The Works Theological, Medical, Political and Miscellaneous of John Jebb* (3 vols, London, 1787), vol. 1, pp. 10, 20.

[7] See, for example, Augustus FitzRoy, duke of Grafton, *Hints Submitted to the Serious Attention of the Clergy, Nobility and Gentry* (London, 1789), pp. 30–1, 41.

In the hands of Enlightened Dissent, concepts of civil religion that had been characterised by latitudinarian moderation within the church establishment throughout the eighteenth century were now to be re-fashioned along congregational and Unitarian lines.[8] By emphasising the centrality of gospel simplicity, Protestant sincerity, and moral egalitarianism, Enlightened Dissenters developed a new vision. Once again, the secular state would prevent the accumulation of priestly power, but it would eventually do so by renouncing all responsibility whatsoever over matters spiritual. The civility of Dissenting religion would depend less on clergy appointed by the state than a multitude of rational congregations engaging in polite and candid debate as well as electing their own learned and pastoral ministers. The civil religion of Enlightened Dissent would emphatically not be the enthusiasm, as rational Dissenters themselves perceived it, of Methodists and the like. A learned clergy was still vital. But it would not need to be trained by the antiquated methods of the universities; the new science and free inquiry of the Dissenting academies would provide a far superior spiritual education.

Casting their programme as a staging post in an ongoing Reformation that had ultimately millennial ends, Enlightened Dissenters pushed the concept of the priesthood of all believers to fuller conclusions. While some, on the radical fringes, rejected religious establishments altogether in favour of a completely free intercourse of Protestant opinion, others were content to worship alongside the Church of England. Their commitment to the congregational election of ministers among myriad small societies of sincere, egalitarian, and perpetually enlightening Protestants rejected the Erastianism of the magisterial Reformation even though they willingly cohabited with it. Superstition was doomed in the face of Dissenting moral optimism and the expectation that free inquiry would purify religion back to its primitive ideal. Gone was reliance on the legal and ecclesiological frameworks of the magisterial Reformation, which was now reduced to a mere milestone in the ongoing process of spiritual flourishing. Gone was the language of the godly prince; the majesty of the Protestant king was eventually to be superseded by the primacy of popular sovereignty. The church establishment was necessary to protect the Protestant nation, in its condition of spiritual imperfection, from over-mighty priests. But with the rise of spiritual enlightenment would come the realisation that all establishments

---

[8] As Knud Haakonssen has explained, care must be taken in defining this group of Dissenters. While the terms 'rational Dissent' and 'Enlightened Dissent' tend to be used interchangeably, they have slightly different meanings. The term 'rational' categorises Dissenters who rejected Calvinism and the necessity of spiritual regeneration and it is, therefore, usually associated with Unitarianism. But the term 'Enlightened' Dissent more broadly encapsulates those, including those of a liberal Calvinist orientation, whose outlook was shared by the Enlightenment in England in seeking to reconcile reason and a spirit of toleration with Christian belief. Since a Dissenting vision of civil religion was advanced by more figures than Unitarians, 'Enlightened Dissent' is a more convenient term here. See Knud Haakonssen, 'Enlightened Dissent: An Introduction', in Haakonssen (ed.), *Enlightenment and Religion*, pp. 1–11, at pp. 4–5.

were institutions of imposture. The civil magistrate might only legitimately intervene in matters spiritual in the instances where belief threatened life, liberty, and estate. Anything else was tyranny.

Anglican comprehension and the subscription controversy

Doubts about the legitimacy of clerical subscription to the Thirty-Nine Articles were not new.[9] Supporters of the Revolution settlement had sought to calm heterodox doubters throughout the century. Bishop Burnet argued in 1699 that the articles had been calibrated in such a manner that Protestants might subscribe to them despite their contradictions.[10] Samuel Clarke presented a fresh justification in his *The Scripture Doctrine of the Trinity* (1712). He explained that Protestants, unlike Roman Catholics, understood all doctrines and institutions were imperfect and fallible because they were of human design. The Anglican clergyman might subscribe to the articles 'whenever he can in any sense at all reconcile them with scripture'.[11] Often the problem was not as radical as anti-Trinitarianism, but lay in the Arminian rejection of Calvinism. Doubters might also have considered the question from the point of view of high churchmen. Daniel Waterland, no Arian he, bridled at what he perceived as the Calvinistic notes struck by the Thirty-Nine Articles, such as the seventeenth article on the doctrine of predestination.[12]

But opponents of subscription extended the Chillingworthian claim that the Bible was the religion of all Protestants to more radical conclusions. Anglican clergymen, they believed, need only profess their faith in the scriptures as the word of God. Anything else was human imposition. Doctrines like the Trinity were not rooted in scripture but were the product of patristic pettifogging and illegitimate church councils. During the heat of the Bangorian controversy, Thomas Herne had argued that the ordinances issued by the established church carried no legitimacy because all civil and ecclesiastical government relied on consent.[13] John Jackson, who had been a student of Clarke's, claimed that doctrines could only be imposed once they had been shown to be clearly expressed in the gospel.[14]

The argument for a comprehensive Anglican civil religion was adumbrated as the subscription controversy erupted. It extended the language of Protestant

---

[9] For an account emphasising the Hoadlyite origins of the subscription controversy, see John Gascoigne, 'Anglican Latitudinarianism and Political Radicalism in the Late Eighteenth Century', *History*, 71:231 (1986), pp. 22–38, at pp. 22–5.
[10] Gilbert Burnet, *An Exposition of the Thirty-Nine Articles of the Church of England* (London, 1699), p. 8.
[11] Samuel Clarke, *The Scripture Doctrine of the Trinity* (London, 1712), pp. ii, ix–xii. See also J. P. Ferguson, *Dr Samuel Clarke* (Kineton, 1976), p. 179.
[12] Daniel Waterland, *The Case of Arian Subscription Considered* (Cambridge, 1721), pp. 39–42.
[13] Thomas Herne, *An Essay on Imposing and Subscribing Articles of Religion* (London, 1718), p. 8.
[14] John Jackson, *The Ground of Civil and Ecclesiastical Government* (London, 1718).

Reformation and the battle against priestcraft and imposture to include aspects of the Hanoverian Church of England. Blackburne argued that the expectation that clergymen would subscribe to imperfect human creeds represented the failure of the Protestant commitment to defend the sincerity of lay consciences against popish creed-making.[15] If 'the rule of a pure religion be taken from the christian scriptures, the temporal peace and safety of any Christian in civil society is but a secondary consideration to the obligation he is under to hold fast his integrity, in *truth* and *sincerity*'.[16] The Feathers Tavern petitioners claimed that the Church held as little legitimate right to prescribe doctrines as to enforce them because they stood among the 'rights and privileges which they [Christians] hold of God only'.[17] It was especially inappropriate for undergraduates 'at an age so immature for their disquisitions and decisions of such moment'. They should be focused on their study rather than 'subscribe their unfeigned assent to a variety of theological propositions'.[18]

To remove the requirement to subscribe would be to enable the church to comprehend all Protestants. Thus, argued Blackburne, the benefits of a church establishment in providing 'methods of public worship, and public edification' would be fully realised. It would better serve 'weekly exhortations to christian piety and virtue' and the zeal 'for the protestant religion and government'.[19] Such a commitment to a broad-based national Christian church moved beyond a commitment to utility. Blackburne dismissed 'the politician's religion' of Warburton's *Alliance*.[20] Removing the requirement to subscribe made good the state's commitment to act as evangelical liberator, since Christians need not be forced to choose between a benign public institution of worship and their tender consciences.

If, Blackburne argued, defenders of church establishments believed in 'their professions of asserting christian liberty', they must not mandate acceptance of 'certain doctrines and modes of worship, for which they have no other than human authority'.[21] Paraphrasing Chillingworth, Blackburne claimed that it was a 'vain conceit' that 'we can speak of the things of God better than in the words of God'. It was little short of popish idolatry, this 'deifying our own interpretations' and 'tyrannous enforcing them upon others'. Moreover, it was 'restraining the word of God from that latitude and generality, and the understandings of men from that liberty, wherein Christ and the Apostles left them'. These errors were

---

[15] *Confessional*, pp. 32–47.
[16] Ibid., pp. 255–6.
[17] Cobbett (ed.), *Parliamentary History*, vol. 17, p. 251.
[18] 'Copy of the Petition of the Clergy, &c. Relative to Subscription to the Thirty-Nine Articles Offered on Thursday 6th of February, 1772', in Francis Blackburne, *The Works, Theological and Miscellaneous of Francis Blackburne* (7 vols, London, 1804), vol. 7, pp. 18–19.
[19] *Confessional*, pp. xviii–xix.
[20] Francis Blackburne, *Reflections on the Fate of a Petition for Relief in the Matter of Subscription* (London, 1772), p. 11.
[21] Ibid., p. xx.

the only 'fountain of the schisms of the church'.²² If the established church were to use creeds, they must be in the simplest possible forms. They must represent the creed of Christ and the apostles.

The Feathers Tavern petitioners put the argument similarly. Loyalty to the established church expressed belonging within a Christian commonwealth that was committed to Protestant individualism. It was desirable that Protestants of all hues might sincerely support the establishment. Why should men subscribe to articles about which 'their private opinions can be of no consequence to the public'? The petition was expressly cast as a defence of 'the right of private judgement' and 'true religion'. Those 'many pious and conscientious men' who agonised over their possible hypocrisy in subscribing were also 'useful subjects of the state' by buttressing social order through Christian teaching.²³ Bishop Law cast the abolition of subscription as the continuation of the Reformation in which lay believers would rationally access the scriptures without the intervention of self-interested priests whose clerical careers depended on the hypocrisy of subscribing to articles with which they did not agree.²⁴ Opposing subscription meant fighting priestly imposture, purging the church of popish superstition, and securing the Christian's relationship with God.

Support for the Feathers Tavern petition was, by extension, justified on the grounds of gospel simplicity. The object of the Reformation was to purge corrupt religion and restore the pure religion espoused by Christ in the gospels. Blackburne insisted that defenders of subscription were 'endeavouring the repair, and *daub with untempered mortar*, certain *strong-holds* and *partition-walls*, which it was the design of the Gospel to throw down and to level'.²⁵ The object of further Reformation was to restore Christ's promise, which 'called all men unto liberty, the glorious liberty of the sons of God, and restored them to the privilege of working out their own salvation by their own understandings and endeavours'. For man's salvation, 'sufficient means are afforded in the holy scriptures, without having sufficient recourse to the doctrines and commandments of men'.²⁶ For Bishop Law, the 'Christian religion as originally constituted' was 'very plain and practical; level to all capacities, and calculated for the common good of mankind, in every station and condition, both here and hereafter'.²⁷ Law believed creeds designed by men corrupted the primitive purity of Christianity. He proposed a revised liturgy to produce a more comprehensive version of the Church of England.²⁸

---

²² Ibid., p. 52n. The relevant passage is from Chillingworth, 'Religion of the Protestants', in *Works*, p. 203.
²³ 'Copy of the Petition of the Clergy', in Blackburne, *Works*, vol. 7, pp. 18–19.
²⁴ Edmund Law, *Considerations on the Propriety of Requiring a Subscription to Articles of Faith* (2nd edn, London, 1774), pp. 7, 48–9, 59, 62.
²⁵ *Confessional*, p. 215.
²⁶ Ibid., pp. 1–2.
²⁷ Law, *Considerations on the Propriety*, p. 2.
²⁸ Ibid., pp. 2–4.

Care must be taken over the relationship between gospel simplicity, revelation, and natural religion. It was common for theorists of civil religion, particularly when deism had been more fashionable during the 1720s and 1730s, to insist that all three were coterminous. But it was not automatic. Often, in seeking to increase toleration within the established church, Anglican reformers were seeking to encompass other forms of religion than natural Christianity. As Young has shown, Blackburne considered himself a Calvinist of the most liberal kind, who opposed natural religion as the infidel faith of polite *literati*. Doubtful of the Arianism of Clarke as well as Socinianism, Blackburne insisted on the pre-existence and divinity of Jesus Christ based on a Chillingworthian *sola scriptura* approach.[29] His opposition to subscription was based on a distaste of the Athanasian notes struck by the Thirty-Nine Articles. For him, they lacked scriptural justification.

Church reform was therefore cast as the fulfilment of the Protestant nation of Whig England. It was the historic mission of Revolution principles to unite all sincere Protestants against the forces of popish Rome. This mission was also a deeply international one. Blackburne was an associate of Thomas Hollis of Lincoln's Inn, whose strident anti-Catholicism has been well documented.[30] Both men had admired the eighteenth-century Swiss divines who opposed the strict Calvinism especially of Geneva and, in 1768, Hollis published a work by Brian Herport entitled *An Essay on Truths of Importance to the Happiness of Mankind*. Both Hollis and Blackburne believed that Roman Catholicism was on the rise in England, and a comprehensive church would allow Protestants to unite against the real enemy.[31] Blackburne remembered that his years as an undergraduate at Cambridge were spent acquiring 'a strong attachment to the principles of ecclesiastical and civil liberty', primarily through the works of Locke and Hoadly.[32] He insisted that true Protestants should tolerate the multiplicity of interpretations that might emerge from a conscientious reading of scripture.[33] The established Church of England should comprehend the entirety of these interpretations.[34] No human church could justifiably 'require assent to a certain sense of scripture, exclusive of other sense, without an unwarrantable interference'.[35] They were all disagreeable 'to the word of God'.[36]

---

[29] Young, *Religion and Enlightenment*, p. 52.
[30] Caroline Robbins, 'The Strenuous Whig, Thomas Hollis of Lincoln's Inn', *William and Mary Quarterly*, 7:3 (1950), pp. 406–53; P. D. Marshall, 'Thomas Hollis (1720–74): The Bibliophile as Libertarian', *Bulletin of the John Rylands Library*, 66:2 (1984), pp. 246–63; W. H. Bond, *Thomas Hollis of Lincoln's Inn: A Whig and His Books* (Cambridge, 1990); Fitzpatrick, 'Latitudinarianism at the Parting of the Ways', pp. 218–19.
[31] Francis Blackburne (ed.), *Memoirs of Thomas Hollis* (2 vols, London, 1780), vol. 1, pp. 302–3, 375.
[32] Blackburne, *Works*, vol. 1, p. iv.
[33] *Confessional*, pp. 4–5.
[34] Ibid., pp. 38–9.
[35] Ibid., pp. 50–1.
[36] Ibid., pp. 419–20.

Reformers sought recourse in the godly prince-in-parliament at the head of the magisterial Reformation. The petitioners appealed to 'this honourable house [of Commons]' and looked 'under God, to the wisdom and justice of a Protestant king'.[37] Revolution principles had subjected ministers of the Church of England to civil control. They must now include a purge of unnecessary creeds that coerced sincere Protestants into conformity. Reformers were rehearsing the common Anglican theme that the transcendental mission of a godly Protestant king was to defend true religion and the spirituality of the lay believer from popery. Opposition to subscription also set a yardstick against which to measure the godliness of England's monarchs. In the preface to the *Confessional*, Blackburne surveyed the history of seventeenth-century Anglicanism and criticised the extent to which Stuart kingship had become the quisling of formalistic and Laudian priests. Favoured topics included the weakness of Stuart kingship at the Hampton Court Conference in 1604, at which churchmen had sought to impose the Thirty-Nine Articles on puritan priests, and the Savoy Conference in 1661 that resulted in the Act of Uniformity of 1662.[38]

Church reform rested on the supposition that human knowledge was progressive in nature and improving continually. Bishop Law explained in *Considerations on the State of the World with Regard to the Theory of Religion* (1745) that all aspects of knowledge advanced with the passage of time. This included the realm of divinity, for 'as we continually advance in the Study of GOD's Works, so we shall come to a proportionally better Understanding of his Word'.[39] It was appropriate that the established church be reformed as human knowledge revealed its articles and creeds to be outmoded. As other institutions had undergone reform on these grounds and as religious knowledge had 'held pace in general with all other Knowledge', the Church of England should not be any different.[40] He later explained, following the failure of the Feathers Tavern petition, that it should be natural for Protestants to place the abolition of subscription alongside 'all fair opportunities to further, and complete their reformation'.[41]

In pressing for the improvement of knowledge, the idea of learned ministry was central to the question of reform. The petition was largely the work of Cambridge graduates and had been signed by the entirety of the Fellowship of Peterhouse. William Samuel Powell, master of St John's College, Cambridge, had previously defended subscription on the classical latitudinarian grounds that no human institution was perfect. The doctrines within the Thirty-Nine Articles were the result of 'the general voice of learned men through the nation' and formed the nearest human estimation to perfection. With the latitude and

[37] 'Copy of the Petition of the Clergy', in Blackburne, *Works*, vol. 7, pp. 18–19.
[38] *Confessional*, pp. xlviii–lii.
[39] Edmund Law, *Considerations on the State of the World with Regard to the Theory of Religion* (3rd edn, Cambridge, 1755), p. 170.
[40] Ibid., p. 212.
[41] Law, *Considerations on the Propriety*, p. 37.

stability that resulted from establishment, reform might follow later theological improvements produced by Protestant learning. In short, the criterion of sincerity should not be prioritised while religious knowledge was imperfect.[42] Blackburne, however, believed such a position neglected the importance of sincerity. It risked reducing the pool from which a learned Anglican clergy might be drawn.[43]

The other function of an endowed clergy was to act as parochial pedagogues and pastoral exemplars of Christian virtue. Since lay interpretations were fallible, the state must endow clergymen to teach the gospel truth. Bishop Law made the passage Micah 6:8 'the Substance of all true religion, and the sole Foundation upon which it is built'.[44] While not denying his divinity, Law placed emphasis on Christ's role on earth as a preacher of simple moral virtue. Strikingly, Law likened Christ with Socrates, Stoicism, monks, and Rousseau.[45] Clerical pastoralia, inculcating moral virtue, provided a means to prevent the rise of enthusiasm. Blackburne proposed to continue the Reformation to purge the Church of England of popish superstition but also to guard the Church against losing adherents to the enthusiasm of Methodism.[46] Blackburne proposed reforms to render clerical functions parochial and pastoral, to restrict their role to teaching the laity as moral exemplars, and to alter the system of emoluments accordingly.[47] In Blackburne's comprehensive church, the clergy would only need to subscribe to those requirements made at the office of ordination. They would merely profess their belief in the divinity of scripture and commit sincerely and conscientiously to act as pastors and pursue knowledge of the scriptures.[48] By such means, clergymen would act as public officeholders of the national church and inculcate true religion.

Anglican latitudinarianism after the parting of the ways

Although a small number of reformers opted to secede from the Church of England, most chose to remain. They continued to defend traditional and comprehensive forms of Anglican civil religion throughout the 1770s and 1780s. But as the reaction to the French Revolution intensified, they found themselves returning to more traditional territory. Whatever their view of comprehension, they now had to put the emphasis on prudence. An example of this shift is the exchange between Bishop Watson and Gilbert Wakefield, who had been a

---

[42] William Samuel Powell, *A Defence of the Subscription Required in the Church of England* (London, 1757), pp. 12–17.
[43] Francis Blackburne, *Remarks on the Revd Dr Powell's Sermons in Defence of Subscription* (London, 1758), p. 3.
[44] Edmund Law, *The True Nature and Intent of Religion* (Newcastle, 1768), p. 3.
[45] Edmund Law, *Reflections on the Life and Character of Christ* (Cambridge, n.d.), pp. 6, 16–18, 22–3, 28, 30, 53–5, 59, 60–75.
[46] *Confessional*, pp. 400–6.
[47] Ibid., p. 403.
[48] Ibid., pp. 421–4.

Fellow at Jesus College, Cambridge, and had stood among the number who left the Church of England following the failure of the Feathers Tavern petition. In 1799 he was prosecuted for publishing a pamphlet in which he criticised Bishop Watson's support for the French war policy of William Pitt the Younger. Wakefield claimed that Pitt's government represented an 'Anti-Christian tyranny' which was being supported by the established church, itself 'a fraudulent usurpation over that liberty "with which Christ has made us free"'.[49]

Bishop Watson represented the surviving rump of Anglican latitudinarians who were increasingly alienated from the likes of Wakefield. He had written an anonymous pamphlet in defence of the Feathers Tavern petition, the principles of which, he later judged, were 'in perfect coincidence with those of Bishop Hoadley'.[50] Watson's support for toleration has been explored especially in the context of his praise for the religious freedoms established by the French National Assembly in 1791.[51] But Watson's initial ardour for the French Revolution faded quickly and he came to defend a more traditional concept of civil religion. In his pamphlet *An Address to the People of Great Britain* (1798), Watson maintained that there were 'great abuses in church and state'. However, 'it is better to tolerate abuses, till they can be reformed by the counsels of the wisest and best men in the kingdom'.[52] He expressly cast his ecclesiastical positions in latitudinarian and Whig terms similar to 'that excellent man', Bishop Law, from whose friendship he had 'derived much knowledge and liberality of sentiment in theology'.[53] Watson's precepts were Revolution principles, those 'of *Locke*, of *Somers*, and of *Hooker*, and in the reign of George the second they were the politics of this University' at Cambridge.[54] He supported an established church without which 'the Ends of civil Government can scarcely be attained'. But he 'cordially' wished to see 'a Reformation of our Religious Establishment'.[55]

Watson put his vision of the Church of England in Chillingworthian terms. He recalled that he 'determined to study nothing but my Bible, being much unconcerned about the opinions of councils, fathers, churches, bishops, and other men as little inspired as myself'.[56] Such interpretations were merely imperfect human understandings of God and, if imposed on other Christians, became forms of priestly superstition and imposture. Instead, 'free disquisition is the best mean of illustrating the doctrine and establishing the truth of Christianity'.[57] He defended

---

[49] Gilbert Wakefield, *A Reply to Some Parts of the Bishop of Llandaff's Address to the People of Great Britain* (London, 1798), p. 39.
[50] Richard Watson, *Anecdotes of the Life of Richard Watson* (London, 1817), p. 43.
[51] T. J. Brain, 'Richard Watson and the Debate on Toleration in the Late Eighteenth Century', *Price-Priestley Newsletter*, 2 (1978), pp. 4–26.
[52] Richard Watson, *An Address to the People of Great Britain* (London, 1798), p. 147.
[53] Watson, *Anecdotes*, p. 8.
[54] Ibid., p. 86.
[55] Richard Watson, *A Letter to the Members of the Honourable House of Commons* (London, 1772), pp. 8, 34.
[56] Watson, *Anecdotes*, p. 39.
[57] Richard Watson, *An Apology for Christianity* (Cambridge, 1776), p. 2.

freedom of inquiry to make intellectual progress.[58] But the limits of human reason, reliant in the end on revelation, meant that ideas of truth were mutable. An open mind opposed to dogma was the only way to achieve the best possible understanding of Christianity.[59]

He repeated standard Anglican defences of learned and pastoral clergy. He published a series of theological tracts in which he recommended a series of readings for Anglican ordinands. First came the Bible: 'the only sure foundation upon which they ought to build every article of faith which they profess'. But lay Christians were not equal in their abilities and even 'the wisest men want on many occasions all the helps of human learning to enable them to understand' the precise meaning of scripture.[60] Support for learned clergymen was his means to prevent a *sola scriptura* system from descending into enthusiasm. It would also be prevented by a pastoral clergy and Watson duly recommended appropriate devotional works.[61] His reforms were both doctrinal and pastoral. He proposed reform to remove the Athanasian creed as well as, despite his own non-residency, reducing episcopal monies better to fund the lower clergy.[62]

Another example of the survival of latitudinarian civil religion was Paley. He had not signed the Feathers Tavern petition. But he believed freedom of inquiry would result in intellectual improvement and a more liberal church settlement.[63] He hoped church reform would come in a more enlightened period of history.[64] If the church proved incapable of reform, it might find itself akin to the master of a family whose servants were more knowledgeable than he. Civil society would be ungovernable. Since scripture did not prescribe any specific form of church government, ecclesiology ought to proceed upon the basis of utility in maintaining civil order.[65] Blackburne and the Feathers Tavern petitioners had been trying to seek church reform on the basis of the alignment between Anglican ecclesiology and the dictates of scripture. Conversely, Paley argued that, since Christ's kingdom was not of this world, temporal establishments in religions should be suited to the societies in which they were to operate. Paley explained that 'Whoever expects to find in the Scriptures a specific direction for every moral doubt that arises, looks for more than he will meet with'. The Thirty-Nine Articles were merely 'articles of *peace*' designed to comprehend all who supported the middle way between Geneva and Rome.

---

[58] Watson, *Anecdotes*, p. 217.
[59] Ibid., p. 227.
[60] Richard Watson, *A Collection of Theological Tracts* (6 vols, Cambridge, 1785), vol. 1, pp. v, xii.
[61] Ibid., vol. 6, p. iii.
[62] See Richard Watson, *A Letter to his Grace the Archbishop of Canterbury* (London, 1783); *Considerations on the Expediency of Revising the Liturgy and the Articles* (London, 1790).
[63] William Paley, 'A Defence of the Considerations on the Propriety of Requiring a Subscription to Articles of Faith', in *Sermons and Tracts by the Late Rev. William Paley* (London, 1808), pp. 41–4.
[64] Ibid., p. 44.
[65] Ibid., p. 58.

But for civil office, there should be '*complete* toleration of all dissenters from the established church'.[66]

There also remained churchmen willing to defend comprehensive Anglican concepts of civil religion after the subscription controversy. Wyvill, despite being suspected of Unitarian inclinations, held Anglican orders throughout his life. Politically, Wyvill had organised the relatively moderate Yorkshire association during the 1770s and 1780s, which had achieved some success in the programme for 'economical reform'.[67] He had also campaigned for the Feathers Tavern programme. Wyvill's view of the established church was one of Protestant comprehension. 'Has not', he asked in 1771, 'the Rigour of our Establishment excluded Multitudes of pious and learned Christians'? Wyvill hoped to don the cloak of respectability to achieve some moderate reform. He was not convinced that more radical moves like seeking to organise Unitarianism would be politically worthwhile. He hoped that 'his sentiments in favour of a moderate Ecclesiastical Reform ... might be more likely to meet a candid reception, and consequently to produce a beneficial effect'.[68]

Wyvill's vision of the Christian commonwealth fits within the category of Anglican civil religion. A truly reformed established church devoid of imposture, superstition, and intolerance would support a Christian commonwealth purged of old corruption by which parliamentary elections were controlled as well as politicians and electors bribed. This duty extended no further than pastoral care for a Protestant flock and pedagogical support in lay interpretation of scripture. Wyvill maintained his support for ecclesiastical reform despite the reaction of the 1790s. He supported abolition of the Test Act which, he claimed, would conclude 'the great work of Tillotson'. Abolition should be followed up, he explained, by a reformation of 'our forms of worship' in a manner of which 'Clarke and Hoadley' as well as 'Locke and Newton would have approved'.[69]

Among political reformers, there were more straightforward utilitarian conceptions of Anglican civil religion. Horne Tooke was an Anglican clergyman who had been associated with John Wilkes and was a friend of Jebb, Disney, and Lindsey. He had been present along with Disney and Lindsey at the Revolution Society on 5 November 1789 when Price gave his infamous sermon. Like this group of reformers, he had been educated at Cambridge. Yet Horne Tooke expressed to Wilkes his regret at having received orders, apologising for the 'infectious hand of a bishop' that 'waved over me'.[70] Nevertheless, he always

---

[66] William Paley, *The Works of William Paley* (6 vols, Cambridge, 1830), vol. 4, pp. 337, 348.
[67] Ian R. Christie, *Wilkes, Wyvill and Reform: The Parliamentary Reform Movement in Eighteenth-Century Britain* (Cambridge, 1994).
[68] Christopher Wyvill, *Thoughts on our Articles of Religion, with Respect to their Supposed Utility to the State* (London, 1771), p. 8.
[69] Christopher Wyvill, *Intolerance the Disgrace of Christians not the Fault of their Religion* (London, 1809), pp. 81, 85.
[70] John Horne Tooke, *Memoirs of John Tooke*, ed. Alexander H. Stephens (2 vols, London, 1813), vol. 1, pp. 320–1.

kept his position as a 'great stickler for the church of England: not on doctrinal points, but on the surer foundation of "civil utility"'.[71] The doctrines of the Church of England gave moral sanction to social order.

As Gascoigne has explained, latitudinarianism was in rapid decline.[72] A central breach in latitudinarianism lay between those, such as Blackburne and Law, who were content to theologise rationally and generously within the confines of orthodoxy and those, including those who seceded from the Anglican fold, who were prepared to acknowledge the potentially Dissenting consequences of a liberal frame of mind. These divisions were exemplified during the parliamentary debate on the Feathers Tavern petition by Burke. To abolish subscription would revive 'the dissensions and animosities, which had slept for a century'. The creeds of the established church should 'remain fixed and permanent like our civil constitution'. Reformers should focus on preserving 'the body ecclesiastical from tyranny and despotism'.[73] In 1792, Burke spoke against Charles James Fox's unsuccessful motion to repeal a number of statutes considered burdensome for Unitarians. 'The principle of your petitioners', he explained, 'is no passive conscientious Dissent on account of an over-scrupulous habit of mind.' Their Dissent was 'fundamental'. It 'goes to the very root'. It was not a question of 'this rite or that ceremony, on this or that school opinion'. It was a question of 'an establishment, as unchristian, unlawful, contrary to the Gospel and to natural right, popish and idolatrous'.[74] Burke believed the language once used to justify Whig England was being used by Dissenters to subvert that very order. He also accused those Dissenters of incivility in religion. They were the inheritors of the puritans of the mid-seventeenth century.

The civil religion of Enlightened Dissent

Despite Burke's fears, the civil religion of Enlightened Dissent remained recognisably Whig. It celebrated the albeit imperfect settlement achieved in 1689 as the basis for a truly reformed Christian commonwealth. As Price preached in 1759, 'our religious liberty is the crown of all our national advantages' and, in that regard, 'we are almost singular and unparalleled'. Dissenters continued to criticise Roman Catholic and high-church justifications for *jure divino* sacerdotal priesthoods. Price warned against 'ignorant pretenders to spiritual authority' across Europe.[75] He later explained that ministers of the gospel 'became, soon after its establishment' by Constantine, 'an independent body of spiritual rulers, nominating one another in perpetual succession, claiming,

---

[71] Ibid., p. 477.
[72] Gascoigne, 'Anglican Latitudinarianism and Political Radicalism', pp. 36–8.
[73] Cobbett (ed.), *Parliamentary History*, vol. 7, pp. 276, 288.
[74] Edmund Burke, 'Speech on a Motion for Leave to Bring a Bill to Repeal and Alter Certain Acts Respecting Religious Opinions, 11 May 1792', in *The Works of the Right Honourable Edmund Burke* (6 vols, London, 1906–7), vol. 3, p. 330.
[75] Price, *Political Writings*, p. 4.

by divine right, the highest powers and forming a hierarchy which by degrees produced a despotism'.[76]

It was even possible for Dissenters tactically to make use of certain Whig shibboleths such as the godly prince-in-parliament. Priestley recalled how James II 'had almost subverted both the civil and religious liberties of his country' before the 'divine being ... raised up William the third, of glorious memory, for our deliverance'.[77] Andrew Kippis appealed for relief for Dissenting ministers on the grounds that Britain enjoyed 'a generous prince of the Brunswick line' supported by 'a seemingly equitable administration' and 'moderate and wise members of both houses'. Kippis added that there were also 'candid bishops' and 'a liberal spirit in all ranks of men' with 'Toleration lifting her voice loudly in Europe'.[78] To this extent, Enlightened Dissenters were at one with standard low-church and Whig conceptions of the Christian commonwealth.

But the Enlightened Dissenting conception of the Christian commonwealth went further than its Anglican counterparts. It cast crucial aspects of the 1689 settlement as nothing more than popish superstition and priestly imposture. The claims once deployed by latitudinarians, Whigs, and low churchmen in defence of the civil religion of Anglican England were now being turned against them. Jebb claimed that any bishop who supported subscription was a 'firm and steady' supporter of civil and religious despotism.[79] Priestley praised Jebb for his 'ardent zeal for the cause of civil and religious liberty in their full extent'.[80] Enlightened Dissenters revived older divisions between Erastian or magisterial and congregational governance of the human church. Price remarked that at the time of the foundation of the present religious establishment, 'the nation was but emerging from Popery'. Was it not possible that the establishment 'should be entirely agreeable to the purity of the Christian doctrine' and that 'it should want no review in order to secure its safety, and adapt it to a more improved and enlightened age'?[81] Pastors who imposed upon the private and tender conscience of the lay Protestant should no longer minster to their flocks. The Church of England, Price concluded, with its creeds, articles, tests and bolstered by its apparatus of state officeholders, represented nothing more than 'Popery reformed'.[82]

Gospel simplicity was as integral to the Dissenting vision of civil religion as the Anglican. It was a point observed wryly by William Pitt the Elder, earl of Chatham, in 1773. The Dissenters 'contend for a scriptural and spiritual

---

[76] Ibid., p. 91.
[77] Joseph Priestley, *Political Writings*, ed. Peter Miller (Cambridge, 1993), p. 22.
[78] Andrew Kippis, *A Vindication of the Protestant Dissenting Ministers with Regard to their Late Application to Parliament* (London, 1772), pp. 51–2.
[79] Jebb, *Works*, vol. 3, pp. 73–5.
[80] See Priestley's dedication in John Jebb, 'Doctrine of Philosophical Necessity', in *Works*, vol. 1, pp. 129–30.
[81] Price, *Political Writings*, p. 10.
[82] Ibid., p. 135.

worship', he explained, but the Church of England had 'a Calvinistic Creed, a Popish liturgy and Arminian clergy'.[83] As Jebb explained, 'the evils of government and the want of felicity in the governed ... arise from the want of a moral and religious principle, which the religion of the gospel, unveiled in its native excellence can alone afford'. The 'right arrangement of political power' could only be achieved by 'philological knowledge of the Scriptures'.[84] Lindsey preached that, by 'its peculiar advantages, its easy doctrines and most powerful motives', the gospel enabled 'men of little worldly account, and wholly uncultivated with learning' to attain 'great wisdom and perfection in virtue'. Gospel study encouraged 'a love of truth, and integrity of heart, and a mind attentive to instruction'.[85] A Christian commonwealth purged of the popish apparatus of the establishment was now to be the best imitation of the principles of primitive Christianity.

For Anglican theorists of civil religion, the history of the pre-Reformation church was the history of superstition and priestly usurpation. Priestcraft and religious mystery had been the tools by which true religion in the form of the pure gospel and primitive Christianity had been subverted into an unwieldy faith. But for Enlightened Dissenters, this history had not concluded during the mid-sixteenth century. Between 1772 and 1804, Priestley published his *Institutes of Natural and Revealed Religion, History of the Corruptions of Christianity, A General History of the Christian Church, Discourses on the Evidences of Revealed Religion*, and *Notes on all the Books of Scripture*. These works formed a grand project recounting the emergence of superstition and clerical imposture in the primitive church, tracing the account into the Reformation church but continuing its history into the eighteenth century. Any form of ritualism in outward worship constituted evidence of superstition. Any mystery, above all the Trinity, signified corruption. Priestley sought to demolish the doctrines of the incarnation and atonement as well as the claim that Christ mediated between God and humankind through his two natures.

In the aftermath of the subscription controversy, Jebb continued the history of corrupt religion into the 1770s. He recounted how the Reformation had freed English Christians from the tyranny of Rome for the supposedly godly king only to become the defender of popish superstition. 'Our boasted Reformation', he argued, 'in fact, was little more than an act of justifiable rebellion against our Spiritual head'. But 'we renounced the dominion of the Universal Monarch' only to 'set up a Spiritual head of our own'.[86] The defenders of the Erastianism that had characterised the English church settlement since the sixteenth century had failed to make good their commitment to the Reformation. Reacting to Warburton's *Alliance*, Jebb announced that 'the Reformation ... is but just

---

[83] Cited in Horton Davies, *Worship and Theology in England: From Watts and Wesley to Maurice, 1690–1850* (Princeton, 1961), p. 139.
[84] Jebb, *Works*, vol. 1, p. 189.
[85] Theophilus Lindsey, *Sermons* (2 vols, London, 1810), vol. 1, p. 29.
[86] John Jebb, *Letters on the Subject of Subscription* (London, 1772), pp. 2–6.

begun'.[87] True religion, understood as the complete liberty for the lay individual to flourish in his exclusive relationship with God, could only be achieved by purging the magisterial justifications for the Reformation from the established church. The first reform must be the abolition of religious tests in favour of a creed based on the principle of *sola scriptura* study.[88] For Disney, too, who campaigned against the Warburtonian positions advanced by the divine and philosopher John Balguy, the failure of the Feathers Tavern petition showed the need for further Reformation.[89]

Price and Priestley provided a neat summary of the Dissenting vision of the ultimate end of the secular civil magistrate. It was, in the words of Price, to protect men in worshipping 'God according to his conscience, and of professing those principles of religion, which he thinks, come nearest to the simplicity of the Gospel'.[90] Because Christ was 'the only law-giver of Christians', there could be 'no such thing as human authority in religious matters'. The office of the civil magistrate was 'not to interpose in any religious differences, but to keep the peace, to secure the civil rights of men, and to protect and encourage all good subjects of all sects and persuasions'.[91] For Priestley, the state could only legitimately intervene if the public good was better served by collective organisation than individual action. The 'good of the whole' dictated that the state subordinate the individual only 'with respect to those things in which the public can make better provision for them than he could for himself'.[92] Religion was not one of these instances. Responding to Warburton's *Alliance* above all, Priestley warned 'Mere Statesmen' that the 'most perfect freedom of inquiry and debate' was a more Protestant value than 'propriety (which is the same as utility)'.[93] However useful an established church might be against practical atheism, its structures retained the popish superstition that withheld spiritual enlightenment.

A minimalist conception of the state radicalised standard conceptions of toleration. Anglicans had sought to tolerate Dissenters whose theologies, they supposed, were wrong. But toleration, the argument ran, was the only means by which civil peace might be secured while an established church might persuade errant Protestants to return to the true religion of the gospel. For Enlightened Dissenters, toleration denoted a generous and comprehensive spirit towards all varieties of thought on the basis that free inquiry, candour, and intellectual progress in all spheres would push Christianity towards the truth. Dissenters chided even latitudinarian heroes for their intolerance towards sceptics and

---

[87] Ibid., p. 15.
[88] Ibid., pp. 16, 19.
[89] See John Disney, *A Letter to the Most Reverend the Lord Archbishop of Canterbury* (London, 1774); *Remarks on Dr. Balguy's Sermon* (London, 1775); *A Short View of the Controversies Occasioned by* The Confessional (2nd edn, London, 1775).
[90] Price, *Political Writings*, p. 4.
[91] Ibid., p. 5.
[92] Priestley, *Political Writings*, p. 134.
[93] Ibid., p. 82.

Roman Catholics. Unitarians like Priestley lined up to criticise Locke for his failure to support the principle of full toleration.[94] Sir George Savile, a member of Priestley's congregation, tabled the Catholic Relief Bill in May 1778. In *Observations on the Importance of the American Revolution* (1785) Price paid tribute to Hume, for 'by attacking, with great ability, every principle of truth and reason, he put me upon examining the ground upon which I stood and taught me not hastily to take any thing for granted'.[95]

By the pen of Priestley, Enlightened Dissenting defences of toleration ran radically deeper than toleration among Christians, encompassing the victims of English civil religion at its most uncivil: the Jews. Priestley believed a *détente* between Jews and Christians must precede the millennium, allowing a consensus to emerge about God's unity. In his *Institutes of Natural and Revealed Religion* (1772–4), Priestley claimed that Judaism and Christianity had 'so close a connection that they must stand and fall together'.[96] Christianity was 'the completion of the whole scheme'. Priestley's 'truly catholic religion' was built from 'the Jewish and Christian religions, jointly'.[97] Unlike the Christians' superstitious preoccupation with neo-Platonism and the Trinity, Jews understood the unity of God. 'Considering how strongly this great article, the worship of one God only,' he explained, 'is guarded in all the books of Scripture, it would seem impossible that it should ever be infringed by any who profess to hold the books of the Old and New Testament for the rule of their faith and practice.'[98] Further, Priestley believed that the Jewish nation 'is still to be distinguished by God, and to be the medium of his communications to the rest of the world'.[99]

Relatedly, Priestley hoped to reunite the Jews and Christians by correcting mistaken Jewish eschatology that failed to identify Jesus as the Messiah. The Jews were still awaiting the Messiah, a future Jewish king of the house of David, 'in whom themselves and all the nations of the earth should be blessed', who would rule them during the messianic age and the world to come. But Jesus was the true Messiah. None of the prophecies had given the Jews 'an idea of any other than a man like themselves in that illustrious character, and no other did they expect, or do they expect to this day'.[100] Similarly, Jesus 'made no other pretensions' than to be human and the apostles had agreed with the prophets that Christ was 'simply a *man*, and not either *God Almighty*, or a *super-angelic being*'. Thus 'the primitive Jewish church was properly

---

[94] Ibid., pp. 59–60.
[95] Price, *Political Writings*, p. 142.
[96] Joseph Priestley, *Institutes of Natural and Revealed Religion* (2nd edn, 2 vols, Birmingham, 1782), vol. 2, p. 279.
[97] Ibid., pp. 363, 364.
[98] Joseph Priestley, *The Theological and Miscellaneous Works of Joseph Priestley* (25 vols, London, 1817–32), vol. 2, 280.
[99] Ibid., p. 368.
[100] Joseph Priestley, *A History of the Corruptions of Christianity* (London, 1871, orig. 1782), p. 1.

Unitarian'.[101] By this reasoning, Priestley hoped that a Unitarian understanding of Christianity would remove the Jews' theological objections to accepting Christ as the promised Messiah.

Part of Priestley's civil religion included an overture to English Jewry. In 1786, Priestley penned an open appeal in his *Letters to the Jews*. Priestley professed to understand the Jews' 'dislike of *Christians*, and your abhorrence of their faith', given 'how much you have suffered by their cruel persecutions, and how contrary their doctrines have been to the fundamental principles of your religion'. However, 'at this day the cruel usage you have met with from Christian nations is happily much abated' and 'you will find that many of them have rejected, as abuses and corruptions of it, those doctrines which you so justly abhor'.[102] A universal spirit of candid toleration provided the means to unite Christians and Jews. As with the enlightenment of Christians, the Jews' conversion must 'be the result of your own diligent study and impartial inquiry'. But, by comparing 'the historical evidence of the two religions', the Jew will find that both were, 'in reality, but one'.[103] Still, for as long as Jews were 'to be distinguished as *Jews*, no less than as *Christians*, it will be more convenient for you to form a separate church, and to keep your sabbath as you do now'.[104] Jews would continue to observe their own rites according to Mosaic law until their reconciliation with Christianity and the dawn of the millennium.

However, the reaction of one Jew, David Levi, to Priestley's *Letters* tellingly reveals the contours of English civil religion as he turned its touchstones against Priestley. In the first of two volumes of *Letters to Dr. Priestly* between 1787 and 1789, Levi claimed that the Jews had been reticent about responding to Priestley because they did not wish to be 'construed as reflecting on, or tending towards disturbing the national religion, as by law established'.[105] Levi had decided to respond because, 'thanks to God, the Reformation, and glorious Revolution', his argument would be treated on its own terms, and 'we live in an enlightened age, in which the investigation of theological points is accounted laudable'.[106] In the tones of the Trinitarian establishment, Levi professed it surprising that a Christian might doubt the miraculous nature of Christ. Levi asked Priestley 'whether you sincerely intend, in this discussion to defend Christianity?'[107] It was not Levi's business to inquire whether 'the generality of Christians have just reason to pay divine honours to Jesus, or not'. That question 'ought to be settled among Christians themselves'. Priestley had not reflected 'how ridiculous it must appear, for you to invite the Jews to embrace, what you yourselves do not rightly understand'. Turning ideas of Enlightened divinity against Priestley, Levi

---

[101] Ibid., pp. 1, 3, 5.
[102] Priestley, *Theological and Miscellaneous Works*, vol. 20, p. 228.
[103] Ibid., p. 250.
[104] Ibid., p. 245.
[105] David Levi, *Letters to Dr. Priestly* (3rd edn, London, 1793), p. 4.
[106] Ibid., p. 6.
[107] Ibid., p. 8.

asked 'how it was possible that a Divine or Philosopher, of your distinguished rank, in the republic of letters' should behave so.[108]

The relationship between English Christians and Jews was especially sensitive for Enlightened Dissenters, since it risked association with the Hebraism of the seventeenth-century puritans now considered to be enthusiasts. But Priestley's Unitarian impulse to unite the Christians with the Jews sat within the broader attempt among Enlightened Dissenters to build a Christian commonwealth broad enough to encompass freedom of conscience without risking enthusiasm, civil disorder, or persecution. Dissenters were still sensible of the Anglican criticism, levelled by Burke, that they were the inheritors of the frenzied and king-killing spirit of the seventeenth-century sects. But, as Priestley explained, 'whether we be called, or call ourselves, christians, papists, protestants, dissenters, heretics, or even deists, (for all are equal here, all are actuated by the same spirit, and all are engaged in the same cause) we stand in need of the same liberty of thinking, debating, and publishing'.[109] Priestley sought to act as the standard-bearer for these ideals and wrote that something 'of the spirit of controversy seems necessary to keep men's attention to religion in general, as well as other things'.[110]

Priestley's project might be compared with Price's *A Review of the Principal Questions of Morals* (1758), in which Price defended the possibility of objective moral judgements made by rational individuals. Priestley also wrote the pamphlet *A Letter of Advice to those Dissenters Who Conduct the Application to Parliament for Relief from Certain Penal Laws* (1769), calling upon fellow-Dissenters to show their Anglican opponents that their communities of rational individuals were capable of intellectual independence, civility, and enlightenment. The pamphlet laid out his central maxims: 'to think with freedom, to speak and write with boldness, to suffer in a good cause with patience, to begin to act with caution, but to proceed with vigour'.[111] In that same year, he founded his *Theological Repository*, which ran until 1772 and was briefly reborn during the 1780s, as a forum for such civilised and candid discussion.

Philip Furneaux made a similar argument in response to Blackstone. In the fourth volume of his *Commentaries*, Blackstone ranked Dissent among such crimes as cursing, witchcraft, sorcery, lewdness, and blasphemy. The Toleration Act represented nothing more than a declaration of parliamentary indulgence of Dissent, a crime which threatened 'those ties and obligations by which all society is kept together' as well as the sovereignty of the state.[112] Furneaux responded that the Test and Corporation Acts should be repealed because

---

[108] Ibid., p. 29.
[109] Priestley, *Political Writings*, p. 122.
[110] Ibid., p. 92.
[111] Joseph Priestley, *A Letter of Advice to those Dissenters Who Conduct the Application to Parliament for Relief from Certain Penal Laws* (London, 1773), p. 455.
[112] Sir William Blackstone, *Commentaries on the Laws of England* (18th edn, 2 vols, New York, 1840), vol. 2, p. 74.

citizens should not be singled out on the sole grounds of their religion. 'Truth can only be propagated and supported by reason and argument', he explained, 'in conjunction with that mild and persuasive insinuation, and that openness and candor, and apparent benevolence in its advocates, which are suited to invite men's attention, and dispose them to examination.' The civil magistrate should make good the commitment to gospel simplicity by following the charitable example of the golden rule. A community of loving and candid Christians was capable of inquiring after truth. No 'civil punishments are adapted to enlighten the understanding, or to conciliate the affections'.[113] Religious tests represented persecution by enabling churches to dominate the secular power and augment their own authority.[114]

A minimalist conception of the state was justified by a faith in human improvability. The coming of Christ relied on the ability of humanity to prepare for it and rational piety was the key tool with which to achieve millennial aspirations.[115] The progressivist mindset of Enlightened Dissent owed a great deal to David Hartley's *Observations on Man* (1749). Hartley had developed doubts about the integrity of subscription to the Thirty-Nine Articles while an undergraduate at Cambridge, eventually opting instead for a career in medicine. Hartley's millenarianism related to his doctrine of 'associationism'. He took advantage of the growth of the new science to argue that the confluence of men's intellectual faculties would progress humankind towards the ultimate truth. Although it was impossible for one person to achieve full truthful understanding alone, the association of inquiring individuals enabled knowledge to grow gradually.

The exercise of reason would result in millenarian achievement. There had once been a state of human knowledge in which those 'who believe can see no reason for their own belief' in Christianity. But 'the diffusion of knowledge' had now spread 'to all ranks and orders of men, to all nations, kindred, tongues, and people'. It 'cannot now be stopped, but proceeds ever with an accelerated velocity'. The result was that 'the number of those who are able to give a reason for their faith increases every day'.[116] To achieve such progress, Hartley made a powerful defence of free inquiry and open discussion. Ultimate truth had been expressed by God in the essentials of scripture and the operation of the world. Human formularies about these truths were both imperfect distractions and impostures. Hartley opposed 'creeds, articles or systems of faith', for it was 'a great insult offered to the truths of religion, to suppose that they want the same kind of assistance as impostures, human projects or

---

[113] Philip Furneaux, *Letters to the Honourable Mr. Justice Blackstone* (2nd edn, London, 1771), p. 43.
[114] Ibid., pp. 164–5.
[115] See Jack Fruchtman Jr, *The Apocalyptic Politics of Richard Price and Joseph Priestley: A Study in Late Eighteenth Century Republican Millennialism* (Philadelphia, 1983).
[116] David Hartley, *Observations on Man, his Frame, his Duty, and his Expectations* (5th edn, 2 vols, London, 1810), vol. 2, pp. 388–9.

worldly designs'.[117] The arrival of the millennium would sweep away all such superstitions and restore a pure faith.

Philosophies like those of Hartley syncretised the rationalism of the new science with Christian revelation to provide a powerful conceptual basis for Enlightened Dissent.[118] The truths of science and theology were coterminous. Revelation was eventually to be attained by means of human reason. As Jebb claimed, 'reason is analogous to the naked eye; revelation to the sight, assisted by the telescope'.[119] Lindsey believed the discoveries of Robert Boyle, Isaac Newton, and Carl Linnaeus furnished Christ 'with new and unceasing songs of praise and adoration'.[120] Alongside gospel simplicity stood an insistence on the convergence between revealed and natural religion. For Jebb, the 'word of God, revealed in the scriptures of both Testaments, like the book of nature, lies open to us all'.[121] Priestley's discovery of oxygen was as much religious as a scientific step forward.

Such moral optimism signified a revision of the role of ministers of the gospel. For Enlightened Dissenters, it was perfectly legitimate for learned clergymen to preach the pure gospel and enable lay consciences to access scripture. But the dictates of the gospel and the growing moral capabilities of the flock meant that the appointment of clergymen lay not in the Erastian church-state but with the votes of gathered congregations. 'Jesus Christ has established among Christians an absolute equality', explained Price. 'He has declared that they have but one master, even himself, and that they are all brethren, and, therefore, has commanded them not to be called masters and, instead of assuming authority over one another, to be ready to wash one another's feet.'[122]

Ministers could only be chosen and removed by the popular sovereignty of the congregation. If the preaching of the elected minister did not accord with the scriptural interpretations of the lay individual, he reserved the power to elect a new minister or join another congregation. The powers of ministers were not those of persecution but 'persuasion and instruction', explained Price, as they were elected by their societies to 'conduct to their worship and to promote their spiritual improvement without any other powers'.[123] Priestley believed the gospels dictated that the 'propagation of Christianity, or reformation in christianity, is comprehended in the general idea of *promoting useful knowledge* of any kind, and this is certainly the duty of every man, in proportion to his ability and opportunity'. Christ 'gives no hint of any difference between *clergy* and *laity* among his disciples'.[124]

---

[117] Ibid., pp. 363, 368.
[118] Rivers, *Reason, Grace, and Sentiment*, vol. 1, pp. 53–9.
[119] Jebb, *Works*, vol. 2, p. 137.
[120] Theophilus Lindsey, *Vindicae Priestlieanae* (London, 1788), pp. 64–5.
[121] Jebb, *Works*, vol. 2, p. 240.
[122] Price, *Political Writings*, p. 90.
[123] Ibid., p. 91.
[124] Priestley, *Political Writings*, p. 68.

In the priesthood of all believers, the ideal of the learned minister ought to extend throughout the laity. Ministers of the gospel must remember, Priestley explained, that men should be, 'as far as possible, self taught' because 'the more liberty is given to everything in a state of growth, the more perfect it will become'.[125] Price celebrated that the 'researches of learned men among us have been pushed farther than ever they were in any nation' thanks to toleration of 'free and publick discussion' and to 'absolute and unbounded scope given to free enquiries of all kinds'.[126] Price imagined the circle of liberty extending to charitable Christians who 'ought to be directed always to the heavenly state, and their whole concern should be so to live and converse together, as to secure a joyful meeting there'.[127]

In 1783, a group of Enlightened Dissenters was involved in founding the Society for the Promotion of the Knowledge of the Scriptures. The Unitarian Society was founded in 1791 expressly to distribute tracts. These new organisations provide more than a faint echo of early eighteenth-century voluntarism including the Society for the Propagation of the Gospel (SPG) and the Society for Promoting Christian Knowledge (SPCK). However, the similarities should not be overstated. These earlier societies had taken the virtuous conduct of the laity as their chief object whereas, while sharing these aims, new societies founded by Dissenters took Christian enlightenment by means of free inquiry as their central message.

The priesthood of all believers required the exercise of reason to achieve millennial truth. Human interpretation was still imperfect, and congregations of sincere Christians were deliberately to elect learned ministers to lead in Christian enlightenment. 'Reason, as well as tradition and revelation', explained Price, 'lead us to expect a more improved and happy state of human affairs.' Light and knowledge had been spreading and 'human life at present, compared with what it once was, is much the same that a youth approaching manhood is compared with an infant'.[128] Thanks to free inquiry, there 'is probably a greater number of rational Christians (that is, of Christians upon enquiry) in England, than in all Popish countries'.[129]

Dissenting scholarship spilled much ink criticising the universities and seeking to advance its own academies. Oxford received most opprobrium. There had been a powerful academic synthesis of Newtonian science and liberal theology at Cambridge led by followers of Hoadly and Clarke.[130] Cambridge had also proven itself capable of at least some reform, resolving in 1772 to abolish subscription for bachelors of the arts, who nonetheless had to declare their

---

[125] Ibid., pp. 113, 111.
[126] Price, *Political Writings*, p. 5.
[127] Richard Price, *Four Dissertations* (London, 1787), p. 351.
[128] Price, *Political Writings*, p. 118.
[129] Ibid., p. 135.
[130] Gascoigne, *Cambridge in the Age of the Enlightenment*.

membership of the Church of England.[131] In 1779 the proposal was extended to bachelors of law, medicine, and music.[132] A similar proposal had failed at Oxford.[133] But the curricula of the two institutions had lagged behind the Dissenting academies from which, supposed the Dissenters, might emerge the learned ministry of a fully reformed Christian commonwealth.

It was also the role of ministry to encourage social perfectibility and Christian virtue by means of pastoral activities. The Enlightened Dissenting vision of social improvability combined the Protestant work ethic with the spirit of trade and the division of labour. It is a familiar refrain that these manufacturers and mill owners, tradesmen and products of the middling sorts, developed a bourgeois sense of Christian respectability.[134] But this is to miss the essential point, for it looks to the sociology of nineteenth-century capitalism rather than the roots of the ideal Christian polity. Political economy was a tool in the fight against popery. In its Dissenting guises, the spirit of Protestant political economy gained ascetic rather than opulent qualities.[135] Priestley bemoaned the lack of industriousness among the poorer sorts whose time was 'spent in alehouses, where they contract the worst habits, and often encourage one another in every kind of vice and licentiousness'.[136] He was struck how Jesus came from among the meek and lowly and did not restrict his words for 'persons of good condition'. He preached to the 'many, and especially those of the middle and lower classes, as standing in most need of instruction, and most likely to receive it with gratitude and without prejudice'.[137] Upon resigning his living in Yorkshire, Lindsey reminded his parishioners that they had a duty to obey their superiors. He also reprimanded them for impious living and 'all those noisy riotous games, always accompanied with profane oaths, and generally ending in the ale-house or worse'.[138]

A further aspect of pastoral Dissenting ministry was the need to purge the uncivil religion of enthusiasm. It behoved ministers of religion to keep their congregations productive in the pursuit of spiritual perfection. As Price explained in his *Review of the Principal Questions in Morals*, human conscience was fallible, and dutiful Christians must continually attempt to right their judgement. 'Moral agents are apt to mistake the circumstances they are in', explained Price, 'and, consequently, to form erroneous judgements concerning their own obligation.' Enthusiasts like the Methodists had fallen into precisely these traps. Instead, it was a duty to inform the conscience 'in the best manner

---

[131] C. H. Cooper, *Annals of Cambridge* (5 vols, Cambridge, 1842–1908), vol. 4, pp. 363–6.
[132] Gascoigne, *Cambridge in the Age of the Enlightenment*, p. 202.
[133] J. R. Green and G. Robertson, *Studies in Oxford History* (Oxford, 1901), pp. 323–4.
[134] Isaac Kramnick, *Republicanism and Bourgeois Radicalism: Political Ideology in Late Eighteenth-Century England and America* (Ithaca, NY, 1990).
[135] Max Weber, *The Protestant Ethic and the Spirit of Capitalism*, trans. Talcott Parsons (London, 1930), pp. 95–183.
[136] Priestley, *Theological and Miscellaneous Works*, vol. 25, p. 315.
[137] Joseph Priestley, *Socrates and Jesus Compared* (London, 1803), pp. 37, 44, 45.
[138] Lindsey, *Farewell Address*, p. 17.

we can'.[139] Claims of authority were equally as repugnant among enthusiasts as they were among established priesthoods. Humanity was engaged in a constant and progressive quest for truthful understanding and it must subject every claim and opinion to the same rational tests of free inquiry.

Dissenting civil religion, ultimately, would not require an established church. The Protestant Reformation, including its magisterial variety in England, was a staging post in the progressive spiritual enlightenment of humankind. Christians were sufficiently unreformed and uninstructed still to require a publicly regulated religion to access the scriptures and guard against superstition and enthusiasm. The secular civil magistrate should defend the liberty of all private congregations, associations, and churches from injury. Hartley conceded that, in its imperfect condition, the Christian commonwealth required a church establishment. He warned against Christians uncharitably criticising each other for subscribing to its imperfect articles of faith. In some cases, 'it may be necessary to submit to some forms'. It was 'only where a plain act of insincerity is required' that it gave 'great offence to others'.[140] As Price wrote in his *Discourse*, 'I see the ardor for liberty catching and spreading, a general amendment beginning in human affairs, the dominion of kings changed for the dominion of laws, and the dominion of priests giving way to the dominion of reason and conscience'.[141] The crucial point was that reform should come as and when the state of the Christian commonwealth merited it.

Priestley also exemplified such moderation. Realising that the abolition of the Church of England was neither necessarily propitious as long as mankind remained in its current state nor politically possible, he claimed not 'to plead against religious establishments in all cases'. Instead he argued 'against fixing every thing so unalterably'.[142] He proposed a series of reforms to make the Church of England more acceptable. First, the articles of faith should be reduced so that subscribers claimed only to believe 'in the religion of *Jesus Christ*, as it is set forth in the *New Testament*'. Second, clerical livings should be reformed so as better to serve the pastoral duties of the clergy and 'the necessary expenses of a liberal education'. Third, no clergyman was to hold civil office by his hierarchic status; therein lay the road to tyrannical pacts between ambitious statesmen and superstitious priests. The episcopal bench was 'a relic of the popish usurpations over the temporal rights of the sovereigns of Europe'. Finally, toleration should be fully established.[143] The abolition of the Church of England would eventually arrive. Millenarian improvement dictated it. Until then, a programme not dissimilar to comprehensive Anglican visions of civil religion would suffice.

---

[139] Richard Price, *A Review of the Principal Questions in Morals*, ed. D. D. Raphael (Oxford, 1974), pp. 177–9.
[140] Hartley, *Observations*, p. 369.
[141] Price, *Political Writings*, p. 195.
[142] Priestley, *Political Writings*, p. 89.
[143] Ibid., p. 87.

In the insistence on the gradual progressivism of human improvement lay a breach within Dissent over the propitious speed of reform. Disney represented the form of radical politics rejected by the likes of Price and Priestley. On 4 November 1792 he gave a sermon to which he gave the title 'The progressive improvement of civil liberty'. The sermon was a manifesto of Unitarian political and ecclesiastical reform, lauding America's achievement in redeeming 'herself from colonial oppression' and celebrating how the revolutionary French had thus far repelled invasion. It located consent, rather than divine right, as the central criterion for the legitimacy of civil institutions and granted the right of revolution in the instance that the contract be broken. Alongside reform to the criminal law, reductions in taxation, and the abolition of slavery stood the disestablishment of the Church of England.[144]

Despite the radical prescriptions of Disney, Enlightened Dissenters were still Whigs and they had to confront the realities of the 1790s. Revolution principles had bequeathed the godly king-in-parliament and the close relationship between the Church of England and the Hanoverian state. Most Enlightened Dissenters believed no set of radically alternative political or religious arrangements might be seriously canvassed while knowledge remained in the state that they found it during the late eighteenth century. Revolution principles had integrated public opinion to some degree within the arrangements of the church-state and therein lay the means of its improvement. The Church of England was unreformed and imperfect. Yet Price was pleased in 1759 that 'a great deal of that shocking rubbish' of popery 'has been cleared among us'. There was, perhaps, 'never a time, since that of the Apostles, in which the nature and design of the Gospel was so well understood'.[145] Persecution, superstition, and enthusiasm were in grand retreat. Reform would follow the progress caused by candid debate and free inquiry. As James Bradley has concluded, the contribution of Nonconformity to political reform lay in its interpretation of the relationship between 'human autonomy' and 'ecclesiastical polity'.[146] Enlightened Dissenters had laid out a vision of a civil religion that did not, upon the arrival of the millennium, need an established church but instead relied on myriad small congregations of rational lay believers with their elected pastors. Until then, the presence of the established church rendered Christian belief conformable with civil ends.

---

[144] John Disney, *Sermons* (2 vols, London, 1793), vol. 1, pp. 221–9.
[145] Price, *Political Writings*, p. 5.
[146] James Bradley, *Religion, Revolution and English Radicalism: Nonconformity in Eighteenth-Century Politics and Society* (Cambridge, 1990), p. 137, n. 46.

Conclusion:
Hanoverian Civil Religion and its Aftermath

> ... something deeper and better than priestcraft and priest-ridden ignorance was at the bottom of the phrase, Church and State, and intitled it to be the form in which so many thousands of men of England clothed the wish for their country's weal.[1]

The varieties of Hanoverian civil religion

Throughout the eighteenth century, English intellectuals sought to solve the problem of the status and public role of the Church of England by transforming it into a civil religion. By its claim to catholic apostolicity, the Church of England held authority over the interpretation of the revealed truth while recognising the fallibility of its articles of faith as a *jure humano* institution. The ministers of the national religion were to preach a civil confession of faith using only the gospel message of Jesus Christ. The civil sovereign secured its ascendancy over the ministers of the gospel, avoiding the problem of superstitious priestly orders destabilising the state, and provided a public option of worship to reduce the threat of enthusiasm. Irrespective of the veracity of the articles of faith of the Church of England, its status as a civil religion meant that all English people should observe its externals. In so doing, the English were to live civilly and piously in this world in anticipation of the next one. The civil religion was one of shared rituals of public worship through which English people expressed their belonging within the Christian commonwealth. Hanoverian intellectuals took seventeenth-century arguments for civil religion and transformed them for the temper of the Enlightenment in England.

There were several varieties of Hanoverian civil religion. Each civil religionist claimed to synthesise civility with piety to construct a church whose structures and beliefs were in accord with the interests of the civil state and the welfare of society. Each sought to harness the ecclesiology of the Reformation with the pastoral and learned ideals of Protestant ministry in constructing a national church whose clergymen preached the precepts of the gospel in a worldly religion of sociability, politeness, and virtue. By the promise of primitive Christianity, ministers would guide the priesthood of all believers in purging civil society of

---

[1] *CCS*, p. 32.

superstition and enthusiasm. The modern Christian civil religion would reconstruct the achievement of the ancient pagans in marrying piety with patriotism. These themes were not comparable with Machiavellian and Rousseauian aspirations for prolonging the life of the city or expanding the martial commonwealth. Rather, the civic potential of English Protestantism was directed towards a peaceful, polite, and sociable commonwealth in which secular relations served enlightenment and civilised society.

The first variety of civil religion, Anglican in character, celebrated the magisterial Reformation as the guarantor of true Christianity and relied on the godly prince to maintain the church-state relationship. It subjected Christian ministers to Erastian control to guarantee the direct soteriological relationship between the lay Christian and God. It was the faith of the defenders of the Revolution settlement in church and state. This variety was the civil religion of Trenchard and Gordon. In its clerical iteration, it defended the sacerdotal status of Christian priests within the Church of England while supporting the superiority of the civil magistrate. This iteration was the civil religion of Gibson and Warburton.

The second variety, more elitist in mood, realised the need for a religious establishment to secure liberty and toleration by regulating priests. This was the civil religion of Shaftesbury, Bolingbroke, Gibbon, and Hume. In the context of the party battles of the Revolution of 1688–9, Shaftesbury went to great lengths to obscure the deistical potential of his arguments. Bolingbroke believed his deistical writings could only be published posthumously. Gibbon felt more confident in the polite world ironically to mock the pretensions of the pompous and fanatical. Hume criticised English civil religion for its residual sacerdotalism and preferred the elective model of Scottish Presbyterianism. His engagement with Christian history also provoked significant controversy and he took great care to intervene in debates without harming the reputation of his Moderate allies. Each of these thinkers believed public religion was an intrinsic aspect of civilised society and developed a principled defence of the church-state relationship bequeathed by the Reformation. They believed civil religion could have a Christian foundation.

The third variety, Anglican, yet heterodox, sought a broad-based and comprehensive establishment for the nation to which all English Protestants might subscribe sincerely. This was the civil faith of clergymen like Blackburne, Law, and Watson. The fourth variety was a fully-fleshed Dissenting vision of civil religion in which an established church would collapse in the face of millennial renewal. Most of its exponents, like Priestley and Price, insisted that the church establishment was necessary to regulate public religion so long as human religious knowledge remained in an imperfect state. Their civil religion existed alongside the national church in myriad small congregations.

The central themes of Hanoverian civil religion rested on the supposition that an established religion, however theologically inaccurate, was a crucial feature of civil life. Reliance on the history of Christian reform allowed civil religionists to defend the supremacy of the civil magistrate over the church and synthesise their Protestant ecclesiology with the ancient pagan faiths, especially by reading Cicero. There was a constant suspicion of priestcraft and superstition in the effort to generate a vision of learned and pastoral established ministry. Civil religionists hoped to separate theology from philosophy and slay their monstrous scholastic offspring. They aimed to reverse perverted historical Christianity with its Greek, Roman, and Hebrew accretions, showing how Enlightened civil religion could become uncivil and slide into anti-Semitism. They hoped to restore true religion by prioritising simplicity in virtue and morals. Theirs was an effort to provide tolerant means of curing religious enthusiasm. They attacked the false virtues of austere Christianity, whether in its monkish Roman Catholic or ascetic Calvinist guises, in favour of a religion congenial to political economy and commercial society. In the age of the Enlightenment, civil religionists sought, first, to render religion safe for the civil state and, second, to civilise it.

It is now common to interpret the eighteenth century in its 'longest' sense.[2] Despite the novelty, created by the Revolution settlement, of the established Church of England enjoying jurisdictional superiority while recognising a degree of statutory toleration, the church-state relationship secured between 1660 and 1662 during the early Restoration remained broadly intact until Roman Catholic emancipation. Following the Quebec Act of 1774 and Catholic Relief Acts of 1778 and 1791, which removed some disabilities, allowing Catholics to worship openly and to build their own churches and chapels, the year 1828 witnessed the repeal of the Test and Corporation Acts. The following year saw Catholic emancipation. These reforms removed one of the central assumptions of Hanoverian civil religion, anti-Catholicism, and presented a fundamental challenge, which Hanoverian civil religionists claimed to have solved, to the problem of the status and public role of the Church of England.

Since a great deal of scholarship has focused on seventeenth-century civil religion, this study has encompassed the age between the Revolution of 1688 and the reaction to the French Revolution during the 1790s. But it is valuable to inquire into the survival of eighteenth-century theories of civil religion by exploring their reception in the thought of Coleridge and the broad-church movement that was so influenced by him. By his move from Enlightened Dissent during the 1790s to his defence of the Church of England during the emancipation debate of the 1820s, Coleridge reveals the evolution of the varieties of Hanoverian civil religion after the French Revolution. He attempted to adapt eighteenth-century civil religion to secure the status and public role of the Church of England in an age of Roman Catholic freedom.

Coleridge and the Church of England in the age of Napoleon Bonaparte

On 15 July 1801, Napoleon produced a document that shook Europe. The Concordat, signed with Pope Pius VII, secured reconciliation between French

---

[2] Clark, *English Society*.

revolutionaries and Roman Catholics as well as the civil status of the Roman Catholic Church. Although the Concordat did not return church lands and endowments confiscated during the 'de-Christianisation' of the 1790s, priests took the accord as a blessing to return from hiding or exile to their parishes. For European Protestants, here was the latest instance of the historic compact between secular and sacerdotal tyranny.[3] In England, Napoleon's actions shocked Coleridge.[4] Writing to his brother in June 1802 about the 'wretched Business', Samuel reflected how the Concordat 'first occasioned me to think accurately & with consecutive Logic on the force & meaning of the word *Established* Church'. He concluded 'very greatly in favor of the Church of England maintained, as it at present is'. Alluding to the language of Warburton's *Alliance*, Coleridge found that his earlier doubts about 'the effects & scriptural propriety of this (supposed) alliance of Church & State were wholly removed'. The 'Church of France' was 'a *standing* church – in the same sense as we say a *standing* army'.[5] It had become an 'instrument of state policy'.[6] Although Coleridge had professed to 'dislike & *suspect*' the 'Warburtonian System', it now seemed to recommend itself.[7]

Coleridge was a Unitarian becoming an Anglican. During his undergraduate years, he had moved in Cantabrigian circles of Enlightened Dissent, rejecting the Test and Corporation Acts and the jurisdictional status of the Church of England. He believed the established church was the next bastion of popish superstition to be dissolved by the progress of Christian reform. The French Revolution represented the next leap in the millennial perfectibility of humankind.[8] In 1793, Coleridge demonstrated in the Vice-Chancellor's Court in support of William Frend, the Unitarian Fellow of Jesus who had resigned his orders, having been accused of 'impugning religion, as by law established' in his critique of the Church of England in *Peace and Union Recommended* (1793).[9] In 1794, Coleridge

---

[3] William Roberts, 'Napoleon, the Concordat of 1801, and Its Consequences', in Frank J. Coppa (ed.), *Controversial Concordats: The Vatican's Relations with Napoleon, Mussolini, and Hitler* (Washington, DC, 1999), pp. 34–80.
[4] For Coleridge, see J. Robert Barth, *Coleridge and Christian Doctrine* (Cambridge, MA, 1969); Basil Willey, *Samuel Taylor Coleridge* (New York, 1973); J. T. Miller, *Ideology and Enlightenment: The Political and Social Thought of Samuel Taylor Coleridge* (New York, 1988); John Morrow, *Coleridge's Political Thought: Property, Morality and the Limits of Traditional Discourse* (Basingstoke, 1990); Peter Allen, 'Morrow on Coleridge's *Church and State*', *JHI*, 50:3 (1989), pp. 485–9.
[5] Samuel Taylor Coleridge to George Coleridge, 3 June 1802, in Earl Leslie Griggs (ed.), *The Collected Letters of Samuel Taylor Coleridge* (6 vols, Oxford, 1956–71), vol. 2, p. 803.
[6] Samuel Taylor Coleridge, *Essays on His Times in* The Morning Post *and* The Courier, ed. David V. Erdman (2 vols, Princeton, 1978), vol. 1, p. 314.
[7] Samuel Taylor Coleridge to George Coleridge, 3 June 1802, in *Collected Letters*, vol. 2, p. 803.
[8] Leonard W. Deen, 'Coleridge and the Radicalism of Religious Dissent', *Journal of English and Germanic Philology*, 61:3 (1962), pp. 496–510.
[9] Frida Knight, *University Rebel: The Life of William Frend, 1751–1841* (London, 1971), pp. 118–19, 140–1, 144.

developed a utopian vision with Robert Southey, which they dubbed 'Pantisocracy' and recommended for the adolescent republic of the United States. In the summer of 1795 he gave a series of lectures on 'revealed religion, its corruption and political views'. It castigated the 'political applications' of Trinitarianism.[10]

During his Unitarian days, Coleridge argued from the precepts of Christian primitivism and the idea of the priesthood of all believers for a religion 'of which every true Christian is the Priest, his own Heart the Altar, the Universe its Temple, and Errors and Vices its only Sacrifices'. Christianity was grounded on the simple truth that 'Immortality [is] made probable to us by the Light of Nature, and proved to us by the Resurrection of Jesus'. The basic instruction of the gospels was that 'Christians must behave towards the majority with loving kindness and submission preserving among themselves a perfect Equality'. In millennial expectation, the kingdom of God would arrive with 'the progressiveness of the moral world'. Coleridge carried the *sola scriptura* ideals of English Protestantism to their Unitarian extreme. It was a Christian duty to 'plea *for* the Oppressed not *to* them'. Reformers must imitate the Methodists in being '*personally* among the poor'. The Bible alone provided the true path of reform among the lower orders: 'By its Simplicity it will meet their comprehension, by its Benevolence soften their affections, by its Precepts it will direct their conduct, by the vastness of its Motives ensure their obedience.' Since Christianity is 'so obvious to the meanest Capacity' that he 'who knows his letters may find everything necessary for him' in the gospels, established churches bore 'the mark of antichrist' and were products of 'an intimate alliance with the powers of this World, which Jesus positively forbids'.[11]

Given Coleridge's language, it is plausible to infer opposition to Warburton's *Alliance*. It is equally plausible to interpret the *jure humano* arguments of the Bangorian controversy taken to their extreme conclusions in Coleridge's repetition of Christ's claim in John 18:36: 'My kingdom is not of this world'. There was no Christian foundation for this 'dear-bought Grace of Cathedrals, this costly defence of Despotism, this nurse of grovelling sentiment and cold-hearted Lip-worship'. The church establishment inspired 'Oppression, while it prompts servility'. It was noteworthy that every bishop, but one, had voted for the French war. Theirs was neither 'the Religion of Peace' nor 'the Religion of the meek and lowly Jesus, which forbids his Disciples all alliance with the powers of this World'. Theirs was the 'Religion of Mitres and Mysteries, the Religion of Pluralities and Persecution, the Eighteen-Thousand-Pound-a-Year Religion of Episcopacy'. Instead of 'the Minister of the Gospels, a Roman might recognise in these Dignitaries the High-priests of Mars'.[12]

---

[10] Samuel Taylor Coleridge, *Lectures 1795: On Politics and Religion*, ed. Lewis Patton and Peter Mann (Princeton, 1971), p. 83. See also David M. Craig, *Robert Southey and Romantic Apostasy: Political Argument in Britain, 1780–1840* (Woodbridge, 2007), pp. 79–100, 189–211.
[11] Coleridge, *Lectures 1795*, pp. 67–8n, 195, 227, 43–4, 209–10.
[12] Ibid., pp. 66–8.

Yet, after the Concordat, Coleridge began to move from the civil religion of Dissenting Protestantism to his defence of the Church of England, especially his conception of a national 'clerisy', in *On the Constitution in Church and State, According to the Idea of Each* (1829).[13] His reaction also took its cue from Burke.[14] Coleridge's concern with the status and public role of the Church of England reflected a more general sense of urgency about the state of the Christian religion in England following the outbreak of the French Revolution. The Church of England underwent a new voluntarist age comparable with the period between 1688 and the 1730s. The Sunday school movement grew rapidly after it had begun to emerge during the 1780s. The following societies were founded during the turn of the century: Proclamation Society (1787), Church Missionary Society (1799), Vice Society (1802), British and Foreign Bible Society (1804), National Society (1811), and Church Building Society (1817). Parliament also acted in its ecclesiological capacity to improve the parochial fabric of the English church in Sir William Scott's Act (1803) and the Church Buildings Act (1818). Pastoral care by Christian ministers was to be furnished with good buildings.

Coleridge and the Church of England in an age of Roman Catholic emancipation

The French Revolution was not the only force, nearing the close of the long eighteenth century, that motivated concern for the Church of England. The year 1828 witnessed the crescendo of decades of debate concerning Catholic relief with the repeal of the Test and Corporation Acts. The year 1829 saw Catholic emancipation. The debate had begun in 1825 with the proposed Relief Bill which, to assuage concerned Protestants, contained provisions to pay clerical livings from a state fund and to raise the property franchise to exclude poorer Catholics. In extending civil rights to Catholics, parliament completely revised the theoretical basis for civil religion. It was during the crisis that unfolded in 1825 that Coleridge began writing *Church and State*.[15] In 1830, Coleridge released a second edition with an attached essay entitled *Aids Toward a Right Judgement of the Late Catholic Bill*.

Coleridge needed to recast Anglican ideas of civil religion for an age of Catholic emancipation. He noted how the issue had turned above all on the central theme of godly kingship. The falls of William Pitt the Younger in 1801 and the 'ministry of all talents' in 1804 were due in part to the belief of George III that his

---

[13] Ben Knights, *The Idea of the Clerisy in the Nineteenth Century* (Cambridge, 1978); Stephen Prickett, 'Coleridge and the Idea of the Clerisy', in W. B. Crawford (ed.), *Reading Coleridge: Approaches and Applications* (Ithaca, NY, 1979), pp. 252–73.
[14] Alfred Cobban, *Edmund Burke and the Revolt against the Eighteenth Century: A Study of the Political and Social Thinking of Burke, Wordsworth, Coleridge and Southey* (2nd edn, London, 1960).
[15] *CCS*, pp. li–lvii.

coronation oath required him to defend 'the laws of God, the true profession of the Gospel, and the Protestant reformed religion established by law'.[16] Similarly, Coleridge noted the importance of anti-Catholicism. He condemned the 'Church Tyranny' and 'the usurpations of their Hierarchy, and Priesthood, under the same name of spiritual authority exercising a temporal Lordship'.[17] But he no longer wished 'to exclude any man from a seat in the Cabinet for worshipping a Wafer'.[18] In return for emancipation, Roman Catholics must promise not to acquire any share of the nation's wealth reserved for the established church.[19] Given that one intellectual justification for exclusion had been that Roman Catholics were incapable of sincere promise-keeping and temporal loyalty, Coleridge's solution showed the difficulties in adapting to the new age.

There was, however, an even bigger problem. Coleridge could no longer defend the church-state relationship on the grounds of the royal supremacy by the crown-in-parliament because growing numbers of Dissenters and Catholics could vote and sit in the Commons. He needed to locate the legitimacy of the national church elsewhere.[20] To do so, he surveyed the ecclesiological history of the long Reformation and developed the proprietorial idea of an independent estate. In a letter of July 1802, he discussed 'a statute of Queen Elizabeth' that confirmed the clergy as 'the great, venerable, third *Estate* of the Realm'. Anglican churchmen and their property 'are an elementary part of our constitution, not created by any Legislature, but really & truly antecedent to any form of Government of England upon which any existing Laws can be built'. The 'Church is not depend[en]t on the Government, nor can the Legislature constit[ution]ally alter it's property without consent of the Proprietor'. This represented an establishment because the Church of England had its 'own foundation'. By comparison, the 'Church of France', under the arrangements of the Concordat, 'has no foundation of it's own – it is a House of Convenience built on the sands of a transient Legislature – & no wise differs from a *standing Army*'.[21] Unlike the French church, the church in England was intrinsically part of the nation and no government could alter or remove its foundation.

However, the proprietorial theme did not imply a return to old sacerdotal Anglican ideas of the Church of England as a distinct society that had struck an alliance with the civil state. The church was an estate of the realm; it was *a priori* part of the nation. Whereas personal property was simply the '*Propriety*' of the realm, the property of the church was the '*Nationalty*'. These were

---

[16] Ibid., p. xxxvi, n. 1.
[17] Samuel Taylor Coleridge, *Aids to Reflection and Confessions of an Inquiring Spirit* (new edn, London, 1884), p. 141n.
[18] Samuel Taylor Coleridge to William Mudford, [28 May 1822], in *Collected Letters*, vol. 5, p. 228.
[19] *CCS*, pp. 156–7.
[20] Ibid., p. 103.
[21] Samuel Taylor Coleridge to George Coleridge, 1 July 1802, in *Collected Letters*, vol. 2, p. 806.

'the two constituent factors, the opposite, but correspondent and reciprocally supporting counter-weights, of the *commonwealth*; the existence of the one being the condition, and the perfecting, of the rightfulness of the other'. Both the civil state and national church were 'two poles of the same magnet; the magnet itself, which is constituted by them, is the CONSTITUTION of the nation'. The church stood beyond parliamentary control and it comprised the '*third* great venerable estate of the realm'. It could not be influenced by a parliament filled with indifferent 'Liberalists' like the philosophic radicals, Protestant Dissenters, and Roman Catholics.[22]

In its new constitutional guise, the Church of England became a truly national institution intrinsic to the state. National churches were the 'Offspring of Human Law'.[23] Their legitimacy was 'visible and public' rather than 'mystic and subjective'. Belonging within the nation implied belonging within its church. The pious Christian inhabited a 'KINGDOM, REALM ... OR STATE ... of the WORLD'. By contrast, the universal church of Christ was 'the *sustaining, correcting, befriending* Opposition of the world'. It was 'the compensating counterforce to the inherent and inevitable evils and defects of the STATE, *as* a State, and without reference to its better or worse construction as a particular state'. The church of Christ was truly an *ecclesia*, a democratic gathering of all otherworldly citizens, but the national church was an 'enclesia' or 'an order of men, chosen in and of the realm'.[24]

The clerisy of the national church was to perform similar functions to the Christian ministry of English civil religion. It was to be learned and pastoral even though its legitimacy no longer lay in employment by the civil state to administer externals of religion by law established. Its legitimacy derived from the Nationalty. Its role was now cultural. In formulating a national clerisy, Coleridge bequeathed to the nineteenth century the idea of an established intellectual cadre of elites.[25] The clerisy was 'grounded in *cultivation*, in the harmonious development of those qualities and faculties that characterise our *humanity*'.[26] Coleridge believed his new vision completed the ideals of learned ministry that had marked the long Reformation. His arguments belonged to the 'diffusion of light and knowledge through this kingdom, by the exertions of the Bishops and clergy, by Episcopalians and Puritans, from Edward VI to the Restoration', which was 'as wonderful as it was praiseworthy, and may be justly placed among the most remarkable facts of history'.[27]

---

[22] *CCS*, pp. 35, 31, 42, 68.
[23] Samuel Taylor Coleridge, *Marginalia*, eds George Whalley and H. J. Jackson (6 vols, Princeton, 1980–2001), vol. 2, p. 747.
[24] *CCS*, pp. 116, 114–15, 45.
[25] Knights, *Idea of the Clerisy*; Peter Allen, 'S. T. Coleridge's *Church and State* and the Idea of an Intellectual Establishment', *JHI*, 46:1 (1985), pp. 87–106; John Morrow, 'The National Church in Coleridge's *Church and State*: A Response to Allen', *JHI*, 47:4 (1986), pp. 640–52.
[26] *CCS*, pp. 42–3.
[27] Coleridge, *Aids to Reflection*, p. 6, n. 2.

Learning was pointless, continued Coleridge, if it was not used for pastoral ends. The clergyman should remain 'neither in the cloistered cell, nor in the wilderness', but become 'a neighbour and family-man'.[28] Coleridge drew from the defences of a national church by Harrington, the edition of whose works by Toland he had consulted, and Baxter, with whose writings Coleridge was familiar.[29] Coleridge also read Bishop Jeremy Taylor and wrote how 'it is really shocking to hear Christian Divines talk in the same way, that a Jewish High-Priest might have done unblameably'. The 'lust of sacerdotal Power is at the bottom of all this'. In true Christianity, ministers were 'only Teachers, Persuaders, Comforters'.[30]

In developing a proprietorial conception of national clerisy, Coleridge believed himself to be improving upon dominant eighteenth-century conceptions of the national church. The idea of the church as a *jure humano* institution under the direct control of the civil magistrate had left clergymen 'neither more or less than Government Cooks in office, to be kept, or dismissed, by the Ministers & Majority of the Houses for the time being'.[31] The 'fatal error into which the peculiar character of the English Reformation threw our church', explained Coleridge in September 1830, 'has borne bitter fruit ever since'. The church clung 'to court and stead, instead of cultivating the people'. The church should be 'a mediator between the people and the government, between the poor and the rich', but it has let 'the hearts of the common people be taken from it'.[32] By this analysis, Coleridge also transformed the relationship between the clerisy and the godly prince. The king was 'Protector and Supreme Trustee of the NATIONALTY' and could only act legitimately with the 'Houses of Convocation', the suspension of which in 1717 showed that 'no great principle was ever invaded or trampled on, that no sooner or later avenge itself on the country'.[33]

This new vision for the church-state relationship developed the relationship between civil religion and political economy. Eighteenth-century civil religionists had sought to reconcile Christian morality with luxury and commerce. But, in Romantic mood, Coleridge was suspicious of the relationship between cultural progress and political economy. Educational reform must lessen the degrading moral and intellectual impact of the spirit of commerciality that had so destabilised France and threatened England by enervating the spirit of their nobles.

---

[28] *CCS*, p. 75.
[29] Coleridge, *Marginalia*, vol. 1, p. 230. See also Peter J. Kitson, '"Our Prophetic Harrington": Coleridge, Pantisocracy, and Puritan Utopias', *The Wordsworth Circle*, 24:2 (1993), pp. 97–102; William Lamont, 'The Two "National Churches" of 1691 and 1829', in Anthony Fletcher and Peter Roberts (eds), *Religion, Culture and Society in Early Modern Britain: Essays in Honour of Patrick Collinson* (Cambridge, 1994), pp. 265–87.
[30] R. F. Brinkley (ed.), *Coleridge on the Seventeenth Century* (Durham, NC, 1955), p. 270.
[31] Samuel Taylor Coleridge to Henry Nelson Coleridge, 7 May 1832, in *Collected Letters*, vol. 6, p. 903.
[32] Samuel Taylor Coleridge, *Specimens of the Table Talk of Samuel Taylor Coleridge*, ed. Henry Nelson Coleridge (2nd edn, London, 1870), p. 109.
[33] *CCS*, pp. 83, 99, and n. 3.

The clerisy tempered the spirits of both commerciality and aristocracy by its proprietorial independence. The story of the commercial invasion of the clerical and aristocratic spheres had begun in the aftermath of the Revolution of 1688 when 'the spirit of the nation became more commercial than it had been before; a learned body, or clerisy, as such, gradually disappeared'.[34] The Nationalty also protected the church from theological trade and popular sermon-gadding. Coleridge criticised the 'mechanic philosophy' and 'spuriousness' of Dissenting education, which showed the 'morbid *symptoms*' of a disease, enthusiasm, that had attempted to destroy an established church with a 'mild and liberal' spirit.[35]

Coleridge's transformation of eighteenth-century civil religion in its latitudinarian and Anglican guise for an age of Roman Catholic emancipation survived in the nineteenth-century Anglican broad-church movement.[36] The idea of the status and public role of the Church of England altered with it. Such men as Thomas Arnold rejected both the intense ritualism of high-churchmanship and Anglo-Catholicism as well as the evangelical tendencies of low-churchmanship. They insisted that the Church of England was a national church capable of tolerating various forms of external worship. For Arnold, the established church was an essential institution of the Christian commonwealth. It was an instrument of godly rule whose members were 'directly called upon to Christianize the nation'. In their 'true moral character', the institutions of church and state were 'perfectly identical'.[37] But, in its Dissenting guise, the civil religion advanced by the likes of Coleridge during the 1790s would also have an afterlife in nineteenth-century socialism. In their millennial iterations, eighteenth-century concepts of civil religion gave forth the religious languages of early English socialism.[38] Couched in the language of the millennial and apocalyptic, nineteenth-century socialists spoke of true religion, returning humankind to its primitive and pristine condition, and casting down priestcraft in favour of the priesthood of all believers.

European and American connections

Although the limits of this study have necessitated a largely English focus, it is valuable to reflect on the relationships between Hanoverian civil religion and,

---

[34] Samuel Taylor Coleridge, 'Literary Lectures, 1818', in Henry Nelson Coleridge (ed.), *The Literary Remains of Samuel Taylor Coleridge* (4 vols, London, 1836), vol. 1, pp. 238–9.
[35] *CCS*, p. 69; Coleridge, *Marginalia*, vol. 1, p. 275.
[36] Richard Sanders, *Coleridge and the Broad Church Movement* (Durham, NC, 1942); Duncan Forbes, *The Liberal Anglican Idea of History* (Cambridge, 1952); Todd E. Jones, *The Broad Church: Biography of a Movement* (Lanham, MD, 2003).
[37] Thomas Arnold, *The Miscellaneous Works of Thomas Arnold D.D.* (New York, 1845), pp. 510, 437, 493.
[38] Gareth Stedman Jones, 'Rethinking Chartism', in Gareth Stedman Jones, *Languages of Class: Studies in English Working Class History, 1832–1982* (Cambridge, 1983), pp. 90–178; 'Religion and the Origins of Socialism', in Gareth Stedman Jones and Ira Katznelson (eds), *Religion and the Political Imagination* (Cambridge, 2010), pp. 171–89.

first, Protestant America and Europe and, second, Roman Catholic Europe. Aside from the relationship between the Church of England and Episcopalianism, concepts of American civil religion developed the Unitarian and congregational potential of Protestantism. They deepened its apocalyptic and millennial impulses by perceiving the new republic as a covenanted nation awaiting the second coming. It was the civil religion of the city upon the hill.[39] It was the product of a revolution that had been motivated in part by the problem of Catholic toleration in the Quebec Bill (1774) and the interposition of Anglican bishops in colonial affairs.[40]

In Protestant Europe, historians are more familiar with the history of civil religion. In Prussia, the idea of a civil religion is often associated with Hegel whose arguments owed much to the religious debates of the late eighteenth century.[41] In ecclesiology, German Lutheranism bore similar rejections of papal temporal jurisdiction to Anglicanism.[42] Theologically, Coleridge had become a student of the 'higher criticism' by touring Germany in 1798–9. He gained access to notes from the lectures of Johann Gottfried Eichhorn, whose criticism of the Old Testament involved philological study of the contexts in which scripture had been composed and who questioned the veracity of several books of the Old Testament as well as the Pauline letters and epistle of Jude.[43] Higher criticism was a product of the clerical Aufklärung, whose exponents, like Friedrich Nicolai, conceptualised the Aufklärung as the product of the Lutheran Reformation.[44] The convergence of Christian reform and the Enlightenment also motivated Frederick the Great in his early writings and later policies regarding the Prussian church-state relationship.[45]

Hanoverian civil religion bore further similarities with themes of eighteenth-century Christian reform in Roman Catholicism. Reformers took aim at the papal priest-king and his army of wealthy bishops. They were anti-curial in temporal matters but recognised the supremacy of the pope in spirituals due to the Petrine inheritance. These were central themes of the English

---

[39] Conrad Cherry, *God's New Israel: Religious Interpretations of American Destiny* (Chapel Hill, NC, 1971); E. L. Tuveson, *Redeemer Nation: The Idea of America's Millennial Role* (Chicago, 1968).
[40] Clark, *Language of Liberty*, pp. 384–91; Philip Lawson, *The Imperial Challenge: Quebec and Britain in the Age of the American Revolution* (Montreal, 1989).
[41] Laurence Dickey, *Hegel: Religion, Economics, and the Politics of Spirit, 1770–1807* (Cambridge, 1987), pp. 1–137; Thomas A. Lewis, *Religion, Modernity, and Politics in Hegel* (Oxford, 2011), pp. 16–56.
[42] Quentin Skinner, *The Foundations of Modern Political Thought* (2 vols, Cambridge, 1978), vol. 2, pp. 3–19.
[43] Morrow, *Coleridge's Political Thought*, pp. 62–3.
[44] Joachim Whaley, 'The Protestant Enlightenment in Germany', in Porter and Teich (eds), *Enlightenment in National Context*, pp. 106–17.
[45] Frederick of Prussia, *The Refutation of Machiavelli's* Prince *or Anti-Machiavel*, trans. Paul Sonnino (Athens, OH, 1981), pp. 1, 80–2, 132. See also Walter Hubatsch, *Frederick the Great: Absolutism and Administration*, trans. Patrick Doran (London, 1973), pp. 190–210.

Catholic Enlightenment.[46] Joseph Berington, John Lingard, and John Joseph Dillon were involved in the Cisalpine movement, which coalesced around such families as the Howards, Petres, and Throckmortons, that opposed Ultramontane papalism in its campaign for Catholic relief.[47] As much as the Scottish Catholic Enlightenment, the church-state writings of the English Catholic Enlightenment represented responses to Catholic Machiavellianism, which cast the pope as a Christian *imperator* and Roman Catholicism as the Christian version of Roman paganism.[48]

The strong relationship between Christian reform and the Enlightenment defined the ecclesiastical state of Mainz ruled by its Archbishop-Elector.[49] Similar themes can be discerned in Austria.[50] In Italy, historians are familiar with the names Ludovico Muratori of Modena and, in the Neapolitan Enlightenment, Giannone and Antonio Genovesi.[51] Genovesi, a priest and professor of philosophy, had studied the writings of Cudworth, Tillotson, Locke, Newton, Clarke, and Bolingbroke.[52] Francesco Longano studied Hobbes, Grotius, and Selden.[53] Francescantonio Grimaldi was a student of Gibbon.[54] Christian reform

---

[46] Geoffrey Scott, *Gothic Rage Undone: English Monks in the Age of Enlightenment* (Bath, 1992); Glickman, *English Catholic Community*; Alexander Lock, *Catholicism, Identity and Politics in the Age of Enlightenment: The Life and Career of Sir Thomas Gascoigne, 1745–1810* (Woodbridge, 2017).

[47] Eamonn Duffy, 'Ecclesiastical Democracy Detected: I (1779–87)', *Recusant History*, 10:4 (1970), pp. 193–209; 'Joseph Berington and the English Catholic Cisalpine Movement, 1772–1803' (PhD thesis, University of Cambridge, 1973); Eamonn Duffy (ed.), *Challoner and His Church: A Catholic Bishop in Georgian England* (London, 1981); C. H. Aveling, *The Handle and the Axe: The Catholic Recusants in England from Reformation to Emancipation* (London, 1976), pp. 322–45; Joseph Chinnici, *The English Catholic Enlightenment: John Lingard and the Cisalpine Movement, 1780–1850* (Shepherdstown, WV, 1980).

[48] Mark Goldie, 'The Scottish Catholic Enlightenment', *JBS*, 30:1 (1991), pp. 20–62; 'Common Sense Philosophy and Catholic Theology in the Scottish Enlightenment', *SVEC*, 302 (1992), pp. 281–320; 'Alexander Geddes at the Limits of the Catholic Enlightenment', *HJ*, 53:1 (2010), pp. 61–86.

[49] T. C. W. Blanning, *Reform and Revolution in Mainz, 1743–1803* (Cambridge, 1974); 'The Enlightenment in Catholic Germany', in Porter and Teich (eds), *Enlightenment in National Context*, pp. 118–26, at pp. 118–22.

[50] Ernst Wangermann, 'Reform Catholicism and Political Radicalism in the Austrian Enlightenment', in Porter and Teich (eds), *Enlightenment in National Context*, pp. 127–40, at pp. 128–33; Peter Dickson, 'Joseph II's Reshaping of the Austrian Church', *HJ*, 36:1 (1993), pp. 89–114; Derek Beales, 'Christians and *Philosophes*: The Case of the Austrian Enlightenment', in Derek Beales and Geoffrey Best (eds), *History, Society and the Churches* (Cambridge, 1985), pp. 169–94; *Enlightenment and Reform in Eighteenth-Century Europe* (London, 2005), pp. 117–20, 211–39.

[51] Owen Chadwick, 'The Italian Enlightenment', in Porter and Teich (eds), *Enlightenment in National Context*, pp. 90–105.

[52] Richard Bellamy, '"Da Metafisico a Mercatante" – Antonio Genovesi and the Development of a New Language of Commerce in Eighteenth-Century Naples', in Pagden (ed.), *Languages of Political Theory*, pp. 277–302; John Robertson, 'Antonio Genovesi: The Neapolitan Enlightenment and Political Economy', *HPT*, 8:2 (1987), pp. 335–44.

[53] Koen Stapelbroek, *Love, Self-Deceit, and Money: Commerce and Morality in the Early Neapolitan Enlightenment* (Toronto, 2008), pp. 62–5.

[54] Edoardo Tortarolo, 'Italian Historical Writing, 1680–1800', in José Rabasa, Masayuki

and the Enlightenment also overlapped in Venetian anti-curialism during the 1760s and at the synod of Pistoria of 1786.

It was, most notoriously, in France that Christian reform in the guise of Jansenism mingled with the Enlightenment. Anton Matytsin has shown how, in an attempt to fashion a Christian civil religion, Catholic and Protestant apologists in France confronted the arguments of the *philosophes* by harnessing worldly justifications for Christianity.[55] The French Revolution, during its earlier and more 'moderate' phase, had roots in Gallican reform.[56] Between 1789 and 1791, the Roman Catholic Church in France saw its right to tithe removed, its property nationalised, its corporate independence ended, its ecclesiastical boundaries redrawn, its regular clergy virtually abolished, and its secular clergy elected and rendered servants of the civil state. The earlier phase owed a great deal to the ecclesiological impact of Jansenism ever since the papal bull *Unigenitus* (1713) had galvanised antipapal reform movements within the French church by condemning opponents of royal absolutism.[57] Although Jansenists revived Augustinian theology, their opposition to royal absolutism, the French episcopacy, and Jesuitical and curial sacerdotalism lent support to Gallicanism.[58] The Civil Constitution of the Clergy was welcomed by such Jansenists as Louis-Adrien Le Paige, who saw it as the reversal of the Constantinean subversion of the church-state relationship, and several Jansenists, sitting on the committee of the National Assembly, had been involved in drafting its articles.[59]

It is necessary to distinguish this phase from the period after 1791, which witnessed the imprisonment, exile, and murder of many clergymen, the introduction of the Revolutionary calendar, iconoclasm, de-Christianisation, the removal of church towers and bells, the temples of reason, and the cult of the supreme being. The 'radicalisation' of the Revolution might be read as a product of the failure of the French Reformation to weaken or remove a superior clerical caste, leaving it to reinforce the sacral dynamics of royal absolutism by its propertied and legal privileges.[60] This failure lent a veneer of plausibility to the arguments of the *philosophes* that political and social utility was the only

---

Sato, Edoardo Tortarolo, and Daniel Woolf (eds), *The Oxford History of Historical Writing: Volume III: 1400–1800* (Oxford, 2012), pp. 364–83, at p. 380.
[55] Anton Matytsin, 'Reason and Utility in French Religious Apologetics', in Bulman and Ingram (eds), *God in the Enlightenment*, pp. 63–82, at pp. 71–6.
[56] Dale van Kley, *The Religious Origins of the French Revolution: From Calvin to the Civil Constitution, 1560–1791* (New Haven, 1996).
[57] Dale van Kley, *The Damiens Affair and the Unraveling of the Ancien Régime, 1750–1770* (Princeton, 1984).
[58] Robert Shackleton, 'Jansenism and the Enlightenment', *SVEC*, 57 (1967), pp. 1387–97.
[59] Dale van Kley, *The Jansenists and the Expulsion of the Jesuits from France* (New Haven and London, 1975).
[60] Alphonse Aulard, *Le Culte de Raison et Le Culte de l'Etre Suprême* (Arras, 1991); Dan Edelstein, *The Terror of Natural Right: Republicanism, the Cult of Nature, and the French Revolution* (Chicago, 2009); Michaël Culoma, *La Religion Civile de Rousseau à Robespierre* (Paris, 2010).

sound basis for civil religion.[61] The argument was put by Diderot's charming old woman, wise in reason but libertine by disposition, in *Jacques le Fataliste et son Maître* (written 1765–80), who said of religion and its laws that 'c'était une paire de béquilles qu'il ne fallait pas ôter à ceux qui avaient les jambes faibles'.[62]

Intriguingly, during the second and more radical stage of the Revolution, the Girondin, Nicolas Bonneville, criticised Warburton's account of the church-state relationship. Bonneville, a bookseller, printer, journalist, and writer, had been expelled from university after scandalising the authorities by refusing to support the claim that Rousseau was an atheist. A translator of d'Alembert and a friend of Tom Paine, he argued in *De l'Espirit des Religions* (1791) that the universal religion was social happiness and its priests were philosophers and scholars. Bonneville situated his civil religion within the debate between Warburton and Rousseau to the extent that it repays quoting the passage in full:

> L'auteur du *Contrat Social* a prétendu que le christianisme *romain* étoit plus *nuisible* qu'utile à la forte constitution d'un état libre. Warburton soutenoit que nulle religion n'étoit utile au corps politique. C'étoit anéantir tous les systêmes religieux; le philosophe anglois est, ce me semble, allé trop loin. Une religion qui feroit de la patrie et des loix l'objet de l'*adoration* de tous les citoyens, seroit aux yeux du sage une religion excellente. Le suprême pontife y seroit le *roi*, le *régisseur* suprême. Mourir pour son pays, seroit aller à *gloire éternelle*, au bonheur *éternel*. Celui qui auroit violé les loix *de son pays*, seroit un impie; et le premier *magistrat* de la nation, pontife et roi, auroit le droit de le dévouer a l'exécration publique, au nom de la société qu'il auroit *offensée*, et au nom du Dieu suprême qui nous a tous *également* soumis à des loix *impartiales*.
>
> Mais où est-elle cette religion qui s'accorde avec une bonne constitution? C'est la *nôtre*, ce sont toutes les religions qui ne sont mauvaises et contradictoires, que par l'altération qu'elles ont éprouvées, par la désunion des deux pouvoirs, autrefois confiés à un même chef librement élu par ses égaux.[63]

---

[61] Ronald I. Boss, 'The Development of Social Religion: A Contradiction of French Free Thought', *JHI*, 34:4 (1973), pp. 577–89.
[62] Trans. 'it was a pair of crutches that one must not remove from those who had weak legs'. Denis Diderot, *Œuvres de Denis Diderot* (7 vols, Paris, 1819), vol. 5, p. 452.
[63] Trans. 'The author of the *Social Contract* has claimed that Roman Christianity was more harmful than useful to the strong constitution of a free state. Warburton maintained that no religion was not useful to the body politic. It was to destroy all religious systems; the English philosopher has, it seems to me, gone too far. A religion that would make of the fatherland and of the laws the object of the adoration of all the citizens, would be in the eyes of the wise man an excellent religion. The supreme pontiff then would be the king, the supreme director. To die for one's country, would be to go to eternal glory, to eternal happiness. He who would have violated the laws of his country, would be an impious man; and the first magistrate of the nation, pontiff and king, would have the right to subject him to public censure, in the name of the society that he would have offended, and in the name of the supreme God who has submitted us all equally to impartial laws. But where is this religion that accords with a good

CONCLUSION

Like Rousseau, Bonneville hoped to replace Christianity with a civil religion that could never separate the temporal and spiritual powers. Given that eighteenth-century Gallicanism had produced several attempts to reconcile the two powers, it is striking that Bonneville alighted upon the exchange between Rousseau, a sometime Genevan, and Warburton, an Englishman. Bonneville, who from 1791 edited the journal of the Cercle Social, *Le Bouche de Fer*, shared the Anglicising impulse of the Cordeliers.[64] Bonneville's discussion reveals the European significance of a debate that throve in England from the time of Hobbes and Harrington to the age of the broad-church movement about the proper contribution of the Christian religion to the peace of the state and the welfare of society. The preserve of clergymen as much as philosophers, this was a debate about civil religion.

It would be fruitful for historians of the Enlightenment to investigate further how Christians who were engaged in the long history of the Reformation, albeit gently and often almost imperceptibly, lent their ecclesiological themes to the eighteenth century. One of the most important of these themes was the idea of a civil religion. Rousseau has given historians and political theorists civil religion in its most deistical and *politique* form. In so doing, he has provided a window onto the influence of Machiavelli and Hobbes throughout the eighteenth century. But it would now be an error to continue to define civil religion on Rousseau's terms alone. English theorists of civil religion developed arguments profoundly divergent from those of Rousseau and his followers during the French Revolution. By studying those with whom Rousseau might not have sympathised, historians will recover political and religious concepts that were once among the most prolific in eighteenth-century Europe and America but, today, have been hidden by secular modernity.

---

constitution? It is ours, it is all the religions that are not bad or contradictory, by the alteration that they have tried, by the disunion of the two powers, once confined to the same leader freely elected by his equals.' Nicolas Bonneville, *De L'Espirit des Religions* (new edn, Paris, 1792), pp. 39–40.

[64] Rachel Hammersley, *French Revolutionaries and English Republicans: The Cordeliers Club, 1790–1794* (Woodbridge, 2005), pp. 30, 52, 61; *The English Republican Tradition and Eighteenth-Century France: Between the Ancients and the Moderns* (Manchester, 2010), pp. 154–97.

Bibliography

Printed primary sources

Contemporary books and articles

Addison, Joseph, and Steele, Richard, *The Spectator*, ed. Smith, Gregory (4 vols, London, 1907).
Anon., *A Letter from a Person of Quality, to his Friend in the Country* (London, 1675).
d'Anvers, Caleb, *The Craftsman* (1726–37).
Arnold, Thomas, *The Miscellaneous Works of Thomas Arnold D.D.* (New York, 1845).
Atterbury, Francis, *A Letter to a Convocation-Man, concerning the Rights, Powers and Privileges of that Body* (London, 1697).
— *The Rights, Powers, and Privileges of an English Convocation* (London, 1700).
Barbeyrac, Jean, *The Spirit of the Ecclesiasticks in all Sects and Ages*, ed. Gordon, Thomas (London, 1722).
Baron, Richard, *The Pillars of Priestcraft and Orthodoxy Shaken* (4 vols, London, 1752).
Baxter, Richard, *A Holy Commonwealth, or Political Aphorisms, opening the True Principles of Government* (London, 1659).
Blackburne, Francis, *The Confessional* (3rd edn, London, 1770).
— *Reflections on the Fate of a Petition for Relief in the Matter of Subscription* (London, 1772).
— *Remarks on the Revd Dr Powell's Sermons in Defence of Subscription* (London, 1758).
— *The Works, Theological and Miscellaneous of Francis Blackburne* (7 vols, London, 1804).
Blackburne, Francis (ed.), *Memoirs of Thomas Hollis* (2 vols, London, 1780).
Blackstone, Sir William, *Commentaries on the Laws of England* (18th edn, 2 vols, New York, 1840).
Bolingbroke, Henry St John, Viscount, *Contributions to the* Craftsman, ed. Varey, Simon (Oxford, 1982).
— *Historical Writings*, ed. Kramnick, Isaac (Chicago and London, 1972).
— *Political Writings*, ed. Armitage, David (Cambridge, 1997).

— *The Works of Lord Bolingbroke* (4 vols, London, 1844).
Bonneville, Nicolas, *De L'Espirit des Religions* (new edn, Paris, 1792).
Boswell, James, *Boswell in Extremes: 1776–1778*, eds Mc. Weis, Charles and Pottle, Frederick A. (London, 1971).
Burke, Edmund, *The Works of the Right Honourable Edmund Burke* (6 vols, London, 1906–7).
Burnet, Gilbert, *A Discourse of the Pastoral Care* (3rd edn, London, 1692).
— *An Exposition of the Thirty-Nine Articles of the Church of England* (London, 1699).
Burton, John Hill (ed.), *Letters of Eminent Persons Addressed to David Hume* (Edinburgh, 1849).
Carlyle, Alexander, *The Autobiography of Alexander Carlyle of Inveresk, 1722–1805*, ed. Burton, John Hill (new edn, London and Edinburgh, 1910).
Cartwright, Major John, *American Independence* (London, 1775).
Chillingworth, William, *The Works of William Chillingworth* (10th edn, London, 1742).
Cicero, Marcus Tullius, *De Natura Deorum, Academica*, trans. Rackham, H. (London and Cambridge, MA, 1933).
— *De Senectute, de Amicitia, de Divinatione*, trans. Falconer, William Armistead (London, 1923).
Clarke, Samuel, *The Scripture Doctrine of the Trinity* (London, 1712).
Cobbett, William (ed.), *The Parliamentary History of England* (36 vols, London, 1806–20).
Coleridge, Henry Nelson (ed.), *The Literary Remains of Samuel Taylor Coleridge* (4 vols, London, 1836).
Coleridge, Samuel Taylor, *Aids to Reflection and Confessions of an Inquiring Spirit* (new edn, London, 1884).
— *Essays on His Times in* The Morning Post *and* The Courier, ed. Erdman, David V. (2 vols, Princeton, 1978).
— *Lectures 1795: On Politics and Religion*, ed. Patton, Lewis and Mann, Peter (Princeton, 1971).
— *Marginalia*, eds Whalley, George and Jackson, H. J. (6 vols, Princeton, 1980–2001).
— *On the Constitution of the Church and State, according to the Idea of Each*, ed. Colmer, John (Princeton, 1979).
— *Specimens of the Table Talk of Samuel Taylor Coleridge*, ed. Coleridge, Henry Nelson (2nd edn, London, 1870).
Cottret, Bernard (ed.), *Bolingbroke's Political Writings: The Conservative Enlightenment* (London and New York, 1997).
Debates and Speeches in Both Houses of Parliament concerning the Schism-Bill (London, 1715).
Diderot, Denis, *Œuvres de Denis Diderot* (7 vols, Paris, 1819).
Disney, John, *A Letter to the Most Reverend the Lord Archbishop of Canterbury* (London, 1774).

— *Reasons for Resigning the Rectory of Panton and Vicarage of Swinderby in Lincolnshire* (2nd edn, London, 1783).
— *Remarks on Dr. Balguy's Sermon* (London, 1775).
— *Sermons* (2 vols, London, 1793).
— *A Short View of the Controversies Occasioned by* The Confessional (2nd edn, London, 1775).
Dodwell, Henry, *A Reply to Mr Baxter's Pretended Confutation* (London, 1681).
Furneaux, Philip, *Letters to the Honourable Mr. Justice Blackstone* (2nd edn, London, 1771).
Gibbon, Edward, *The Autobiographies of Edward Gibbon*, ed. Murray, John (London, 1897).
— *The English Essays of Edward Gibbon*, ed. Craddock, Patricia (Oxford, 1972).
— *The History of the Decline and Fall of the Roman Empire*, ed. Womersley, David (3 vols, London, 1994).
— *Le Journal de Gibbon à Lausanne, 17 août 1763–19 avril 1764*, ed. Bonnard, Georges (Lausanne, 1945).
— *Memoirs of My Life*, ed. Radice, Betty (London, 1984).
— *Miscellanea Gibboniana*, eds de Beer, G. R., Bonnard, George, and Jounod, Louis (Lausanne, 1952).
Gibson, Edmund, *The Bishop of London's Pastoral Letter* (London, 1728).
— *The Bishop of London's Second Pastoral Letter* (London, 1730).
— *Codex Juris Ecclesiastici Anglicani* (2 vols, London, 1713).
— *The Dispute Adjusted* (Dublin, 1733).
— *Some Considerations upon Pluralities, Non-Residence and Salaries of Curates* (London, 1737).
Gordon, Thomas, *A Political Dissertation upon Bull-Baiting and Evening Lectures. With Occasional Meditations on the 30th of January* (London, 1718).
Grafton, Augustus FitzRoy, duke of, *Hints Submitted to the Serious Attention of the Clergy, Nobility and Gentry* (London, 1789).
Greig, J. Y. T. (ed.), *The Letters of David Hume* (2 vols, Oxford, 1932).
Griggs, Earl Leslie (ed.), *The Collected Letters of Samuel Taylor Coleridge* (6 vols, Oxford, 1956–71).
Harrington, James, *The Political Works of James Harrington*, ed. Pocock, J. G. A. (Cambridge, 1977).
Hartley, David, *Observations on Man, his Frame, his Duty, and his Expectations* (5th edn, 2 vols, London, 1810).
Herne, Thomas, *An Essay on Imposing and Subscribing Articles of Religion* (London, 1718).
Hickes, George, *The Constitution of the Catholic Church* (London, 1716).
Hobbes, Thomas, *Leviathan*, ed. Tuck, Richard (revised edn, Cambridge, 1996).
Home, John, *A Sketch of the Character of Mr. Hume and Diary of a Journey from Morpeth to Bath*, ed. Norton, David Fate (Edinburgh, 1976).

Hooker, Richard, *Of the Laws of Ecclesiastical Polity*, ed. McGrade, Arthur Stephen (3 vols, Oxford, 2013).
Hume, David, *Dialogues* and *Natural History of Religion*, ed. Gaskin, J. C. A. (Oxford, 1993).
— *An Enquiry concerning Human Understanding*, ed. Beauchamp, Tom L. (Oxford, 1999).
— *An Enquiry concerning the Principles of Morals*, ed. Beauchamp, Tom L. (Oxford, 1998).
— *Essays Moral, Political, and Literary*, ed. Miller, E. F. (Indianapolis, 1985).
— *The History of England from the Invasion of Julius Caesar to the Revolution in 1688* (6 vols, Indianapolis, 1983).
— *A Treatise of Human Nature*, eds. Norton, David Fate and Norton, Mary J. (Oxford, 2000).
Jackson, John, *The Ground of Civil and Ecclesiastical Government* (London, 1718).
Jebb, John, *Letters on the Subject of Subscription* (London, 1772).
— *A Short State of the Reasons for a Late Resignation* (Cambridge, 1773).
— *The Works Theological, Medical, Political and Miscellaneous of John Jebb* (3 vols, London, 1787).
Johnson, Samuel, *A Letter to Mr. Jonathan Dickinson* (Boston, 1747).
Kippis, Andrew, *A Vindication of the Protestant Dissenting Ministers with Regard to their Late Application to Parliament* (London, 1772).
Lashmore-Davies, Adrian (ed.), *The Unpublished Letters of Henry St John, First Viscount Bolingbroke* (5 vols, London, 2013).
The Last Will and Testament of the Late Rt. Hon. Henry St. John, Lord Viscount Bolingbroke (London, 1752).
Law, Edmund, *Considerations on the Propriety of Requiring a Subscription to Articles of Faith* (2nd edn, London, 1774).
— *Considerations on the State of the World with Regard to the Theory of Religion* (3rd edn, Cambridge, 1755).
— *Reflections on the Life and Character of Christ* (Cambridge, n.d.).
— *The True Nature and Intent of Religion* (Newcastle, 1768).
Levi, David, *Letters to Dr. Priestly* (3rd edn, London, 1793).
Lindsey, Theophilus, *A Farewell Address to the Parishioners of Catterick* (London, 1774).
— *A Sermon Preached at the Opening of the Chapel in Essex-House, Essex-Street* (London, 1774).
— *Sermons* (2 vols, London, 1810).
— *Vindicae Priestlieanae* (London, 1788).
Locke, John, *A Letter Concerning Toleration and Other Writings*, ed. Goldie, Mark (Indianapolis, 2010).
Low, D. M. (ed.), *Gibbon's Journal to January 28th. 1763* (London, 1929).
Ludlow, Edmund, *A Voyce from the Watch Tower, Part V: 1660–1662*, ed. Worden, Blair (Camden Fourth Series, vol. 21, London, 1978).

MacCulloch, Diarmaid (ed.), *The Book of Common Prayer* (London, 1999).
Machiavelli, Niccolò, *Discourses on Livy*, trans. Bondanella, Julia Conway and Bondanella, Peter (Oxford and New York, 1997).
Mandeville, Bernard, *The Fable of the Bees: Or Private Vices, Publick Benefits* (2 vols, London, 1732).
Marvell, Andrew, *The Rehearsal Transpos'd* (London, 1672).
Middleton, Conyers, *A Free Inquiry into the Miraculous Powers, which are Supposed to have Subsisted in the Christian Church, from the Earliest Ages through Several Centuries* (London, 1749).
— *The History of the Life of Marcus Tullius Cicero* (3 vols, London, 1741).
— *A Letter from Rome* (London, 1729).
— *A Letter to Dr. Waterland* (London, 1731).
Molesworth, Robert, *An Account of Denmark, with Francogallia and Some Considerations for the Promoting of Agriculture and Employing the Poor*, ed. Champion, Justin (Indianapolis, 2011).
Norton, J. E. (ed.), *The Letters of Edward Gibbon* (3 vols, London, 1956).
Paley, William, *Sermons and Tracts by the Late Rev. William Paley* (London, 1808).
— *The Works of William Paley* (6 vols, Cambridge, 1830).
Powell, William Samuel, *A Defence of the Subscription Required in the Church of England* (London, 1757).
Price, Richard, *Four Dissertations* (London, 1787).
— *Political Writings*, ed. Thomas, D. O. (Cambridge, 1991).
— *A Review of the Principal Questions in Morals*, ed. Raphael, D. D. (Oxford, 1974).
Priestley, Joseph, *A History of the Corruptions of Christianity* (London, 1871, orig. 1782).
— *Institutes of Natural and Revealed Religion* (2nd edn, 2 vols, Birmingham, 1782).
— *A Letter of Advice to those Dissenters Who Conduct the Application to Parliament for Relief from Certain Penal Laws* (London, 1773).
— *Political Writings*, ed. Miller, Peter (Cambridge, 1993).
— *Socrates and Jesus Compared* (London, 1803).
— *The Theological and Miscellaneous Works of Joseph Priestley* (25 vols, London, 1817–32).
Prussia, Frederick of, *The Refutation of Machiavelli's* Prince *or Anti-Machiavel*, trans. Sonnino, Paul (Athens, OH, 1981).
Rand, Benjamin (ed.), *The Life, Unpublished Letters, and Philosophical Regimen of Anthony, Earl of Shaftesbury* (London, 1900).
Rousseau, Jean-Jacques, *The Social Contract and Other Later Political Writings*, ed. Gourevitch, Victor (Cambridge, 1997).
Sacheverell, Henry, *The Character of a Low Churchman* (London, 1702).
— *The Political Union* (London, 1702).

Sambrook, James (ed.), *Liberty, the Castle of Indolence, and Other Poems* (Oxford, 1986).
Shaftesbury, Anthony Ashley Cooper, third earl of, *Characteristicks of Men, Manners, Opinions, Times*, ed. Uyl, Douglas den (3 vols, Indianapolis, 2001).
— *Characteristics of Men, Manners, Opinions, Times*, ed. Klein, Lawrence E. (Cambridge, 1999).
— *Several Letters Written by a Noble Lord to a Young Man at the University* (London, 1716).
Sherburn, George (ed.), *The Correspondence of Alexander Pope* (5 vols, Oxford, 1956).
Skelton, Philip, *Ophiomaches, or Deism Revealed* (London, 1749).
Swift, Jonathan, *The Works of Jonathan Swift*, ed. Scott, Walter (19 vols, Edinburgh, 1814).
Tacitus, Publius Cornelius, *The Works of Tacitus*, ed. Gordon, Thomas (2nd edn, 4 vols, London, 1737).
Tillotson, John, *The Works of the Most Reverend Dr. John Tillotson* (London, 1707).
Tindal, Matthew, *Rights of the Christian Church* (London, 1706).
Tocqueville, Alexis de, *The Old Regime and the Revolution*, ed. Furetand, François and Mélonio, Françoise, trans. Kahan, Alan S. (2 vols, Chicago and London, 1998).
Tooke, John Horne, *Memoirs of John Tooke*, ed. Stephens, Alexander H. (2 vols, London, 1813).
Trenchard, John and Gordon, Thomas, *Cato's Letters or Essays on Liberty, Civil and Religious, and other Important Subjects*, ed. Hamowy, Ronald (2 vols, Indianapolis, 1995).
— *A Collection of Tracts* (2 vols, London, 1751).
— *The Independent Whig* (7th edn, 2 vols, London, 1743).
Wakefield, Gilbert, *A Reply to Some Parts of the Bishop of Llandaff's Address to the People of Great Britain* (London, 1798).
Warburton, William, *The Alliance between Church and State* (4th edn, London, 1766).
— *A Critical and Philosophical Commentary on Mr. Pope's* Essay on Man (London, 1742).
— *The Doctrine of Grace* (London, 1763).
— *Remarks on Mr. David Hume's* Essay on the Natural History of Religion (London, 1757).
— *A View of Lord Bolingbroke's Philosophy* (3 vols, London, 1754–6).
— *A Vindication of Mr. Pope's* Essay on Man (London, 1739).
— *The Works of the Right Reverend William Warburton* (12 vols, London, 1811).
Waterland, Daniel, *The Case of Arian Subscription Considered* (Cambridge, 1721).
Watson, Richard, *An Address to the People of Great Britain* (London, 1798).
— *Anecdotes of the Life of Richard Watson* (London, 1817).

— *An Apology for Christianity* (Cambridge, 1776).
— *A Collection of Theological Tracts* (6 vols, Cambridge, 1785).
— *Considerations on the Expediency of Revising the Liturgy and the Articles* (London, 1790).
— *A Letter to his Grace the Archbishop of Canterbury* (London, 1783).
— *A Letter to the Members of the Honourable House of Commons* (London, 1772).
Whichcote, Benjamin, *Select Sermons* (London, 1698).
Williams, E. Neville (ed.), *The Eighteenth-Century Constitution* (Cambridge, 1960).
Williams, Harold (ed.), *The Correspondence of Jonathan Swift* (5 vols, Oxford, 1963–5).
Wyvill, Christopher, *Intolerance the Disgrace of Christians not the Fault of their Religion* (London, 1809).
— *Thoughts on our Articles of Religion, with Respect to their Supposed Utility to the State* (London, 1771).
Yorke, P. C. (ed.), *The Life and Correspondence of Philip Yorke, Earl of Hardwicke* (3 vols, Cambridge, 1913).

Secondary sources

Books and journal articles

Abbott, William M., 'Anticlericalism and Episcopacy in Parliamentary Debates, 1640–1641: Secular versus Spiritual Functions', in Sharp, Buchanan and Fissel, Mark (eds), *Law and Authority in Early Modern England* (Newark, DE, 2007), pp. 147–85.
Ajello, R. J. (ed.), *L'Età dei Lumi: Studi Storici sul Settecento Europeo in Onore di Franco Venturi* (Naples, 1985).
Aldridge, Alfred Owen, 'Shaftesbury and Bolingbroke', *Philological Quarterly*, 31:1 (1952), pp. 1–16.
— 'Shaftesbury and the Deist Manifesto', *Transactions of the American Philosophical Society*, new ser., 41:2 (1951), pp. 297–382.
Allen, Peter, 'Morrow on Coleridge's *Church and State*', *JHI*, 50:3 (1989), pp. 485–9.
— 'S. T. Coleridge's *Church and State* and the Idea of an Intellectual Establishment', *JHI*, 46:1 (1985), pp. 87–106.
Andre, Shane, 'Was Hume an Atheist?', *HS*, 19:1 (1993), pp. 141–66.
Aston, Nigel and Cragoe, Matthew (eds), *Anticlericalism in Britain, c.1500–1914* (Stroud, 2000).
Aston T. H. (ed.), *The History of the University of Oxford*, vol. 5, Sutherland, L. S. and Mitchell., L. G. (eds), *The Eighteenth Century* (Oxford, 1986), pp. 565–91.
Aulard, Alphonse, *Le Culte de Raison et Le Culte de l'Etre Suprême* (Arras, 1991).

Aveling, C. H., *The Handle and the Axe: The Catholic Recusants in England from Reformation to Emancipation* (London, 1976).
Ayres, Philip, *Classical Culture and the Idea of Rome in Eighteenth-Century England* (Cambridge, 1997).
Bailyn, Bernard, *The Ideological Origins of the American Revolution* (Cambridge, MA, 1967).
Baker, Derek (ed.), *Reform and Reformation in England and the Continent, c.1500–c.1750* (Oxford, 1979).
— *Renaissance and Renewal in Christian History* (Oxford, 1977).
Ball, Terence, Farr, James, and Hanson, Russell (eds), *Political Innovation and Conceptual Change* (Cambridge, 1989).
Barbour, Reid, *John Selden: Measures of the Holy Commonwealth in Seventeenth-Century England* (Toronto, 2004).
Barducci, Marco, 'Clement Barksdale, Translator of Grotius: Erastianism and Episcopacy in the English Church, 1651–1658', *The Seventeenth Century*, 25:2 (2010), pp. 265–80.
Barnett, S. J., *The Enlightenment and Religion: The Myths of Modernity* (Manchester, 2003).
— *Idol Temples and Crafty Priests: The Origins of Enlightenment Anticlericalism* (Basingstoke, 1999).
Barth, J. Robert, *Coleridge and Christian Doctrine* (Cambridge, MA, 1969).
Beales, Derek, 'Christians and *Philosophes*: The Case of the Austrian Enlightenment', in Beales, Derek and Best, Geoffrey (eds), *History, Society and the Churches* (Cambridge, 1985), pp. 169–94.
— *Enlightenment and Reform in Eighteenth-Century Europe* (London, 2005).
Beales, Derek, and Best, Geoffrey (eds), *History, Society and the Churches* (Cambridge, 1985).
Becker, Carl, *The Heavenly City of the Eighteenth-Century Philosophers* (2nd edn, New Haven and London, 2003, orig. 1932).
Beddard, Robert (ed.), *The Revolutions of 1688* (Oxford, 1991).
Beier, A. L., Cannadine, David, and Rosenheim, J. M. (eds), *The First Modern Society: Essays in English History in Honour of Lawrence Stone* (Cambridge, 1989).
Beiner, Ronald, *Civil Religion: A Dialogue in the History of Political Philosophy* (Cambridge, 2011).
Bejan, T. M., *Mere Civility: Disagreement and the Limits of Toleration* (Cambridge, MA, 2017).
Bellah, Robert N., *The Broken Covenant: American Civil Religion in Time of Trial* (2nd edn, Chicago and London, 1975).
Bellamy, Richard, '"Da Metafisico a Mercatante" – Antonio Genovesi and the Development of a New Language of Commerce in Eighteenth-Century Naples', in Pagden, Anthony (ed.), *The Languages of Political Theory in Early-Modern Europe* (Cambridge, 1987), pp. 277–302.

Bennett, G. V., *The Tory Crisis in Church and State: The Career of Francis Atterbury, Bishop of Rochester* (Oxford, 1975).
Bennett, G. V. and Walsh, J. D. (eds), *Essays in Modern English Church History: In Memory of Norman Sykes* (Oxford, 1966).
Berg, J. van den, 'Priestley, the Jews and the Millennium', in Katz, David S. and Israel, Jonathan I. (eds), *Sceptics, Millenarians and Jews* (Leiden, 1990), pp. 256–74.
Berger, Peter, *The Desecularization of the World: Resurgent Religion and World Politics* (Washington, DC, 1999).
— *The Sacred Canopy* (Garden City, NJ, 1967).
Berman, David, 'Anthony Collins's Essays in the *Independent Whig*', *Journal of the History of Philosophy*, 13:4 (1975), pp. 463–9.
— *A History of Atheism in Britain from Hobbes to Russell* (London, 1988).
Black, Jeremy, *The British and the Grand Tour* (London, 1985).
Blanning, T. C. W., 'The Enlightenment in Catholic Germany', in Porter, Roy and Teich, Mikuláš (eds), *The Enlightenment in National Context* (Cambridge, 1981), pp. 118–26.
— *Reform and Revolution in Mainz, 1743–1803* (Cambridge, 1974).
Bloom, Edward Alan and Bloom, Lilly D., *Joseph Addison's Sociable Animal: In the Marketplace, on the Hustings, in the Pulpit* (Providence, RI, 1971), pp. 151–202.
Blumenthal, Uta-Renate, *The Investiture Controversy: Church and Monarchy from the Ninth to the Twelfth Century* (Philadelphia, 1988).
Bond, Harold L., *The Literary Art of Edward Gibbon* (Oxford, 1960).
Bond, W. H., *Thomas Hollis of Lincoln's Inn: A Whig and His Books* (Cambridge, 1990).
Bongie, Laurence L., *David Hume: Prophet of the Counter-Revolution* (Oxford, 1965).
Boss, Ronald I., 'The Development of Social Religion: A Contradiction of French Free Thought', *JHI*, 34:4 (1973), pp. 577–89.
Bouwsma, W. J., 'Venice and the Political Education of Europe', in Hale, John R. (ed.), *Renaissance Venice* (London, 1973), pp. 445–66.
Bowersock, G. W., Clive, John, and Graubard, Stephen (eds), *Edward Gibbon and the Decline and Fall of the Roman Empire* (Cambridge, MA, 1977).
Bradley, James, 'Anti-Catholicism as Anglican Anticlericalism: Nonconformity and the Ideological Origins of Radical Disaffection', in Aston, Nigel and Cragoe, Matthew (eds), *Anticlericalism in Britain, c.1500–1914* (Stroud, 2000), pp. 67–92.
— 'The Changing Shape of Religious Ideas in Enlightened England', in Chapman, Alister, Coffey, John, and Gregory, Brad S. (eds), *Seeing Things Their Way: Intellectual History and the Return of Religion* (Notre Dame, IN, 2009), pp. 175–201.
— 'The Public, Parliament and the Protestant Dissenting Deputies, 1732–1740', *PH*, 24:1 (2005), pp. 71–90.

— *Religion, Revolution and English Radicalism: Nonconformity in Eighteenth-Century Politics and Society* (Cambridge, 1990).
Bradley, James and Kley, Dale van (eds), *Religion and Politics in Enlightenment Europe* (Notre Dame, IN, 2001).
Brain, T. J., 'Richard Watson and the Debate on Toleration in the Late Eighteenth Century', *Price-Priestley Newsletter*, 2 (1978), pp. 4–26.
Brewer, John, *The Sinews of Power: War, Money, and the English State, 1688–1783* (Cambridge, MA, 1990).
Brinkley, R. F. (ed.), *Coleridge on the Seventeenth Century* (Durham, NC, 1955).
Browning, Reed, *Political and Constitutional Ideas of the Court Whigs* (Baton Rouge, 1982).
Brumfitt, J. H., *Voltaire and Warburton* (Geneva, 1961).
Bulman, William J., *Anglican Enlightenment: Orientalism, Religion and Politics in England and Its Empire, 1648–1715* (Cambridge, 2015).
— 'Introduction: Enlightenment for the Culture Wars', in Bulman, William J. and Ingram, Robert G. (eds), *God in the Enlightenment* (Oxford, 2016), pp. 1–41.
Bulman, William J. and Ingram, Robert G. (eds), *God in the Enlightenment* (Oxford, 2016).
Bush, George R., 'Dr Codex Silenced: *Middleton* v *Crofts* Revisited', *Journal of Legal History*, 24:1 (2007), pp. 23–58.
Butterfield, Herbert, *The Whig Interpretation of History* (New York, 1965, orig. 1931).
Cameron, Euan, *Enchanted Europe: Superstition, Reason, and Religion, 1250–1750* (Oxford, 2010).
Campbell, Ted A., 'John Wesley and Conyers Middleton on Divine Intervention in History', *Church History*, 55:1 (1986), pp. 39–49.
Capaldi, Nicholas, 'Hume's Philosophy of Religion: God without Ethics', *IJPR*, 1:4 (1970), pp. 233–40.
Capaldi, Nicholas and Livingston, Donald W. (eds), *Liberty in Hume's* History of England (Dordrecht, 1990).
Casanova, José, *Public Religions in the Modern World* (Chicago and London, 1994).
Chadwick, Owen, 'Gibbon and the Church Historians', in Bowersock, G. W., Clive, John, and Graubard, Stephen (eds), *Edward Gibbon and the Decline and Fall of the Roman Empire* (Cambridge, MA, 1977), pp. 219–31.
— 'The Italian Enlightenment', in Porter, Roy and Teich, Mikuláš (eds), *The Enlightenment in National Context* (Cambridge, 1981), pp. 90–105.
Champion, Justin, 'Godless Politics: Hobbes and Public Religion', in Bulman, William J. and Ingram, Robert G. (eds), *God in the Enlightenment* (Oxford, 2016), pp. 42–62.
— *Pillars of Priestcraft Shaken: The Church of England and Its Enemies, 1660–1730* (Cambridge, 1992).

— *Republican Learning: John Toland and the Crisis of Christian Culture, 1696–1722* (Manchester and New York, 2003).
Chapman, Alister, Coffey, John, and Gregory, Brad S. (eds), *Seeing Things Their Way: Intellectual History and the Return of Religion* (Notre Dame, IN, 2009).
Chappell, V. C. (ed.), *Hume: A Collection of Critical Essays* (New York, 1966).
Cherpeck, Clifton, 'Warburton and the *Encyclopédie*', *Comparative Literature*, 7 (1955), pp. 226–39.
Cherry, Conrad, *God's New Israel: Religious Interpretations of American Destiny* (Chapel Hill, NC, 1971).
Chinnici, Joseph, *The English Catholic Enlightenment: John Lingard and the Cisalpine Movement, 1780–1850* (Shepherdstown, WV, 1980).
Christi, Marcela, 'Durkheim's Political Sociology: Civil Religion, Nationalism and Globalisation', in Hvithamar, Annika, Warburg, Margit, and Jacobsen, Brian (eds), *Holy Nations and Global Identities: Civil Religion, Nationalism and Globalisation* (Leiden, 2009), pp. 47–78.
Christianson, Paul, *Reformers and Babylon: English Apocalyptic Visions from the Reformation to the Eve of the Civil War* (Toronto, 1978).
Christie, Ian R., *Wilkes, Wyvill and Reform: The Parliamentary Reform Movement in Eighteenth-Century Britain* (Cambridge, 1994).
Clark, J. C. D., *English Society, 1660–1832* (2nd edn, Cambridge, 2000).
— *The Language of Liberty: Political Discourse and Social Dynamics in the Anglo-American World* (Cambridge, 1994).
— 'On Hitting the Buffers: The Historiography of England's Ancien Regime: A Response', *Past & Present*, 117:1 (1987), pp. 195–207.
— *Revolution and Rebellion: State and Society in England in the Seventeenth and Eighteenth Centuries* (Cambridge, 1986).
— 'Secularization and Modernization: The Failure of a "Grand Narrative"', *HJ*, 55:1 (2012), pp. 161–94.
Claydon, Tony, *William III and the Godly Revolution* (Cambridge, 1996).
Claydon, Tony and McBride, Ian (eds), *Protestantism and National Identity: Britain and Ireland, c. 1650 – c. 1850* (Cambridge, 1998).
Cobban, Alfred, *Edmund Burke and the Revolt against the Eighteenth Century: A Study of the Political and Social Thinking of Burke, Wordsworth, Coleridge and Southey* (2nd edn, London, 1960).
Coffey, John, *John Goodwin and the Puritan Revolution: Religion and Intellectual Change in Seventeenth-Century England* (Woodbridge, 2006).
Colley, Linda, *Britons: Forging the Nation, 1707–1832* (New Haven and London, 1992).
— *In Defiance of Oligarchy: The Tory Party, 1714–60* (Cambridge, 1982).
Collini, Stefan, Whatmore, Richard, and Young, Brian (eds), *History, Religion, and Culture: British Intellectual History, 1750–1950* (Cambridge, 2000).
Collins, Jeffrey R., 'The Restoration Bishops and the Royal Supremacy', *Church History*, 68:3 (1999), pp. 549–80.
Collinson, Patrick, *The Birthpangs of Protestant England: Religious and*

Cultural Change in the Sixteenth and Seventeenth Centuries (Basingstoke, 1988).

— 'If Constantine, then also Theodosius: St Ambrose and the Integrity of the Elizabethan *Ecclesia Anglicana*', *JEH*, 30:2 (1979), pp. 205–29.

Connell, Philip, *Secular Chains: Poetry and the Politics of Religion from Milton to Pope* (Oxford, 2016).

Cooper, C. H., *Annals of Cambridge* (5 vols, Cambridge, 1842–1908).

Coppa, Frank J. (ed.), *Controversial Concordats: The Vatican's Relations with Napoleon, Mussolini, and Hitler* (Washington, DC, 1999).

Cornwall, Robert D. and Gibson, William (eds), *Religion, Politics and Dissent, 1660–1832: Essays in Honour of James E. Bradley* (Farnham, 2010).

Costelloe, Timothy M., '"In Every Civilized Community": Hume on Belief and the Demise of Religion', *IJPR*, 55:3 (2004), pp. 171–85.

Coudert, Allison P. and Shoulson, Jeffrey S. (eds), *Hebraica Veritas? Christian Hebraists and the Study of Judaism in Early Modern Europe* (Philadelphia, 2004).

Craig, David M., *Robert Southey and Romantic Apostasy: Political Argument in Britain, 1780–1840* (Woodbridge, 2007).

Crawford, W. B. (ed.), *Reading Coleridge: Approaches and Applications* (Ithaca, NY, 1979).

Cruickshanks, Eveline (ed.), *Ideology and Conspiracy: Aspects of Jacobitism, 1689–1759* (Edinburgh, 1982).

Culoma, Michaël, *La Religion Civile de Rousseau à Robespierre* (Paris, 2010).

Curran, Mark, *Atheism, Religion and Enlightenment in Pre-Revolutionary Europe* (Woodbridge, 2012).

Darnton, Robert, 'The Case for the Enlightenment: George Washington's False Teeth', in Darnton, Robert, *George Washington's False Teeth: An Unconventional Guide to the Eighteenth Century* (New York and London, 2003), pp. 3–24.

— *George Washington's False Teeth: An Unconventional Guide to the Eighteenth Century* (New York and London, 2003).

— 'In Search of the Enlightenment: Recent Attempts to Create a Social History of Ideas', *JMH*, 43:1 (1971), pp. 113–32.

Davies, Horton, *Worship and Theology in England: From Watts and Wesley to Maurice, 1690–1850* (Princeton, 1961).

Davis, R. W. (ed.), *Lords of Parliament: Studies, 1714–1914* (Stanford, 1995).

Day, Matthew, 'The Sacred Contagion: John Trenchard, Natural History, and the Effluvial Politics of Religion', *History of Religions*, 50:2 (2010), pp. 144–61.

Deen, Leonard W., 'Coleridge and the Radicalism of Religious Dissent', *Journal of English and Germanic Philology*, 61:3 (1962), pp. 496–510.

Dickey, Laurence, *Hegel: Religion, Economics, and the Politics of Spirit, 1770–1807* (Cambridge, 1987).

Dickinson, H. T., *Bolingbroke* (London, 1970).

Dickson, Peter, 'Joseph II's Reshaping of the Austrian Church', *HJ*, 36:1 (1993), pp. 89–114.
Ditchfield, G. M., 'The Changing Nature of English Anticlericalism, *c*.1750– *c*.1800', in Aston, Nigel and Cragoe, Matthew (eds), *Anticlericalism in Britain, c.1500–1914* (Stroud, 2000), pp. 93–114.
— 'The Subscription Issue in British Parliamentary Politics, 1772–79', *PH*, 7:1 (1988), pp. 45–80.
Duffy, Eamonn, 'Correspondence Fraternelle: the SPCK, the SPG and the Churches of Switzerland in the War of the Spanish Succession', in Baker, Derek (ed.), *Reform and Reformation in England and the Continent, c.1500– c.1750* (Oxford, 1979), pp. 251–80.
— 'Ecclesiastical Democracy Detected: I (1779–87)', *Recusant History*, 10:4 (1970), pp. 193–209.
— 'Primitive Christianity Reviv'd: Religious Renewal in Augustan England', in Baker, Derek (ed.), *Renaissance and Renewal in Christian History* (Oxford, 1977), pp. 287–300.
— 'The SPCK and Europe', *Pietismus und Neuzeit*, 7 (1981), pp. 28–42.
Duffy, Eamonn (ed.), *Challoner and His Church: A Catholic Bishop in Georgian England* (London, 1981).
Dwyer, Philip G. (ed.), *Modern Prussian History, 1830–1947* (London and New York, 2001).
East, K. A., *The Radicalization of Cicero: John Toland and Strategic Editing in the Early Enlightenment* (London, 2017).
Edelstein, Dan, *The Enlightenment: A Genealogy* (Chicago, 2010).
— *The Terror of Natural Right: Republicanism, the Cult of Nature, and the French Revolution* (Chicago, 2009).
Ellenzweig, Sarah, *The Fringes of Belief: English Literature, Ancient Heresy, and the Politics of Freethinking, 1660–1760* (Stanford, 2008).
Endelman, Todd M., *The Jews of Georgian England, 1714–1830* (Ann Arbor, 1999).
Evans, A. W., *Warburton and the Warburtonians: A Study in Some Eighteenth-Century Controversies* (London, 1932).
Falkenstein, Lorne, 'Hume on "Genuine", "True", and "Rational" Religion', *Eighteenth Century Thought*, 4 (2009), pp. 171–201.
Farooq, Jennifer, *Preaching in Eighteenth-Century London* (Woodbridge, 2013).
Felsenstein, Frank, *Anti-Semitic Stereotypes: A Paradigm of Otherness in English Popular Culture, 1660–1832* (Baltimore, 1999).
Ferguson, J. P., *Dr Samuel Clarke* (Kineton, 1976).
Figgis, J. N., 'Erastus and Erastianism', *Journal of Theological Studies*, 2 (1901), pp. 66–101.
Firth, Katherine, *The Apocalyptic Tradition in Reformation Britain, 1530–1645* (Oxford, 1979).
Fitzpatrick, Martin, 'Latitudinarianism at the Parting of the Ways: A Suggestion', in Walsh, John, Haydon, Colin, and Taylor, Stephen (eds), *The Church of*

England, c. 1689 – c. 1833: From Toleration to Tractarianism (Cambridge, 1993), pp. 209–27.

Fletcher, Anthony and Roberts, Peter (eds), *Religion, Culture and Society in Early Modern Britain: Essays in Honour of Patrick Collinson* (Cambridge, 1994).

Flew, Anthony, Livingston, Donald W., Mavrodes, George I., and Norton, David Fate (eds), *Hume's Philosophy of Religion: The Sixth James Montgomery Hester Seminar* (Winston-Salem, NC, 1986).

Forbes, Duncan, *Hume's Philosophical Politics* (Cambridge, 1975).

— *The Liberal Anglican Idea of History* (Cambridge, 1952).

Fruchtman, Jack, Jr, *The Apocalyptic Politics of Richard Price and Joseph Priestley: A Study in Late Eighteenth Century Republican Millennialism* (Philadelphia, 1983).

Garnett, Jane and Matthew, Colin (eds), *Revival and Religion since 1700: Essays for John Walsh* (London, 1993).

Garrett, Don, 'What's True about Hume's "True Religion"?', *JSP*, 10:2 (2012), pp. 199–220.

Gascoigne, John, 'Anglican Latitudinarianism and Political Radicalism in the Late Eighteenth Century', *History*, 71:231 (1986), pp. 22–38.

— *Cambridge in the Age of the Enlightenment: Science, Religion and Politics from the Restoration to the French Revolution* (Cambridge, 1989).

— 'Church and State Allied: The Failure of Parliamentary Reform of the Universities, 1688–1800', in Beier, A. L., Cannadine, David, and Rosenheim, J. M. (eds), *The First Modern Society: Essays in English History in Honour of Lawrence Stone* (Cambridge, 1989), pp. 401–29.

— 'The Unity of Church and State Challenged: Responses to Hooker from the Restoration to the Nineteenth-Century Age of Reform', *JRH*, 21:1 (1997), pp. 60–79.

Gaskin, J. C. A., 'Hume's Attenuated Deism', *Archiv für Geschichte der Philosophie*, 65:2 (1983), pp. 160–73.

— *Hume's Philosophy of Religion* (2nd edn, Basingstoke, 1988).

Gay, Peter, *The Enlightenment: An Interpretation* (2 vols, London, 1966–9).

Gerrard, Christine, *The Patriot Opposition to Walpole* (Oxford, 1994).

Ghosh, Peter, 'Gibbon's First Thoughts: Rome, Christianity and the *Essai sur l'Etude de la Littérature*, 1758–61', *Journal of Roman Studies*, 85 (1995), pp. 148–64.

Gibson, William and Ingram, Robert G. (eds), *Religious Identities in Britain, 1660–1832* (Burlington, VT, 2005).

Gillespie, Michael Allen, *The Theological Origins of Modernity* (Chicago, 2008).

Gilley, Sheridan, 'Christianity and Enlightenment', *History of European Ideas*, 1:2 (1981), pp. 103–121.

Gipson, Alice Edna, *John Home: A Study of His Life and Works* (Caldwell, ID, [1917]).

Glickman, Gabriel, *The English Catholic Community, 1688–1745: Politics, Culture and Ideology* (Woodbridge, 2009).

Goldie, Mark, 'Alexander Geddes at the Limits of the Catholic Enlightenment', *HJ*, 53:1 (2010), pp. 61–86.

— 'Civil Religion and the English Enlightenment', in Schochet, Gordon (ed.), *Politics, Politeness, and Patriotism* (Washington, DC, 1993), pp. 31–46.

— 'The Civil Religion of James Harrington', in Pagden, Anthony (ed.), *The Languages of Political Theory in Early-Modern Europe* (Cambridge, 1987), pp. 197–222.

— 'Common Sense Philosophy and Catholic Theology in the Scottish Enlightenment', *SVEC*, 302 (1992), pp. 281–320.

— 'Ideology', in Ball, Terence, Farr, James, and Hanson, Russell (eds), *Political Innovation and Conceptual Change* (Cambridge, 1989), pp. 266–91.

— 'John Locke and Anglican Royalism', *Political Studies*, 31:1 (1983), pp. 61–85.

— 'John Locke, Jonas Proast, and Religious Toleration, 1688–1689', in Walsh, John, Haydon, Colin, and Taylor, Stephen (eds), *The Church of England, c. 1689 – c. 1833: From Toleration to Tractarianism* (Cambridge, 1993), pp. 143–71.

— 'The Nonjurors, Episcopacy, and the Origins of the Convocation Controversy', in Cruickshanks, Eveline (ed.), *Ideology and Conspiracy: Aspects of Jacobitism, 1689–1759* (Edinburgh, 1982), pp. 15–35.

— 'The Political Thought of the Anglican Revolution', in Beddard, Robert (ed.), *The Revolutions of 1688* (Oxford, 1991), pp. 102–36.

— 'Priestcraft and the Birth of Whiggism', in Phillipson, Nicholas and Skinner, Quentin (eds), *Political Discourse in Early Modern Britain* (Cambridge, 1993), pp. 209–31.

— 'The Scottish Catholic Enlightenment', *JBS*, 30:1 (1991), pp. 20–62.

— 'The Theory of Religious Intolerance in Restoration England', in Grell, Ole Peter, Israel, Jonathan, and Tyacke, Nicholas (eds), *From Persecution to Toleration: The Glorious Revolution and Religion in England* (Oxford, 1991), pp. 331–68.

— 'Toleration and the Godly Prince in Restoration England', in Morrow, John and Scott, Jonathan (eds), *Liberty, Authority, Formality: Political Ideas and Culture, 1600–1900* (Exeter, 2008), pp. 45–66.

Goldsmith, M. M., 'Liberty, Virtue, and the Rule of Law, 1689–1770', in Wootton, David (ed.), *Republicanism, Liberty, and Commercial Society* (Stanford, 1994), pp. 197–232.

Gorski, Philip, *American Covenant: A History of Civil Religion from the Puritans to the Present* (Princeton, 2017).

Gorski, Philip S., Kim, David Kyuman, Torpey, John, and VanAntwerpen, Jonathan (eds), *The Post-Secular in Question: Religion in Contemporary Society* (New York and London, 2012).

Grean, Stanley, *Shaftesbury's Philosophy of Religion and Ethics: A Study in Enthusiasm* (Athens, OH, 1967).
Greaves, R. W., 'The Working of an Alliance: A Comment on Warburton', in Bennett, G. V. and Walsh, J. D. (eds), *Essays in Modern English Church History: In Memory of Norman Sykes* (Oxford, 1966), pp. 163–80.
Green, J. R. and Robertson, G., *Studies in Oxford History* (Oxford, 1901).
Gregory, Jeremy, 'The Eighteenth-Century Reformation: The Pastoral Task of the Anglican Clergy after 1689', in Walsh, John, Haydon, Colin, and Taylor, Stephen (eds), *The Church of England, c. 1689 – c. 1833: From Toleration to Tractarianism* (Cambridge, 1993), pp. 67–85.
— *Restoration, Reformation and Reform: Archbishops of Canterbury and Their Diocese* (Oxford, 2000).
Grell, Ole Peter, Israel, Jonathan, and Tyacke, Nicholas (eds), *From Persecution to Toleration: The Glorious Revolution and Religion in England* (Oxford, 1991).
Gunnoe, Charles D., *Thomas Erastus and the Palatinate: A Renaissance Physician in the Second Reformation* (Leiden, 2010).
Guy, John, *Tudor England* (Oxford, 1988).
Haakonssen, Knud, 'Enlightened Dissent: An Introduction', in Haakonssen, Knud (ed.), *Enlightenment and Religion: Rational Dissent in Eighteenth-Century Britain* (Cambridge, 1996), pp. 1–11.
Haakonssen, Knud (ed.), *Enlightenment and Religion: Rational Dissent in Eighteenth-Century Britain* (Cambridge, 1996).
Habermas, Jürgen, 'Notes on Post-Secular Society', *New Perspectives Quarterly*, 25:4 (2008), pp. 17–29.
— 'Religion in the Public Sphere', *European Journal of Philosophy*, 14:1 (2006), pp. 1–25.
— *The Structural Transformation of the Public Sphere* (Cambridge, MA, 1989, orig. 1962).
Habermas, Jürgen and Hendieta, Eduardo, *Religion and Rationality: Essays on Reason, God and Modernity* (Cambridge, 2002).
Habermas, Jürgen and Ratzinger, Joseph, *Dialectics of Secularization: On Reason and Religion* (San Francisco, 2006).
Hale, John R. (ed.), *Renaissance Venice* (London, 1973).
Haller, William, *Foxe's Book of Martyrs and the Elect Nation* (London, 1963).
Hammersley, Rachel, *The English Republican Tradition and Eighteenth-Century France: Between the Ancients and the Moderns* (Manchester, 2010).
— *French Revolutionaries and English Republicans: The Cordeliers Club, 1790–1794* (Woodbridge, 2005).
Hamowy, Ronald, 'Cato's Letters, John Locke, and the Republican Paradigm', *HPT*, 11:2 (1990), pp. 273–94.
Hanley, Ryan Patrick, 'Hume's Critique and Defense of Religion', in Nadon, Christopher (ed.), *Enlightenment and Secularism: Essays on the Mobilization of Reason* (Lanham, MD, 2013), pp. 89–101.

Harris, James A., *Hume: An Intellectual Biography* (Cambridge, 2015).
Harris, M. R. A., 'Figures Relating to the Printing and Distribution of the *Craftsman* 1726 to 1730', *Bulletin of the Institute of Historical Research*, 43:108 (1970), pp. 233–42.
Harrison, Peter, *'Religion' and the Religions in the English Enlightenment* (Cambridge, 2002).
Haydon, Colin, *Anti-Catholicism in Eighteenth-Century England: A Political and Social Study* (London, 1993).
Hayton, David, 'The "Country" Interest and the Party System', in Jones, Clyve (ed.), *Party and Management in Parliament, 1660–1784* (New York, 1984), pp. 37–85.
— 'Moral Reform and Country Politics in the Late-Seventeenth-Century House of Commons', *Past & Present*, 128:1 (1990), pp. 48–89.
Herdt, Jennifer A., *Religion and Faction in Hume's Moral Philosophy* (Cambridge, 1997).
Herold, A. L., '"The Chief Characteristical Mark of the True Church": John Locke's Theology of Toleration and His Case for Civil Religion', *Review of Politics*, 76:2 (2014), pp. 195–221.
Heyd, Michael, *'Be Sober and Reasonable': The Critique of Enthusiasm in the Seventeenth and Early Eighteenth Centuries* (Leiden and New York, 1995).
Hilson, J. C., Jones, M. M. B., and Watson, J. R. (eds), *Augustan Worlds: Essays in Honour of A. R. Humphreys* (Leicester, 1978).
Hirschmann, A. O., *The Passions and the Interests: Political Arguments for Capitalism before Its Triumph* (Princeton, 1977).
Hoak, Dale (ed.), *Tudor Political Culture* (Cambridge, 1995).
Holden, Thomas, *Spectres of False Divinity: Hume's Moral Atheism* (Oxford, 2010).
Holmes, Geoffrey, *The Trial of Dr Sacheverell* (London, 1973).
Hone, Joseph, *Literature and Party Politics at the Accession of Queen Anne* (Oxford, 2017).
Hope, Nicholas, 'Prussian Protestantism', in Dwyer, Philip G. (ed.), *Modern Prussian History, 1830–1947* (London and New York, 2001), pp. 188–208.
Hubatsch, Walter, *Frederick the Great: Absolutism and Administration*, trans. Doran, Patrick (London, 1973).
Hudson, Wayne, Lucci, Diego, and Wigelsworth, Jeffrey R. (eds), *Atheism and Deism Revalued: Heterodox Religious Identities in Britain, 1650–1800* (Farnham, 2014).
Hunter, Michael and Wootton, David (eds), *Atheism from the Reformation to the Enlightenment* (Oxford, 1992).
Hvithamar, Annika, Warburg, Margit, and Jacobsen, Brian (eds), *Holy Nations and Global Identities: Civil Religion, Nationalism and Globalisation* (Leiden, 2009).
Immerwahr, John, 'Hume's Aesthetic Theism', *HS*, 22:2 (1996), pp. 225–338.

Ingram, Robert G., *Reformation without End: Religion, Politics and the Past in Post-Revolutionary England* (Manchester, 2018).
— *Religion, Reform and Modernity in the Eighteenth Century: Thomas Secker and the Church of England* (Woodbridge, 2007).
— '"The Weight of Historical Evidence": Conyers Middleton and the Eighteenth-Century Miracles Debate', in Cornwall, Robert D. and Gibson, William (eds), *Religion, Politics and Dissent, 1660–1832: Essays in Honour of James E. Bradley* (Farnham, 2010), pp. 85–109.
— 'William Warburton, Divine Action, and Enlightened Christianity', in Gibson, William and Ingram, Robert G. (eds), *Religious Identities in Britain, 1660–1832* (Burlington, VT, 2005), pp. 97–117.
Innes, Joanna, 'Jonathan Clark, Social History, and England's "Ancien Regime"', *Past & Present*, 115:1 (1987), pp. 165–200.
— 'Parliament and Church Reform: Off and on the Agenda', in Pentland, Gordon and Davis, Michael T. (eds), *Property and Popular Politics: England and Scotland, 1760–1832* (Cambridge, 1989), pp. 39–57.
Isaacs, Tina, 'The Anglican Hierarchy and the Reformation of Manners, 1688–1738', *JEH*, 33:3 (1982), pp. 391–411.
Israel, Jonathan, *Enlightenment Contested: Philosophy, Modernity, and the Emancipation of Man, 1670–1752* (Oxford, 2006).
— *Radical Enlightenment: Philosophy and the Making of Modernity, 1650–1750* (Oxford, 2001).
Jacob, James R., *Henry Stubbe, Radical Protestantism and the Early Enlightenment* (Cambridge, 1983).
Jacob, Margaret C., *Living the Enlightenment: Freemasonry and Politics in Eighteenth-Century Europe* (New York, 1991).
— *The Radical Enlightenment: Pantheists, Freemasons, and Republicans* (London, 1981).
Jacob, W. M., *The Clerical Profession in the Long Eighteenth Century* (Oxford, 2007).
James, D. G., *The Life of Reason: Hobbes, Locke, Bolingbroke* (London, 1949).
Johnston, Warren, 'Revelation and the Revolution of 1688–1689', *HJ*, 48:2 (2005), pp. 351–89.
— *Revelation Restored: The Apocalypse in Later Seventeenth-Century England* (Woodbridge, 2011).
Jones, Clyve (ed.), *Party and Management in Parliament, 1660–1784* (New York, 1984).
Jones, M. G., *The Charity School Movement* (London, 1964).
Jones, Peter, *Hume's Sentiments: Their Ciceronian and French Context* (Edinburgh, 1982).
Jones, Peter (ed.), *The Reception of David Hume in Europe* (London, 2005).
Jones, Todd E., *The Broad Church: Biography of a Movement* (Lanham, MD, 2003).
Jordan, David, *Gibbon and His Roman Empire* (Urbana, 1971).

Katz, David S., *The Jews in the History of England, 1485–1850* (Oxford, 1994).
Katz, David S. and Israel, Jonathan I. (eds), *Sceptics, Millenarians and Jews* (Leiden, 1990).
Kidd, Colin, 'Constructing a Civil Religion: Scots Presbyterians and the Eighteenth-Century British State' in Kirk, J. (ed.), *The Scottish Churches and the Union Parliament, 1707–1999* (Edinburgh, 2001), pp. 1–21.
— *Subverting Scotland's Past: Scottish Whig Historians and the Creation of an Anglo-British Identity, 1689–c.1830* (Cambridge, 1993).
King, John N., 'The Royal Image, 1535–1603', in Hoak, Dale (ed.), *Tudor Political Culture* (Cambridge, 1995), pp. 104–32.
Kirk, J. (ed.), *The Scottish Churches and the Union Parliament, 1707–1999* (Edinburgh, 2001).
Kitson, Peter J., '"Our Prophetic Harrington": Coleridge, Pantisocracy, and Puritan Utopias', *The Wordsworth Circle*, 24:2 (1993), pp. 97–102.
Klein, Lawrence E., *Shaftesbury and the Culture of Politeness: Moral Discourse and Cultural Politics in Early Eighteenth-Century England* (Cambridge, 1994).
— 'Shaftesbury, Politeness and the Politics of Religion', in Phillipson, Nicholas and Skinner, Quentin (eds), *Political Discourse in Early Modern Britain* (Cambridge, 1993), pp. 283–301.
Klein Lawrence E. and La Vopa, Anthony (eds), *Enthusiasm and Enlightenment in Europe, 1650–1850* (San Marino, CA, 1998).
Kley, Dale van, *The Damiens Affair and the Unraveling of the Ancien Régime, 1750–1770* (Princeton, 1984).
— *The Jansenists and the Expulsion of the Jesuits from France* (New Haven and London, 1975).
— *The Religious Origins of the French Revolution: From Calvin to the Civil Constitution, 1560–1791* (New Haven, 1996).
Klibansky, Raymond and Mossner, Ernest C. (eds), *New Letters of David Hume* (Oxford, 1954).
Knight, Frida, *University Rebel: The Life of William Frend, 1751–1841* (London, 1971).
Knights, Ben, *The Idea of the Clerisy in the Nineteenth Century* (Cambridge, 1978).
Knights, Mark, 'Occasional Conformity and the Representation of Dissent: Hypocrisy, Sincerity, Moderation and Zeal', *PH*, 24:1 (2005), pp. 41–57.
Knox, Ronald A., *Enthusiasm: A Chapter in the History of Religion* (Notre Dame, IN, 1950).
Koch, Bettina, 'Priestly Despotism: The Problem of Unruly Clerics in Marsilius of Padua's *Defensor Pacis*', *JRH*, 36:2 (2012), pp. 165–83.
Koontz, Theodore J., 'Religion and Political Cohesion: John Locke and Jean Jacques Rousseau', *Journal of Church and State*, 23:1 (1981), pp. 950–1115.
Kors, Alan Charles, 'The French Context of Hume's Philosophical Theology', *HS*, 21:2 (1995), pp. 221–36.

Kramnick, Isaac, *Bolingbroke and His Circle: The Politics of Nostalgia in the Age of Walpole* (London, 1968).
— *Republicanism and Bourgeois Radicalism: Political Ideology in Late Eighteenth-Century England and America* (Ithaca, NY, 1990).
Laborie, Lionel, *Enlightening Enthusiasm: Prophecy and Religious Experience in Early Eighteenth-Century England* (Manchester, 2015).
Lacey, Andrew, *The Cult of King Charles the Martyr* (Woodbridge, 2003).
Lamont, William, *Godly Rule: Politics and Religion, 1603–60* (London, 1963).
— *Marginal Prynne, 1600–69* (London, 1963).
— *Richard Baxter and the Millennium* (London, 1980).
— 'The Two "National Churches" of 1691 and 1829', in Fletcher, Anthony and Roberts, Peter (eds), *Religion, Culture and Society in Early Modern Britain: Essays in Honour of Patrick Collinson* (Cambridge, 1994), pp. 265–87.
Lawson, Philip, *The Imperial Challenge: Quebec and Britain in the Age of the American Revolution* (Montreal, 1989).
Lemmens, Willem, '"Beyond the Calm Sunshine of the Mind": Hume on Religion and Morality', *Aufklärung und Kritik*, 37 (2011), pp. 214–50.
Lerner, Ralph, 'Gibbon's Jewish Problem', in Lerner, Ralph, *Naïve Readings: Reveilles Political and Philosophic* (Chicago, 2016), pp. 92–118.
— *Naïve Readings: Reveilles Political and Philosophic* (Chicago, 2016).
Levine, Joseph M., *The Battle of the Books: History and Literature in the Augustan Age* (Ithaca, NY, 1991).
Levitin, Dmitri, *Ancient Wisdom in the Age of the New Science: Histories of Philosophy in England, c. 1640–1700* (Cambridge, 2015).
— 'Matthew Tindal's Rights of the Christian Church (1706) and the Church-State Relationship', *HJ*, 54:3 (2011), pp. 717–40.
Lewis, Thomas A., *Religion, Modernity, and Politics in Hegel* (Oxford, 2011).
Livesay, J. L., *Venetian Phoenix: Paolo Sarpi and Some of His English Friends* (Lawrence, KS, 1973).
Livingston, Donald W., 'Hume's Conception of "True Religion"', in Flew, Anthony, Livingston, Donald W., Mavrodes, George I., and Norton, David Fate (eds), *Hume's Philosophy of Religion: The Sixth James Montgomery Hester Seminar* (Winston-Salem, NC, 1986), pp. 33–73.
— 'Hume's Historical Conception of Liberty', in Capaldi, Nicholas and Livingston, Donald W. (eds), *Liberty in Hume's History of England* (Dordrecht, 1990), pp. 105–53.
— *Hume's Philosophy of Common Life* (Chicago and London, 1984).
— *Philosophical Melancholy and Delirium: Hume's Pathology of Philosophy* (Chicago, 1998).
Lock, Alexander, *Catholicism, Identity and Politics in the Age of Enlightenment: The Life and Career of Sir Thomas Gascoigne, 1745–1810* (Woodbridge, 2017).
Lockwood, Shelley, 'Marsilius of Padua and the Case for the Royal Ecclesiastical

Supremacy', *Transactions of the Royal Historical Society*, 5th ser., 1 (1991), pp. 89–119.

Luckmann, Thomas, *The Invisible Religion: The Problem of Religion in Modern Society* (New York, 1967).

Lym, Paul, *Mystery Unveiled: The Crisis of the Trinity in Early Modern England* (Oxford, 2012).

Malherbe, Michael, 'Hume's Reception in France', in Jones, Peter (ed.), *The Reception of David Hume in Europe* (London, 2005), pp. 34–97.

Mandelbrote, Scott, 'Biblical Hermeneutics and the Sciences, 1700–1900: An Overview', in Mandelbrote, Scott and van der Meer, Jitse (eds), *Nature and Scripture in the Abrahamic Religions* (4 vols, Leiden, 2008), vol. 2, pp. 3–40.

Mandelbrote, Scott and van der Meer, Jitse (eds), *Nature and Scripture in the Abrahamic Religions* (4 vols, Leiden, 2008).

Mansfield, Harvey C., Jr, *Statesmanship and Party Government: A Study of Burke and Bolingbroke* (London, 1965).

Manuel, Frank, *The Eighteenth Century Confronts the Gods* (Cambridge, MA, 1959).

Marshall, John, 'The Ecclesiology of the Latitude-Men, 1660–89: Stillingfleet, Tillotson and "Hobbism"', *JEH*, 36:3 (1985), pp. 407–27.

— *John Locke, Toleration and Early Enlightenment Culture* (Cambridge, 2006).

Marshall, P. D., 'Thomas Hollis (1720–74): The Bibliophile as Libertarian', *Bulletin of the John Rylands Library*, 66:2 (1984), pp. 246–63.

Martin, Dale B., *The Invention of Superstition: From the Hippocratics to the Christians* (Cambridge, MA, 2004).

Mather, F. C., 'Georgian Churchmanship Reconsidered: Some Variations in Anglican Public Worship, 1714–1830', *JEH*, 36:2 (1985), pp. 255–83.

Matytsin, Anton, 'Reason and Utility in French Religious Apologetics', in Bulman, William J. and Ingram, Robert G. (eds), *God in the Enlightenment* (Oxford, 2016), pp. 63–82.

McKendrick, Neil (ed.), *Historical Perspectives: Studies in English Thought and Society in Honour of J. H. Plumb* (London, 1974).

McKitterick, Rosamond and Quinault, Roland (eds), *Edward Gibbon and Empire* (Cambridge, 1997).

McMahon, Marie, *The Radical Whigs, John Trenchard and Thomas Gordon: Libertarian Loyalists to the New House of Hanover* (Lanham, MD, 1990).

Mendieta, Eduardo, and VanAntwerpen, Jonathan (eds), *The Power of Religion in the Public Sphere* (New York, 2011).

Merrill, Thomas W., *Hume and the Politics of the Enlightenment* (New York, 2015).

Merrill, Walter Mackintosh, *From Statesman to Philosopher: A Study in Bolingbroke's Deism* (London, 1949).

Miller, J. T., *Ideology and Enlightenment: The Political and Social Thought of Samuel Taylor Coleridge* (New York, 1988).

Mitchell, Annie, 'Character of an Independent Whig – "Cato" and Bernard Mandeville', *History of European Ideas*, 29:3 (2003), pp. 291–311.

— 'A Liberal Republican *Cato*', *American Journal of Political Science*, 48:3 (2004), pp. 588–603.

Moore, James, 'Utility and Humanity: The Quest for the *Honestum* in Cicero, Hutcheson, and Hume', *Utilitas*, 14:3 (2002), pp. 365–86.

Morrow, John, *Coleridge's Political Thought: Property, Morality and the Limits of Traditional Discourse* (Basingstoke, 1990).

— 'The National Church in Coleridge's *Church and State*: A Response to Allen', *JHI*, 47:4 (1986), pp. 640–52.

Morrow, John and Scott, Jonathan (eds), *Liberty, Authority, Formality: Political Ideas and Culture, 1600–1900* (Exeter, 2008).

Mossner, Ernest Campbell, *The Life of David Hume* (2nd edn, Oxford, 1980).

Nadon, Christopher (ed.), *Enlightenment and Secularism: Essays on the Mobilization of Reason* (Lanham, MD, 2013).

Nelson, Eric, *The Hebrew Republic: Jewish Sources and the Transformation of European Political Thought* (Cambridge, MA, 2010).

Neufeld, Matthew, *The Civil Wars after 1660: Public Remembering in Late Stuart England* (Woodbridge 2013).

Nockles, Peter, *The Oxford Movement in Context* (Cambridge, 1994).

Noonkester, Myron C., 'Gibbon and the Clergy: Private Virtues, Public Vices', *Harvard Theological Quarterly*, 83:4 (1990), pp. 399–414.

Norton, David Fate and Popkin, Richard H. (eds), *David Hume: Philosophical Historian* (Indianapolis, 1965).

Noxon, James, 'Hume's Agnosticism', in Chappell, V. C. (ed.), *Hume: A Collection of Critical Essays* (New York, 1966), pp. 361–83.

Orr, Robert, *Reason and Authority: The Thought of William Chillingworth* (Oxford, 1967).

Pagden, Anthony (ed.), *The Languages of Political Theory in Early-Modern Europe* (Cambridge, 1987).

Paknadel, Felix, 'Shaftesbury's Illustrations of *Characteristics*', *Journal of the Warburg and Courtauld Institutes*, 37 (1974), pp. 290–312.

Parkin, Jon and Stanton, Timothy (eds), *Natural Law and Toleration in the Early Enlightenment* (Oxford, 2013).

Parsons, Talcott, 'The Theoretical Development of the Sociology of Religion', *JHI*, 5:2 (1944), pp. 176–90.

Paulson, Ronald, *Hogarth's Harlot: Sacred Parody in Enlightenment England* (Baltimore and London, 2003).

Peltonen, Markku, 'Politeness and Whiggism, 1688–1732', *HJ*, 48:2 (2005), pp. 391–414.

Penelhum, Terence, *Themes in Hume: The Self, the Will, Religion* (Oxford, 2003).

Pentland, Gordon and Davis, Michael T. (eds), *Property and Popular Politics: England and Scotland, 1760–1832* (Cambridge, 1989).

Perry, Thomas W., *Propaganda and Politics in Eighteenth-Century England: A Study of the Jew Bill of 1753* (Cambridge, MA, 1962).
Petersen, Grethe B. (ed.), *The Tanner Lectures on Human Values*, vol. 11 (Salt Lake City, 1988).
Pettit, Alexander, *Illusory Consensus: Bolingbroke and the Polemical Response to Walpole, 1730–1737* (London, 1997).
Phillipson, Nicholas, *David Hume: The Philosopher as Historian* (revised edn, New Haven and London, 2012).
— 'Politics and Politeness in the Reigns of Anne and the Early Hanoverians', in Pocock, J. G. A. with Schochet, Gordon and Schwoerer, Lois (eds), *The Varieties of British Political Thought, 1500–1800* (Cambridge, 1996), pp. 229–35.
— 'Propriety, Property, and Prudence: David Hume and the Defence of the Revolution', in Phillipson, Nicholas and Skinner, Quentin (eds), *Political Discourse in Early Modern Britain* (Cambridge, 1993), pp. 302–20.
Phillipson, Nicholas and Skinner, Quentin (eds), *Political Discourse in Early Modern Britain* (Cambridge, 1993).
Plumb, J. H., *The Growth of Political Stability in England, 1675–1725* (London, 1967).
Pocock, J. G. A., *Barbarism and Religion* (6 vols, Cambridge, 1999–2015).
— 'Between Machiavelli and Hume: Gibbon as Civic Humanist and Philosophical Historian', *Daedalus*, 105:3 (1976), pp. 152–69.
— 'Clergy and Commerce: The Conservative Enlightenment in England', in Ajello, R. J. (ed.), *L'Età dei Lumi: Studi Storici sul Settecento Europeo in Onore di Franco Venturi* (Naples, 1985), pp. 523–68.
— 'A Discourse of Sovereignty: Observations on the Work in Progress', in Phillipson, Nicholas and Skinner, Quentin (eds), *Political Discourse in Early Modern Britain* (Cambridge, 1993), pp. 377–428.
— 'Edward Gibbon in History: Aspects of the Text in *The History of the Decline and Fall of the Roman Empire*', in Petersen, Grethe B. (ed.), *The Tanner Lectures on Human Values*, vol. 11 (Salt Lake City, 1988), pp. 289–364.
— 'Enthusiasm: The Antiself of Enlightenment', in Klein, Lawrence E. and La Vopa, Anthony (eds), *Enthusiasm and Enlightenment in Europe, 1650–1850* (San Marino, CA, 1998), pp. 7–28.
— 'Gibbon and the Primitive Church', in Collini, Stefan, Whatmore, Richard, and Young, Brian (eds), *History, Religion, and Culture: British Intellectual History, 1750–1950* (Cambridge, 2000), pp. 48–68.
— 'Gibbon's *Decline and Fall* and the World View of the Late Enlightenment', in Pocock, J. G. A., *Virtue, Commerce, and History: Essays on Political Thought and History, Chiefly in the Eighteenth Century* (Cambridge, 1985), pp. 143–56.
— 'Hume and the American Revolution: The Dying Thoughts of a North Briton', in Pocock, J. G. A., *Virtue, Commerce, and History: Essays on*

Political Thought and History, Chiefly in the Eighteenth Century (Cambridge, 1985), pp. 125–41.
— *The Machiavellian Moment: Florentine Political Thought and the Atlantic Republican Tradition* (Cambridge, 1975).
— *Politics, Language, and Time: Essays on Political Thought and History* (Chicago and London, 1981).
— 'Post-Puritan England and the Problem of the Enlightenment', in Zagorin, Perez (ed.), *Culture and Politics from Puritanism to the Enlightenment* (Berkeley, 1980), pp. 91–111.
— 'Superstition and Enthusiasm in Gibbon's History of Religion', *Eighteenth-Century Life*, 8:1 (1982), pp. 83–94.
— 'Time, History, and Eschatology in the Thought of Thomas Hobbes', in Pocock, J. G. A., *Politics, Language, and Time: Essays on Political Thought and History* (Chicago and London, 1981), pp. 148–201.
— *Virtue, Commerce, and History: Essays on Political Thought and History, Chiefly in the Eighteenth Century* (Cambridge, 1985).
Pocock, J. G. A. with Schochet, Gordon and Schwoerer, Lois (eds), *The Varieties of British Political Thought, 1500–1800* (Cambridge, 1996).
Popper, Karl, *The Open Society and Its Enemies* (2 vols, London, 1945).
Porter, Roy, *English Society in the Eighteenth Century* (Harmondsworth, 1982).
— *Enlightenment: Britain and the Creation of the Modern World* (London, 2000).
— 'The Enlightenment in England', in Porter, Roy and Teich, Mikuláš (eds), *The Enlightenment in National Context* (Cambridge, 1981), pp. 1–18.
Porter, Roy and Teich, Mikuláš (eds), *The Enlightenment in National Context* (Cambridge, 1981).
Potkay, Adam, 'Hume's "Supplement to Gulliver": The Medieval Volumes of the *History of England*', *Eighteenth-Century Life*, 25:2 (2001), pp. 32–46.
Price, Martin, '"The Dark and Implacable Genius of Superstition": An Aspect of Gibbon's Irony', in Hilson, J. C., Jones, M. M. B., and Watson, J. R. (eds), *Augustan Worlds: Essays in Honour of A. R. Humphreys* (Leicester, 1978), pp. 241–59.
Prickett, Stephen, 'Coleridge and the Idea of the Clerisy', in Crawford, W. B. (ed.), *Reading Coleridge: Approaches and Applications* (Ithaca, NY, 1979), pp. 252–73.
Quantin, Jean-Louis, *The Church of England and Christian Antiquity* (Oxford, 2009).
Rabasa, José, Sato, Masayuki, Tortarolo, Edoardo, and Woolf, Daniel (eds), *The Oxford History of Historical Writing: Volume III: 1400–1800* (Oxford, 2012).
Rivers, Isabel, *Reason, Grace, and Sentiment: A Study of the Languages of Religion and Ethics in England, 1660–1780* (2 vols, Cambridge, 1991–2000).
Robbins, Caroline, *The Eighteenth-Century Commonwealthman* (Cambridge, MA, 1959).

— 'The Strenuous Whig, Thomas Hollis of Lincoln's Inn', *William and Mary Quarterly*, 7:3 (1950), pp. 406–53.
Roberts, William, 'Napoleon, the Concordat of 1801, and Its Consequences', in Coppa, Frank J. (ed.), *Controversial Concordats: The Vatican's Relations with Napoleon, Mussolini, and Hitler* (Washington, DC, 1999), pp. 34–80.
Robertson, John, 'Antonio Genovesi: The Neapolitan Enlightenment and Political Economy', *HPT*, 8:2 (1987), pp. 335–44.
— *The Case for the Enlightenment: Scotland and Naples, 1680–1760* (Cambridge, 2005).
— 'Universal Monarchy and the Liberties of Europe: David Hume's Critique of an English Whig Doctrine', in Phillipson, Nicholas and Skinner, Quentin (eds), *Political Discourse in Early Modern Britain* (Cambridge, 1993), pp. 349–73.
Robertson, John and Mortimer, Sarah (eds), *The Intellectual Consequences of Religious Heterodoxy, 1600–1750* (Leiden, 2012).
Rogers, G. A. J., and Sorell, Tom (eds), *Hobbes and History* (London and New York, 2000).
Rose, Craig, 'The Origins of the SPCK, 1699–1716', in Walsh, John, Haydon, Colin, and Taylor, Stephen (eds), *The Church of England, c. 1689 – c. 1833: From Toleration to Tractarianism* (Cambridge, 1993), pp. 172–90.
Rose, Jacqueline, *Godly Kingship in Restoration England: The Politics of the Royal Supremacy, 1660–1688* (Cambridge, 2011).
Rosenblatt, Jason P., 'John Selden's *De Jure Naturalis ... Juxta Disciplinam Ebraeorum* and Religious Toleration', in Coudert, Allison P. and Shoulson, Jeffrey S. (eds), *Hebraica Veritas? Christian Hebraists and the Study of Judaism in Early Modern Europe* (Philadelphia, 2004), pp. 102–24.
— *Renaissance England's Chief Rabbi: John Selden* (Oxford, 2006).
Russell, Paul, *The Riddle of Hume's Treatise: Skepticism, Naturalism, and Irreligion* (Oxford, 2008).
Ryley, Robert M., *William Warburton* (Boston, MA, 1984).
Sambrook, James, *James Thomson, 1700–1748: A Life* (Oxford, 1991).
Sanders, Richard, *Coleridge and the Broad Church Movement* (Durham, NC, 1942).
Schneewind, J. B., *The Invention of Autonomy: A History of Modern Political Philosophy* (Cambridge, 1998).
Schochet, Gordon (ed.), *Politics, Politeness, and Patriotism* (Washington, DC, 1993).
Schwartz, Hillel, *The French Prophets: The History of a Millenarian Group in Eighteenth-Century England* (Berkeley and Los Angeles, 1980).
— *Knaves, Fools, Madmen and That Subtle Effluvium: A Study of the Opposition to the French Prophets in England, 1706–1710* (Gainesville, FL, 1978).
Scott, Geoffrey, *Gothic Rage Undone: English Monks in the Age of Enlightenment* (Bath, 1992).
Scott, Mary Jane W., *James Thomson, Anglo-Scot* (Athens, GA, 1988).

Serjeantson, Richard, 'Hume's *Natural History of Religion* (1757) and the Demise of Modern Eusebianism', in Robertson, John and Mortimer, Sarah (eds), *The Intellectual Consequences of Religious Heterodoxy, 1600–1750* (Leiden, 2012), pp. 267–95.

Shackleton, Robert, 'Jansenism and the Enlightenment', *SVEC*, 57 (1967), pp. 1387–97.

Shagan, Ethan, *Catholics and the 'Protestant Nation': Religious Politics and Identity in Early Modern England* (Manchester, 2005).

— *The Rule of Moderation: Violence, Religion and the Politics of Restraint in Early Modern England* (Cambridge, 2011).

Sharp, Buchanan and Fissel, Mark (eds), *Law and Authority in Early Modern England* (Newark, DE, 2007).

Shaw, Jane, *Miracles in Enlightenment England* (New Haven and London, 2006).

Sheehan, Jonathan, *The Enlightenment Bible: Translation, Scholarship, Culture* (Princeton, 2005).

— 'Enlightenment, Religion, and the Enigma of Secularization: A Review Essay', *American Historical Review*, 108:4 (2003), pp. 1061–80.

Sher, Richard, *Church and University in the Scottish Enlightenment: The Moderate Literati of Edinburgh* (Princeton, 1985).

Short, K. R. M., 'The English Indemnity Acts, 1726–1867', *Church History*, 42:3 (1973), pp. 366–76.

Sichel, Walter, *Bolingbroke and His Times: The Sequel* (New York, 1968).

Siebert, Donald T., *The Moral Animus of David Hume* (Newark, DE, 1990).

Silk, Mark, 'Numa Pompilius and the Idea of Civil Religion in the West', *Journal of the American Academy of Religion*, 72:4 (2004), pp. 863–96.

Sirota, Brent, *The Christian Monitors: The Church of England in the Age of Benevolence, 1680–1730* (New Haven and London, 2014).

— 'The Occasional Conformity Controversy, Moderation and the Anglican Critique of Modernity, 1700–1714', *HJ*, 57:1 (2014), pp. 81–105.

— 'The Trinitarian Crisis in Church and State: Religious Controversy and the Making of the Post-Revolutionary Church of England, 1687–1701', *JBS*, 52:1 (2013), pp. 26–54.

Skinner, Quentin, *The Foundations of Modern Political Thought* (2 vols, Cambridge, 1978).

— 'The Principles and Practice of Opposition: The Case of Bolingbroke versus Walpole', in McKendrick, Neil (ed.), *Historical Perspectives: Studies in English Thought and Society in Honour of J. H. Plumb* (London, 1974), pp. 93–128.

Slinn, Sara, *The Education of the Anglican Clergy, 1780–1839* (Woodbridge, 2017).

Smith, David Dillon, 'Gibbon in Church', *JEH*, 35:3 (1984), pp. 452–63.

Smith, Hannah, *Georgian Monarchy: Politics and Culture, 1714–1760* (Cambridge, 2006).

Smith, R. J., *The Gothic Bequest: Medieval Institutions in British Thought, 1688–1863* (Cambridge, 1987).
Smith, Ruth, *Handel's Oratorios and Eighteenth-Century Thought* (Cambridge, 1995).
Sommerville, J. P., 'Hobbes, Selden, Erastianism, and the History of the Jews', in Rogers, G. A. J., and Sorell, Tom (eds), *Hobbes and History* (London and New York, 2000), pp. 160–88.
Sorkin, David, *The Religious Enlightenment: Protestants, Jews, and Catholics from London to Vienna* (Princeton, 2008).
— 'A Wise, Enlightened and Reliable Piety': The Religious Enlightenment in Central and Western Europe, 1689–1789 (Southampton, 2002).
Speck, W. A., *Tory and Whig: The Struggle in the Constituencies, 1701–1715* (London, 1970).
Spurr, John, 'The Church of England, Comprehension and the Toleration Act of 1689', *English Historical Review* 104:413 (1989), pp. 927–46.
— 'The Church, the Societies, and the Moral Revolution of 1688', in Walsh, John, Haydon, Colin, and Taylor, Stephen (eds), *The Church of England, c. 1689 – c. 1833: From Toleration to Tractarianism* (Cambridge, 1993), pp. 127–42.
— 'Latitudinarianism and the Restoration Church', *HJ*, 31:1 (1988), pp. 61–82.
— '"Rational Religion" in Restoration England', *JHI*, 49:4 (1988), pp. 564–58.
— *The Restoration Church of England* (New Haven, 1991).
Stanton, Timothy, 'Locke and the Fable of Liberalism', *HJ*, 61:3 (2018), pp. 597–622.
Stapelbroek, Koen, *Love, Self-Deceit, and Money: Commerce and Morality in the Early Neapolitan Enlightenment* (Toronto, 2008).
Stark, Rodney, 'Atheism, Faith, and the Social Scientific Study of Religion', *Journal of Contemporary Religion*, 14:1 (1999), pp. 41–62.
Starkie, Andrew, *The Church of England and the Bangorian Controversy* (Woodbridge, 2007).
Stedman Jones, Gareth, *Languages of Class: Studies in English Working Class History, 1832–1982* (Cambridge, 1983).
— 'Religion and the Origins of Socialism', in Stedman Jones, Gareth and Katznelson, Ira (eds), *Religion and the Political Imagination* (Cambridge, 2010), pp. 171–89.
— 'Rethinking Chartism', in Stedman Jones, Gareth, *Languages of Class: Studies in English Working Class History, 1832–1982* (Cambridge, 1983), pp. 90–178.
Stedman Jones, Gareth and Katznelson, Ira (eds), *Religion and the Political Imagination* (Cambridge, 2010).
Stephen, Leslie, *History of English Thought in the Eighteenth Century* (2 vols, London, 1881).
Stevens, Ralph, *Protestant Pluralism: The Reception of the Toleration Act, 1689–1720* (Woodbridge, 2018).

Stuart-Buttle, Tim, *From Moral Theology to Moral Philosophy: Cicero, Christianity and Humanity from Locke to Hume* (Oxford, 2018).
Sullivan, Robert E., *John Toland and the Deist Controversy: A Study in Adaptions* (Cambridge, MA, 1982).
Susato, Ryu, 'Taming "the Tyranny of Priests": Hume's Advocacy of Religious Establishments', *JHI*, 73:2 (2012), pp. 273–93.
Sutcliffe, Adam, *Judaism and the Enlightenment* (Cambridge, 2003).
Swain, Joseph, *Edward Gibbon the Historian* (London, 1966).
Sykes, Norman, *Edmund Gibson, Bishop of London, 1669–1748: A Study in Politics and Religion in the Eighteenth Century* (London, 1926).
Talmon, J. L., *The Origins of Totalitarian Democracy* (London, 1952).
Taylor, Stephen, '"Dr. Codex" and the Whig "Pope": Edmund Gibson, Bishop of Lincoln and London, 1716–1748', in Davis, R. W. (ed.), *Lords of Parliament: Studies, 1714–1914* (Stanford, 1995), pp. 9–28.
— 'Sir Robert Walpole, the Church of England, and the Quakers Tithe Bill of 1736', *HJ*, 28:1 (1985), pp. 51–77.
— 'Whigs, Bishops and America: The Politics of Church Reform in Mid-Eighteenth-Century England', *HJ*, 36:2 (1993), pp. 331–56.
— 'Whigs, Tories and Anticlericalism: Ecclesiastical Courts Legislation in 1733', *PH*, 19:3 (2000), pp. 329–55.
— 'William Warburton and the Alliance of Church and State', *JEH*, 43:2 (1992), pp. 271–86.
Temple, Liam P., *Mysticism in Early Modern England* (Woodbridge, 2019).
Thomas, Keith, *Religion and the Decline of Magic* (London, 1971).
Thompson, Andrew, 'Contesting the Test Acts: Dissent, Parliament and the Public in the 1730s', *PH*, 24:1 (2005), pp. 58–70.
— 'Popery, Politics, and Private Judgement in Early Hanoverian Britain', *HJ*, 45:2 (2002), pp. 333–56.
Toomer, G. J., *John Selden: A Life in Scholarship* (2 vols, Oxford, 2009).
Toon, Peter (ed.), *Puritans, the Millennium and the Future of Israel: Puritan Eschatology, 1600–1660* (Cambridge and London, 1970).
Torrey, Norman, *Voltaire and the English Deists* (New Haven, 1930).
Tortarolo, Edoardo, 'Italian Historical Writing, 1680–1800', in Rabasa, José, Sato, Masayuki, Tortarolo, Edoardo, and Woolf, Daniel (eds), *The Oxford History of Historical Writing: Volume III: 1400–1800* (Oxford, 2012).
Townend, G. M., 'Religious Radicalism and Conservatism in the Whig Party under George I: The Repeal of the Occasional Conformity and Schism Acts', *PH*, 7:1 (1988), pp. 24–44.
Trevor-Roper, Hugh, 'From Deism to History: Conyers Middleton', in Trevor-Roper, Hugh, *History and the Enlightenment* (New Haven, 2010), pp. 71–119.
— *History and the Enlightenment* (New Haven, 2010).
— *Religion, the Reformation and Social Change* (London, 1967).
— 'The Religious Origins of the Enlightenment', in Trevor-Roper, Hugh, *Religion, the Reformation and Social Change* (London, 1967), pp. 193–236.

Tuck, Richard, 'The "Christian Atheism" of Thomas Hobbes', in Hunter, Michael and Wootton, David (eds), *Atheism from the Reformation to the Enlightenment* (Oxford, 1992), pp. 111–30.
— 'The Civil Religion of Thomas Hobbes', in Phillipson, Nicholas and Skinner, Quentin (eds), *Political Discourse in Early Modern Britain* (Cambridge, 1993), pp. 120–38.
— *Natural Rights Theories: Their Origin and Development* (Cambridge, 1979).
— *Philosophy and Government, 1572–1651* (Cambridge, 1993).
Tucker, Robert, *Philosophy and Myth in Karl Marx* (Cambridge, 1961).
Turnbull, Paul, 'Gibbon and Pastor Allamand', *JRH*, 16:3 (1991), pp. 280–91.
— 'Gibbon's Exchange with Priestley', *BJECS*, 14:2 (1991), pp. 139–58.
— 'The "Supposed Infidelity" of Edward Gibbon', *HJ*, 25:1 (1982), pp. 23–41.
Tuveson, E. L., *Millennium and Utopia* (Gloucester, MA, 1972).
— *Redeemer Nation: The Idea of America's Millennial Role* (Chicago, 1968).
Tyacke, Nicholas (ed.), *England's Long Reformation, 1500–1800* (London, 1998).
Varey, Simon, 'Introduction', in Bolingbroke, Henry St John, Viscount, *Contributions to the* Craftsman, ed. Varey, Simon (Oxford, 1982), pp. xiii–xv.
Venturi, Franco, *Utopia and Reform in the Enlightenment* (Cambridge, 1971).
Virgin, Peter, *The Church in an Age of Negligence* (Cambridge, 1989).
Voitle, Robert, *The Third Earl of Shaftesbury, 1671–1713* (Baton Rouge and London, 1984).
Wallace, Ruth A., 'Emile Durkheim and the Civil Religion Concept', *Review of Religious Research*, 18:3 (1977), pp. 287–90.
Walsh, John, Haydon, Colin, and Taylor, Stephen (eds), *The Church of England, c. 1689 – c. 1833: From Toleration to Tractarianism* (Cambridge, 1993).
Walzer, Michael, *Exodus and Revelation* (New York, 1985).
Wangermann, Ernst, 'Reform Catholicism and Political Radicalism in the Austrian Enlightenment', in Porter, Roy and Teich, Mikuláš (eds), *The Enlightenment in National Context* (Cambridge, 1981), pp. 127–40.
Ward, W. R., 'The Eighteenth-Century Church: A European View', in Walsh, John, Haydon, Colin, and Taylor, Stephen (eds), *The Church of England, c. 1689 – c. 1833: From Toleration to Tractarianism* (Cambridge, 1993), pp. 285–98.
Waterman, A. M. C., 'A Cambridge "Via Media" in Late Georgian Anglicanism', *JEH*, 42:3 (1991), pp. 419–36.
Webb, Mark, 'The Argument of the *Natural History*', *HS*, 17:2 (1991), pp. 141–59.
Weber, Max, *The Protestant Ethic and the Spirit of Capitalism*, trans. Parsons, Talcott (London, 1930).
Whaley, Joachim, 'The Protestant Enlightenment in Germany', in Porter, Roy and Teich, Mikuláš (eds), *The Enlightenment in National Context* (Cambridge, 1981), pp. 106–17.

Whelan, Frederick G., *Hume and Machiavelli: Political Realism and Liberal Thought* (Lanham, MD, 2004).
Wilbur, E. M., *A History of Unitarianism* (Cambridge, MA, 1952).
Willey, Basil, *Samuel Taylor Coleridge* (New York, 1973).
Willis, André C., 'The Potential Value of Hume's "Religion"', *JSP*, 13:1 (2015), pp. 1–15.
— *Toward a Humean True Religion: Genuine Moderate Hope, Practical Morality* (University Park, PA, 2014).
Wilson, Bryan, *Religion in Secular Society* (London, 1966).
Womersley, David, 'Gibbon and the "Watchmen of the Holy City": Revision and Religion in the *Decline and Fall*', in McKitterick, Rosamond and Quinault, Roland (eds), *Edward Gibbon and Empire* (Cambridge, 1997), pp. 190–216.
— *Gibbon and the 'Watchmen of the Holy City': The Historian and His Reputation, 1776–1815* (Oxford, 2002).
— 'Gibbon's Apostasy', *BJECS*, 11:1 (1988), pp. 51–70.
Womersley, David (ed.), *Religious Scepticism: Contemporary Responses to Gibbon* (Bristol, 1997).
Wootton, David, *Paolo Sarpi: Between Renaissance and Enlightenment* (Cambridge, 1983).
Wootton, David (ed.), *Republicanism, Liberty, and Commercial Society* (Stanford, 1994).
Worden, Blair, 'Introduction', in Ludlow, Edmund, *A Voyce from the Watch Tower, Part V: 1660–1662*, ed. Worden, Blair (Camden Fourth Series, vol. 21, London, 1978), pp. 1–80.
Yandell, Keith, *Hume's 'Inexplicable Mystery': His Views on Religion* (Philadelphia, 1990).
Yolton, J. W., 'Schoolmen, Logic and Philosophy', in Aston T. H. (ed.), *The History of the University of Oxford*, vol. 5, Sutherland, L. S. and Mitchell. L. G. (eds), *The Eighteenth Century* (Oxford, 1986), pp. 565–91.
Young, B. W., 'Conyers Middleton: The Historical Consequences of Orthodoxy', in Robertson, John and Mortimer, Sarah (eds), *The Intellectual Consequences of Religious Heterodoxy, 1600–1750* (Leiden, 2012), pp. 235–65.
— 'A History of Variations: The Identity of the Eighteenth-Century Church of England', in Claydon, Tony and McBride, Ian (eds), *Protestantism and National Identity: Britain and Ireland, c. 1650 – c. 1850* (Cambridge, 1998), pp. 105–28.
— 'John Jortin, Ecclesiastical History, and the Christian Republic of Letters', *HJ*, 55:4 (2012), pp. 961–81.
— '"Knock-Kneed Giants": Victorian Representations of Eighteenth-Century Thought', in Garnett, Jane and Matthew, Colin (eds), *Revival and Religion since 1700: Essays for John Walsh* (London, 1993), pp. 79–93.
— *Religion and Enlightenment in Eighteenth-Century England: Theological Debate from Locke to Burke* (Oxford, 1998).

— 'Religious History and the Eighteenth-Century Historian', *HJ*, 43:3 (2000), pp. 849–68.
— '"Scepticism in Excess": Gibbon and Eighteenth-Century Christianity', *HJ*, 41:1 (1998), pp. 179–99.
— *The Victorian Eighteenth Century* (Oxford, 2007).
Zagorin, Perez (ed.), *Culture and Politics from Puritanism to the Enlightenment* (Berkeley, 1980).

Unpublished theses

Craig, A. G., 'The Movement for the Reformation of Manners, 1688–1715' (PhD thesis, University of Edinburgh, 1980).
Duffy, Eamonn, 'Joseph Berington and the English Catholic Cisalpine Movement, 1772–1803' (PhD thesis, University of Cambridge, 1973).
Fitzpatrick, Martin, 'Rational Dissent in the Late Eighteenth Century with Particular Reference to the Growth of Toleration' (PhD thesis, University of Wales, 1982).
Taylor, Stephen, 'Church and State in England in the Mid-Eighteenth Century: The Newcastle Years 1742–62' (PhD thesis, University of Cambridge, 1987).

Index

Abernathy, John 77
absolutism 48, 73, 98, 124, 205
Academics 12, 57
Act in Restraint of Appeals (1533) 14
Act of Submission of the Clergy (1534) 14, 15
Act of Uniformity (1662) 14, 23, 175
Addison, Joseph 21, 23, 34, 43, 63
Addison, Lancelot 34
adiaphora 23, 167
Ainsworth, Michael 43, 48, 49, 50, 54
d'Alembert, Jean le Rond 126, 206
Alexander II, Pope 149
Alexander Severus, Emperor 148
Alexandre, Noël 149
Ambrose, bishop of Milan, Saint 67, 144
America 33–4, 59, 169, 192, 202–3, 207
Anabaptism 77, 91, 114, 159
Anderson, George 128
Anglicanism *see* Church of England
Anglo-Saxons 36, 99, 116–17
Anne, Queen 16, 38, 62, 72, 80, 82, 84
anticlericalism 1–2, 17–19, 34, 37–8
   and the Enlightenment 30
   legal anticlericalism 36
antisemitism 7–9, 195
Antonines 137–40, 142, 143, 162–3
apocalyptic 20, 55, 202, 203
Apollonius of Tyana 157
apostles 5
Arianism 171, 174
Arius 1, 5
Arminianism 4, 18, 31, 156, 171, 182
Arnold, Thomas 202
articles of faith *see* Thirty-Nine Articles
Athanasian creed 143, 174, 178
Athanasius, of Alexandria, Saint 1, 5, 9
Atterbury, Francis, bishop of Rochester 16, 62
Aufklärung 203
Augustine, of Hippo, Saint 24, 28
Austria 10, 204

Bacon, Francis 88
Baker, John Holroyd, earl of Sheffield 163, 164
Balguy, John 183
Bangorian controversy (1717–21) 24, 29, 38, 85, 171, 197
   and Trenchard and Gordon 59–62, 78
Bannatine, Hugh 127
Barbeyrac, Jean 60, 64, 65, 67, 88
Baron, Richard 29–30
Basil, Saint 67
Bastwick, John 72
Baxter, Richard 18, 19, 201
Bayle, Pierre 53, 134–5, 156–7
Beaufort, Louis de 152
Becket, Thomas, Saint, archbishop of Canterbury 6, 117
Bedford, Hilkiah 84
Berington, Joseph 204
Blackburne, Francis, archdeacon of Cleveland 18, 172–6, 178, 194
   and Calvinism 174
   and comprehension 23
   and Switzerland 10
   and the subscription controversy 168–9
   and the Thirty-Nine Articles 174
   anti-sacerdotalism of 16
   latitudinarianism of 23, 180
Blackstone, William 151, 186
Blair, Hugh 127–8
Blount, Charles 40
Bolingbroke, Henry St John, Viscount
   and Cicero 96, 103–4
   and Constantine 89, 96–7
   and deism 81, 87–8, 96–7, 100–1, 106–7
   and Erastianism 80–1, 90–1, 96, 99, 103
   and Gibson 80, 85
   and high-churchmanship 80–4, 102
   and Jewish history 88–9
   and the apostolic church 99–100

and the Church of England 80–4, 96, 101–2, 104
and the church-state relationship 80–3, 89–92, 96, 99, 104–6
and the clergy 81, 87, 89–90, 94, 99, 101, 103, 107
and the royal supremacy 80–1, 99
and the Thirty-Nine Articles 81, 90, 96, 98, 101, 104, 107
and the Trinity 87, 90, 96, 107
and Toryism 80–2, 84–5, 103
and Whiggism 80, 84–5, 95, 103, 105
Bonaparte, Napoleon 38, 195–6
Bonar, John 128
Bonneville, Nicolas 206–7
Boswell, James 129
Bottens, Polier de 155
Boyle, Richard, earl of Burlington 105
Boyle, Robert 188
Bramhall, John, bishop of Armagh 77–8
Britain 10, 32, 59
and Enlightened Dissent 177, 181
and Hume 122–3, 127–8
and the 'patriot' opposition 95, 104–7
British and Foreign Bible Society 198
broad-church movement 195, 202, 207
Brutus, Marcus Junius, 'the Younger' 64
Burgess, Daniel 82
Burke, Edmund 38, 163, 165, 169, 180, 186, 198
Burnet, Gilbert, bishop of Salisbury 10, 19, 23–4, 94, 171
and Gibbon 159
and Shaftesbury 49, 53
and Trenchard and Gordon 75
and Warburton 93
Burton, Robert 65
Butler, James, second duke of Ormond 68
Butler, Joseph, bishop of Bristol 134

Calvinism 4, 22, 31, 171, 195
in America 34
in Scotland 127
in Switzerland 10, 174
'Cambridge Platonists' 22
Cambyses II, king of Persia 46
Camisards 19–20, 56, 77
candour 170, 179, 181, 183, 185–7, 192
Carlyle, Alexander 127, 128
Carolingians 149
Casaubon, Méric 65
Catholic emancipation 29, 38–9, 195, 198–9, 202, 204

Catholic Relief Acts (1778 and 1791) 154–5, 184, 195
Cato, 'the Younger' 64
Cercle Social 207
charity school movement 68–9
Charles I, king of England, Scotland, and Ireland 9, 20, 62, 68, 72, 98, 124
Charles II, king of England, Scotland, and Ireland 9, 15, 68, 70, 72
Childeric III, king of the Franks 149
Chillingworth, William 17, 23, 54, 77, 93, 153, 156–7, 171–4, 177
Christ Church, Oxford 154
Church Buildings Act (1818) 198
Church Building Society 198
church councils 5, 42–3, 46, 48–9, 51, 67, 89, 99, 143, 147, 157, 171, 177
council of Nicaea 9, 89, 143, 161
Church Missionary Society 198
Church of England 13–14, 18–26, 29, 35–8, 166–71, 176–80
and civil religion 1–5, 9, 193–5
Church of Scotland 32, 68, 109, 116, 126–31, 132, 135
Church Rates and Repairs Bill (1733) 83
church-state relationship 4, 13–15, 24, 193–5, 199–201, 203–6
and Bolingbroke 80–3, 89–92, 96, 99, 104–6
and Enlightened Dissent 188, 192
and Gibbon 140
and Hume 111, 116–19, 121–3, 132–3, 135
and Shaftesbury 41–9, 57
and Trenchard and Gordon 59–61, 70
Cicero, Marcus Tullius 5, 12–13, 28, 37, 194–5
Cisalpinism 204
citizenship 1–2, 5, 28, 42, 44, 63–4, 75, 97–8, 100–1, 103, 135, 165
civic humanism 41
Civil Constitution of the Clergy 205
civil society 21–2, 25, 30–1, 34–5, 90, 138, 172
'Clarendon code' 7, 14–15, 84, 186
Clarke, Godfrey 163
Clarke, Samuel 93, 156, 171, 174, 179, 189, 204
Cleanthes 111, 125
clergy
and Bolingbroke 81, 87, 89–90, 94, 99, 101, 103, 107
and civil religion 5, 193–4, 207

240

INDEX

and Coleridge   199–201
and Enlightened Dissent   167–73, 176, 178, 179, 181–2, 188, 191
and Gibbon   137, 146–50, 152–3, 155–7, 159, 162–3
and Hume   110, 116, 119–20, 122–4, 126–34
and 'latitudinarianism'   22
and Shaftesbury   40–4, 48–9, 51–3, 56
and the Enlightenment   28–32
and Trenchard and Gordon   59–63, 65–6, 69–77, 79
in the French Revolution   205
learned clergy   17–20, 26–7
of the Church of England   3, 13–16, 24–6
pastoral clergy   17–20, 26–7
clerisy   198, 200–2
Cocks, Sir Richard   36
Coleridge, Samuel Taylor   38–9, 195–202, 203
Collins, Anthony   40, 60–1
commercial society   21, 130–1, 195
common good   2, 47, 55–6, 61, 64, 75, 80, 97–8, 100, 103–4, 173, 183
common law   36
'commonwealth' political theory   59
Commodus, Emperor   138, 140
comprehension   7, 23, 37, 39, 102, 166–8, 171–6, 178–9, 183, 191, 194, 197
Concordat (1801)   195–6, 198, 199
conformity   41–2, 64–5, 80–1, 99, 167, 175
Constantine, Emperor   5–6, 9, 141, 180, 205
Conventicle Act (1664) *see* 'Clarendon code'
Convocation   14, 70, 72
  Convocation controversy   16, 25, 38
  suspension of (1717)   62, 201
Copel, Jean François, 'Père Elysée'   155
Cordeliers Club   207
Corinth   146, 148
Corporation Act (1661)   14, 84, 186–7, 196
  campaigns against   36, 83
  repeal of   195, 198
corruption   4–5, 17–18, 45–8, 61–4, 68–9, 87–9, 96–7, 99, 105, 110–11, 137–53, 163–5, 166–7, 173, 182–5, 197
court of high commission   98
Cranmer, Thomas, archbishop of Canterbury   71, 159

Cromwell, Oliver   8, 154–5
crown-in-parliament   14–16, 34, 60, 72–3, 80–1, 99, 175, 181, 192, 199
Cudworth, Ralph   22, 54, 77, 93, 204

Darby, John   53–4
Davenant, William   52
deism   22, 25, 28, 37, 174, 194, 207
  and Bolingbroke   81, 87–8, 96–7, 100–1, 106–7
  and Gibbon   161
  and Hume   108, 114, 135
  and Priestley   186
  and Shaftesbury   40–1
  and Trenchard and Gordon   78
  deist controversy   35
  in the French Revolution   30
Diderot, Denis   126, 155, 206
Dillon, John Joseph   204
Dionysius of Halicarnassus   152
Disney, John   169, 179, 183, 192
Dissent *see also* Enlightened Dissent
  and civil religion   37–9, 166–71, 180–92, 194–202
  and 'conventicling'   20
  and 'radicalism'   29–30
  and the movement for the reformation of manners   21
  persecution of   14, 81–4
  toleration of   7, 15, 23–4, 36, 68–9, 72, 76–8, 94, 102–6, 125, 131–2, 162–5, 178–80
Dissenting academies   19, 81–2, 170, 189, 190
divine right
  monarchy   29, 68, 125, 192,
  priesthoods   29, 38, 68, 70, 91–4, 180–1
Dodwell, Henry   24
dogmatism   4–5, 85, 112, 126, 140, 178
Domitian, Emperor   138, 140
Donation of Constantine   149
dualism   150–1
Durkheim, Emile   33

ecclesiastical courts   22, 36, 77, 151
Ecclesiastical Courts Bills (1733 and 1734)   83
ecclesiology   1–2, 5–7, 14, 16–17, 24–6, 37–8, 41, 47–50, 70, 93, 99, 106–7, 121–3, 137, 146, 170, 178, 193–5, 199, 203–5, 207
edict of Nantes   56
Edmonstoune, James   133

241

Edward VI, king of England and Ireland 158, 159, 200
Egypt 8, 44–6, 87, 88, 89, 101, 142
Eichhorn, Johann Gottfried 203
Elibank, Patrick Murray, Lord 128
Elizabeth I, queen of England and Ireland 9, 14, 68, 70, 72, 98, 124, 158, 199
Elliot, Gilbert 126–7, 128
Enlightened Dissent 31–2, 169, 181–2
   and Erastianism 170, 181–2, 188
   and high-churchmanship 180
   and the church-state relationship 188, 192
   and the clergy 167–73, 176, 178, 179, 181–2, 188, 191
   Whiggism of 166, 174, 177, 180–1, 192
Enlightenment
   and Jews 7
   Catholic 203–7
   in England 17, 28–32, 34, 193
   in France 1, 30, 35, 59, 205–7
   in Germany 203
   in Italy 204–5
   in Scotland 32
enthusiasm 19–22, 31, 45, 50, 54–57, 62, 66–7, 76–8, 93–4, 106, 110–16, 123–4, 129–31, 134, 150, 154–5, 159, 164–5, 170, 176–, 178, 186, 190–2, 193–5, 202
Ephesus 146, 148
Epicureans 12, 57, 135
episcopacy 14–15, 29, 32, 53–4, 67–8, 72–3, 80, 83, 85, 89, 93–4, 96, 98, 122, 146–512, 177–9, 181, 191, 197, 200, 203, 205
Episcopalianism 203
Erasmianism 17, 23, 42, 47, 156, 165
Erasmus 156, 165
Erastianism 6, 8–9, 24, 26, 36, 38, 94, 194
   and Bolingbroke 80–1, 90–1, 96, 99, 103
   and Enlightened Dissent 170, 181–2, 188
   and Hume 116, 121
   and Shaftesbury 47, 49
   and Trenchard and Gordon 59–61, 70–4, 79
Erastus, Thomas 6, 70–1
eschatology 9, 11, 184
Essex Street chapel, London 169
ethics 4, 52
Ethiopia 46

Eunapius 144
exoteric philosophy 28, 37, 50, 96, 161
external worship 7, 42, 50, 57–8, 92–3, 112, 124, 139

Feathers Tavern petition 168, 172, 173, 175, 177, 178, 179, 180, 183
Ferguson, Adam 126–8
fiscal-military state 41, 84
Fitzroy, Augustus, duke of Grafton 169
Five Mile Act (1665) *see* 'Clarendon code'
Fletcher, Andrew 41
Foster, John 155
Foster, Sir Michael 36
Fox, Charles James 163, 180
Foxe, John 9
France 10, 55, 72, 85, 86, 98, 114, 196, 199, 201
Franklin, Benjamin 169
Frederick I, Barbarossa, Emperor 149
Frederick II, king of Prussia, 'the Great' 203
Frederick, Prince of Wales 80, 85, 90, 105
freedom of inquiry 177–8, 183
freethinking 22, 25, 35, 57, 74, 104, 105–6, 158
French Revolution 164–5, 205–7
   and 'de-Christianisation' 196, 205
Frend, William 196
Furneaux, Philip 186–7

Gallicanism 149, 205, 207
Gardiner, Stephen, bishop of Winchester 131
Gauls 139
Geneva 54, 98, 146, 174, 178, 207
Genovesi, Antonio 204
George II, king of Great Britain and Ireland 90
George III, king of Great Britain and Ireland 38, 198–9
Giannone, Pietro 149, 204
Gibbon, Edward
   and Calvinism 157
   and Cicero 139, 152, 159, 161
   and Constantine 30, 139, 149
   and deism 161
   and Jewish history 8–9, 142–3
   and Price 164–5
   and the apostolic church 140, 146–8, 164
   and the Church of England 137–9, 151, 154, 158–9

and the church-state relationship   140
and the clergy   137, 146–50, 152–3, 155–7, 159, 162–3
and the royal supremacy   151
and the subscription controversy   162–5
and the Thirty-Nine Articles   137–8, 157, 161–2
and the Trinity   143, 157, 162
and Toryism   59–62, 69, 71, 77
and Whiggism   151
Gibson, Edmund, bishop of London   17, 26, 36, 93–4, 194
  and Bolingbroke   80, 85
  and the 'church-Whig' alliance   26, 29, 38, 62, 83, 105
  and Toryism   93–4
  and voluntary Anglicanism   21–2
Girondins   206
'Glorious Revolution' (1688–9)   11, 15, 59–60, 62, 68–9, 122–3, 151, 185, 202
  Revolution principles   70, 72–3, 83–5, 96, 105, 174–5, 177, 192
  Revolution settlement   12, 24–5, 38, 41–4, 47, 49, 92, 166–7, 171, 194–5
Gnosticism   151
godly prince   4, 9–10, 15, 42, 46, 49, 68, 72–3, 81, 83, 93, 96–8, 104, 107, 122–4, 151–2, 170, 175, 181–2, 192, 194, 198–9, 201
godly rule   19, 202
Goodwin, John   18
Gordon riots   38, 154
Gordon, Thomas
  and Calvinism   71, 76
  and deism   78
  and Erastianism   59–61, 70–4, 79
  and high-churchmanship   59–62, 68–9, 71, 77–8
  and Jewish history   63, 65
  and sociability   62–3
  and the apostolic church   71, 75–6
  and the church-state relationship   59–61, 70
  and the clergy   59–63, 65–6, 69–77, 79
  and the royal supremacy   59, 71–3
  anticlericalism of   78
  Whiggism of   59–60, 62, 70, 72–3
grand tour   18, 75, 105, 141, 142
Gratian, Emperor   139
Grecian Coffee House, Devereux Court   62

Greece   5, 51–3, 57–8, 87–9, 105, 142–4, 146–7, 154, 155, 157–8, 195
Grimaldi, Francescantonio   204
Grotius, Hugo   156, 204
Guelphs and Ghibellines   6, 97, 150

Hadrian, Emperor   142–3
Hampton Court Conference (1604)   9, 175
Handel, George Frederick   7–8
Hannibal   139
Hanoverian succession (1714)   10, 62, 96
Hare, Francis, bishop of Chichester   83
Harley, Robert, earl of Oxford   72, 82
Harrington, James   3, 7, 8, 34, 207
  and Bolingbroke   98–9
  and Coleridge   201
  and Hume   121–2
  and Shaftesbury   43–5, 47, 50, 55
  and Trenchard and Gordon   61, 64, 70
Hartley, David   187–8, 191
  'associationism' of   187
Hay, William   36
Hebraism   7–9
Hegel, G. W. F.   32, 203
Helvétius, Claude Adrien   126
Henry II, king of England   6, 117
Henry III, king of France   98
Henry IV, king of France   98
Henry IV, king of the Germans   6, 149
Henry V, king of the Germans   149
Henry VII, king of England   70, 98–9
Henry VIII, king of England and Ireland   9, 13, 45, 70, 98–9, 123, 151
Henry, Robert   128
Herne, Thomas   171
Herport, Brian   174
Hickes, George   16
high churchmanship   15–16, 18, 21–6, 29, 31, 35, 37, 93–4, 171, 202
  and Bolingbroke   80–4, 102
  and Enlightened Dissent   180,
  and Hume   114, 129
  and Shaftesbury   41–3, 48, 54–5, 56
  and Trenchard and Gordon   59–62, 68–9, 71, 77–8
'higher criticism'   203
Hoadly, Benjamin, bishop of Bangor   16, 29, 60, 85, 189
  and Blackburne   174
  and Gibbon   156
  and Trenchard and Gordon   70, 71, 78
  and Watson   177

and Wyvill 179
Hobbes, Thomas 2, 3, 7, 11, 32, 204, 207
 and Bolingbroke 89
 and Shaftesbury 49, 52
 and Trenchard and Gordon 73–4
Hogarth, William 26–7
d'Holbach, Baron 59, 126
Hollis, Thomas 174
Home, Henry, Lord Kames 134
Home, John 127, 128, 133
homoiousios 143
homoousios 143
Hooker, Richard 7, 9, 93, 146, 153, 177
Horne Tooke, John 168, 179
Howard, Sir Robert 34
Howards 204
Huguenots 19–20, 60, 82
humanism 2, 17, 18, 41
Hume, David
 and Calvinism 127, 129–30
 and Cicero 110, 129–30, 133–5
 and common sense 112–13, 118
 and Constantine 118
 and deism 108, 114, 135
 and Erastianism 116, 121
 and high-churchmanship 114, 129
 and Price 127, 184
 and prudence 114, 121–5, 131–5, 139–40
 and sociability 127, 129–30, 133, 135
 and the Church of England 121, 123–4
 and the church-state relationship 111, 116–19, 121–3, 132–3, 135
 and the clergy 110, 116, 119–20, 122–4, 126–34
 and the royal supremacy 116, 123
 and Toryism 114
 and Whiggism 114, 122–3
 anticlericalism of 123
Hutcheson, Francis 129
Hyde, Henry, Viscount Cornbury 85

idolatry 42, 141, 142, 143, 148, 172
imperator 9, 12, 46, 96, 152, 204
imperium in imperio 4, 31, 92, 97, 113, 117
imposture 42, 48, 67, 76, 112, 123, 141–2, 157, 160, 170–1, 182, 187–8
incarnation 143, 182
Independency 3, 77
indulgence 24, 68, 102, 103, 125
 declarations of indulgence (1672 and 1687) 15

parliamentary 15, 186
Innocent III, Pope 149
Interregnum 3, 9, 34, 43, 155
investiture controversy 6, 149
Ireland 38, 77, 122
irreligion 28–9, 34, 37, 41, 50, 108, 126, 139
Israelites 5, 7, 96
Italy 75, 77, 105, 149, 204–5

Jackson, John 171
Jacobitism 10, 18, 24–5, 38, 61, 68, 69, 80, 83, 84, 96
James II, king of England, Scotland, and Ireland 15, 62, 68, 84, 125, 181
James VI and I, king of England, Scotland, and Ireland 9, 68, 70, 72, 98, 125
Jansenism 149, 205
Jardine, John 127, 128
Jebb, John 168–9, 179, 181, 182–3, 188
Jerome, Saint 67
Jerusalem 113, 143, 146
Jesuits 205
Jesus College, Cambridge 176–7, 196
Joseph 46
Josephus 142
junto Whiggism 41

Keith, George 66
Kippis, Andrew 181

latitudinarianism 22–4, 62, 92–3, 114, 135, 156, 165, 167–8, 170, 175–81, 183–4, 202
Laud, William, archbishop of Canterbury 9, 72, 124–5
 Laudianism 3, 72, 124, 175
Launoy, Jean de 149
Lausanne 10, 150, 155, 158–9
Law, Edmund, bishop of Carlisle 16, 23, 168–9, 173, 175–80, 194
Lechmere, Nicholas 82
Le Clerc, Jean 156
Leechman, William 131
legal anticlericalism 36
Le Paige, Louis-Adrien 205
Leslie, Charles 84
Levi, David 8, 185–6
liberalism 29, 33, 40, 59
Limborch, Philipp van 156
Lindsey, Theophilus 169, 179, 182, 188, 190

244

Lingard, John 204
Linnaeus, Carl 188
liturgy 7, 124, 173, 178, 181–2
Livy 152
Locke, John 5, 31, 34, 59–60, 204
  and Blackburne 174
  and Bolingbroke 87
  and Gibbon 153
  and Priestley 184
  and Trenchard and Gordon 75, 77–8
  and Warburton 91, 93
  and Watson 177
  and Wyvill 179
Longano, Francesco 204
Louis XIV, king of France 72, 157
low churchmanship 16–18, 21–4, 34, 37, 41, 43, 49, 60, 62, 65, 69, 79, 181, 202
Lowth, Robert, bishop of London 153
Lucian 165
Lutheranism 131, 146, 158, 203
luxury 105, 130–1, 201–2
Lyttleton, George, Baron 105

Machiavelli, Niccolò 1, 28, 194, 204
  and Bolingbroke 81, 100–1
  and Gibbon 144
  and Hume 118–19, 121, 132–3
  and Rousseau 1, 32, 207
Magdalen College, Oxford 153–4, 155
Magdalene College, Cambridge 160
Magi 46, 65
Mainz 204
Mallet, David 86, 105
Mandeville, Bernard 40, 69
Manicheanism 45, 150–1
manners 19, 43–4, 120, 127, 130, 146, 152, 154
Manton, Thomas 82
Markham, William, bishop of Gloucester 154
Marsilius of Padua 6, 9, 97, 150
Martyr, Justin 46
Mary I, queen of England and Ireland 131
Melchoir, Friedrich, Baron von Grimm 126
Merovingians 149
Mesopotamia 46
Methodism 20, 26, 170, 176, 190, 197
Middleton, Conyers 16, 36, 39, 141–2, 159–61
militia 44, 65, 122
millenarianism 8, 56, 163–4, 187, 191

millennialism 19, 55, 166, 169–70, 187, 189, 194, 196, 197, 202–3
moderation 22–3, 31, 43, 52, 54–5, 76–7, 98, 123–5, 130–1, 135, 153, 156, 170, 179, 181, 191
Moderatism 126–8, 131, 133–5, 194
modernisation theory 29, 32–4, 207
Molesworth, Robert 11, 17, 41, 61
monasticism 120–1, 144–5, 149, 150, 159
Montagu, Richard, bishop of Chichester 72
More, Henry 22, 54, 65–6
mortmain 46, 148
Mortmain Act (1736) 29, 83
Mosaic dispensation 8, 147, 185
Moses 8, 46, 88, 101, 143
Mosheim, Johann Lorenz von 146–7, 152
Moyle, Walter 41, 60, 61, 152
Muratori, Ludovico 204

National Assembly 177, 205
National Society 198
natural religion 12, 23, 63–5, 76–9, 81, 86–91, 97, 100, 102, 107, 115, 133, 135, 159–60, 174
Nazarenes 9
neo-Harringtonianism 34
  and Bolingbroke 98–9
  and Hume 121–2
  and Shaftesbury 43–5, 47, 55
  and Trenchard and Gordon 61, 64, 70
Nerva, Emperor 138
Neville, Henry 34
new science 31, 51, 66, 167, 170, 187–9
Newton, Isaac 179, 188, 204
Nicolai, Friedrich 203
Nonconformity 14–15, 18–19, 24, 82, 169, 192
non-jurors 16, 25
North, Frederick, earl of Guildford, 'Lord North' 163
Numa Pompilius 12, 101, 117, 125, 139, 152

occasional conformity 25, 29
Occasional Conformity Act (1711) 29, 81–2, 103
  repeal of 62
old corruption 179
Osterwald, Jean Frederick 10
Oxford movement 25

paganism

and civil religion 1–3, 5, 28, 58, 101, 108–9, 117–19, 121, 130, 135, 194–5
  Greek 5, 51–3, 57–8, 87–9, 142–4, 146–7, 154, 157, 195
  Roman 46, 51, 61, 63–5, 79, 137–44, 152, 158–60, 165, 204
Pagi, Antoine 149
Paine, Tom 206
Paley, William 168, 178–9
papacy 6, 9, 14, 31, 36, 97, 98, 148–50, 154, 186, 203–5
parliament 14–16, 25, 36, 48, 60, 62–3, 72–3, 80–5, 124, 154, 163, 179–80, 186, 198, 200
  House of Commons 73, 84–5, 124, 163, 168, 175, 199
  House of Lords 73, 80
passions 54–7, 64–6, 89, 104, 110, 115–16, 118, 120, 129–30, 134–5, 145
patriotism 1, 5, 11–12, 33, 38, 61, 79, 97, 100–1, 104–5, 137–8, 145, 147, 158–9, 165, 194
'patriot' opposition 80, 84–5, 105
patristics 18, 25, 48–9, 67, 171
Paul, Saint 5, 7, 87, 89, 151, 157–8, 203
Paul V, Pope 150
Paulicians 150–1
Pavillard, Daniel 158
penal laws see 'Clarendon code'
Pepin, king of the Franks, 'the Short', 149
persecution 2, 8–9, 15, 17, 22–5, 44, 50, 56–7, 72, 76–7, 90, 101–3, 105, 111–12, 118, 120, 123, 128–32, 143, 157–9, 161, 165, 179, 183–8, 192, 197
Persia 46, 65
Peter, Saint 141, 148, 149, 203
Peterhouse, Cambridge 168–9, 175
Petres 204
Philip IV, king of France, 'the Fair' 6, 97, 150
Philo 111, 125, 134
philology 17–18, 51, 110, 126, 146, 152, 182, 203
philosophes 30, 126, 205–6
Philosophical Society 127
philosophy 5, 12–13, 28–31, 37, 47, 49–57, 81, 86–9, 96, 101, 109–13, 118, 121, 126–8, 130, 132–6, 138–40, 143–4, 153–65, 169, 185–6, 188, 195, 200, 202, 204–7

piety 1, 4, 11–12, 18, 21, 30, 36, 50, 53–4, 56, 63–5, 68–9, 74, 78, 82, 90, 125, 127–8, 131, 141, 143–5, 147–8, 150, 153, 157–8, 160, 163–5, 172–3, 179, 187, 190, 193–4, 200
Pistoria 205
Pitt, William, first earl of Chatham, 'the Elder' 181–2
Pitt, William, 'the Younger' 177, 198–9
Pius VII, Pope 195–6
Plato 64, 131
Platonism 18, 22, 57, 87, 143, 145, 148, 151, 164, 184
plebeians 139–40
pluralism 3, 24, 26, 28, 33, 38
Pole, Reginald, Cardinal 131
politeness 40, 20–1, 43–4, 47–8, 51–4, 58, 62–3, 95, 117–18, 126–7, 130, 133–5, 166, 169–70, 174, 193–4
political economy 195, 201
  and Enlightened Dissent 190
  and Gibbon 148, 154
  and Hume 119–21, 130–1
  and Trenchard and Gordon 74–5
polytheism 88, 141
Pompey 139
Pope, Alexander 86, 90, 94, 99, 104, 105, 106
Popular party 127–8
'post-secular turn' 33–4
Powell, William Samuel, archdeacon of Colchester 175–6
praemunire 11, 31, 68, 72, 113
Presbyterianism 11, 18, 19, 25, 32, 91, 109
  English 43, 71, 77
  Irish 77
  Scottish 32, 68, 110, 121–2, 136, 194
  Swiss 10, 158–9
presbyters 146–7
Price, Richard 32, 36, 39, 169, 179, 180–1, 183–4, 186, 188–92, 194
  and Gibbon 164–5
  and Hume 127, 184
  and the apostolic church 192
  and the Church of England 31–2, 181
Prideaux, Humphrey, dean of Norwich 65, 67
priestcraft 4, 9, 20, 29–30, 34, 40, 43–7, 53, 55, 60–9, 78, 81, 86–90, 95–6, 105, 107, 108–13, 116, 121–2, 124–5, 159, 165, 166, 171–2, 182, 193–5, 202

priesthood of all believers 4, 9, 16, 25, 42, 47, 100, 170, 189, 193, 197, 202
Priestley, Joseph
   and deism 186
   and the apostolic church 184–5
   and the Church of England 191
   and the Trinity 182, 184–5
   seeks unity with Jews 8, 184–6
primitive Christianity 3–5, 11, 20, 21, 23, 43, 52–3, 57–8, 61, 63–4, 81, 86–7, 91–2, 97, 99–102, 104, 107, 133, 137–48, 161, 164–5, 166, 170, 173, 182, 193, 202
Proclamation Society 198
Protestant ethic 190
prudence 13, 40, 67, 71, 75, 96, 98, 102, 107, 144, 148, 157, 165, 176–7
   in Hume 114, 121–5, 131–5, 139–40
Prussia 10, 32, 203
Prynne, William 19
public sphere 20–1, 44
Pufendorf, Samuel 65
Pulteney, William, earl of Bath 85
puritanism 7, 8, 14, 18, 20, 22, 43, 82–3, 94, 98, 124, 154, 164, 175, 180, 186, 200,
Pythagoreans 57, 157
Pythian oracle 133

Quakers 66, 77, 91
Quakers Tithe Bill (1736) 29, 83
Quebec 38
Quebec Act (1774) 195, 203

'radical' Whiggism 41, 59
raillery 47, 48, 53, 57
reason 20, 22–3, 29–31, 33–4, 42–3, 51, 53, 56–8, 63–7, 71, 78, 81, 84, 86–9, 102–7, 112–18, 123–4, 131–9, 141–4, 150, 153, 154–63, 165, 167, 170, 173, 177–8, 180, 184–92, 205–6
recusancy 7, 14
Reformation 4–7, 28–32, 42–50, 57–8, 61, 67–75, 78–9, 81, 93, 97–102, 107, 110–11, 116–24, 134, 137–8, 150–2, 156–60, 163, 165, 166–7, 170–3, 175–7, 180–5, 191–2, 193–5, 199, 203–7
   'long Reformation' 10–12, 17–19, 199–200
   magisterial Reformation 2, 9, 13–16, 35–6, 201

reformation of manners 10, 21–2, 69, 92
republicanism 3, 5, 12, 34, 35, 41, 61, 157
   civic 43–4, 47–8, 61, 63–4, 74–5, 80, 98, 105, 117, 121–2, 132–3, 165
   Roman 57, 109, 138–9, 154
republic of letters 41, 90, 185–6
revelation 1–3, 12, 20, 23, 35–6, 63, 67, 86–8, 101, 106–7, 137, 143, 160, 164, 174, 178, 188–9, 193, 197
Revolution Society 169, 179
Robertson, William 126–8
Robespierre, Maximilien 30 32
Roman Catholicism 4–5, 10, 15, 20, 25, 29, 31, 38–9, 42, 45, 47–8, 54, 65, 67, 72, 76, 82–4, 86, 90, 97, 104, 110, 113–14, 116–17, 120, 123–5, 132, 141–4, 150, 153–8, 160, 166–7, 171, 174, 180, 183–4, 193–207
Roman Empire 46, 89–90, 144–5, 148–50, 152, 161
Roman law 12
Roman republic 5, 101, 175
Romanticism 201–2
Rome 12, 46–7, 57–8, 98, 105, 131, 137, 139–43, 146, 148–51, 174, 178–9, 182
Romulus 12, 13
Rousseau, Jean-Jacques 1–2, 3, 5, 11, 194, 206–7
   and Hume 118–19, 121, 132
   and Law 176
   and Warburton 106–7, 206–7
   influence of 32–3
royal supremacy 4, 7, 9, 15–17, 25–6
   and Bolingbroke 80–1, 99
   and Coleridge 194–5, 199, 201
   and Gibbon 151
   and Gibson 93
   and Hume 116, 123
   and Shaftesbury 42
   and Trenchard and Gordon 59, 71–3
Rundle, Thomas, bishop of Derry 83

sacerdotalism 1, 16–17, 21, 23–6, 34–5, 40, 42, 48, 61–3, 71, 73, 87, 90–5, 99, 106–7, 113, 116, 121, 137, 139, 146–51, 159, 162–3, 166, 180, 194, 196, 199–201, 205
Sacheverell, Henry 15–16, 21–2, 25, 38
St John's College, Cambridge 175
Sarpi, Paolo 6–7, 150
Savile, Sir George 184

Savoy Conference (1661)   9, 175
scepticism   12–13, 28, 32–4, 37, 45–6, 51,
    88, 108, 122–3, 125–6, 128, 134,
    138–41, 157–61, 164–5, 183–4
Schism Act (1714)   81–2, 103
    repeal of   62
scholasticism   17, 18, 24, 42, 47, 51, 67, 87,
    105, 110, 112–13, 145, 154, 195
Scotland   32, 60, 68, 105, 109, 110, 114,
    116, 121–22, 126–8, 131–2, 125,
    194, 204
secularisation   11, 24, 33–4
secularism   40
Selden, John   7, 204
Select Society   127
Seneca   142
separation between church and state   24,
    32–3, 40, 59
Septennial Act (1716)   62
Shaftesbury, Anthony Ashley Cooper, third
    earl of
    and Calvinism   54, 56
    and Cicero   55
    and Constantine   46
    and deism   40–1
    and Erastianism   47, 49
    and high-churchmanship   41–3, 48–9,
        54–6
    and Jewish history   45–6
    and sociability   43–4, 47, 53, 56
    and the Church of England   41–3, 54–5
    and the church-state relationship   41–9,
        57
    and the clergy   40–4, 48–9, 51–3, 56
    and the royal supremacy   42
    and the Thirty-Nine Articles   49
    and Toryism   41, 43, 48, 54, 56
    Whiggism of   41, 43–4, 47–9
Sherlock, Thomas, bishop of London   85
sincerity   1, 22–3, 37, 50, 53, 78–9, 94,
    102–4, 130–1, 133, 161, 166–76,
    185, 189, 191, 194, 199
Sir William Scott's Act (1803)   198
Smith, Adam   127
Spencer, John   45
sociability   4, 20–1, 193–4
socialism   202
Society for Promoting Christian
    Knowledge   21, 189
Society for the Promotion of the Knowledge
    of the Scriptures   189
Society for the Propagation of the
    Gospel   189

Socinianism   31, 167, 174
Socrates   64, 160, 176
sola scriptura   17, 23, 54, 77–8, 166–8,
    174, 178, 183, 197
Solemn League and Covenant (1643)   14
Somers, John, first Baron   41, 43, 47, 48,
    53, 177
soteriology   15, 20, 79, 194
Southey, Robert   196–7
South Sea crisis   60, 61, 62
sovereignty   2, 4–6, 9, 11–12, 14–16, 35,
    44–5, 48–9, 73–4, 91–3, 117, 134,
    149, 155, 170, 186, 191, 193
Spanheim, Ezekiel, Freiherr von   146, 152
Spinoza, Baruch   8, 89
standing army   41, 60, 61, 196, 199
Stanhope, James, Viscount   62
Stanley, Hans   163
Steele, Richard   21, 23, 43, 63
Stephens, William   34
Stillingfleet, Edward, bishop of
    Worcester   19, 24, 93
Stuart, James Francis Edward, 'the Old
    Pretender'   80, 83
Stuart, John, earl of Bute   127
Stubbe, Henry   35
subscription controversy   24, 37–8, 162–4,
    167–76, 180–2, 189–90
Sunderland, Charles Spencer, third earl
    of   62
superstition   4–8, 12–13, 17, 19–20, 33,
    42, 44–50, 54–7, 60–9, 76, 81, 85,
    88–90, 93–6, 99, 101, 103–5, 107,
    109–16, 118–24, 126–36, 137–44,
    148, 150, 152–7, 159–60, 162–5,
    166, 170, 173, 176–9, 181–4,
    191–2, 193–6
Swift, Jonathan   82, 87, 106
Switzerland   10, 158–9, 174
Symmachus, Quintus Aurelius   139–40,
    144
Syria   142

Tacitus, Publius Cornelius   46, 60, 142
Taylor, Jeremy, bishop of Down and
    Connor   54, 201
Tension, Thomas, archbishop of
    Canterbury   69
Test Acts (1673 and 1678)   14, 84, 92, 94,
    102–3, 179, 181, 183, 186–7
    campaigns to repeal   36, 83, 196
    repeal of   195, 198
Theodosius, Emperor   67–8

INDEX

theology 1, 5, 17, 19, 24, 28, 37, 40, 47, 51–3, 61, 86–90, 106–7, 112–13, 125, 131–2, 141–3, 150–2, 154–6, 163, 167, 172, 175–8, 180, 183–6, 188–9, 194–5, 202–3, 205
Thirty-Nine Articles 3–4, 35–7, 193
  in the subscription controversy 167–72, 175–9
Thomson, James 105
Throckmortons 204
Tillotson, John, archbishop of Canterbury 54, 67, 77, 88, 94, 156, 179, 204
Tindal, Matthew 16, 40, 49
Tithe Bill (1731) 83
Tocqueville, Alexis de 28–9
Toland, John 8, 35, 40, 41, 61, 201
toleration 2–5, 7–8, 15, 18–20, 22–4, 34, 41, 43, 50, 53–8, 59–62, 72–9, 83–4, 92–8, 101–10, 114, 125, 130–2, 139, 143, 156–63, 165–8, 169, 172, 174, 177–9, 181, 183–6, 189–91, 194–5, 202, 203
Toleration Act (1689) 7, 15, 23–4, 62, 76, 92, 186
Toryism 20–6, 29, 37–8
  ecclesiology of 15–16, 21–2, 25–6, 34–5, 94
Tractarianism 25, 26
Trenchard, John
  and Calvinism 71, 76
  and deism 78
  and Erastianism 59–61, 70–4, 79
  and high-churchmanship 59–62, 68–9, 71, 77–8
  and Jewish history 63, 65
  and sociability 62–3
  and the apostolic church 71, 75–6
  and the Church of England 60, 68–9, 72, 77
  and the church-state relationship 59–61, 70
  and the clergy 59–63, 65–6, 69–77, 79
  and the royal supremacy 59, 71–3
  and Toryism 59–62, 69, 71, 77
  anticlericalism of 78
  Whiggism of 59–60, 62, 70, 72–3
Trinitarianism 15, 23, 31, 37, 167, 171
Trinity College, Cambridge 141
Turretini, Jean-Alphonse 10
tyranny 4, 17, 44, 46–8, 65, 68–9, 76, 83, 94–6, 98, 111–12, 130, 142, 144–5, 149–51, 155, 159, 172–3, 177, 180, 182, 191, 196, 199

Ultramontanism 204
Unitarianism 8, 38–9, 163, 167–70, 179–80, 184–6, 189, 192, 196–7, 203
Unitarian Society 189
University College, Oxford 43
University of Cambridge 18–19, 51, 54, 85, 153–4, 156, 168–9, 174, 175–7, 179, 187, 189–90
University of Oxford 18–19, 48, 50, 68–9, 146, 153–4, 158, 189–90

Venice 6–7
Vice Society 198
virtue 12, 43–4, 47–8, 50, 53–6, 61, 64, 69, 74, 83, 92, 97–8, 105, 112–14, 128–30, 135, 138, 149, 156, 160, 172, 176, 182, 190, 193–5
Voltaire, François-Marie Arouet 29, 165

Wakefield, Gilbert 176–7
Wake, William, archbishop of Canterbury 62
Walpole, Sir Robert 29, 38, 61, 62, 80, 83–6, 95, 105
Warburton, William, bishop of Gloucester 17, 25–6, 31, 35–6, 38–9, 90–5, 194
  and Blackburne 172
  and Bolingbroke 80, 90, 94–5, 99, 106–7
  and Bonneville 206–7
  and Coleridge 196, 197
  and Hume 127
  and Jebb 182–3
  and Priestley 183
  and Rousseau 106–7
  and the Thirty-Nine Articles 80–1
  and Toryism 93–4
wars of religion 9, 11, 24, 28, 56, 61, 66, 114
Waterland, Daniel 160, 171
Watson, Richard, bishop of Llandaff 168, 176–8, 194
Weber, Max 33
Werenfels, Samuel 10
Westminster Assembly 6
Wharton, Thomas, marquess of 82
Whichcote, Benjamin 41, 53–5, 57
Whiggism

249

and churchmanship 22, 26, 37–8, 62, 69
and godly kingship 10, 15
and politeness 20
and toleration 24, 36
anticlericalism of 17, 18–19, 34
ecclesiology of 16, 21
Wilkes, John 179
Wilkie, William 128
William III, king of England, Scotland, and Ireland, 'William of Orange' 10, 72, 181

will of Matilda 149
Wyndham, Sir William 83, 86, 87–8, 103
Wyvill, Christopher 168, 179

Xenophon 133

Yorke, Philip, earl of Hardwicke 36, 106

Zachary, Pope 149
Zoroaster 65, 101
Zoroastrians 46, 65

STUDIES IN MODERN BRITISH RELIGIOUS HISTORY

Previously published volumes in this series

I
Friends of Religious Equality
Non-Conformist Politics in Mid-Victorian England
Timothy Larsen

II
Conformity and Orthodoxy in the English Church, c.1560–1660
edited by Peter Lake and Michael Questier

III
Bishops and Reform in the English Church, 1520–1559
Kenneth Carleton

IV
Christabel Pankhurst
Fundamentalism and Feminism in Coalition
Timothy Larsen

V
The National Church in Local Perspective
The Church of England and the Regions, 1660–1800
edited by Jeremy Gregory and Jeffrey S. Chamberlain

VI
Puritan Iconoclasm during the English Civil War
Julie Spraggon

VII
The Cult of King Charles the Martyr
Andrew Lacey

VIII
Control of Religious Printing in Early Stuart England
S. Mutchow Towers

IX
The Church of England in Industrialising Society
The Lancashire Parish of Whalley in the Eighteenth Century
M. F. Snape

X
Godly Reformers and their Opponents in Early Modern England
Religion in Norwich, c.1560–1643
Matthew Reynolds

XI
Rural Society and the Anglican Clergy, 1815–1914
Encountering and Managing the Poor
Robert Lee

XII
The Church of England and the Holocaust
Christianity, Memory and Nazism
Tom Lawson

XIII
Religious Politics in Post-Reformation England
edited by Kenneth Fincham and Peter Lake

XIV
The Church of England and the Bangorian Controversy, 1716–1721
Andrew Starkie

XV
Martyrs and Martyrdom in England, c.1400–1700
edited by Thomas S. Freeman and Thomas F. Mayer

XVI
John Henry Williams (1747–1829): 'Political Clergyman'
War, the French Revolution, and the Church of England
Colin Haydon

XVII
Religion, Reform and Modernity in the Eighteenth Century
Thomas Secker and the Church of England
Robert G. Ingram

XVIII
The Royal Army Chaplains' Department, 1796–1953
Clergy under Fire
Michael Snape

XIX
Women, Reform and Community in Early Modern England
Katherine Willoughby, Duchess of Suffolk, and Lincolnshire's Godly Aristocracy,
1519–1580
Melissa Franklin Harkrider

XX
A History of the Mothers' Union
Women, Anglicanism and Globalisation, 1876–2008
Cordelia Moyse

XXI
National Religion and the Prayer Book Controversy, 1927–1928
John Maiden

XXII
The Problem of Pleasure
Sport, Recreation and the Crisis of Victorian Religion
Dominic Erdozain

XXIII
The Reformation and Robert Barnes
History, Theology and Polemic in Early Modern England
Korey D. Maas

XXIV
Syon Abbey and its Books
Reading, Writing and Religion, c.1400–1700
edited by E. A. Jones and Alexandra Walsham

XXV
Modern Spiritualism and the Church of England, 1850–1939
Georgina Byrne

XXVI
Conscience, Consciousness and Ethics in
Joseph Butler's Philosophy and Ministry
Bob Tennant

XXVII
Revelation Restored: The Apocalypse in Later Seventeenth-Century England
Warren Johnston

XXVIII
The Culture of Controversy: Religious Arguments in Scotland, 1660–1714
Alasdair Raffe

XXIX
Religion and the Demographic Revolution: Women and Secularisation in Canada,
Ireland, UK and USA since the 1960s
Callum G. Brown

XXX
Preaching in Eighteenth-Century London
Jennifer Farooq

XXXI
Evangelicalism and the Church of England in the Twentieth Century
Reform, Resistance and Renewal
edited by Andrew Atherstone and John Maiden

XXXII
Scandal and Religious Identity in Early Stuart England
A Northamptonshire Maid's Tragedy
Peter Lake and Isaac Stephens

XXXIII
The Origins of Primitive Methodism
Sandy Calder

XXXIV
Catholicism, Identity and Politics in the Age of Enlightenment: The Life and Career of Sir Thomas Gascoigne, 1745–1810
Alexander Lock

XXXV
The Education of the Anglican Clergy, 1780–1839
Sara Slinn

XXXVI
'This Great Firebrand': William Laud and Scotland, 1617–1645
Leonie James

XXXVII
Protestant Pluralism: The Reception of the Toleration Act, 1689–1720
Ralph Stevens

XXXVIII
Mysticism in Early Modern England
Liam Peter Temple

XXXIX
Protestant Dissent and Philanthropy in Britain, 1660–1914
edited by Clyde Binfield, G. M. Ditchfield and David L. Wykes

www.ingramcontent.com/pod-product-compliance
Lightning Source LLC
Chambersburg PA
CBHW051607230426
43668CB00013B/2019